The Public Years of Sarah and Angelina Grimké

SELECTED WRITINGS, 1835–1839

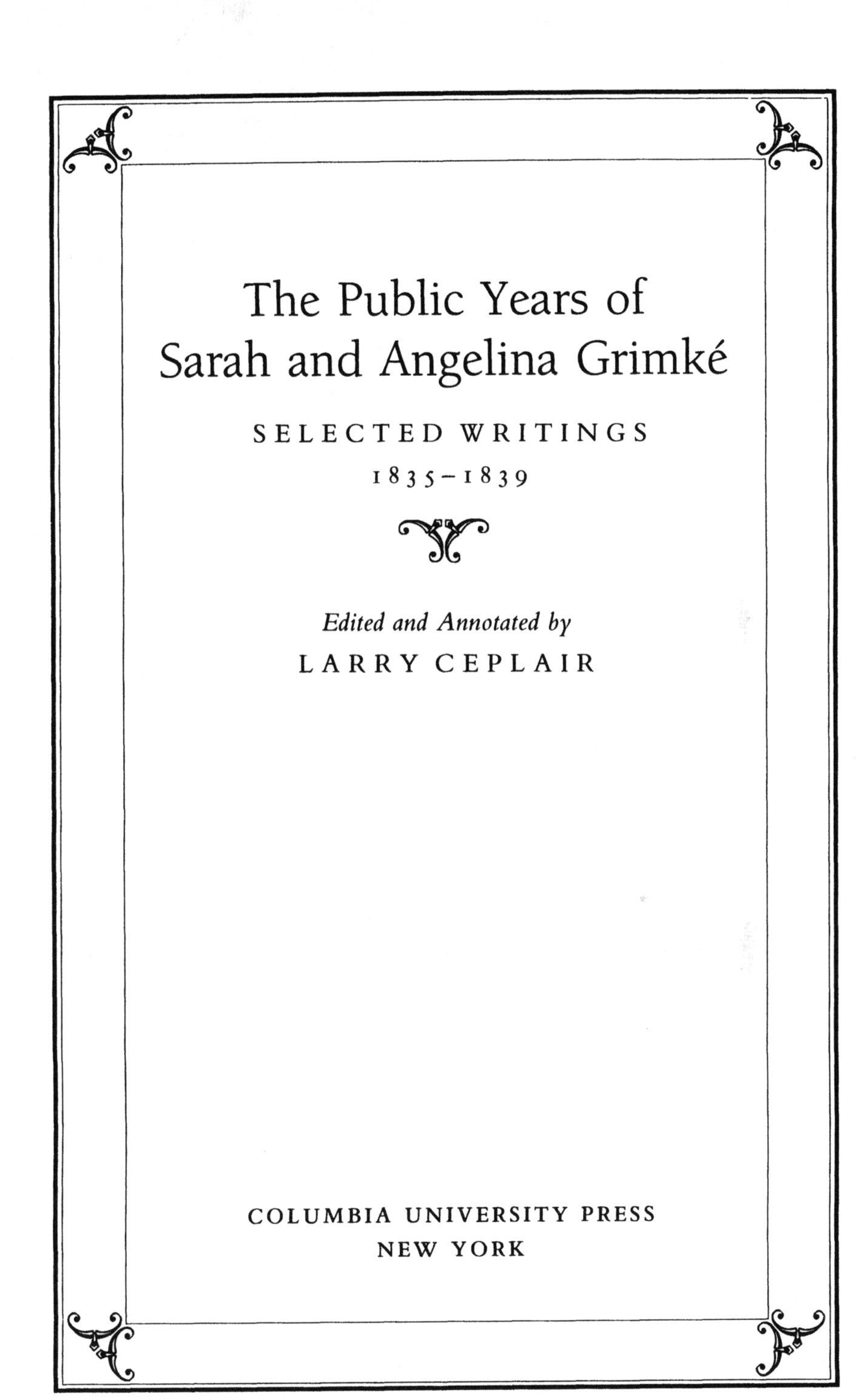

The Public Years of Sarah and Angelina Grimké

SELECTED WRITINGS
1835–1839

Edited and Annotated by

LARRY CEPLAIR

COLUMBIA UNIVERSITY PRESS
NEW YORK

The frontispiece shows the first page of a letter from Angelina to Sarah Grimké, dated July 19, 1836. Courtesy of the William L. Clements Library.

Columbia University Press
New York Oxford

Library of Congress Cataloging-in-Publication Data
The Public years of Sarah and Angelina Grimké : selected writings, 1835–1839 / edited and annotated by Larry Ceplair.
p. cm.
Bibliography: p.
Includes index.
ISBN 0-231-06800-X
ISBN 0-231-06801-8 (pbk.)
1. Grimké, Angelina Emily, 1805–1879—Archives.
2. Grimké, Sarah Moore, 1792–1873—Archives.
3. Slavery—United States—Anti-slavery movements—Sources.
4. Women's rights—United States—History—Sources.
I. Grimké, Angelina Emily, 1805–1879. Selections, 1989.
II. Grimké, Sarah Moore, 1792–1873. Selections. 1989.
III. Ceplair, Larry.
E449.G865P83 1989
322.4'4'092—dc20
89-7055
CIP

Book design by Jennifer Dossin

Casebound editions of Columbia University Press books are Smyth-sewn and printed on permanent and durable acid-free paper

Printed in the United States of America
c 10 9 8 7 6 5 4 3 2 1
p 10 9 8 7 6 5 4 3 2

To Mimi Flood, the most gifted of educators
and the finest of friends

Contents

Major Documents

ABBREVIATIONS

B/D Gilbert H. Barnes and Dwight L. Dumond, *Letters of Theodore Dwight Weld, Angelina Grimké Weld, and Sarah Grimké, 1822–1844.*

BPL Rare Books and Manuscripts, Boston Public Library.

W/G Weld-Grimké Papers, William L. Clements Library, University of Michigan, Ann Arbor.

Preface

SARAH and Angeline Grimké were revolutionaries, increasingly conscious that they were blazing a public path for women of courage who had seen a light or heard a voice of truth. They emerged from an improbable milieu to chart a new course for women who fervently believed in social change and social activism. And yet they shone in the public eye for a relatively short period, from 1835 to 1838. The sisters anticipated that Angelina's marriage to Theodore Dwight Weld, in May 1838, would allow them to meld domesticity and political activity, but the results were different than they had imagined.

Nevertheless, the words they wrote and spoke between September 1835 and May 1838 moved and inspired many who read and heard them then and in subsequent periods. The pages of their books and letters emit a crystal clear tone of morality, integrity, piety, intelligence, and strength of purpose. But too much of what they wrote remains hidden in archives and scattered among reprints of individual works that go in and out of print, various anthologies, and specialized periodicals. Their public statements and their accounts of their private struggles deserve to be better known. Hence this book.

The material gathered here is by no means a complete record. I have chosen to focus on their public years and to select and shape the material to form a historical narrative that does not distort events or perceptions. Therefore, I have used only those portions of their letters (and letters written to them) that reflect the sisters' political thinking and activity, and their responses to political events and controversies affecting them. Because I have excluded "chatty" material, very few of the letters are reprinted in their entirety.

Catherine H. Birney, who knew the sisters, informs us that Sarah asked the recipients of the letters she wrote to her family from Philadelphia, during the period 1821–1836, to destroy them upon receipt. Whether she destroyed others in the intervening years or simply wrote fewer letters than her sister is not known, but in any event we have many more letters by Angelina than by Sarah for the years covered in this book.

I have used original manuscripts, with three exceptions: three letters that are lost, for which I have relied on Catherine H. Birney, *The Grimké Sisters,*

Sarah and Angelina Grimké: The First American Women Advocates of Abolition and Woman's Rights (Boston, Mass.: Lee and Shepard, 1885; Westport, Conn.: Greenwood, 1969); two speeches by Angelina Grimké, for which I have relied on contemporary reports; and the manuscripts for their four books and contributions to *American Slavery As It Is,* for which I have relied on the first printed editions.

I have annotated all of the historical and literary references, again with three exceptions. I have chosen not to annotate most of the biblical references, because the sisters refer to the Bible so frequently that such annotations would overwhelm the text. I have tried and failed to discover the authors of the unattributed quotations that appear in their books. In the case of the names of minor historical characters, to whom passing reference is made and for whom the context makes their position clear, I have chosen to provide only the data necessary to make the reference to them understandable. All annotations from the original sources are indicated.

I have retained Angelina's peculiar spelling (based on an orthographical system developed by her brother, Thomas), which she used between 1835 and 1837, but I have replaced many of the sisters' ubiquitous dashes with commas and periods and added commas and periods where necessary to make the texts more intelligible.

I am deeply indebted to my editor, Kate Wittenberg, for her enthusiasm and critical support. Galen Wilson, former curator of manuscripts at the William L. Clements Library (University of Michigan), provided assistance and amenities far beyond the dictates of duty. An anonymous reader, asked by Columbia University Press to read both the proposal and the manuscript, provided a detailed, intelligent, and valuable critique of both.

Roy Kiplinger (William L. Clements Library) and Albert W. Fowler (Friends Historical Library of Swarthmore College) were remarkably generous toward and patient with my many requests. Other archivists and librarians who proved invaluable were: Alicia Jones Helsley (South Carolina Department of Archives and History), Louise T. Jones (The Historical Society of Pennsylvania), Diane F. Matzke (Department for Libraries and Archives, Commonwealth of Kentucky), Giuseppe Bisaccia and Eugene Zepp (Boston Public Library), Susan Eltsher (United Methodist Commission of Archives and History), Joyce Ann Tracy and Joanne D. Chaison (American Antiquarian Society), Peter Dummery (Massachusetts Historical Society), Emily Epstein (Oberlin College Library), James L. Hansen (The State Historical Society of Wisconsin), Mary K. Sine and Donald L. Morecock (Virginia State Library and Archives), Caroline Lewis Kardell (General Society of Mayflower Descendants), Fay Greenleaf (Lynn Historical Society), E. F. Donnelly (Lexington Historical Society), Helen J. Fife (Arch Street Meeting House), and Darla Parkes (Missouri State Library).

For their generous responses to my small but important requests, I wish to thank Kathryn Kish Sklar, Eugene Genovese, and Bertram Wyatt-Brown.

For permission to reprint documents, I am grateful to the director of the

William L. Clements Library, the trustees of the Boston Public Library, the Historical Society of Pennsylvania, and Special Collections, Oberlin College Library.

Finally, anyone who works in this area owes a huge debt of gratitude to Gilbert H. Barnes, Dwight L. Dumond, and Gerda Lerner. Their detailed and scholarly efforts greatly eased my tasks.

Addenda—for paperback edition

Maria W. Stewart (1803–1879), an African-American was the first United States woman to speak to a mixed audience. She delivered four speeches in Boston between 1832 and 1833, focusing on the need for free blacks to educate themselves (p. 1, line 10).

Oberlin Collegiate Institute was renamed Oberlin College in 1850 (p. 6, line 10; p. 293, footnote).

Mary S. Parker (1801–1841) was one of four sisters from New Hampshire, three of whom maintained a boarding house in Boston, which was frequented by antislavery people. She served as president of the Boston Female Anti-Slavery Society from 1834–1840 (p. 86, footnote).

In her letter to Henry C. Wright, excerpted on p. 287, Sarah wrote: "In the next two weeks I shall take up the subject of the ministry of women and those I do not expect Wm. S. Porter [editor of the *Spectator*] will publish." Thus it is possible that the unnumbered letter was rejected by Porter (p. 204, footnote).

Chronology

1792	November 26: Birth of Sarah Moore Grimké, sixth child (second daughter) of John Faucheraud and Mary Smith Grimké.
1805	February 20: Birth of Angelina Emily Grimké, fourteenth and youngest child of John and Mary Grimké. Sarah is named her godmother.
1807	Thomas Smith Grimké, second-born son of John and Mary Grimké, returns from Yale College, a convert to Timothy Dwight's brand of revivalism, determined to become a minister, but his father insists he become a lawyer.
1811	Judge Grimké nearly impeached by the South Carolina House of Representatives.
1817	After four years of sliding between the "gay life" and religious revival, Sarah converts to Presbyterianism.
1818	Angelina refuses confirmation in the Episcopal church.
1819	April: Sarah accompanies her dying father to Philadelphia.
	August 8: Judge Grimké dies. During her voyage home Sarah makes the acquaintance of a Quaker family and is given a copy of the memoirs of John Woolman, an eighteenth-century Quaker abolitionist.
1820	A confused Sarah is sent to North Carolina for respite from her spiritual travail; on her return, she converts to Quakerism.
1821	May 15: Sarah leaves Charleston to live in Philadelphia; she is accompanied by her widowed sister, Anna Frost.
1823	May 29: Sarah accepted into the Fourth and Arch Street Meeting of the Philadelphia Society of Friends.
1825	Mary Smith Grimké undergoes a conversion experience but remains within the Episcopalian church.

1826 April: Angelina converts to Presbyterianism.

September 26: Israel Morris proposes marriage to Sarah. (Although she believed she loved him, she chose not to accept.)

1827 October: Sarah visits Charleston to "save" Angelina.

1828 Spring: Angelina begins attending Friends' meeting.

July–November: Angelina visits Philadelphia. She returns to Charleston committed to Quaker principles and convinced that slavery is an outrage.

1829: May: Angelina is expelled from the Presbyterian church, charged with neglect of her duties.

November: Angelina leaves Charleston for Philadelphia.

1831: April 28: Angelina is accepted into the Fourth and Arch Street Meeting, but in May, dissatisfied with her performance as a teacher at an infant school, she writes to Catharine Beecher at the Hartford Seminary. Ms. Beecher travels to Philadelphia to meet Angelina and invites her to come to Hartford.

May: Edward Bettle begins to "visit" Angelina.

July 4: Angelina travels to Hartford, likes what she sees, and makes plans to attend. But the Friends refuse her permission.

November: Sarah's last visit to Charleston.

1832 March: Angelina moves to sister Anna's house.

October: Edward Bettle dies from cholera; the Bettles tell Angelina her presence is not desired at the mourning or funeral.

1832 Early months: Angelina begins reading abolitionist newspapers.

September: Thomas Grimké visits Philadelphia; he and Angelina debate the slavery issue.

October 12: Thomas Grimké dies suddenly.

Last months: Sarah makes an effort to form a Peace Society among Friends but surrenders the idea when she meets resistance.

1835 February 12: Angelina attends a lecture sponsored by the Philadelphia Female Anti-Slavery Society.

March 3: Angelina attends a speech given by the British abolitionist, George Thompson.

May: First appearance of Angelina's name in the minutes of the Philadelphia Female Anti-Slavery Society.

August 30: Angelina writes the letter to William Lloyd Garrison that signals her commitment to abolitionism.

1836 Summer: Angelina writes *Appeal to the Christian Women of the South*. Sarah leaves Philadelphia.

October: The sisters travel to New York to attend an agent-training convention sponsored by the American Anti-Slavery Society, and they begin their agency.

December: Sarah writes *An Epistle to the Clergy of the Southern States*.

1837 May: The sisters attend the first Anti-Slavery Convention of American Women (New York City).

June: The sisters arrive in Boston.

July: Angelina begins to write her *Letters to Catherine [sic] E. Beecher* and Sarah her *Letters on the Equality of the Sexes*.

November: The Massachusetts tour ends with Angelina deathly ill.

1838 February: Angelina testifies before a committee of the Massachusetts legislature on the subject of slavery.

March: Sarah and Angelina deliver six lectures in Boston on the subject of women.

May: Angelina weds Theodore Dwight Weld; the sisters attend the Anti-Slavery Convention of American Women (Philadelphia).

July: Angelina, Theodore, and Sarah settle in Fort Lee, New Jersey. The sisters work in local petition campaigns. They are disowned by the Quakers: Angelina for marrying out of the faith, Sarah for attending the wedding.

November: They begin work on *American Slavery As It Is*.

1839 April: Sarah writes a statement for the British Friends concerning racial discrimination within the American Society of Friends.

December 14: Charles Stuart Faucheraud Weld born.

1840 March: Weld purchases a fifty-acre farm near Belleville, New Jersey. The family takes on the responsibility for caring for an ex-slave of the Grimké family.

April: They remain uncomfortably neutral when the American Anti-Slavery Society splits over the questions of the participation of women and political activity.

1841	January 3: Theodore Grimké Weld born.
	December: Weld goes to Washington to lobby against the gag rule.
1844	March 22: Sarah Grimké Weld born.
1848	October: Weld opens a coeducational institution—the Belleville Boarding School; Angelina and Sarah assist with the administration and teaching.
1850	Angelina elected as a member of the Central Committee of the Woman's Rights Convention (Worcester, Mass.), but is unable to attend.
1851	Angelina attends the Woman's Rights Convention, held in Rochester, N.Y.
1852	Angelina and Sarah contribute, by letter, to the Woman's Rights Convention, held in Syracuse.
1853–54	Sarah moves away as the sisters disagree, ostensibly over control of money, but actually over Sarah's mothering of Angelina and her children.
1854	All three join the Raritan Bay Union (Perth Amboy, N.J.) and Weld starts the Eagleswood School. The union failed in 1856, but the school continued, with Angelina and Sarah teaching there.
1862	Eagleswood graduates its last class.
1863	The family moves to West Newton, Mass. Sarah and Angelina teach at Diocletian Lewis' Young Ladies Boarding School until it burns down in 1867.
	May: Angelina attends a national convention of women held in New York City.
1865	The family works on behalf of the freedmen.
1868	February: Angelina learns that she and Sarah have two mulatto nephews (Archibald Henry Grimké and Francis James Grimké) attending Lincoln College in Pennsylvania; they communicate and form a close relationship. Sarah, Angelina, and Weld serve as officers of the Massachusetts Woman Suffrage Association; Sarah and Angelina circulate petitions.
1870	Sarah and Angelina, with fifty-eight other women, deposit ballots in a local election.
1873	December: Sarah dies.
1879	October 26: Angelina dies.
1895	February 3: Weld dies.

The Public Years of Sarah and Angelina Grimké

SELECTED WRITINGS, 1835–1839

Introduction

PERHAPS no decade in United States history contained more social and intellectual energy than the 1830s. A period of unprecedented economic growth, it fairly burst with radical hopes, plans, and activities, on the one hand, and reaction, on the other. Violent words and deeds frequently fell on those who advocated change.

Midway through that decade, there appeared two unique and unlikely women. Sarah Moore Grimké and Angelina Emily Grimké were not the first women to write or speak on behalf of the abolition of slavery and the right and duty of women to speak publicly, but they were the first women of a slaveholding family to speak; the first women to tour as agents of the American Anti-Slavery Society and to speak before mixed audiences; and the first women within the abolitionist movement to defend publicly, and at length, their right as women to speak.

They were the products of two worlds: a southern world that had strict expectations of women and was becoming increasingly rigid in defense of the institution of slavery but was still infused with a deep sense of spirituality and steeped in biblical knowledge; and a northern world that was undergoing unsettling economic, political, and social transformations, which in turn provoked profound cultural changes. An outburst of voluntarism, in the form of religious revival, benevolent reform, militant reform, and utopian reform was in evidence by the time Angelina joined Sarah in Philadelphia in 1829. Though the Society of Friends provided the bridge across which they walked from South to North, and northern women's groups and abolition societies provided them with a supportive set of institutions, it was, ultimately, their closeness, profound religious faith, and biblical knowledge that sustained them as they broke through the barriers enclosing the "woman's sphere" and marched onto hostile terrain.

Religious devotion carried many nineteenth-century women from the private to the public realms. A Protestant evangelical revival bloomed in

New England in the late 1790s and blossomed forth as the "Second Great Awakening" in Kentucky and Tennessee in 1800. Itinerant Presbyterian and Methodist ministers repudiated Calvinist predestination, assured listeners of the possibility of redemption for those who sincerely sought it, and urged worshipers to renounce personal sin and eliminate social evils. From the midst of the hundreds of thousands of converts there emerged a significant number of reformers of both sexes, who formed, during the 1820s, a united Christian front.[1]

Women's voluntary organizations preceded, indeed anticipated, the formation of this front; they proliferated during the early years of the nineteenth century as women searched for means to establish an identity and respond to urban problems.[2] At first, these women pursued goals and utilized methods that would not provoke unnecessary criticism of them, but as the number of charitable associations multiplied, their goals became more specialized and women grew more confident. Still, they did not challenge their assigned social roles. When broad-based women's reform organizations began to emerge during the early 1830s whose concerns included temperance, peace, and abolition, they tended, with the notable exception of the Moral Reform Societies, to be formed under the aegis of men's organizations.[3]

THE ABOLITION MOVEMENT

ON THE twenty-seventh anniversary of the American Anti-Slavery Society in 1860, Elizabeth Cady Stanton* said: "Yes, this is the only organization on God's footstool where the humanity of woman is recognized, and these are the only men who have ever echoed back her cries for justice and equality. . . . No the mission of this Radical Anti-Slavery Movement is not to the African slave alone, but to the slaves of custom, creed and sex, as well, and most faithfully has it done its work."[4]

There had been quarrels and divisions along the way, though. The motto of radical abolition, the "immediate emancipation" of the slaves, connoted different meanings and means to those who professed to live by it. In addition, several streams had merged to form the most important immediatist organization, the American Anti-Slavery Society, but

* Elizabeth Cady (1815–1902), cousin of the abolitionist Gerrit Smith, married the abolitionist Henry B. Stanton in 1840. She was a coconvenor of the Woman's Rights Convention that met at Seneca Falls, N.Y. in July 1848.

the currents remained distinct and would ultimately follow different channels.

These streams cannot be, despite the attempts of the movement's first historians, narrowly identified with a handful of major personalities; nor can they be divided into two distinct channels. Contemporary historians have, by looking more closely at a wider range of elements, notably the psychological, social, and cultural aspects of abolitionists, placed personalities and ideologies into a larger, interlocking grid of factors. Thus the tensions and differences within the movement are now located in "cliques" and "clusters" rather than blocs. The movement is now seen by its most convincing analysts as a composite of tendencies that altered and overlapped depending on issues, personalities, and the impact of outside forces. These historians (Ronald G. Walters, Lawrence J. Friedman, James Brewer Stewart, and Lewis Perry) present the movement as a meld of nearly converging parts rather than a neat, sharp bifurcation of opposites.[5]

The Society of Friends in Pennsylvania initiated the abolitionist movement. Four Germantown Quakers issued a written statement in 1688 opposing the slave trade; the Philadelphia Yearly Meeting registered its opposition to slavery in 1754 and prohibited slaveholding among its members in 1776. Quakers had been in the forefront of those who organized the Pennsylvania Society for Promoting the Abolition of Slavery, the Relief of Negroes Unlawfully Held in Bondage, and for Improving the Conditions of the African Race (1775); the American Convention for Promoting the Abolition of Slavery and Improving the Conditions of the African Race (1794); the Free Produce movement (boycotting products made with slave labor); and the American Colonization Society (1816). Quaker antislavery activity, however, declined markedly at the end of the 1820s, the result of a doctrinal schism and the shift of the abolition movement toward a more aggressive mode. When a new generation of abolitionists, many from the evangelical ranks, began demanding "immediate emancipation," many Quaker leaders began to discourage involvement in antislavery activity, even disciplining and disowning those who were deemed too active.[6]

The founders of the first important national organization dedicated to solving the problem of slavery, the American Colonization Society (ACS), attempted to solve the United States' slave and race problem simultaneously, by establishing a voluntary process for transporting freed blacks to Africa. It attracted members such as Henry Clay, James Madison, and John Marshall (and the Quaker Benjamin Lundy); won the support of churches, state legislatures, southern planters, and northern philanthropists; secured approval from the British antislavery movement; hired agents; published reams of material; and collected large sums of money from the public and state governments. By 1830, however, it had sent only 1,421 blacks to Liberia,[7] slavery had been extended further west, and opposition to the colonizationist approach was becoming significant both from within and without. Frustrated by these results, a significant nucleus of men—the Tappan brothers (Arthur and Lewis), Theodore Dwight Weld, Gerrit Smith, Amos A. Phelps, and James Gillespie Birney—departed the ACS to join the ranks of the "immediatists."

The move toward immediatism was influenced by the British Society for the Mitigation and Gradual Abolition of Slavery, the revivalism of Charles Grandison Finney, and the personal intensity of William Lloyd Garrison. The British abolition society had been founded in 1823, embraced immediatism in 1830, and formed an agitational auxiliary, the Agency Committee, in 1831. Its example and the works and advice of Britons such as William Wilberforce, Thomas Clarkson, Elizabeth Heyrick, Charles Stuart, and George Thompson contributed significantly to United States abolitionism.

Finney (1792–1875) began his revival in upstate New York in 1824, preaching that man, not God, was the measure of all things. He was the most successful evangelist of the Second Great Awakening. Conversion, he believed, was the path of human progress, and personal moral reform, not legislative or political activity, the best path to social reform. He instructed his young converts: "set out with a determination *to aim at being useful in the highest degree possible.*"[8] He did not join any reform organization, and he did not endorse radical abolitionism, but he and his mentor, George Gale (1789–1862), converted or influenced an entire generation of immediatists.

William Lloyd Garrison (1805–1879) was not the first immediatist, but his intensity, militancy, and confrontational approach vaulted immediatism to the front of the abolitionist movement, where it remained for a full decade. Raised by a strict Baptist mother in Newburyport, Mass., he became an intense and ambitious printer. Garrison converted to the cause of gradual abolition following his meeting with Benjamin Lundy (1789–1839), a Quaker who, in 1821, had founded *The Genius of Universal Emancipation* and begun to travel around the United States promoting antislavery and colonization. Garrison coedited *The Genius* for several months, 1829–1830, until he was jailed on a libel charge.

Bailed out by the Tappans, he wound up in Boston, where he began publishing *The Liberator* in January 1831. One year later, he organized the New England Anti-Slavery Society.

One of his first and most enduring targets was the American Colonization Society. In *The Liberator,* on April 23, 1831, Garrison labeled the ACS a "CONSPIRACY AGAINST HUMAN RIGHTS." Two months later, in an "Address to the People of Color," Garrison called the colonizationist approach "a libel upon humanity and justice—a libel upon republicanism—a libel upon the Declaration of Independence—a libel against Christianity," and said of the society: "Its pretences are false, its doctrine odious, its means contemptible." He reprinted this speech in a 232-page elaboration of his diatribe, published the following year as *Thoughts on African Colonization: or An Impartial Exhibition of the Doctrines, Principles and Purposes of the American Colonization Society.*[9]

Many of the other important personalities of the abolitionist movement of the 1830s came, with Garrison, from the Protestant evangelical tradition and embraced the cause of immediate emancipation as though it were a "sacred vocation," requiring the damnation of rival schools of thought. Immediate emancipation was not so much a program or method as it was a goal, a state of mind, and a vehicle of self-liberation. Animated by visions of a purified United States and a mass of repentant Americans, immediatism, in the early years of the movement, meant nongradual emancipation as an end and intense, undauntable moral pressure as a means.[10]

But those who came into the antislavery movement under the influence of Gale and Finney were never comfortable with Garrison. Foremost among them were Theodore Dwight Weld and Arthur and Lewis Tappan. Weld (1803–1895) had been converted by Finney in 1826. He had preached revival, reform, and gradual abolition until 1832, when he became an immediatist under the influence of his closest male friend, Charles Stuart (1793–c. 1865), and three professors at Western Reserve College: Beriah Green (1795–1874), Elizur Wright, Jr. (1804–1885), and Charles B. Storrs (1794–1833). He became one of the most successful antislavery agents in the West, and he convinced the Tappans to support Lane Seminary in Cincinatti as a theological seminary. When the Lane students became actively involved in abolition and working with blacks in black neighborhoods, the board of trustees moved to end such activities. Weld led a "debate" on the issue in February and March 1834, and, when the trustees passed a set of censoring rules, he and forty other students (the "Lane rebels") left the seminary in October. They established themselves at Oberlin College, intensifying and widening their efforts to convert people to immediate emancipation.

Weld wielded much influence with Arthur (1786–1865) and Lewis (1788–1873) Tappan, wealthy silk merchants who assisted in the organizing, administering, and funding of benevolent reform societies (Bible, tract, missionary, Sunday school, temperance, and seamen), abolitionist organizations (the New York Anti-Slavery Society, the American Anti-Slavery Society, and the American and Foreign Anti-Slavery Society), reform-oriented schools (Oneida Institute, Lane Seminary, and Oberlin College), and made several efforts to create schools for blacks, which were aborted by the violent opposition of local whites.

The various immediatist elements joined together in December 1833, at Philadelphia, when the American Anti-Slavery Society was formed. And yet the single most concerned element of the national antislavery movement, blacks, were woefully underrepresented there: only three of the sixty-two delegates were black.[11] Indeed, although black abolitionists actively involved themselves in antislavery activity, they were not generally accepted by white abolitionists as full partners. Therefore, blacks developed their own organizations, though their tactics and strategies tended to parallel those of whites. By the end of the 1820s several free blacks expressed strong criticism of colonization in particular and gradual abolition in general. The first black newspaper in the United States, *Freedom's Journal* (1827–1829), condemned colonization as a scheme to exile free blacks and perpetuate slavery.[12] And David Walker, in his *Appeal* of 1829, warned white Americans: "we must and shall be free and enlightened as you are. . . . And wo, wo, will be to you if we have to obtain our freedom by fighting."[13] The twenty-six blacks who met in Philadelphia in September 1830, however, to found the American Society of the Free People of Color, took a moderate stance: they encouraged free blacks to emigrate to Canada. Though this society met annually for the next five years, its delegates did not develop a coherent program or a practical plan of action for free or enslaved blacks.[14] Nevertheless, free blacks, with white assistance, constructed and operated for thirty years the underground railway, which aided the escapes of hundreds of slaves from the South.

WOMAN'S RIGHTS

INDIVIDUAL women had publicly objected to slavery and the status of women prior to the 1830s. Prominent among them was Frances Wright (1775–1852), a Scotswoman, who visited the United States in 1820 and published an account of her impressions, *Views of Society and Manners in America*. She wrote that slavery was an "evil" and that women's education was neglected.[15]

She returned to the United States in 1824 and decided to implement a plan for abolition based on cooperative labor, industrial education, and colonization. She outlined it in *A PLAN For the Gradual Abolition of Slavery in the United States, without danger or loss to the Citizens of the South,* and tried to implement a model community at Nashoba, Tennessee. It was not a success, and sexual scandal was attached to it and her. Undaunted, she embarked on a lecture tour of the West, speaking to mixed audiences on the subject of social change, the power of knowledge, and free inquiry. She prescribed universal education as the cure for society's ills: "until women assume the place in society which good sense and good feeling alike assign to them, human improvement must advance but feebly."[16]

Another British woman, the Quaker Elizabeth Heyrick (1769–1831), proved much more influential to the cause of abolition in the United States with her powerful pamphlet, *Immediate, not Gradual Emancipation,* which was reprinted in Philadelphia in 1824. She called gradual abolition "the marplot of human virtue and happiness;—the very master-piece of satanic policy," and though she offered no precise plan to gain immediate emancipation, she did urge her readers: "Let the produce of slave labour,—henceforth and for ever,—be regarded as *'the accursed thing'*, and refused admission into our houses."[17]

Shortly after Heyrick's pamphlet appeared in the United States, and coincident with Wright's efforts to establish Nashoba, a Philadelphia Quaker, Elizabeth Chandler (1807–1834), began sending antislavery contributions to *The Genius of Universal Emancipation*. Three years later, in 1829, she was placed in charge of its "Ladies Repository" section. She wrote numerous poems on the subject and, when attacked, defended her right as a woman to speak out against slavery and the rights of all women to extend their sphere to activities of the mind. They should, she wrote, use their powers

> in advancing the cause of the oppressed, in exciting the compassion of the the proud lords of the creation, for the thousands of her fellow-creatures, of her own sex, too, doomed to drain its very dregs, of the horrors of a cup of bitterness. . . . [S]hould we not, every women of us, north and south, east and west, rise up with one accord, and demand for our miserable sisters a restitution of the rights and privileges of her sex?[18]

She penned a series of letters "To the Ladies of Baltimore," pointing out the horrors of the domestic slave trade, appealing to women of the South to act against the institution, calling on American women to emulate British female abolitionists by supporting the Free Produce movement, and reprinting extracts from Heyrick's *NO British Slavery*.[19]

Collective efforts began in 1829. Three years after men had formed Free Produce societies in Wilmington, Delaware, and Philadelphia, a few Quaker women met in Ohio to organize against using cane sugar, and the American Convention for Promoting the Abolition of Slavery created a Female Association for Promoting the Manufacture and Use of Free Cotton.[20]

The Liberator inaugurated a "Ladies' Department" on January 7, 1832, reprinting Chandler's essay "Our Own Sex." "In their hands," wrote Garrison, "is the destiny of the slaves." Six months later, announcing the formation of the first female antislavery society in New England—the Providence Female Anti-Slavery Society—he added his hope that it would be the forerunner of similar organizations in every part of the country: "The cause of bleeding humanity is always, legitimately, the cause of WOMAN. Without her powerful assistance, its progress must be slow, difficult, imperfect."[21]

He did not, however, open his institutional door to them. Instead, Maria Weston Chapman (1806–1888), three of her sisters (Caroline, Anne, and Deborah), and eight other women organized the Boston Female Anti-Slavery Society. It began as a fund-raising auxiliary for the New England Anti-Slavery Society but soon began to initiate petition campaigns. The Chapman home became the main gathering place for Garrisonian abolitionists in Boston, and Mrs. Chapman was second only to Garrison in the compass and importance of her antislavery activities.

The very next year, 1833, Lydia Maria Child (1802–1880) wrote the first antislavery work to be published in book form in the United States. She was a Unitarian and one of the country's most popular authors. Her husband, David, had been one of the twelve charter members of the

New England Anti-Slavery Society. *An Appeal in Favor of that Class of Americans Called Africans* was a thoroughly researched, logically structured, clearly written critique of the myths propagated about blacks and the slave institution. In it she refuted the colonization scheme and supported immediate emancipation. Although the book's argument was powerfully presented, she was reticent on the subject of women, limiting herself to a sarcastic aside in the Preface—"Read it, from sheer curiosity to see what a woman (who had much better tend to her household concerns) will say upon such a subject"—and, on the last page, almost in passing, noted that women should sign petitions to Congress calling for the abolition of slavery in the District of Columbia.[22]

Samuel J. May (1797–1871), looking back over the formative years of the abolitionist movement, remembered: "That such an author—ay, such an *authority*—should espouse our case just at that crisis, I do assure you, was a matter of no small joy, yes exultation."[23] But Child's literary career suffered: sales of her books plummeted, she lost so many subscriptions that she had to cease publishing her children's magazine, and the Boston Athenaeum revoked her reading privileges. Nevertheless she continued to produce antislavery material, including *The Evils of Slavery and the Cure of Slavery* and *Anti-Slavery Catechism*.[24]

Two years later, in 1835, she compiled a second factual, historical treatise: *Brief History of the Condition of Women, in Various Ages and Nations*. It was not, however, a call to action. She wrote, in the Preface: "This volume is not an essay upon woman's rights, or a philosophical investigation of what is or ought to be the relation of the sexes. . . . I have simply endeavored to give an accurate history of the condition of women, in language sufficiently concise for popular use."[25]

Yet when some sixty delegates met in Philadelphia in December 1833 to organize the American Anti-Slavery Society, no women were invited. On the second day, though, the delegates sent an invitation to the city's antislavery women. Lucretia Coffin Mott* and three other women responded, attending as "spectators and listeners." Although Mott spoke effectively on several occasions, when it came time to prepare the final document, the "Declaration of Sentiments and Purposes," May remembered: "No one suggested that it would be well to invite the women to

* Lucretia Coffin Mott (1793–1880) became a Quaker minister in 1821 and gained renown as one of the most eloquent speakers in the Society of Friends. A few years later, she dedicated herself to support of the Free Produce movement and became one of the best-known and most-respected woman abolitionists. She met Elizabeth Cady Stanton at the World's Antislavery Convention (1840), and eight years later they convened the first Woman's Rights Conference at Seneca Falls, N.Y.

enroll their names as members of the Convention and sign the Declaration. It was not thought of in season."[26] Mott remembered: "I do not think it occurred to any of us that there would be a propriety in our signing the [Declaration]."[27] The male delegates did, however, adopt a resolution thanking "our female friends for the deep interest they have manifested in the cause of anti-slavery, during the long and fatiguing sessions of this Convention."[28]

Indeed, the buttresses supporting separate sexual roles for men and women were still so strong that Mott, when she, on the morrow of the founding of the American Anti-Slavery Society, organized the Philadelphia Female Anti-Slavery Society, she asked James McCrummell, a black man, to preside over it. The women established as their main goal the furthering of the principles and aims of the national organization. In addition to sponsoring petitions calling for the abolition of slavery in the District of Columbia and the territories and promoting the sale of anti-slavery literature throughout the city and adjoining counties, they supported the Free Produce movement, undertook social work among the city's blacks, and sponsored a school for black children.[29]

In sum, a female network existed. Intelligent, active women were making themselves known and their presences felt, but there was no crossover into "man's sphere." May wrote that "though [they] constantly attended our meetings, and often *suggested* the best things that were said and done at them, they could not be persuaded to utter their thoughts aloud. They were bound to silence by the almost universal sentiment and custom which forbade 'women to speak in meetings.' "[30] In addition, the letters exchanged by abolitionists in the United States and Great Britain reveal that males corresponded almost exclusively with males and females with females.[31]

ONE
The Sisters

TOGETHER, Sarah and Angelina Grimké, two daughters of a prominent slaveholding family of South Carolina, changed the nature of female activism in the United States. They have, with one notable exception, received equal treatment from historians: there have been two biographies on the sisters, a biography of Angelina, and a collection of Sarah's writings on women.[1] But Elizabeth Cady Stanton, when she coedited the multivolume *History of Woman Suffrage,* contributed a fifteen-page appreciation of Angelina, appending to it one paragraph on Sarah.[2] To be sure, Angelina was the motivating force in their public activity and delivered the most celebrated of their public speeches. Sarah, however, possessed an equally powerful intellect, wrote with a commanding prose style, and investigated in impressive depth the legal, economic, and social constraints entrapping women in the United States in the nineteenth century.

Historians do diverge, however, on the question of the sisters' radicalism. All concur that Sarah and Angelina's activities and words caused radical results, but Catherine H. Birney and Katherine Du Pre Lumpkin label the sisters as "courageous" and "heroic" women,[3] while Gerda Lerner, Ellen Carol DuBois, and Blanche Glassman Hersh explicitly describe them as conscious radical feminists.[4] The best evidence, Sarah's and Angelina's writings, clearly supports the latter thesis.

Southern girls, however, were not trained or expected to be radical feminists or courageous heroines. Instead, they were trained from earliest childhood to be submissive. *The Rosebud,* a children's magazine published in Charleston, South Carolina, the Grimkés' home, regularly featured fiction filled with pious, obedient little girls. The lessons, institutions, and traditions of southern society, according to Anne Firor Scott, all carried the warning that unladylike behavior would result in rejection, loss of love, and perhaps starvation.[5] Although Scott provides ample evidence that some southern women found their "sphere" confining and their lack of education irksome, and hated the institution of slavery, she concludes that most would not have tried, or known how, to free themselves from their assigned niches.[6] Catherine Clinton, from her detailed examination of the lives of plantation mistresses, concludes that southern culture provided no primary role for unmarried daughters. Unlike unmarried women in the North, who could use independent incomes to live together, unmarried southern women were required to live either with their parents or married siblings.[7]

So powerful was this stricture that, aside from the Grimké sisters, Scott cites only one southern woman who openly worked to end slavery —Mary Berkely Minor Blackford (1802–1896), a Virginia aristocrat, who spent her own and her friends' money to buy slaves and send them to their freedom in Liberia.[8] Clinton notes that Mary Telfair of Savannah, Georgia gave up using black waiting maids, but that Elizabeth Yates of Charleston, despite repeated protestations against holding slaves, could not convince her husband or children to free the family's slaves.[9] Another Virginia woman, Anne R. Page (b. 1781), an evangelical Episcopalian, converted and freed her slaves and sent them to Liberia.[10]

The strength and independence displayed by Sarah and Angelina Grimké can, at least partially, be attributed to the Grimké family. Their father, John Faucheraud Grimké, a legislator and a judge, had intellectual qualities of a high order and a strong belief in one's right to think for oneself. His favorite subject was moral discipline, and he compiled three volumes on law and legal practice. Although he provided the sisters with little formal education, he allowed them access to his large personal library and allowed Sarah to participate in the debates he used to prepare his sons for the law. His death, before they began their serious rebellion from southern standards of womanhood, probably eased their path. Their mother, Mary Smith Grimké, was understanding and affectionate. She was intelligent and had a taste for reading, especially theological works. Rigid and formal in her own duties, she allowed her daughters great leeway and did not disown them for the paths they chose.

Two of their brothers, Thomas and Frederick, were successful lawyers and men of broad learning and high intellect. Thomas Smith Grimké (1786–1834), the second-born child, was at the top of his class at the College of Charleston and Yale, perhaps the most successful lawyer in Charleston, a very generous philanthropist, and one of the most learned of southern men.[11] He delivered numerous orations and addresses and authored well over thirty substantial published pamphlets. He helped organize the American Peace Society and the Colonization Society of

South Carolina, supported the temperance movement, served in the South Carolina Senate (1826–1830), and wrote and spoke heatedly against the efforts of South Carolina politicians to "nullify" (refuse to enforce) the federal tariffs of 1828 and 1832. Grimké wrote extended essays on the fallacies of nullification, denounced it in an open letter to the leading politicians of the state, and spoke against it in the state senate.* He also successfully defended two state militia officers who had refused to take a newly passed oath of allegiance to the state. The sisters regularly corresponded with him, helped him prepare and distribute his peace pamphlets, and wrote, following his death: "None of us may expect to equal, but all of us may grow better and wiser by recollecting the great and holy man who once livd and movd amongst us."[12]

Frederick (1792–1863) also attended Yale and became a lawyer. He moved to Ohio, where he was named a judge of the Court of Common Pleas and then of the Supreme Court of Ohio (1836–1842). He retired from the bench to write *Considerations Upon the Nature and Tendency of Free Institutions,* a detailed philosophical analysis of politics in the United States.[13] Unlike Thomas, who thrilled at the prospects of Christian-inspired reform, Frederick did not believe in the power of moral persuasion, the potential of reform, or the motives of reformers. He believed that blacks were "an inferior and unenlightened order of men" who could not be introduced into white society or transported; hence, he concluded, "there is but one alternative: to retain the institution of slavery."[14]

In sum, a rich lode of strength of mind and resolution ran through the family of John and Mary Grimké. Still, for women to mine it required independence of a higher magnitude than any of the progeny had yet demonstrated.

Sarah displayed few rebellious signs as a child or young woman, but she possessed a fierce determination to find a purpose for herself. She was hampered by the rigid southern framework of expectations and her own lack of confidence in her judgments, but built a foundation for her later work on her father's confidence in her intellect, her own (secret) studies of the law, and her knowledge of the Bible. She gained personal strength after accompanying her father North for medical reasons and attending, alone, to his dying and death in that alien region. During her lone voyage home, she met a Quaker family, the Morrises. Israel Morris

* When a special state convention (November 1832) issued an ordinance of nullification, declaring the tariffs void, President Andrew Jackson promised to use force, if necessary, to enforce federal law. Congress empowered the president by means of a Force Act, which became law on the same day, March 2, 1833, as a compromise tariff. South Carolina then withdrew its ordinance.

gave her a copy of John Woolman's journal.* Finding, on her return, that nothing in her accustomed world offered her spiritual comfort, she read his journal and came to a momentous conclusion: she could not continue to live in Charleston.

Accompanied by her widowed sister Anna Frost, who, though a supporter of the slave institution, wanted to raise her daughter free from its malign influences, Sarah moved to Philadelphia in 1821. Mrs. Frost opened a school, a venture not likely to have been approved in Charleston, and Sarah began attending the Fourth and Arch Street Meeting of the Philadelphia Society of Friends. She did not, however, find a vocation that suited her; her efforts to prepare herself for the ministry foundered on her shyness, her lack of ease in speaking before groups, and the coldness and indifference male members of her meeting displayed toward her halting efforts. She never received a formal "recommendation" from her monthly meeting; neither did she openly challenge her treatment.

Sarah also appears to have accepted quietly the schism that occurred in the Philadelphia Yearly Meeting in 1827, separating the followers of Elias Hicks (1748–1830) from the established orthodox leadership. Hicks represented a democratically inclined, mainly rural group of Friends who resented the increasingly rigid, centralized control of the meeting by prosperous city elders. The Hicksites looked with disapproval on what they saw as the increasing influence of British evangelicals on the American Society of Friends and a growing reliance on Scripture rather than the Inner Light. The elders of the Fourth and Arch Street Meeting were staunchly anti-Hicksite.[15]

They also, like many other elders of other Meetings, did not practice precisely what their doctrine preached about the equality of people. Though the society was the first religious sect based on the principle that men and women possessed equal spiritual qualities, and though it seemed to allow women an equal role within the church's government and discipline, in fact men and the men's monthly meeting exercised far greater policymaking and disciplinary powers.

An equal divergence between concept and practice complicated the relation blacks had with the Society of Friends. American Friends had been speaking against the evils of slavery since 1688, had helped establish

* John Woolman, *A Journal of the Life, Gospel Labours and Christian Experience of that Faithful Minister of Jesus Christ, John Woolman, Late of Mt. Holly in the Province of New Jersey, North America* (Philadelphia, Pa.: Cruikshank, 1774). Woolman (1720–1772) was among the most quietly influential abolitionists of the eighteenth century. He made two trips to the South, published the reports of his observations, and convinced the Philadelphia Yearly Meeting to begin abolishing traffic in slaves among its membership. His *Journal* influenced a large and diverse number of nineteenth-century thinkers and activists.

many of the earliest organizations designed to abolish slavery and aid free blacks, and constituted one-third of the delegates at the founding convention of the American Anti-Slavery Society and forty percent of female abolitionists.[16] Yet blacks who were not members of the Society of Friends found many Friends condescending, and blacks who converted were not admitted to membership in the meetings. The Philadelphia Yearly Meeting of 1796 had tried to overcome this contradiction by agreeing to entertain applications for membership without "distinction of color." Although this decision seemed to open the way for blacks to become full members of a local meeting, most meeting houses retained what were called "Negro benches" or "Negro pews" situated usually in a corner or under the stairs. (At the Fourth and Arch Street Meeting, which Sarah and Angelina joined, blacks had to sit on a back bench.)

Though Sarah had led the way to religious conversion and to Philadelphia, the far more critical and less self-censorious Angelina would blaze the trail to commitment, purpose, and vocation. Although Angelina also suffered bouts of agonizing self-doubt, she possessed much greater confidence in her judgments and in her ability to distinguish right from wrong. Though both expressed, in their diaries, feelings of helpless suffering over the institution of slavery, Angelina spoke out much earlier. Sarah, however, provided Angelina with antislavery material on several occasions and in 1829 pledged money to the American Colonization Society.[17]

Angelina had refused confirmation in the Episcopal church when she was thirteen and converted to Presbyterianism seven years later. She taught Bible classes, organized an interfaith female prayer meeting, and held daily prayer meetings for her family's slaves. She also urged every church member to speak out against slavery. Frustrated with her family and Christianity as practiced in the South, she began to record her thoughts in a diary on January 10, 1828.

Angelina wrote regularly in her diary for five years, recording the details of her increasing frustration with the institution of slavery and those who supported it or mistreated their slaves (notably, her brothers); she also wrote of her conflict over her desire to leave the South and her feelings of duty toward her mother.

A stay of several months in Philadelphia in 1828, regular pressure from Sarah, and growing frustration with southern attitudes finally decided the issue, and Angelina left Charleston for Philadelphia in November 1829. There she was much less humble than Sarah before the restrictions she discovered in the Friends' movement. Angelina was immediately and regularly critical of the shortcomings of the Society of Friends and its members, and she did not remain quiet when she believed that she had been unfairly criticized.

Nevertheless, by the spring of 1831 Angelina had become a member of the Fourth and Arch Street Meeting. She joined Sarah in charity work, trained herself to be a teacher in an infant school, and, when she felt inadequate to that task, sought professional training. She wrote to Catharine E. Beecher (1800–1878) at the Hartford Seminary, met her, visited Hartford, and decided to enroll. However, the meeting would not allow it.

At about that time, Angelina evinced an interest in events outside the Friends' milieu. She began reading abolitionist literature and, when Thomas visited Angelina and Sarah in 1834, she challenged him to forsake colonization and examine the virtues of immediate emancipation. Angelina attended her first antislavery lecture in February 1835 and joined the Philadelphia Female Anti-Slavery Society that spring. Although Sarah did neither of these things, she joined her sister in the Free Produce movement, in questioning the racially segregated seating at meetings, and in pleading with Mrs. Grimké to free her slaves.

*Angelina E. Grimké, diary entry, Charleston, January 10, 1828**

[W/G, Box 22.]

Jany 10. This text rests much on my mind: "I have many things to say unto you, but you cannot hear them now." It does appear to me, & it has appeared so ever since I had a hope that there was a work before me to which all my other duties & trials were only preparatory. I have no idea what it is, & I may be mistaken, but it does seem that *if* I am obedient to the still small voice of Jesus in my heart that he will lead into more difficult paths & cause me to glorify Him in a more honorable & trying work than any in which I have yet been engaged.

* Angelina's diary consists of five paper-covered booklets covering the period from January 10, 1828 through May 1833. There are also eight-odd diary pages written between November 1834 and October 1835.

Angelina E. Grimké, diary entry, Charleston, February 6, 1829

2d Month 6th. I have been suffering for the last two days on account of H[enry]'s boy having run away, because he threatened to whip him. O, who can paint the horrors of slavery & yet so hard is the natural heart that I am continually told that their situation is very good, much better than that of their owners. How strange that anyone should believe such an absurdity or try to make others credit it. No wonder poor John ran away at the threat of a flogging, when H has told me more than once that when he (H) last whipped him, he felt it physically for one week afterwards—so I dont know how the boy must have felt. Indeed, that night was a night of agony to me, for it was not only dreadful to hear him beating him, but the oaths & curses he uttered went like daggers to my heart, & this was done too in the house of one who is regarded as a light in the Church. . . . [H]aving the occasion to go into his room for something, [I] broached the subject as guardedly & mildly as possible, first passing my arm around him & leaning my head on his shoulder. He very openly acknowledged that he meant to give him such a whipping he would cure him of doing the same thing again & that he deserved to be whipped till he could not stand. I remarked that would be treating him worse than he would treat his horse. He now became excited & replied that he considered his *horse* no *comparison better* than *John* & would not beat *it* so. By this time my heart was full & I felt so
sick
much overcome as to be compelled to rest myself or rather to fall into a chair before him. I dont think he knew this—the conversation proceeded—I pled the cause of humanity. He grew very angry & said I had no business to be meddling with him, that he never did it with me. I said if I had ever done any thing to offend him, I was very sorry for it but that I had [been] very careful to do every thing I could to oblige him. He said I had come from the No[rth] expressly to make myself miserable & every body in the house & that I had much better go & live at the North. I told him I was not ignorant that both C[harles]* & himself would be very glad if I did & that as soon as I felt released from Carolina I would go. . . .

* Henry and Charles Grimké, brothers of Sarah and Angelina.

Angelina E. Grimké, diary entry, Charleston, September 11, 1829

11. Much as I have suffered here, yet I find the very idea of leaving poor Mother extremely painful. I think I can truly say it is so painful as to counter-balance the satisfaction felt at the prospect of leaving the land of Slavery. The *only* thing which seems to turn the balance in favour of my going is the consideration that if there is a human being to whose happiness I may contribute, it is my beloved Sister, & when I remember *all* she has done for me from childhood, & look at the deep trials thro' which she has been passing, & the comfort I believe (under the divine blessing) I might be to her, it seems as tho' *I* had no right to refuse to walk in that path which has been so evidently set out before me. I feel very sensibly that last Spring was *my* time for going, but *now* is the Lords time.

Angelina E. Grimké, diary entry, Charleston, September 29, 1829

29. Sometimes when I think of leaving poor Mother, I feel as tho' I cannot do it, & yet when I remember how steadily she has always refused to listen to my advice [about freeing her slaves], *I* cannot hope to be of any service to her, but think the great work will be effected by some other means than my living here & admonishing & reproving with all long-suffering. It appears to me to plain that nothing but her refusing to listen to me has caused this separation. . . .

Angelina E. Grimké, diary entry, Philadelphia, July 20, 1830

7th Mo-20. In the beginning of last month E T and M C* paid me a visit as observers†—& much freedom of expression was used, & *I* found it a satisfactory one, but yesterday they called again to inform me they could not see their way in taking my case to the Monthly Meeting, &

* Unable to identify. The membership roster, "Members of Philadelphia Monthly Meeting: 1829," lists twelve "M. C.'s" and eight "E. T.'s." (Friends Historical Library, Swarthmore College.)

† Meeting officials who monitored candidates for membership.

wished to know whether I still wished it left with them or was willing to make a fresh application when my mind was drawn to do so. I told them that as near as I could judge I had applied at the right time & having done what I believed required of *me,* I preferred it being left entirely with them as I did not think *I* had any more to do in it, adding I was very sure I had not made the application in my own will. A great deal passed, which was exceedingly trying, & which I scarcely knew how to bear. M C further said that one of the testimonies the Society has always supported was duties of children to parents—that the fact of my having embraced different opinions did not release me from my obligations as a child. I told him [?] I did not understand her [?]—(for truly I was totally at a loss to know why he should speak thus as I was unconscious of any dereliction of duty). She went on to query whether *we* were in the path of duty whilst separated from our aged Mother & whether having found new associations & friendships, there was not reason to fear we would invisibly lose that affection for her wh[ic]h we ought to cherish & a good deal more to that purpose. My tears, which had before only stolen down my cheeks, now flowed in torrents. I sobbed aloud. . . . As soon as I could command myself, I remarked that it felt deeply humbling & wounding to me that [she] should think we had committed a breach of duty in leaving Mother—that she was in excellent health & had other daughters with her & that I believed the circumstances must be very peculiar which would render it binding on any one who embraced the principles of Friends to live in a Slave Country, & that I could not feel it my duty to subject myself to the suffering of mind necessarily occasioned by it. That if we were walking in the path of duty, I did not believe our affections would be withdrawn from her, as I tho't the more Religion gained an influence over the mind, the more we should feel the sacred obligations we owed to our relations—and added that it was not only with her consent that we left C.[harleston], but that knowing how much we suffered there she did not wish to see us live there. M C said she did not want to judge of the case but felt compelled to leave it for my consideration.

Angelina E. Grimké, diary entry, Philadelphia, May 12, 1834

5th 12th. Five months have elapsed since I wrote in this diary, since which time I have become deeply interested in the subject of abolition. I had long regarded this cause as utterly hopeless, but since I have examined Antislavery principles, I find them so full of the power of Truth, that I am confident not many years will roll over before the horrible traffic in human beings will be destroyed in this land of Gospel privileges. My soul has measurably stood in the stead of the poor slave & my earnest prayers hav been pourd out that the Lord would be pleasd to permit me to [be] instrumental of good to these degraded, oppressed & suffering fellow creatures. Truly I often feel as if I were ready to go to prison & to death in this cause of justice, mercy & love, but perhaps I may be just like Peter, who was frightened into a triple denial of his Master. O! I think I do know my own weaknesses too well to suppose I can do any thing of myself, but "thro' Christ strengthening me I can do all things," & I do fully believe that if I am able to go back to Carolina, it will not be long before I shall suffer persecution of some kind or other.

TWO

The Commitment

THE VIOLENCE increasingly surrounding abolitionist activity, while driving many Friends away from the American Anti-Slavery Society, proved to be the catalyst that pushed Angelina toward it. Oliver Johnson* wrote about the year 1835: "True, the pro-slavery mobs neither began nor ended with that year, but they were more numerous than at any previous or subsequent time."[1] They were also, he might have added, more prone to violence. Violent antiabolitionist mob activity peaked in August 1835.[2] Garrison countered with two powerful editorials. "Reign of Terror," in the August 15 edition of *The Liberator,* proclaimed Garrison's pledge "that we shall never desist from our practice of publishing the truth, the whole truth, and nothing but the truth, respecting [the South's] thievous and murderous acts, while life remains, or a slave pines in bondage."[3] In the next week's issue, he wrote his "Appeal to our Fellow Citizens," in which he vowed: "WE SHALL NOT YIELD AN INCH."[4]

Angelina, who was spending the summer in Shrewsbury, New Jersey, with Margaret and James Parker, a more liberal cast of Friends, read these stories and decided that she had to express her feelings in writing. Upon receiving her letter, Garrison wrote to a friend: "Angelina E. Grimké, sister of the lamented [Thomas Smith] Grimké, has sent me a soul-thrilling epistle."[5]

Garrison printed Angelina's letter in *The Liberator,* and it was reprinted in several religious and reform newspapers and in two American Anti-Slavery Society pamphlets. It provoked harsh disapproval from elders of the Philadelphia Society of Friends, who pressured Angelina to recant. Sarah also expressed disapproval and tried to dissuade Angelina from pursuing the path of radical abolitionism, but Angelina held firm.

Angelina began to read everything she could find on the subject of

* Oliver Johnson (1808–1889) helped Garrison found the New England Anti-Slavery Society and assisted him with *The Liberator.*

antislavery, to correspond with woman abolitionists, and to speak critically at Friends' meetings. Her letters to Sarah convey a general sense of expectation of a call and the readiness to receive it but do not mention the antislavery movement. There are no letters from Sarah to Angelina during this period, and Sarah's diary hardly mentions her. Sarah's thoughts were focused on her own unhappiness with the meetings (their "oppressiveness"), her fervent desire to find spiritual peace, and confessions of her weakness and sinfulness.

The sisters' growing alienation from the Philadelphia Friends increased when they attended the Providence Yearly Meeting in February 1836, and met many convinced and active abolitionists. Feeling straitened by the Philadelphia Friends, who were in the midst of a debate that would end in 1837 with a rejection of involvement in immediate emancipation, the sisters decided that they could not continue to live with Catherine Morris. At the beginning of the summer, Angelina returned to Shrewsbury and Sarah went to live with a family in Burlington, New Jersey. Angelina began to receive letters from abolitionists who had read her letter to Garrison in *The Liberator*.

The most significant letter came from Elizur Wright, Jr., corresponding secretary of the American Anti-Slavery Society, inviting her, in the name of its Executive Committee, to come to New York to meet with sewing circles of Christian women in private parlors to impart to them her knowledge of slavery. She did not know how to respond. While she was struggling with the prospect, she experienced a revelation: "It has all come to me; God had shown me what I can do; I can write an appeal to Southern women, one which, thus inspired, will touch their hearts, and lead them to use their influence with their husbands and brothers. I will speak to them in such tones that they *must* hear me, and, through me, the voice of justice and humanity."[6]

The result, the *Appeal to the Christian Women of the South,* proved popular with abolitionists—"It sells rapidly," Garrison wrote[7]—but not with the Philadelphia Friends, and certainly not with the South. It was burned in Charleston, and the mayor warned Mrs. Grimké that Angelina would not be allowed to visit the city. If she tried to do so, he said, she would be held on the ship until it returned to the North. Wright was deeply moved by the *Appeal* and renewed the Executive Committee's invitation to her.

Sarah, meanwhile, was essaying a break with Philadelphia and the Philadelphia Friends. About a week after she had written to Angelina approving her antislavery work, Sarah was peremptorily and publicly silenced at the Orange Street Meeting by one of the male elders. She wrote in what would be her final diary entry: "it seems to be one more evidence that my dear Savior designs to bring me out of this place."[8] She then went to Burlington, New Jersey, hoping that "the Lord may be pleased to cast our [her and Angelina's] lot somewhere together."[9]

Unexpectedly, and without precedent, the Executive Committee of the American Anti-Slavery Society invited Angelina to attend a convention of agents scheduled to meet in New York in early November. The Executive Committee, impressed with the success of Weld and the "Lane rebels" in the West, had decided to shift its propaganda thrust from pamphlets to agents. Weld, Henry B. Stanton, and John Greenleaf Whittier were assigned to recruit the candidates;* Weld was to conduct the sessions.

The recruits were called "The Seventy"—"After this the Lord appointed others, seventy in number, and dispatched them ahead of him in pairs to every town and place that he himself intended to visit" (Luke 10:1). The experienced agents from Ohio were sent directly into the field; the others (about thirty) met from November 8 to November 27. Angelina was the only woman invited, although Sarah would join her at all of the sessions. Garrison wrote to his wife: "Our convention has unanimously invited the Grimkés . . . to speak whenever they think proper, and to state such facts respecting slavery as they may choose."[10]

The day after the convention ended, Garrison wrote: "With the exception of the meeting which organized the New England Anti-Slavery Society, and that which was held in Philadelphia in 1833, I regard this convention of Agents as of higher importance than any meeting or convocation which has been held to advance the anti-slavery cause. . . . Weld was the central luminary around which they all revolved."[11]

This convention proved critically important for the immediatist abolition movement. The Seventy dispersed throughout the Northeast, energizing the older societies and creating hundreds of new ones. By the spring of 1837, there were over 1,000 auxiliaries and 100,000 members in the American Anti-Slavery Society. (The following year the society would claim 1,350 auxiliaries and 250,000 members.)[12] Although Pennsylvania was one of the least organized large states—with 32 auxiliaries, as compared to 274 in New York, 213 in Ohio, and 145 in Massachusetts[13]—

* Henry B. Stanton (1805–1887) had been converted by Finney and was one of the Lane "rebels." He was one of the best abolitionist speakers and became financial secretary of the American Anti-Slavery Society. He married Elizabeth Cady in 1840.

John Greenleaf Whittier (1807–1892), a Quaker poet, whose early work was regularly printed in *The Liberator*, had attended the founding convention of the American Anti-Slavery Society.

a combination of factors determined that Sarah and Angelina would not return to Philadelphia to commence their agency. Given their problems with the Philadelphia Friends and their lack of a suitable home, the sisters were probably not eager to return there. They had been living comfortably in New York City for two months; New York State had the largest network of antislavery organizations and membership totals in the nation, and the women there, though they had long been involved in revival and reform activity, were not radically inclined. In sum, it seemed a venue in which the first female abolitionist agents could most comfortably be situated.

Angelina E. Grimké to William Lloyd Garrison, August 30, 1835

[*The Liberator,* September 19, 1835, p. 150.]

CHRISTIAN HEROISM

The following epistle is from a sister of the departed GRIMKÉ. Whether it was sent for our private consolation and encouragement exclusively, or whether it is meekly committed to the disposal of our judgment either for individual or general perusal, we are not certain. We know that its excellent authoress ordinarily shuns public observation, and that nothing but a willingness to bear odium for Christ's sake, or the hope of advancing his cause, would allow her to obtrude her thoughts upon the attention of others. We are thrilled—subdued—strengthened—soul-animated, on reading it. It comes to us as the voice of an angel. Its spirit, dignity, endurance, faith, devotion, are such as have never been excelled by the noblest exhibition of Christian martyrdom even since the days of the apostles. We cannot, we dare not suppress it, nor the name of her who indited it. We publish it, that our cruel assailants may perceive how heavenly is that temper, and how pure that principle, which they are branding as fanaticism and madness. We publish it, that all who are toiling with us for the redemption of the bodies and souls of perishing millions, may be with us quickened and confirmed in our good work. We publish it, especially, that female abolitionists may derive support and comfort from its perusal, in the midst of danger and distress. . . .

This letter will be read widely—attentively, *now:* it will be read with admiration and thanksgiving by *posterity*. It has been written in the midst of universal anarchy and peril—when scorn and insult are the certain portion of those who advocate the right of the bondman to instant emancipation from his fetters—when worldly prudence and policy are crying silence—when many of the clergy and the church are acting the part of traitors to God and their dying fellow men—when to espouse the cause of the black man is to place one's self among the offscouring of all the earth. This makes the gold of Ophir* as dross in comparison with its value.

Philadelphia, 8th month 30th.

Respected Friend:

It seems as if I was compelled at this time to address thee, notwithstanding all of my reasonings against intruding on thy valuable time, and the uselessness of so insignificant a person as myself offering thee the sentiments of sympathy at this alarming crisis.

I can hardly express to thee the deep and solemn interest with which I have viewed the violent proceedings of the last few weeks. Although I expected opposition, yet I was not prepared for it so soon—it took me by surprise, and I greatly feared Abolitionists would be driven back in the first onset, and thrown into confusion. So fearful was I, that though I clung with unflinching firmness to our *principles,* yet I was afraid of even opening one of thy papers, lest I should see some indications of compromise, some surrender, some palliation. Under these feelings, I was urged to read thy Appeal to the Citizens of Boston. Judge, then, what were my feelings, on finding that my fears were utterly groundless, and that thou stoodest firm in the midst of the storm, determined to suffer and to die, rather than yield one inch. My heart was filled with thanksgiving and praise to the Preserver of men; I thanked God, and took courage, earnestly desiring that thousands may adopt thy language, and be *prepared* to meet the Martyr's doom, rather than give up the principle you (i.e., Abolitionists) have adopted. The ground upon which you stand is holy ground; never—never surrender it. If you surrender it, the hope of the slave is extinguished, and the chains of his servitude will be strengthened a hundred fold. But let no man take your crown, and success is as certain as the rising of tomorrow's sun. But remember you must be willing to suffer the loss of all things—willing to be the scorn and reproach of *professor* and profane. You must obey our great masters' injunction: "Fear *not* them that kill the body, and after that, have nothing more that they can do." You must, like Apostles, "count

* A place or region mentioned in the Old Testament where fine gold was obtained (Job 22:24).

not your lives dear unto yourselves, so that you may finish your course with joy."

Religious persecution always begins with *mobs:* it is always unprecedented in the age or country in which it *commences,* and therefore there are no *laws,* by which Reformers can be punished; consequently a lawless breed of unprincipled men determine to take the matter into their hands, and set out in *mobs,* what they know are the *principles* of a large majority of those who are too high in *Church* and State to *condescend* to mingle with them, tho' they *secretly* approve and rejoice over their violent measures. The first martyr who ever died was stoned by a *lawless mob;* and if we look at the rise in various sects—Methodists, Friends, &c.—we shall find that *mobs began* the persecution against them, and it was not until *after* the people had thus spoken out their wishes, that laws were framed to fine, imprison, and destroy them. Let us, then, be prepared for the enactment of laws even in our *Free* States, against Abolitionists. And how ardently has the prayer been breathed, that God would prepare us for *all* he is preparing for us; that he would strengthen us in the hour of conflict, and cover our heads (if consistent with his holy will) in the day of battle! But O! how earnestly have I desired, *not* that we may escape suffering, but that we may be willing to endure unto the end. If we call upon the slaveholder to suffer the loss of what he calls property, then let us show him we make this demand from a deep sense of duty, by being ourselves willing to suffer the loss of character, property—yea, and life itself, in what we believe to be the cause of bleeding humanity.

My mind has been especially turned toward those, who are standing in the forefront of battle, and the prayer has gone up for *their* preservation—not the preservation of their lives, but the preservation of their minds in humility and patience, faith, hope and *charity*—that charity which is the bond of perfectness. If persecution is the means which God has ordained for the accomplishment of this great end, EMANCIPATION; then, in dependence *upon him* for strength to bear it, I feel as if I could say, LET IT COME; for it is my deep, solemn, deliberate conviction, that *this is a cause worth dying for.* I say so, from what I have seen, and heard, and known in a land of slavery, where rests the darkness of Egypt, and where is found the sin of Sodom. Yes! LET IT COME—let *us* suffer, rather than insurrections should arise.

At one time, I thought this system would be overthrown in blood, with the confused noise of the warrior; but a hope gleams across my mind, that *our* blood will be spilt, instead of the slaveholders'; *our* lives will be taken, and theirs spared—I say a *hope,* for of all things I desire to be spared the anguish of seeing our beloved country desolated with the horrors of a servile war. If persecution can abolish slavery, it will purify the Church; and who that stands between the porch and altar, weeping over the sins of the people, will not be willing to suffer, if such immense good will be accomplished. Let us endeavor, then, to put on the *whole* armor of God, and, having done all, to stand ready for whatever is before us.

I have just heard of Dresser's* being flogged: it is no surprise at all; but the language of our Lord has been sweetly revived—"Blessed are ye when men shall revile you, and persecute you, and say all manner of evil against you *falsely,* for my sake. Rejoice and be exceeding glad, for great is your reward in heaven." O! for a willingness and strength to suffer! But we shall have false brethren now, just as the Apostles had, and this will be one of our greatest griefs.

A. E. Grimké.

Sarah M. Grimké, diary entry, Philadelphia, September 25, 1835†

25. The suffering which my precious sister has brought upon herself, by her connection with the anti slavery society, which has been a sorrow of heart to me, is another proof how dangerous it is to slight the clear convictions of Truth. But, like myself, she listened to the voice of the tempter, & oh that she may learn obedience by the things that she suffers. Of myself, I can say the Lord brought me out of the horrible pit, & my prayer for her is that she may be willing to bear the first chastisement *patiently*.

Angelina E. Grimké to Sarah M. Grimké

[Catherine H. Birney, *The Grimké Sisters; Sarah and Angelina Grimké: The First American Women Advocates of Abolition and Woman's Rights* (Boston, Mass.: Lee

* Amos Dresser, a Lane Seminary student, had left Cincinnati on July 1, 1835, to sell "Cottage Bibles" in the South. He carried with him antislavery material and distributed some tracts to sympathetic people he met along the way. His arrival in Nashville, Tennessee, on July 11 aroused suspicions, his box was searched and the antislavery material discovered, and he was summoned to appear before the city's Committee of Vigilance. His "trial" resulted in a verdict of "guilty" and a sentence of twenty lashes on his bare back laid on by a heavy cowhide in the public square. He left in disguise the next morning, carrying only the clothes on his back. His account appeared in *The Liberator* on September 26, 1835, p. 156, and was then published as a pamphlet: *The Personal Narrative of Amos Dresser . . .* (New York: American Anti-Slavery Society, 1836).

† Sarah's diary (W/G, Box 22) consists of eight paper-covered booklets covering the years from August 1819 to August 3, 1836.

and Shepard, 1885; Westport, Conn.: Greenwood, 1969), pp. 126–128; original not found.]

[Shrewsbury, N.J., September 27, 1835]

My Beloved Sister: I feel constrained in all the tenderness of a sister's love to address thee, though I hardly know what to say, seeing that I stand utterly condemned by the standard which thou hast set up to judge me by—the opinion of my friends. This thou seemest to feel an infallible criterion. If it is, I have not so learned Christ, for He says, "he that loveth father or mother more than me is not worthy of me," etc. I do most fully believe that had I done what I have done in a church capacity, I should justly incur their censure, because they disapprove of any intermeddling with the question, but what I did was done in a private capacity, on my own responsibility. Now, my precious sister, I feel willing to be condemned by all but thyself, *without* a hearing; but to thee I owe the sacred duty of vindication, though hardly one ray of hope dawns on my mind that I shall be acquitted even by *thee*. If I know mine own heart, I desire *not* to be acquitted; if I have erred, or if this trial of my faith is needful for me by Him who knoweth with what food to feed His poor dependent ones, thou hast been with me in heights and in depths, in joy and in sorrow, therefore to thee I speak. Thou knowest what I have passed through on the subject of slavery; thou knowest I am an exile from the home of my birth because of slavery—therefore, to thee I speak.

Previous to my writing this letter, I believe four weeks elapsed, during which time, though I passed through close and constant exercise, I did not read anything on the subject of abolition, except the pieces in the Friends' paper and the *Pennsylvanian* relative to the insurrection and the bonfires in Charleston.* I was afraid to read. After this, I perused the Appeal. I confess I could not read it without tears, so much did its spirit harmonize with my own feelings. This introduced my mind into deep sympathy with Wm. Lloyd Garrison. I found in that piece the spirit of my Master; my heart was drawn out in prayer for him, and I felt as if I would like to write to him, but forebore until this day four weeks ago, when it seemed to me I *must* write to him. I put it by and sat

* Angered by the efforts of the American Anti-Slavery Society to inundate the country with antislavery propaganda—the "postal campaign"—a group of Charlestonians broke into a United States post office on the evening of July 29, 1835 and stole bags of mail from New York City containing antislavery pamphlets. On the following evening, a crowd burned the pamphlets and hanged effigies of William Lloyd Garrison and Arthur Tappan.

down to read, but I could not read. I then thought that perhaps writing would relieve *my own mind,* without it being required to send what I wrote. I wrote the letter and laid it aside, desiring to be preserved from sending it if *it* was *wrong* to do so. On Second Day night [Monday], on my bended knees, I implored Divine direction, and next morning, after again praying over it, I felt easy to send it, and, after committing it to the office, felt anxiety removed, and as though I had nothing more to do with it. Thou knowest what has followed. I think on Fifth day [Thursday] I was brought as low as I ever was. After what my Heavenly Father was pleased in great mercy to open the windows of heaven, and pour out upon my grief-bound, sin-sick soul, the showers of His grace, and in prayer at the footstool of mercy I found that relief which human hearts denied me. A little light seemed to arise. I remembered how often, in deep and solemn prayer, I had told my Heavenly Father I was willing to suffer anything if I could only aid the great cause of emancipation, and the query arose whether *this* suffering was not the peculiar kind required of *me*. Since then I have been permitted to enjoy a portion of that peace which human hands cannot rob me of, though great sadness covers my mind; for I feel as though my character had sustained a deep injury in the opinion of those I love and value most—how justly, they will best know at a future day. Silent submission is my portion, and in the everlasting strength of my Master, I humbly trust I shall be enabled to bear whatever is put upon me.

I have now said *all* I have to say, and I leave this text with thee: "Judge not by appearance, but judge righteous judgment"; and again, "Judge nothing before the time." Farewell. In the love of the blessed Gospel of God's Son, I remain thy afflicted sister.

A. E. G.

Angelina E. Grimké, diary entry, Philadelphia, September 1835

9th mo. I believe it is right, when we hav passed thro' deep trials to record our feelings & exercises under them. It is now more than 4 weeks since I tho't I felt it right to write W L G a letter of sympathy & encouragement in regard to the efforts of Abolitionists & the violent opposition made to them. As far as I can possibly judge, I believe that letter, pennd under right feeling, in the spirit of prayer. I felt that it might involve me in some difficulty, & therefore it was written in fear. And after it was written, I hardly knew whether to send it or not, &

therefore again implored divine direction. At last I sent it to the Office & felt a degree of peace in doing so & as tho' I had nothing more to do with it than if I had never written it.

I had some idea it would be published but did not feel [at] liberty to say it must not be, for I had no idea of my name being attached to it if it was. As 3 wks lapsed & I heard nothing of my letter, I concluded it had been broken open in the Office & destroyd; that was just what I hoped would be done if it was wrong in me to hav written it. I think I had no will at all about it, but committed it wholly to the divine disposal.

To my great surprise, last 4th day [Wednesday], Friend B.* came to tell me a letter of mine had been published in the Liberator. He was most exceedingly tried at my having written it & also its publication. He wished me to reexamine the letter, &, if I could, to write to W L G disapproving the publication & altering some expressions in the letter. His visit was, I fully believ, prompted by the affection he bore me, but he appeard utterly incapable of understanding the depth of feeling with which it was written. The Editor's remarks were deeply trying to him. He seemd to think they were the ravings of a fanatic & that the bare mention of my precious brother's name, was a disgrace to his character when coupled with mine, in such a cause, advocated in such a way. I was so perplexd, astonishd & tried that I hardly knew what to say & said very little, declining, however, to write to W L G & expressing my belief that silent, patient suffering would be far better for me than any thing I could possibly do.

That night, I hardly slept at all, & the next day I was sunk as low as I ever hav been, involv'd in great darkness & desiring to feel utterly condemned, if I had done wrong. I was truly miserable, believing my character was altogether gone among my dearest, most valuable friends. My grief-bound heart could not weep, but was sick of sorrow until evening, when I was enabled to throw myself as a helpless sinner at the foot of the Cross & plead for sight & for strength to undo, or to bear just what was required. I was indeed brought to the brink of despair as the vilest of sinners. A little light dawnd, & I remembered how often I had told the Lord if he would only prepare me to be & make me instrumental in the great work of Emancipation, I would be willing to bear any suffering, & the query arose, whether this was not the peculiar

* Samuel Bettle, a wealthy Quaker philanthropist and overseer of the Arch Street Meeting whose son, Edward, had been in love with Angelina. When Edward died, in late 1832, the Bettles refused to allow Angelina to pay them a condolence call.

kind allotted to me. O! the extreme strain of extravagant praise—to be held up as a saint in a public newspaper before thousands of people, when I felt I was the chief of sinners. Blushing & confusion of face were mine, & I tho't the walls of a prison would hav been preferable to such an exposure. Then again, to hav my name, not so much *my* name, as the name of Grimké associated with that of the despised Garrison, seemd like bringing disgrace upon my *family,* not myself alone. I felt as tho' the name had been tarnished in the eye of thousands who had before lovd & reverd it. Nevertheless, I was helpd with a little strength, and tho' I sufferd so deeply, I could not blame the publication of my letter, nor would I have recalld it if I could. I believd I had done right, that tho' condemnd by human judges, I was acquitted by him whom I believ qualifyd me to write it, & I feel willing to bear all, if it was only made instrumental of good. I felt my great unworthiness of being used in such a work but rememberd that "God hath chosen the *weak things* of this world to confound the wise" & so was comforted. Since this time, my greatest trial is the continued opposition of my precious sister S. She thinks I have been given over to blindness of mind & that I do not know light from darkness & right from wrong. Her grief is that I cannot see it was wrong in me ever to hav written the letter at all, & she seems to think I deserv all the suffering I have brought upon myself.

Angelina E. Grimké, diary entry, Philadelphia, October 1835

10 mo—O, the goodness & mercy of God. He has been graciously pleasd to deliver me from the trial & the apprehension of trial with regard to the writing of that letter. The storm seems to hav gone over for the present. Condemnation I do not feel, & I think I hav been enabled to cast the responsibility on Him by whose direction I *think* I wrote it. . . . O, I sometimes feel as if I am willing to become any thing if the Lord will only purify & refine & make me useful in his Church militant & prepare me at last for her [manuscript breaks off].

Angelina E. Grimké to the Ladies Anti-Slavery Society, Concord, New Hampshire

[Pennsylvania Abolition Society Papers, The Historical Society of Pennsylvania, Box 11A, Folder 3.]

[Burlington, N.J.?] 3d Mo., 16, 1836.

Respected Friends,

. . . My heart was indeed refreshed and comforted by the spirit of love which breathed through every part of your letter & I rejoice, that, among abolitionists, there are thousands who can adopt its language. As a Southerner, I cannot be too thankful that they are almost universally advocates for *Peace,* as well as *Emancipation;* thus affording to the masters the strongest evidence that, through them, they have nothing to fear from insurrection and murder. I think it very important that every member of an Anti Slavery Society should belong to a Peace Society, also, and allow me, dear friends, in the freedom of the gospel to bring this consideration home to each one of you. Let me exhort you, first, to examine the doctrine of non-resistance by the Sermon on the Mount, by secret & social prayer to seek for that wisdom which cometh down from above, which is first pure, then *peaceable,* gentle & easy to be entrusted, full of mercy & good fruits. Then look at this subject by the light of our great Master's example; follow him through his life of suffering & contempt, despised and rejected of man; ["]a man of sorrow & acquainted with grief." Ponder in your hearts those divine precepts which he registered in characters of light & love in his own living experience, "leaving us an example that we might walk in his steps," & then decide whether christians, under the glorious dispensation of the gospel can *ever* resist evil, either in an individual or corporate capacity, in private or in public, without swerving from the purity of his example. . . . Suffer me, then, to suggest whether the formation of a Female Peace Society in Concord, would not be a valuable auxiliary to the Anti Slavery Society of which you are members. Several have already been formed in our country; one, about ten days since, in this city of brotherly love, & another, the week before, at Newark, N.J., besides two others in New England. Any information you may desire on this subject, may be obtained, by addressing a letter to Wm. Ladd, of Minot, Maine. . . .*

With feelings of christian regard,
I remain your Friend,

A. E. Grimké.

* William Ladd (1778–1841), one of the founders of the American Peace Society, its president, and editor of its newspaper.

Angelina E. Grimké to Sarah M. Grimké

[W/G, Box 3.]

[Shrewsbury, N.J.] First day—[July 10, 1836]

My Beloved sister

. . . 2d day [Monday] morning, after breakfast, I was sitting in silence & desiring to know why I had been bro't here & what the Lord would hav me to do. It seemd as tho' my designs of modernizing Gough* & writing the history of the U S on peace principles hav both been frustrated, & I hardly know what to do. At first, I tho't I would write a little book on the beauty & duty of Forgiveness as illustrated by Josephs history; then I tho't if I was going to write on Scripture characters, I might as well begin at Adam. I finally concluded to commence a Sacred History of the Bible, just writing down all the information I can gather from Horne, Calmet &c,† interspersed with original remarks &c. I accordingly began, & I am sure *I* shall be materially benefitted by it, tho' it may never pass thro' the proofs. My whole mornings are thus passd in studying Townsend‡ & writing out the history according to his arrangement.

Thine very affy Angelina

Angelina E. Grimké to Sarah M. Grimké

[W/G, Box 3.]

[Shrewsbury, N.J.] 3d day morning, [July] 19th [1836]

My Beloved sister

. . . The lack of usefulness among others seems to hav been thrown open in a most unexpected & wonderful manner, whilst this loss of usefulness in our S F [Society of Friends] seems as if it was hard & double-locked to me. I feel no opening among frds. My spirit is oppressed & heavy-laden & wrout up in passion. What then am I to do? The only relief I experience is in writing letters & pieces for the Peace &

* John Gough, *A History of the people called Quakers, from their first rise to the present time [1764]. Compiled from authentic records, etc.* (Dublin: 1789–1790).

† Thomas Hartwell Horne, *An Introduction to the Critical Study and Knowledge of Holy Scriptures*, 4 vols., 5th ed. (London: 1825); Augustin Calmet, *Antiquities Sacred and Profane; or A collection of critical dissertations on the Old and New Testament . . . Done into English, with additional notes by N. Tindal . . .* (London: Roberts, 1727).

‡ George Townsend, *The Old Testament arranged in historical and chronological order; The New Testament arranged in chronological and historical order, with notes, etc.* (London: Rivington, 1821 and 1825).

Anti Slavery causes, & this makes me think my influence is to reach beyond our own limits.

As to E W's proposal, I cannot think of acceding to it, because I hav seen so clearly that my work, at least, must be a sacrifice in the reformations of the day, but if it is engaged in a school, my brain would not be my own. No money that could be given could induce me to bind myself, my body, mind & soul, so completely in Phila. There is no lack of light as to the right decision about this.

4th day [Wednesday]. I had written so far, Dearest, when I got so unwell that I spent at most the whole of the rest of the day in bed, for, besides my periodical troubles, Elizur Wright's letter threw my mind into such a state of deep suffering the night previous that I hardly slept at all. The bare idea that such a thing may be required is truly alarming & that thy mind should be at all resignd to it increases the fear I feel that probably I may have to do it. Thou mayest remember that is just what Friends in New England wanted me to do, for it does not appear by the letter that it is expected that I should extend my labors *out* of our Society. One thing, however, I do see clearly that I am not to do it now, for I hav begun to write "An Appeal to Christian Women of the South," which I feel must be finished first. . . .

My wish is to submit it to the publishing committee of the An A S Sy [American Anti-Slavery Society] of New York for revision & correction, to be published by them with my name attachd, for I well know my name is worth more than myself & will add weight to it. Now, Dearest, what dost thou think of it—a pretty bold step, I know, & one my friends will highly disapprove, but this is a day in which I believe I must act indifferently of consequences to myself, for of how little consequence will my trials be if the cause of Truth is only helped forward one inch. . . . This, my beloved sister, has been a subject of deep reflection & solemn prayer, & I trust I am not touching the Ark with unholy, lewd hands. Pray for me, then, that I may be helped in this undertaking, for I feel it to be a great one, & one in which I need divine aid. I mean to write to E. Wright by tomorrow's mail, informing him that I am writing such a pamphlet at present & feel as if the proposition of the tour is one of too g[reat im]portance either to refuse or accept without more reflection than I have yet been able to give it. It would indeed be a great trial to me to hav to [word missing] their [Friends'] secret & quiet reproof, but if duty calls, I must go.

Farewell dearest of all in the bonds of gospel love

A. E. Gé

Sarah M. Grimké, diary entry, Burlington, July 19, 1836

19th. Amidst much to try & exercise me on account of my precious sister & myself, I have not yet been favored, for the most part, with a quiet mind & been enabled at this eventful crisis to leave our concerns in his hands, believing that he will not permit her to do wrong, but will enable her to see whether the proposal for her to enter into active service in the Anti Slavery cause is in accordance with his holy will. And for myself, whether or not I must still continue in this city of bonds. . . .

Angelina E. Grimké to Sarah M. Grimké

[W/G, Box 3.]

[Shrewsbury, N.J.] First day evening—[July 31, 1836]

My dearest Sister

I have just finished my Appeal to Southern Women. It has furnished work for two weeks, having been extended to 46 pages of foolscap paper. How much I wish I could have you here, if it were only for 3 or 4 hours, that we might read it over together before I send it to Elizur Wright. . . .

I have just received thy precious letter. . . . I cannot be too thankful for the change in thy feelings with regard to the A S Society & feel no desire at all to blame thee for former opposition, believing as I do that it was permitted in order to drive me closer to my Savior & into a deeper examination as to the ground upon which I was standing. . . . O, sister, I feel as if I could not only giv up friends, but life itself, for the slave, if it is called for. I feel as if I could go anywhere to serve him even down to the South, if I am calld there. . . . The conviction deepens & strengthens, as retirement affords fuller opportunity for calm reflection, that the cause of Emancipation is a cause worth suffering, yea, dying for, if need be. With regard to the proposed decision [regarding Wright's proposal], I can see nothing about it, & never did any poor creature feel more unfit to do anything than I do to undertake it. May the Lord's will be done in me & thro' me & by me is all I crave every day. . . .

It really seems as if Friends were determined we should not be useful among them, when I can truly say I desired to be so & would have sacrificed any thing if I could; but it is all right just as it is. I feel completely shut up among them & as tho' I hav nothing to do with them, unless it is on the subject of slavery. . . . I sometimes feel frightend to think of how long I was standing idle in the market place, & I cannot help attributing it, in a great measure, to the doctrine of nothingness so consistently preachd up in our society. It is the most paralyzing, zeal-quenching doctrine that ever was preachd in the Church, & I believe has produced its legitimate fruit of nothingness introducing us to nothing, when we might have been a light in the Christian Ch[urch]. . . .

Thy aff A.

Angelina Emily Grimké, Appeal to the Christian Women of the South*

> Then Mordecai commanded to answer Esther. Think not within thyself that thou shalt escape in the king's house more than all the Jews. For if thou altogether holdest thy peace at this time, then shall there enlargement and deliverance arise to the Jews from another place: but thou and thy father's house shall be destroyed: and who knoweth whether thou art come to the kingdom for such a time as this. And Esther bade them return Mordecai this answer: —and so will I go unto the king, which is not according to law, and *if I perish, I perish.* Esther IV. 13–16.

RESPECTED FRIENDS,

It is because I feel a deep and tender interest in your present and eternal welfare that I am willing thus publicly to address you. Some of you have loved me as a relative, and some have felt bound to me in Christian sympathy, and Gospel friendship; and even when compelled by a strong sense of duty, to break those outward bonds of union which bound us together as members of the same community, and members of the same religious denomination, you were generous enough to give me credit, for sincerity as a Christian, though you believed I had been most strangely deceived. I thanked you then for your kindness, and I ask you *now,* for the sake of former confidence, and friendship, to read the following pages in the spirit of calm investigation and fervent prayer. It is because you have known me, that I write thus unto you.

But there are other Christian women scattered over the Southern States, a very large number of whom have never seen me, and never

* (New York: [American Anti-Slavery Society], 1836; New York: Arno and *New York Times,* 1969).

heard my name, and who feel *no* interest whatever in *me.* But I feel an interest in *you,* as branches of the same vine from whose root I daily draw the principle of spiritual vitality—Yes! Sisters in Christ I feel an interest in *you,* and often has the secret prayer arisen on your behalf, Lord "open thou their eyes that they may see wondrous things out of thy Law"—It is then, because I *do feel* and *do pray* for you, that I thus address you upon a subject about which of all others, perhaps you would rather not hear any thing; but, "would to God ye could bear with me a little in my folly, and indeed bear with me, for I am jealous over you with godly jealousy." Be not afraid then to read my appeal; it is *not* written in the heat of passion or prejudice, but in that solemn calmness which is the result of conviction and duty. It is true, I am going to tell you unwelcome truths, but I mean to speak those *truths in love,* and remember Solomon says, "faithful are the *wounds* of a friend." I do not believe the time has yet come when *Christian women* "will not endure sound doctrine," even on the subject of slavery, if it is spoken to them in tenderness and love, therefore I now address *you.*

To all of you then, known or unknown, relatives or strangers, (for you are all *one* in Christ,) I would speak. I have felt for you at this time, when unwelcome light is pouring in upon the world on the subject of slavery; light which even Christians would exclude, if they could, from our country, or at any rate from the southern portion of it, saying, as its rays strike the rock bound coasts of New England and scatter their warmth and radiance over her hills and valleys, and from thence travel onward over the Palisades of the Hudson, and down the soft flowing waters of the Delaware and gild the waves of the Potomac, "hitherto shalt thou come and no further"; I know that even professors of His name who has been emphatically called the "Light of the world" would, if they could, build a wall of adamant around the Southern States whose top might reach unto heaven, in order to shut out the light which is bounding from mountain to mountain and from the hills to the plains and valleys beneath, through the vast extent of our Northern States. But believe me, when I tell you, their attempts will be as utterly fruitless as were the efforts of the builders of Babel; and why? Because moral, like natural light, is so extremely subtle in its nature as to overleap all human barriers, and laugh at the puny efforts of man to control it. All the excuses and palliations of this system must inevitably be swept away, just as other "refuges of lies" have been, by the irresistible torrent of a rectified public opinion. "The *supporters* of the slave system," says Jonathan Dymond in his admirable work on the Principles of Morality,* "will *hereafter* be regarded with the *same* public feeling, as he who was an advocate for the slave trade *now is.*" It will be, and that very soon, clearly perceived and fully acknowledged by all the virtuous and the candid, that in *principle* it is as sinful to hold a human being in bondage who has been born in Carolina, as one who has been born in Africa. All that sophistry of argument which has been employed to prove, that although it is sinful to send to Africa to procure men and women as slaves, who have never been in slavery, that still, it is not sinful to keep those in bondage who have come down by inheritance, will be utterly overthrown. We must come back to the good old doctrine of our forefathers who declared to the world, "this self evident truth that *all* men are created equal, and that they have certain *inalienable* rights among which are life, *liberty,* and the pursuit of happiness." It is even a greater absurdity to suppose a man can be legally born a slave under *our free Republican* Government, than under the petty despotisms of barbarian Africa. If then, we have no right to enslave an African, surely we can have none to enslave an American; if it is a self evident truth that *all* men, every where and of every color are born equal, and have an *inalienable right to liberty,* then it is equally true that *no* man can be born a slave, and no man can ever *rightfully* be reduced to *involuntary* bondage and held as a slave, however fair may be the claim of his master or mistress through will and title-deeds.

But after all, it may be said, our fathers were certainly mistaken, for the Bible sanctions Slavery, and that is the highest authority. Now the Bible is my ultimate appeal in all matters of faith and practice, and it is to *this test* I am anxious to bring the subject at issue between us. Let us then begin with Adam and examine the charter of privileges which was given to him. "Have dominion over the fish of the sea, and over the fowl of the air, and over every living thing that moveth upon the earth." In the eighth Psalm we have a still fuller description of this charter which through Adam was given to all mankind. "Thou madest him to have dominion over the works of thy hands; thou hast put all things under his feet. All sheep and oxen, yea, and the beasts of the field, the fowl of the air, the fish of the sea, and whatsoever passeth through the paths of the seas." And after the flood when this charter of human rights was renewed, we find *no additional* power vested in man. "And the fear

* Jonathan Dymond (1796–1828), a British Quaker moralist, published *An Enquiry into the Accordancy of War with the Principles of Christianity* . . . in 1823 and founded a peace society in Exeter in 1825. *Essays on the principles of morality, and on the private and political rights of mankind* was published posthumously in England in 1829. The sisters edited a version of it with notes by Thomas S. Grimké (Philadelphia, Pa.: Ashmead, 1834).

of you and the dread of you shall be upon every beast of the earth, and every fowl of the air, and upon all that moveth upon the earth, and upon all the fishes of the sea, into your hand are they delivered." In this charter, although the different kinds of *irrational* beings are so particularly enumerated, and supreme dominion over *all of them* is granted, yet *man is never* vested with this dominion *over his fellow man;* he was never told that any of the human species were put *under his feet;* it was only *all things,* and man, who was created in the image of his Maker, *never* can properly be termed a *thing,* though the laws of Slave States do call him a "chattel personal"; *Man* then, I assert *never* was put *under the feet of man,* by that first charter of human rights which was given by God, to the Fathers of the Antediluvian and Postdiluvian worlds, therefore this doctrine of equality is based on the Bible.

But it may be argued, that in the very chapter of Genesis from which I have last quoted, will be found the curse pronounced upon Canaan, by which his posterity was consigned to servitude under his brothers Shem and Japheth. I know this prophecy was uttered, and was most fearfully and wonderfully fulfilled, through the immediate descendants of Canaan, i.e. the Canaanites, and I do not know but it has been through all the children of Ham, but I do know that prophecy does *not* tell us what *ought to be,* but what actually does take place, ages after it has been delivered, and that if we justify America for enslaving the children of Africa, we must also justify Egypt for reducing the children of Israel to bondage, for the latter was foretold as explicitly as the former. I am well aware that prophecy has often been urged as an excuse for Slavery, but be not deceived, the fulfilment of prophecy will *not cover one sin* in the awful day of account. Hear what our Saviour says on this subject; "it must needs be that offences come, but *woe unto that man through whom they come"*—Witness some fulfilment of this declaration in the tremendous destruction of Jerusalem, occasioned by that most nefarious of all crimes the crucifixion of the Son of God. Did the fact of that event having been foretold, exculpate the Jews from sin in perpetrating it; No —for hear what the Apostle Peter says to them on this subject, "Him being delivered by the determinate counsel and foreknowledge of God, *ye* have taken, and by *wicked* hands have crucified and slain." Other striking instances might be adduced, but these will suffice.

But it has been urged that the patriarchs held slaves, and therefore, slavery is right. Do you really believe that patriarchal servitude was like American slavery? Can you believe it? If so, read the history of these primitive fathers of the church and be undeceived. Look at Abraham, though so great a man, going to the herd himself and fetching a calf from thence and serving it up with his own hands, for the entertainment of his guests. Look at Sarah, that princess as her name signifies, baking cakes upon the hearth. If the servants they had were like Southern slaves, would they have performed such comparatively menial offices for themselves? Hear too the plaintive lamentation of Abraham when he feared he should have no son to bear his name down to posterity. "Behold thou hast given me no seed, &c, one born in my house *is mine* heir." From this it appears that one of his *servants* was to inherit his immense estate. Is this like Southern slavery? I leave it to your own good sense and candor to decide. Besides, such was the footing upon which Abraham was with *his* servants, that he trusted them with arms. Are slaveholders willing to put swords and pistols into the hands of their slaves? He was as a father among his servants; what are planters and masters generally among theirs? When the institution of circumcision was established, Abraham was commanded thus; "He that is eight days old shall be circumcised among you, *every* man-child in your generations; he that is born in the house, or bought with money of any stranger which is not of thy seed." And to render this command with regard to his *servants* still more impressive it is repeated in the very next verse; and herein we may perceive the great care which was taken by God to guard the *rights of servants* even under his "dark dispensation." What too was the testimony given to the faithfulness of this eminent patriarch. "For I know him that he will command his children and his *household* after him, and they shall keep the way of the Lord to do justice and judgment." Now my dear friends many of you believe that circumcision has been superseded by baptism in the Church; *Are you* careful to have *all* that are born in your house or bought with money of any stranger, baptized? Are *you* as faithful as Abraham to command *your household to keep the way of the Lord?* I leave it to your own consciences to decide. Was patriarchal servitude then like American Slavery?

But I shall be told, God sanctioned Slavery, yea commanded Slavery under the Jewish Dispensation. Let us examine this subject calmly and prayerfully. I admit that a species of *servitude* was permitted to the Jews, but in studying the subject I have been struck with wonder and admiration at perceiving how carefully the servant was guarded from violence, injustice and wrong. I will first inform you how these servants became servants, for I think this a very important part of our subject. From consulting Horne, and the Bible, I find there were six different ways by which the Hebrews became servants legally.

1. If reduced to extreme poverty, a Hebrew might sell himself, i.e. his services, for six years, in which case *he* received the purchase money *himself.* Lev. xxv, 39.

2. A father might sell his children as servants, i.e. his *daughters,* in which circumstance it was understood the daughter was to be the wife or daughter-in-law of the man who bought her, and the *father* received the price. In other words, Jewish women were sold as *white women* were in the first settlement of Virginia—as *wives, not* as slaves. Ex. xxi, 7.

3. Insolvent debtors might be delivered to their creditors as servants. 2 Kings iv, 1.

4. Thieves not able to make restitution for their thefts, were sold for the benefit of the injured person. Ex. xxii, 3.

5. They might be born in servitude. Ex. xxi, 4.

6. If a Hebrew had sold himself to a rich Gentile, he might be redeemed by one of his brethren at any time the money was offered; and he who redeemed him, was *not* to take advantage of the favor thus conferred, and rule over him with rigor. Lev. xxv, 47–55.

Before going into an examination of the laws by which these servants were protected, I would just ask whether American slaves have become slaves in any of the ways in which the Hebrews became servants. Did they sell themselves into slavery and receive the purchase money into their own hands? No! Did they become insolvent, and by their own imprudence subject themselves to be sold as slaves? No! Did they steal the property of another, and were they sold to make restitution for their crimes? No! Did their present masters, as an act of kindness, redeem them from some heathen tyrant to whom *they had sold themselves* in the dark hour of adversity? No! Were they born in slavery? No! No! not according to *Jewish Law,* for the servants who were born in servitude among them, were born parents who had *sold themselves* for six years: Ex. xxi, 4. Were the female slaves of the South sold by *their* fathers? How shall I answer this question? Thousands and tens of thousands never were, *their* fathers *never* have received the poor compensation of silver or gold for the tears and toils, the suffering, and anguish, and hopeless bondage of *their* daughters. They labor day by day, and year by year, side by side, in the same field, if haply their daughters are permitted to remain on the same plantation with them, instead of being as they often are, separated from their parents and sold into distant states, never again to meet on earth. But do the *fathers of the South ever sell their daughters?* My heart beats, and my hand trembles, as I write the awful affirmative, Yes! The fathers of this Christian land often sell their daughters, *not* as Jewish parents did, to be the wives and daughters-in-law of the man who buys them, but to be the abject slaves of petty tyrants and irresponsible masters. Is it not so, my friends? I leave it to your own candor to corroborate my assertion. Southern slaves then have *not* become slaves in any of the six different ways in which Hebrews became servants, and I hesitate not to say that American masters *cannot* according to *Jewish law* substantiate their claim to the men, women, or children they now hold in bondage.

But there was one way in which a Jew might illegally be reduced to servitude; it was this, he might be *stolen* and afterwards sold as a slave, as was Joseph. To guard most effectually against this dreadful crime of manstealing, God enacted this severe law. "He that stealeth a man and selleth him, or if he be found in his hand, he shall surely be put to death."* As I have tried American Slavery by *legal* Hebrew servitude, and found, (to your surprise, perhaps,) that Jewish law cannot justify the slaveholder's claim, let us now try it by *illegal* Hebrew bondage. Have the Southern slaves then been stolen? If they did not sell themselves into bondage; if they were not sold as insolvent debtors or as thieves; if they were not redeemed from a heathen master to whom *they had sold themselves;* if they were not born in servitude according to Hebrew law; and if the females were not sold by their fathers as wives and daughters-in-law to those who purchased them; then what shall we say of them? what can we say of them? but that according *to Hebrew Law they have been stolen.*

But I shall be told that the Jews had other servants who were absolute slaves. Let us look a little into this also. They had other servants who were procured in two different ways.

1. Captives taken in war were reduced to bondage instead of being killed; but we are not told that their children were enslaved. Deut. xx, 14.

2. Bondmen and bondmaids might be bought from the heathen round about them; these were left by fathers to their children after them, but it does not appear that the *children* of these servants ever were reduced to servitude. Lev. xxv, 44.

I will now try the right of the southern planter by the claims of Hebrew masters over their *heathen* slaves. Were the southern slaves taken captive in war? No! Were they bought from the heathen? No! for surely,

* And again, "If a man be found stealing any of his brethren of the children of Israel, and maketh merchandise of him, or selleth him; then *that thief shall die,* and thou shalt put away evil from among you." Deut. xxiv, 7. [Footnote in original.]

no one will *now* vindicate the slave-trade so far as to assert that slaves were bought from the heathen who were obtained by that system of piracy. The only excuse for holding southern slaves is that they were born in slavery, but we have seen that they were *not* born in servitude as Jewish servants were, and that the children of heathen slaves were not legally subjected to bondage even under the Mosaic Law. How then have the slaves of the South been obtained?

I will next proceed to an examination of those laws which were enacted in order to protect the Hebrew and the Heathen servant; for I wish you to understand that *both* are protected by Him, of whom it said "his mercies are over *all* his works." I will first speak of those which secured the rights of Hebrew servants. This code was headed thus:

1. Thou shalt *not* rule over him with *rigor,* but shalt fear thy God.

2. If thou buy a Hebrew servant, six years shall he serve, and in the seventh year he shall go out free for nothing. Ex. xxi, 2.*

3. If he come in by himself, he shall go out by himself; if he were married, then his wife shall go out with him.

4. If his master have given him a wife and she have borne him sons and daughters, the wife and her children shall be his master's, and he shall go out by himself.

5. If the servant shall plainly say, I love my master, my wife, and my children; I will not go out free; then his master shall bring him unto the Judges, and he shall bring him to the door, or unto the door-post, and his master shall bore his ear through with an awl, and he shall serve him *forever*. Ex. xxi, 5–6.

6. If a man smite the eye of his servant, or the eye of his maid, that it perish, he shall let him go *free* for his eye's sake. And if he smite out his man servant's tooth or his maid servant's tooth, he shall let him go *free* for his tooth's sake. Ex. xxi, 26, 27.

7. On the Sabbath rest was secured to servants by the fourth commandment. Ex. xx, 10.

8. Servants were permitted to unite with their masters three times in every year in celebrating the Passover, the feast of Pentecost, and the feast of Tabernacles; every male throughout the land was to appear before the Lord at Jerusalem with a gift; here the bond and the free stood on common ground. Deut. xvi.

9. If a man smite his servant or his maid with a rod, and he die under

* And when thou sendest him out free from thee, thou shalt not let him go away empty: Thou shalt furnish him *liberally* out of thy flock and out of thy floor, and out of thy wine-press: of that wherewith the Lord thy God hath blessed thee, shalt thou give unto him. Deut. xv, 13, 14. [Footnote in original.]

his hand, he shall be surely punished. Notwithstanding, if he continue a day or two, he shall not be punished, for he is his money. Ex. xxi, 20, 21.

From these laws we learn that Hebrew men servants were bound to serve their masters *only six* years, unless their attachment to their employers, their wives and children, should induce them to wish to remain in servitude, in which case, in order to prevent the possibility of deception on the part of the master, the servant was first taken before the magistrate, where he openly declared his intention of continuing in his master's service, (probably a public register was kept of such) he was then conducted to the door of the house, (in warm climates doors are thrown open,) and *there* his ear was *publicly* bored, and by submitting to this operation he testified his willingness to serve him *forever,* i.e. during his life, for Jewish Rabbins who must have understood Jewish *slavery,* (as it is called,) "affirm that servants were set free at the death of their masters and did *not* descend to their heirs": or that he was to serve him until the year of Jubilee, when *all* servants were set at liberty. To protect servants from violence, it was ordained that if a master struck out the tooth or destroyed the eye of a servant, that servant immediately became *free,* for such an act of violence evidently showed he was unfit to possess the power of a master, and therefore that power was taken from him. All servants enjoyed the rest of the Sabbath and partook of the privileges and festivities of the three great Jewish Feasts; and if a servant died under the infliction of chastisement, his master was surely to be punished. As a tooth for a tooth and life for life was the Jewish law, of course he was punished with death. I know that great stress has been laid upon the following verse: "Notwithstanding, if he continue a day or two, he shall not be punished, for he is his money."

Slaveholders, and the apologists of slavery, have eagerly seized upon this little passage of scripture, and held it up as the masters' Magna Charta,* by which they were licensed by God himself to commit the greatest outrages upon the defenceless victims of their oppression. But, my friends, was it designed to be so? If our Heavenly Father would protect by law the eye and the tooth of a Hebrew servant, can we for a moment believe that he would abandon that same servant to the brutal rage of a master who would destroy even life itself. Do we rather not see in this, the *only* law which protected masters, and was it not right

* The "Great Charter" was forced on King John of England in 1215 by his nobles. It curbed some of his arbitrary powers and is considered the first step on England's constitutional road.

that in case of the death of a servant, one or two days after chastisement was inflicted, to which other circumstances might have contributed, that the master should be protected when, in all probability, he never intended to produce so fatal a result? But the phrase, "he is his money" has been adduced to show that Hebrew servants were regarded as mere *things,* "chattels personal"; if so, why were so many laws made to *secure their rights as men,* and to ensure their rising into equality and freedom? If they were mere *things,* why were they regarded as responsible beings, and one law made for them as well as for their masters? But I pass on now to the consideration of how the *female* Jewish servants were protected by *law.*

1. If she please not her master, who hath betrothed her to himself, then shall he let her be redeemed: to sell her unto another nation he shall have no power, seeing he hath dealt deceitfully with her.

2. If he have betrothed her unto his son, he shall deal with her after the manner of daughters.

3. If he take him another wife, her food, her raiment, and her duty of marriage, shall he not diminish.

4. If he do not these three unto her, then shall she go out *free* without money.

On these laws, I will give you Calmet's remarks; "A father could not sell his daughter as a slave, according to the Rabbins, until she was at the age of puberty, and unless he were reduced to the utmost indigence. Besides when a master bought an Israelitish girl, it was *always* with the presumption that he would take her to wife. Hence Moses adds, 'if she please not her master, and he does not think fit to marry her, he shall set her at liberty,' or according to the Hebrew, 'he shall let her be redeemed.' 'To sell her to another nation he shall have no power, seeing he hath dealt deceitfully with her'; as to the engagement implied, at least of taking her to wife. 'If he have betrothed her unto his son, he shall deal with her after the manner of daughters,' i.e. he shall take care that his son uses her as his wife that he does not despise or maltreat her. If he make his son marry another wife, he shall give her her dowry, her clothes and compensation for her virginity; if he does none of these three, she shall *go out free* without money." Thus were the *rights of female servants carefully secured by law* under the Jewish Dispensation; and now I would ask, are the rights of females slaves at the South thus secured? Are *they* sold only as wives and daughters-in-law, and when not treated as such, are they allowed to *go out free?* No! They have *all* not only been illegally obtained as servants according to Hebrew law, but they are also illegally *held* in bondage. Masters at the South and West have all forfeited their claims, *(if they ever had any,)* to their female slaves.

We come now to examine the case of those servants who were "of the heathen round about"; Were *they* left entirely unprotected by law? Horne in speaking of the law, "Thou shalt not rule over him with rigor, but shalt fear thy God," remarks, "this law Lev. xxv, 43, it is true speaks expressly of slaves who were of Hebrew descent; but as *alien born* slaves were ingrafted into the Hebrew Church by circumcision, *there is no doubt* but that it applied to *all* slaves"; if so, then we may reasonably suppose that the other protective laws extended to them also; and that the only difference between Hebrew and Heathen servants lay in this, that the former served but six years unless they chose to remain longer, and were always freed at the death of their masters; whereas the latter served until the year of Jubilee, though that might include a period of forty-nine years,—and were left from father to son.

There are however two other laws which I have not yet noticed. The one effectually prevented *all involuntary* servitude, and the other completely abolished Jewish servitude every fifty years. They were equally operative upon the Heathen and the Hebrew.

1. "Thou shalt *not* deliver unto his master the servant that is escaped from his master unto thee. He shall dwell with thee, even among you, in that place which he shall choose, in one of thy gates where it liketh him best: thou shalt *not* oppress him." Deut. xxiii, 15, 16.

2. "And ye shall hallow the fiftieth year, and proclaim *Liberty* throughout *all* the land, unto *all* the inhabitants thereof: it shall be a jubilee unto you." Lev. xxv, 10.

Here, then, we see that by this first law, the *door of Freedom was opened wide to every servant who* had any cause whatever for complaint; if he was unhappy with his master, all he had to do was to leave him, and *no man* had a right to deliver him back to him again, and not only so, but the absconded servant was to *choose* where he should live, and no Jew was permitted to oppress him. He left his master just as our Northern servants leave us; we have no power to compel them to remain with us, and no man has any right to oppress them; they go and dwell in that place where it chooseth them, and live just where they like. Is it so at the South? Is the poor runaway slave protected *by law* from the violence of that master whose oppression and cruelty has driven him from his plantation or his house? No! no! Even the free states of the North are compelled to deliver unto his master the servant that is escaped from his master into them. By *human* law, under the *Christian Dispensation,* in the *nineteenth century we* are commanded to do, what *God* more than *three thousand* years ago, under the *Mosaic Dispensation, positively commanded* the Jews *not* to do. In the wide domain even of our free states, there is not *one* city of refuge for the poor runaway fugitive; not one spot upon which he can stand and say, I am a free man—I am protected in my rights as a *man,* by the strong arm of the law; no! *not one.* How long the North will thus shake hands with the South in sin, I know not. How long she will stand by like the persecutor Saul, *consenting* unto the death of Stephen, and keeping the raiment of them that slew him[?] I know not; but one thing I do know, the *guilt of the North* is increasing in a tremendous ratio as light is pouring in upon her on the subject and the sin of slavery. As the sun of righteousness climbs higher and higher in the moral heavens, she will stand still more and more abashed as the query is thundered down into her ear, "*Who* hath required *this* at thy hand?" It will be found *no* excuse then that the Constitution of our country required that *persons bound to service* escaping from their masters should be delivered up; no more excuse than was the reason which Adam assigned for eating the forbidden fruit. *He* was *condemned and punished because* he hearkened to the voice of *his wife,* rather than to the command of his Maker; and *we* will assuredly be condemned and punished for obeying *Man* rather than *God,* if we do not speedily repent and bring forth fruits meet for repentance. Yea, are we not receiving chastisement even *now?*

But by the second of these laws a still more astonishing fact is disclosed. If the first effectually prevented *all involuntary servitude,* the last absolutely forbade even *voluntary servitude being perpetual.* On the great day of atonement every fiftieth year the Jubilee trumpet was sounded through the land of Judea, and *Liberty* was proclaimed to *all* the inhabitants thereof. I will not say that the servants' *chains* fell off and their *manacles* were burst, for there is no evidence that Jewish servants *ever* felt the weight of iron chains, and collars, and handcuffs; but I do say that even the man who had voluntarily sold himself and the *heathen* who had been sold to a Hebrew master, were set free, the one as well as the other. This law was evidently designed to prevent the oppression of the poor, and the possibility of such a thing as *perpetual servitude* existing among them.

Where, then, I would ask, is the warrant, the justification, or the palliation of American Slavery from Hebrew servitude? How many of the southern slaves would now be in bondage according to the laws of

Moses; Not one. You may observe that I have carefully avoided using the term *slavery* when speaking of Jewish servitude; and simply for this reason, that *no such thing* existed among that people; the word translated servant does *not* mean *slave,* it is the same that is applied to Abraham, to Moses, to Elisha and the prophets generally. *Slavery* then *never* existed under the Jewish Dispensation at all, and I cannot but regard it as an aspersion on the character of Him who is "glorious in Holiness" for any one to assert that *"God sanctioned, yea commanded slavery* under the old dispensation." I would fain lift my feeble voice to vindicate Jehovah's character from so foul a slander. If slaveholders are determined to hold slaves as long as they can, let them not dare to say that the God of mercy and of truth *ever* sanctioned such a system of cruelty and wrong. It is blasphemy against Him.

We have seen that the code of laws framed by Moses with regard to servants was designed to *protect them* as *men and women,* to secure to them their *rights* as *human beings,* to guard them from oppression and defend them from violence of every kind. Let us now turn to the Slave laws of the South and West and examine them too. I will give you the substance only, because I fear I shall trespass too much on your time, were I to quote them at length.

1. *Slavery* is hereditary and perpetual, to the last moment of the slave's earthly existence, and to all his descendants to the latest posterity.

2. The labor of the slave is compulsory and uncompensated; while the kind of labor, the amount of toil, the time allowed for rest, are dictated solely by the master. No bargain is made, no wages given. A pure despotism governs the human brute; and even his covering and provender, both as to quantity and quality, depend entirely on the master's discretion.*

3. The slave being considered a personal chattel may be sold or pledged, or leased at the will of his master. He may be exchanged for marketable commodities, or taken in execution for the debts or taxes either of a living or dead master. Sold at auction, either individually, or

* There are laws in some of the slave states, limiting the labor which the master may require of the slave to fourteen hours daily. In some of the states there are laws requiring the masters to furnish a certain amount of food and clothing, as for instance, *one quart* of corn per day, or *one peck* per week, or *one bushel* per month, and "*one* linen shirt and pantaloons for the summer, and a linen shirt and woolen great coat and pantaloons for the winter," &c. But "still," to use the language of Judge Stroud "the slave is entirely under the control of his master,—is unprovided with a protector,—and, especially as he cannot be a witness or make complaint in any known mode against his master, the *apparent* object of these laws may *always* be defeated." Ed. [Footnote in original. See George McDowell Stroud, *A Sketch of the Law Relating to Slavery in the Several States of the United States of America* (Philadelphia, Pa.: Kimber and Sharpless, 1827).]

in lots to suit the purchaser, he may remain with his family, or be separated from them for ever.

4. Slaves can make no contracts and have no *legal* right to any property, real or personal. Their own honest earnings and the legacies of friends belong in point of law to their masters.

5. Neither a slave nor a free colored person can be a witness against any *white,* or free person, in a court of justice, however atrocious may have been the crimes they have seen him commit, if such testimony would be for the benefit of a *slave;* but they may give testimony *against a fellow slave,* or free colored man, even in cases affecting life, if the *master* is to reap the advantage of it.

6. The slave may be punished at his master's discretion—without trial—without any means of legal redress; whether his offence be real or imaginary; and the master can transfer the same despotic power to any person or persons, he may choose to appoint.

7. The slave is not allowed to resist any free man under *any* circumstances, *his* only safety consists in the fact that his *owner* may bring suit and recover the price of his body, in case his life is taken, or his limbs rendered unfit for labor.

8. Slaves cannot redeem themselves, or obtain a change of masters, though cruel treatment may have rendered such a change necessary for their personal safety.

9. The slave is entirely unprotected in his domestic relations.

10. The laws greatly obstruct the manumission of slaves, even where the master is willing to enfranchise them.

11. The operation of the laws tends to deprive slaves of religious instruction and consolation.

12. The whole power of the laws is exerted to keep slaves in a state of the lowest ignorance.

13. There is in this country a monstrous inequality of law and right. What is a trifling fault in the *white* man, is considered highly criminal in the *slave;* the same offences which cost a white man a few dollars only, are punished in the negro with death.

14. The laws operate most oppressively upon free people of color.*

Shall I ask you now my friends, to draw the *parallel* between Jewish *servitude* and American *slavery?* No! For there is *no likeness* in the two systems; I ask you rather to mark the contrast. The laws of Moses

* See Mrs. Child's Appeal, Chap. II. [Footnote in original; see Lydia Maria Child, *An Appeal in Favor of that Class of Americans Called Africans* (Boston, Mass.: Allen and Ticknor, 1833; New York: Arno and *New York Times,* 1968).]

protected servants in their *rights* as *men and women,* guarded them from oppression and defended them from wrong. The Code Noir* of the South *robs the slave of all his rights* as a *man,* reduces him to a chattel personal, and defends the *master* in the exercise of the most unnatural and unwarantable power over his slave. They each bear the impress of the hand which formed them. The attributers of justice and mercy are shadowed out in the Hebrew code; those of injustice and cruelty, in the Code Noir of America. Truly it was wise in the slaveholders of the South to declare their slaves to be "chattels personal"; for before they could be robbed of wages, wives, children, and friends, it was absolutely necessary to deny they were human beings. It is wise in them, to keep them in abject ignorance, for the strong man armed must be bound before we can spoil his house—the powerful intellect of man must be bound down with the iron chains of nescience before we can rob him of his rights as a man; we must reduce him to a *thing* before we can claim the right to set our feet upon his neck, because it was only *all things* which were originally *put under the feet of man* by the Almighty and Beneficent Father of all, who has declared himself to be *no respecter* of persons, whether red, white or black.

But some have even said that Jesus Christ did not condemn slavery. To this I reply that our Holy Redeemer lived and preached among the Jews only. The laws which Moses had enacted fifteen hundred years previous to his appearance among them, had never been annulled, and these laws protected every servant in Palestine. If then He did not condemn Jewish servitude this does not prove that he would not have condemned such a monstrous system as that of American *slavery,* if that had existed among them. But did not Jesus condemn slavery? Let us examine some of his precepts. "*Whatsoever* ye would that men should do to you, do *ye even so to them*[.]" Let every slaveholder apply these queries to his own heart; Am *I* willing to be a slave—Am *I* willing to see *my* wife the slave of another—Am *I* willing to see my mother a slave, or my father, my sister or my brother? If *not,* then in holding others as slaves, I am doing what I would *not* wish to be done to me or any relative I have; and thus have I broken this golden rule which was given *me* to walk by.

But some slaveholders have said, "we were never in bondage to any man," and therefore the yoke of bondage would be insufferable to us, but slaves are accustomed to it, their backs are fitted to the burden.

* The slave code written for the French West Indies in 1685. It was one of the most oppressive of the codes and provided the basis for some of the codes used by southern states, notably Louisiana.

Well, I am willing to admit that you who have lived in freedom would find slavery even more oppressive than the poor slave does, but then you may try this question in another form—Am I willing to reduce *my little child* to slavery? You know that *if it is brought up a slave* it will never know any contrast, between freedom and bondage, its back will become fitted to the burden just as the negro child's does—*not by nature*—but by daily, violent pressure, in the same way that the head of the Indian child becomes flattened by the boards in which it is bound. It has been justly remarked that *"God never made a slave,"* he made man upright; his back was *not* made to carry burdens, nor his neck to wear a yoke, and the *man* must be crushed within him, before *his* back can be *fitted* to the burden of perpetual slavery; and that his back is *not* fitted to it, is manifested by the insurrections that so often disturb the peace and security of slaveholding countries. Who ever heard of a rebellion of the beasts of the field; and why not? simply because *they* were all placed *under the feet of man,* into whose hand they were delivered; it was originally designed that they should serve him, therefore their necks have been formed for the yoke, and their backs for the burden; but *not so with man,* intellectual, immortal man! I appeal to you, my friends, as mothers; Are you willing to enslave *your* children? You start back with horror and indignation at such a question. But why, if slavery is *no wrong* to those upon whom it is imposed? why, if as has often been said, slaves are happier than their masters, free from the cares and perplexities of providing for themselves and their families: why not place *your children* in the way of being supported without your having the trouble to provide for them, or they for themselves? Do you not perceive that as soon as this golden rule of action is applied to *yourselves* that you involuntarily shrink from the test; as soon as *your* actions are weighed in *this* balance of the sanctuary that *you are found wanting?* Try yourselves by another of the Divine precepts, "Thou shalt love thy neighbor as thyself." Can we love a man *as* we love *ourselves*[;] if we do, and continue to do unto him, what we would not wish any one to do to us? Look too, at Christ's example, what does he say of himself, "I came *not* to be ministered unto, but to minister." Can you for a moment imagine the meek, and lowly, and compassionate Saviour, *a Slaveholder?* do you not shudder at this thought as much as at that of his being *a warrior?* But why, if slavery is not sinful?

Again, it has been said, the Apostle Paul did not condemn Slavery, for he sent Onesimus back to Philemon. I do not think it can be said he sent him back, for no coercion was made use of. Onesimus was not thrown into prison and then sent back in chains to his master, as your runaway slaves often are—this could not possibly have been the case, because you know Paul as a Jew, was *bound to protect* the runaway, *he had no right* to send any fugitive back to his master. The state of the case then seems to have been this. Onesimus had been an unprofitable servant to Philemon and left him—he afterwards became converted under the Apostle's preaching, and seeing that he had been to blame in his conduct, and desiring by future fidelity to atone for past error, he wished to return, and the Apostle gave him the letter we now have as a recommendation to Philemon, informing him of the conversion of Onesimus, and entreating him as "Paul the aged" "to receive him, *not* now as a *servant,* but *above* a servant, a brother beloved, especially to me, but how much more unto thee, both in the flesh and in the Lord. If thou count *me* therefore as a partner, *receive him as myself.*" This then surely cannot be forced into a justification of the practice of returning runaway slaves back to their masters, to be punished with cruel beatings and scourgings as they often are. Besides the word *ζουλος* here translated servant,* is the same that is made use of in Matt. xvii, 27. Now it appears that this servant owed his lord ten thousands talents; he possessed property to a vast amount. Onesimus could not then have been a *slave,* for slaves do not own their wives, or children; no, not even their own bodies, much less property. But again, the servitude which the apostle was accustomed to, must have been very different from American slavery, for he says, "the heir (or son), as long as he is a child, differeth *nothing from a servant,* though he be lord of all. But is under *tutors* and governors until the time appointed of the father." From this it appears, that the means of *instruction* were provided for *servants* as well as children; and indeed we know it must have been so among the Jews, because their servants were not permitted to remain in perpetual bondage, and therefore it was absolutely necessary they should be prepared to occupy higher stations in society than those of servants. Is it so at the South, my friends? Is the daily bread of instruction provided for *your slaves?* are their minds enlightened, and they gradually prepared to rise from the grade of menials into that of *free,* independent members of the state? Let your own statute book, and your own daily experience, answer these questions.

If this apostle sanctioned *slavery,* why did he exhort masters thus in his epistle to the Ephesians, "and ye, masters, do the same things unto them (i.e. perform your duties to your servants as unto Christ, not unto

* *Zoulos* is translated as *slave* in most modern Greek-English lexicons.

me) *forbearing threatening;* knowing that your master also is in heaven, neither is *there respect of persons with him.*" And in Colossians, "Masters give unto your servants that which is *just and equal,* knowing that ye also have a master in heaven." Let slaveholders only *obey* these injunctions of Paul, and I am satisfied slavery would soon be abolished. If he thought it sinful even to *threaten* servants, surely he must have thought it sinful to flog and to beat them with sticks and paddles; indeed, when delineating the character of a bishop, he expressly names this as one feature of it, *"no striker."* Let masters give unto their servants that which is *just* and *equal,* and all that vast system of unrequited labor would crumble into ruin. Yes, and if they once felt they had no right to the *labor* of their servants without pay, surely they could not think they had a right to their wives, their children, and their own bodies. Again, how can it be said Paul sanctioned slavery, when, as though to put this matter beyond all doubt, in that black catalogue of sins enumerated in his first epistle to Timothy, he mentions *"menstealers,"* which word may be translated *"slavedealers."* But you may say, we all despise slavedealers as much as any one can; they are never admitted into genteel or respectable society. And why not? Is it not because even you shrink back from the idea of associating with those who make their fortunes by trading in the bodies and souls of men, women, and children? whose daily work it is to break human hearts, by tearing wives from their husbands, and children from their parents? But why hold slavedealers as despicable, if their trade is lawful and virtuous? and why despise them more than the *gentlemen of fortune and standing* who employ them as *their* agents? Why more than the *professors of religion* who barter their fellow-professors to them for gold and silver? We do not despise the land agent, or the physician, or the merchant, and why? Simply because their professions are virtuous and honorable; and if the trade of men-jobbers were honorable, you would not despise them either. There is no difference in *principle,* in *Christian ethics,* between the despised slavedealer and the *Christian* who buys slaves from, or sells slaves to him; indeed, if slaves were not wanted by the respectable, the wealthy, and the religious in that community, there would be no slaves in that community, and of course no *slavedealers.* It is then the *Christians* and the *honorable men* and *women* of the South, who are the *main pillars* of this grand temple built to Mammon and to Moloch. It is the *most enlightened* in every country who are *most* to blame when any public sin is supported by public opinion, hence Isaiah says, *"When* the Lord hath performed his whole work upon mount *Zion* and on *Jerusalem,* (then) I will punish the fruit of the stout heart of the king of Assyria, and the glory of his high looks." And was it not so? Open the historical records of that age, was not Israel carried into captivity B.C. 606, Judah B.C. 588, and the stout heart of the heathen monarchy not punished until B.C. 536, fifty-two years *after* Judah's, and seventy years *after* Israel's captivity, when it was overthrown by Cyrus, king of Persia? Hence, too, the apostle Peter says, "judgment must *begin at the house of God.*" Surely this would not be the case, if the *professors of religion* were not *most worthy* of blame.

But it may be asked, why are *they* most culpable? I will tell you, my friends. It is because sin is imputed to us just in proportion to the spiritual light we receive. Thus the prophet Amos says, in the name of Jehovah, "*You only* have I known of all the families of the earth: *therefore* I will punish *you* for all your iniquities." Hear too the doctrine of our Lord on this important subject; "The servant who *knew* his Lord's will and *prepared not* himself, neither did according to his will, shall be beaten with *many* stripes": and why? "For unto whomsoever *much* is given, of *him* shall *much* be required; and to whom men have committed *much,* of *him* they will ask the *more.*" Oh! then that the *Christians* of the south would ponder these things in their hearts, and awake to the vast responsibilities which rest *upon them* at this important crisis.

I have thus, I think, clearly proved to you seven propositions, viz.: First, that slavery is contrary to the declaration of our independence. Second, that it is contrary to the first charter of human rights given to Adam, and renewed to Noah. Third, that the fact of slavery having been the subject of prophecy, furnishes *no* excuse whatever to slavedealers. Fourth, that no such system existed under the patriarchal dispensation. Fifth, that *slavery never* existed under the Jewish dispensation; but so far otherwise, that every servant was placed under the *protection of law,* and care taken not only to prevent all *involuntary* servitude, but all *voluntary perpetual* bondage. Sixth, that slavery in America reduces a *man* to a *thing,* a "chattel personal," *robs him* of *all* his rights as a *human being,* fetters both his mind and body, and protects the *master* in the most unnatural and unreasonable power, whilst it *throws him out* of the protection of law. Seventh, that slavery is contrary to the example and precepts of our holy and merciful Redeemer, and of his apostles.

But perhaps you will be ready to query, why appeal to *women* on this subject? *We* do not make the laws which perpetuate slavery. *No* legislative power is vested in *us; we* can do nothing to overthrow the system, even if we wished to do so. To this I reply, I know you do not make the laws, but I also know that *you are the wives and mothers, the sisters and daughters of those who do;* and if you really suppose *you* can do nothing to overthrow slavery, you are greatly mistaken. You can do much in every way: four things I will name. 1st. You can read on this subject. 2d. You can pray over this subject. 3d. You can speak on this subject. 4th. You can *act* on this subject. I have not placed reading before praying because I regard it more important, but because, in order to pray aright, we must understand what we are praying for; it is only then we can "pray with the understanding and the spirit also."

1. Read then on the subject of slavery. Search the Scriptures daily, whether the things I have told you are true. Other books and papers might be a great help to you in this investigation, but they are not necessary, and it is hardly probable that your Committees of Vigilance* will allow you to have any other. The *Bible* then is the book I want you to read in the spirit of inquiry, and the spirit of prayer. Even the enemies of Abolitionists, acknowledge that their doctrines are drawn from it. In the great mob in Boston last autumn,† when the books and papers of the Anti-Slavery Society were thrown out of the windows of their office, an individual laid hold of the Bible and was about tossing it out to the ground, when another reminded him that it was the Bible he had in his hand. *"O! 'tis all one,"* he replied, and out went the sacred volume along with the rest. We thank him for the acknowledgment. Yes, *"it is all one,"* for our books and papers are mostly commentaries on the Bible, and the Declaration. Read the *Bible* then, it contains the words of Jesus, and they are spirit and life. Judge for yourselves whether *he sanctioned* such a system of oppression and crime.

2. Pray over this subject. When you have entered into your closets, and shut to the doors, then pray to your father, who seeth in secret, that he would open your eyes to see whether slavery is *sinful,* and if it is, that he would enable you to bear a faithful, open and unshrinking testimony against it, and to do whatsoever your hands find to do, leaving the

* Self-appointed groups of southern white males organized to confiscate what Southerners termed "incendiary," i.e. abolitionist, literature and generally suppress antislavery speech.

† On October 21, 1835 a Boston Female Anti-Slavery Society meeting was surrounded by a mob, erroneously believing that the British abolitionist, George Thompson, was going to appear. The women reluctantly agreed to adjourn, but the mob, frustrated, tore up the office, seized Garrison, tore his clothes, and put a rope around his chest. He would have been hanged, reports May, if not for the efforts of "several gentlemen, assisted by some of the police and a vigorous hack driver," who then put him in the Leverett Street Jail for safekeeping. Samuel J. May, *Some recollections of our antislavery conflict* (Boston, Mass.: Fields, Osgood, 1869), p. 156.

George Thompson (1804–1878), a brilliant orator, was invited by Garrison to make a lecture tour of the United States. He arrived in September 1834, planning to stay three years, but he became the focal point of antiabolitionist mobs, being greeted by twenty in fourteen months. He departed hastily in November 1835. The speeches he gave, however, made a strong impression, especially on New England Methodists.

consequences entirely to him, who still says to us whenever we try to reason away duty from the fear of consequences, *"What is that to thee, follow thou me."* Pray also for that poor slave, that he may be kept patient and submissive under his hard lot, until God is pleased to open the door of freedom to him without violence or bloodshed. Pray too for the master that his heart may be softened, and he made willing to acknowledge, as Joseph's brethren did, "Verily we are guilty concerning our brother," before he will be compelled to add in consequence of Divine judgment, "therefore is all this evil come upon us." Pray also for all your brethren and sisters who are laboring in the righteous cause of Emancipation in the Northern States, England and the world. There is great encouragement for prayer in these words of our Lord. "Whatsoever ye shall ask the Father *in my name,* he *will give* it to you"—Pray then without ceasing, in the closet and the social circle.

3. Speak on this subject. It is through the tongue, the pen, and the press, that truth is principally propagated. Speak then to your relatives, your friends, your acquaintances on the subject of slavery; be not afraid if you are conscientiously convinced it is *sinful,* to say so openly, but calmly, and to let your sentiments be known. If you are served by the slaves of others, try to ameliorate their condition as much as possible; never aggravate their faults, and thus add fuel to the fire of anger already kindled in a master and mistress's bosom; remember their extreme ignorance, and consider them as your Heavenly Father does the *less* culpable on this account, even when they do wrong things. Discountenance *all* cruelty to them, all starvation, all corporal chastisement; these may brutalize and *break* their spirits, but will never bond them to willing, cheerful obedience. If possible, see that they are comfortably and *seasonably* fed, whether in the house or the field; it is unreasonable and cruel to expect slaves to wait for their breakfast until eleven o'clock, when they rise at five or six. Do all you can, to induce their owners to clothe them well, and to allow them many little indulgences which would contribute to their comfort. Above all, try to persuade your husband, father, brothers and sons, that *slavery is a crime against God and man,* and that it is a great sin to keep *human beings* in such abject ignorance; to deny them the privilege of learning to read and write. The Catholics are universally condemned, for denying the Bible to the common people, but, *slaveholders must not* blame them, for *they* are doing the *very same thing,* and for the very same reason, neither of these systems can bear the light which bursts from the pages of that Holy Book. And

lastly, endeavour to inculcate submission on the part of the slaves, but whilst doing this be faithful in pleading the cause of the oppressed.

> Will *you* behold unheeding,
> Life's holiest feelings crushed,
> Where *woman's* heart is bleeding,
> Shall *woman's* heart be hushed?

4. Act on this subject. Some of you *own* slaves yourselves. If you believe slavery is *Sinful,* set them at liberty, "undo the heavy burdens and let the oppressed go free." If they wish to remain with you, pay them wages, if not let them leave you. Should they remain teach them, and have them taught the common branches of an English education; they have minds and those minds, *ought to be improved.* So precious a talent as intellect, never was given to be wrapt in a napkin and buried in the earth. It is the *duty* of all, as far as they can, to improve their own mental faculties, because we are commanded to love God with *all our minds,* as well as with all our hearts, and we commit a great sin, if we *forbid or prevent* that cultivation of the mind in others, which would enable them to perform this duty. Teach your servants then to read &c, and encourage them to believe it is their *duty* to learn, if it were only that they might read the Bible.

But some of you will say, we can neither free our slaves nor teach them to read, for the laws of our state forbid it. Be not surprised when I say such wicked laws *ought to be no barrier* in the way of your duty, and I appeal to the Bible to prove this position. What was the conduct of Shiphrah and Puah, when the king of Egypt issued his cruel mandate, with regard to the Hebrew children? "*They* feared *God,* and did *not* as the King of Egypt commanded them, but saved the men children alive." Did these *women* do right in disobeying that monarch? "*Therefore* (says the sacred text,) *God dealt well* with them, and made them houses." Ex. i. What was the conduct of Shadrach, Meshach, and Abednego, when Nebuchadnezzar set up a golden image in the plain of Dura, and commanded all people, nations, and languages to fall down and worship it? "Be it known, unto thee, (said these faithful *Jews*) O king, that *we will not* serve thy gods, nor worship the image which thou hast set up." Did these men *do right in disobeying the law* of their sovereign: Let their miraculous deliverance from the burning fiery furnace, answer; Dan. iii. What was the conduct of Daniel, when Darius made a firm decree that no one should ask a petition of any man or God for thirty days? Did the prophet cease to pray? No! "When Daniel *knew that the writing was signed,* he went into his house, and his windows being *open* towards Jerusalem, he kneeled upon his knees three times a day, and prayed and gave thanks before his God, as he did aforetime." Did Daniel do right thus to *break* the law of his king? Let his wonderful deliverance out of the mouths of the lions answer; Dan. vii. Look, too, at the Apostles Peter and John. When the rulers of the Jews, *"commanded them not* to speak at all, nor teach in the name of Jesus," what did they say? "Whether it be right in the sight of God, to hearken unto you more than unto God, judge ye." And what did they do? "They spake the word of God with boldness, and with great power gave the Apostles witness of the *resurrection* of the Lord Jesus"; although *this* was the very doctrine, for the preaching of which, they had just been cast into prison, and further threatened. Did these men do right? I leave *you* to answer, who now enjoy the benefits of their labors and sufferings, in that Gospel they dared to preach when positively commanded *not to teach any more* in the name of Jesus; Acts iv.

But some of you may say, if we do free our slaves, they will be taken up and sold, therefore there will be no use in doing it. Peter and John might just as well have said, we will not preach the gospel, for if we do, we shall be taken up and put in prison, therefore there will be no use in our preaching. *Consequences,* my friends, belong no more to *you,* than they did to these apostles. Duty is ours and events are God's. If you think slavery is sinful, all *you* have to do is to set your slaves at liberty, do all you can to protect them, and in humble faith and fervent prayer, commend them to your common Father. He can take care of them; but if for wise purposes he sees fit to allow them to be sold, this will afford you an opportunity of testifying openly, wherever you go, against the crime of *manstealing.* Such an act will be *clear robbery,* and if exposed, might, under the Divine direction, do the cause of Emancipation more good, than any thing that could happen, for "He makes even the wrath of man to praise him, and the remainder of wrath he will restrain."

I know that this doctrine of obeying *God,* rather than man, will be considered as dangerous and heretical by many, but I am not afraid openly to avow it, because it is the doctrine of the Bible; but I would not be understood to advocate resistance to any law however oppressive, if, in obeying it, I was not obliged to commit *sin.* If for instance, there was a law, which imposed imprisonment or a fine upon me if I manumitted a slave, I would on no account resist that law, I would set the slave free, and then go to prison or pay the fine. If a law commands me to *sin I will break it;* if it calls me to *suffer,* I will let it take its course *unresistingly*. The doctrine of blind obedience and unqualified submission to *any human* power, whether civil or ecclesiastical, is the doctrine of despotism, and ought to have no place among Republicans and Christians.

But you will perhaps say, such a course of conduct would inevitably expose us to great suffering. Yes! my christian friends, I believe it would, but this will *not* excuse you or any one else for the neglect of *duty*. If Prophets and Apostles, Martyrs, and Reformers had not been willing to suffer for the truth's sake, where would the world have been now? If they had said, we cannot speak the truth, we cannot do what we believe is right, because the *laws of our country or public opinion are against us,* where would our holy religion have been now? The Prophets were stoned, imprisoned, and killed by the Jews. And why? Because they exposed and openly rebuked public sins; they opposed public opinion; had they held their peace, they all might have lived in ease and died in favor with a wicked generation. Why were the Apostles persecuted from city to city, stoned, incarcerated, beaten, and crucified? Because they dared to *speak the truth;* to tell the Jews, boldly and fearlessly, that *they* were the *murderers* of the Lord of Glory, and that, however great a stumbling-block the Cross might be to them, there was no other name given under heaven by which men could be saved, but the name of Jesus. Because they declared, even at Athens, the seat of learning and refinement, the self-evident truth, that "they be no gods that are made with men's hands," and exposed to the Grecians the foolishness of worldy wisdom, and the impossibility of salvation but through Christ, whom they despised on account of the ignominious death he died. Because at Rome, the proud mistress of the world, they thundered out the terrors of the law upon that idolatrous, war-making, and slaveholding community. Why were the martyrs stretched upon the rack, gibbeted and burnt, the scorn and diversion of a Nero,* whilst their tarred and burning bodies sent up a light which illuminated the Roman capital? Why were the Waldenses† hunted like wild beasts upon the mountains of Piedmont, and slain with the sword of the Duke of Savoy and the proud monarch of France [Philip II]? Why were the Presbyterians chased like the partridge over the highlands of Scotland—the Methodists pumped, and stoned, and pelted with rotten eggs—the Quakers incarcerated in filthy prisons, beaten, whipped at the cart's tail, banished and hung?

* Emperor of Rome, A.D. 54–68.

† Valdens preached a form of primitive Christianity, akin to that of the Apostles, in Lyons (1170–1176). His followers were excommunicated in 1184, and eighty were burned in 1211.

Because they dared to *speak* the *truth,* to *break* the unrighteous *laws* of their country, and chose rather to suffer affliction with the people of God, "not accepting deliverance," even under the gallows. Why were Luther and Calvin persecuted and excommunicated, Cranmer, Ridley, and Latimer burnt?* Because they fearlessly proclaimed the truth, though that truth was contrary to public opinion, and the authority of Ecclesiastical councils and conventions. Now all this vast amount of human suffering might have been saved. All these Prophets and Apostles, Martyrs, and Reformers, might have lived and died in peace with all men, but following the example of their great pattern, "they despised the shame, endured the cross, and are now set down on the right hand of the throne of God," having received the glorious welcome of "well *done* good and faithful servants, enter ye into the joy of your Lord."

But you may say we are *women,* how can *our* hearts endure persecution? And why not? Have not *women* stood up in all the dignity and strength of moral courage to be the leaders of the people, and to bear a faithful testimony for the truth whenever the providence of God has called them to do so? Are there no *women* in that noble army of martyrs who are now singing the song of Moses and the Lamb? Who led out the women of Israel from the house of bondage, striking the timbrel, and singing the song of deliverance on the banks of that sea whose waters stood up like walls of crystal to open a passage for their escape? It was a *woman;* Miriam, the prophetess, the sister of Moses and Aaron. Who went up with Barak to Kadesh to fight against Jabin, King of Canaan, into whose hand Israel had been sold because of their iniquities? It was a *woman!* Deborah the wife of Lapidoth, the judge, as well as the prophetess of that backsliding people; Judges iv, 9. Into whose hands was Sisera, the captain of Jabin's host delivered? Into the hand of a *woman.* Jael the wife of Heber! Judges vi, 21. Who dared to *speak the truth* concerning those judgments which were coming upon Judea, when Josiah, alarmed at finding that his people "had not kept the word of the Lord to do after all that was written in the book of the Law," sent to enquire of the Lord concerning these things? It was a *woman.* Huldah the prophetess, the wife of Shallum; 2, Chron. xxxiv, 22. Who was chosen to deliver the whole Jewish nation from that murderous decree of Persia's King, which wicked Haman had obtained by calumny and fraud? It

* Martin Luther (1483–1546) and John Calvin (1509–1564) broke with the Roman Catholic church and laid the basis for Protestant Christianity. Thomas Cranmer (1489–1556) was the first Protestant archbishop of Canterbury; Nicholas Ridley (c. 1503–1555) was bishop of Rochester and London; Hugh Latimer (1485–1555) had been bishop of Worcester. The latter three were burned as heretics by order of the Catholic queen of England, Mary I.

was a *woman;* Esther the Queen; yes, weak and trembling *woman* was the instrument appointed by God, to reverse the bloody mandate of the eastern monarch, and save the *whole visible church* from destruction. What human voice first proclaimed to Mary that she should be the mother of our Lord? It was a *woman!* Elizabeth, the wife of Zacharias; Luke i, 42, 43. Who united with the good old Simeon in giving thanks publicly in the temple, when the child, Jesus, was presented there by his parents, "and spake of him to all them that looked for redemption in Jerusalem"? It was a *woman!* Anna the prophetess. Who first proclaimed Christ as the true Messiah in the streets of Samaria, once the capital of the ten tribes? It was a *woman!* Who ministered to the Son of God whilst on earth a despised and persecuted Reformer, in the humble garb of a carpenter? They were *women!* Who followed the rejected King of Israel, as his fainting footsteps trod the road to Calvary? "A great company of people and of *women":* and it is remarkable that to *them alone,* he turned and addressed the pathetic language, "Daughters of Jerusalem, weep not for me, but weep for yourselves and your children." Ah! who sent unto the Roman Governor when he was set down on the judgment seat, saying unto him, "Have thou nothing to do with that just man, for I have suffered many things this day in a dream because of him"? It was a *woman!* the wife of Pilate. Although *"he knew* that for envy the Jews had delivered Christ," yet *he* consented to surrender the Son of God into the hands of a brutal soldiery, after having himself scourged his naked body. Had the *wife* of Pilate sat upon that judgment seat, what would have been the result of the trial of this "just person"?

And who last hung around the cross of Jesus on the mountain of Golgotha? Who first visited the sepulchre early in the morning on the first day of the week, carrying sweet spices to embalm his precious body, not knowing that it was incorruptible and could not be holden by the bands of death? These were *women!* To whom did he *first* appear after his resurrection? It was to a *woman!* Mary Magdalene; Mark xvi, 9. Who gathered with the apostles to wait at Jerusalem, in prayer and supplication, for "the promise of the Father"; the spiritual blessing of the Great High Priest of his Church, who had entered, *not* into the splendid temple of Solomon, there to offer the blood of bulls, and of goats, and the smoking censer upon the golden altar, but into Heaven itself, there to present his intercessions, after having "given himself for us, an offering and a sacrifice to God for a sweet smelling savor"? *Women* were among that holy company; Acts, i, 14. And did *women* wait in vain? Did those who had ministered to his necessities, followed in his train, and wept at his crucifixion, wait in vain? No! No! Did the cloven tongues of fire descend upon the heads of *women* as well as men? Yes, my friends, "it sat upon *each of them";* Acts ii, 3. *Women* as well as men were to be living stones in the temple of grace, and therefore *their* heads were consecrated by the descent of the Holy Ghost as well as those of men. Were *women* recognized as fellow laborers in the gospel field? They were! Paul says in his epistle to the Philippians, "help those *women* who labored with men, in the gospel"; Phil. iv, 3.

But this is not all. Roman *women* were burnt at the stake, *their* delicate limbs were torn joint from joint by the ferocious beasts of the Amphitheatre, and tossed by the wild bull in his fury, for the diversion of that idolatrous, warlike, and slaveholding people. Yes, *women* suffered under the ten persecutions of heathen Rome, with the most unshrinking constancy and fortitude; not all the entreaties of friends, nor the claims of new born infancy, nor the cruel threats of enemies could make *them* sprinkle one grain of incense upon the altars of Roman idols. Come now with me to the beautiful valleys of Piedmont. Whose blood stains the green sward, and decks the wild flowers with colors not their own, and smokes on the sword of persecuting France? It is *woman's,* as well as man's? Yes, *women* were accounted as sheep for the slaughter, and were cut down as the tender saplings of the wood.

But time would fail me, to tell of all those hundreds and thousands of *women,* who perished in the Low countries of Holland, when Alva's* sword of vengeance was unsheathed against the Protestants, when the Catholic Inquisitions of Europe became the merciless executioners of vindictive wrath, upon those who dared to worship God, instead of bowing down in unholy adoration before "my Lord God the *Pope,"* and when England, too, burnt her Ann Ascoes† at the stake of martyrdom. Suffice it to say, that the Church, after having been driven from Judea to Rome, and from Rome to Piedmont, and from Piedmont to England, and from England to Holland, at last stretched her fainting wings over the dark bosom of the Atlantic, and found on the shores of a great wilderness, a refuge from tyranny and oppression—as she thought, but *even here,* (the warm blush of shame mantles my cheeks as I write it,) *even there, woman* was beaten and banished, imprisoned, and hung upon the gallows, a trophy to the Cross.

* Fernando, third duke of Alba (1507–1582), commanded Charles V's army in a vain attempt to stamp out Lutheranism from Germany and then led the equally unsuccessful effort to crush Protestantism in the Spanish Netherlands.

† Anne Askew was burnt, with three men, on July 16, 1546 for refusing to accept the doctrine of transubstantiation.

And what, I would ask in conclusion, have *women* done for the great and glorious cause of Emancipation? Who wrote that pamphlet which moved the heart of Wilberforce* to pray over the wrongs, and his tongue to plead the cause of the oppressed African? It was a *woman,* Elizabeth Heyrick. Who labored assiduously to keep the sufferings of the slave continually before the British public? They were *women.* And how did they do it? By their needles, paint brushes and pens, by speaking the truth, and petitioning Parliament for the abolition of slavery. And what was the effect of their labors? Read it in the Emancipation bill† of Great Britain. Read it, in the present state of her West India Colonies. Read it, in the impulse which has been given to the cause of freedom in the United States of America. Have English women then done so much for the negro, and shall American women do nothing? Oh no! Already are there sixty female Anti-Slavery Societies in operation. These are doing just what the English women did, telling the story of the colored man's wrongs, praying for his deliverance, and presenting his kneeling image constantly before the public eye on bags and needle-books, card-racks, pen-wipers, pin-cushions, &c. Even the children of the north are inscribing on their handy work, "May the points of our needles prick the slaveholder's conscience." Some of the reports of these Societies exhibit not only considerable talent, but a deep sense of religious duty, and a determination to persevere through evil as well as good report, until every scourge, and every shackle, is buried under the feet of the manumitted slave.

The Ladies' Anti-Slavery Society of Boston was called last fall, to a severe trial of their faith and constancy. They were mobbed by "the gentlemen of property and standing," in that city at their anniversary meeting, and their lives were jeoparded by an infuriated crowd; but their conduct on that occasion did credit to our sex, and affords a full assurance that they will *never* abandon the cause of the slave. The pamphlet, Right and Wrong in Boston,‡ issued by them in which a particular account is given of that "mob of broad cloth in broad day," does equal credit to the head and the heart of her who wrote it. I wish my Southern

* William Wilberforce (1759–1833), a British philanthropist and reformer who led the fight to end the slave trade and slavery in the British Empire.

† Parliament, on August 29, 1833, passed a bill, to take effect eleven months hence, freeing slave children under the age of six, and holding the other slaves in an apprenticeship system (six years for field hands, four years for others). Slaveowners were paid twenty million pounds in compensation. Antigua and Bermuda waived the apprenticeship system, and the other colonies so abused it that the act was amended on April 11, 1838, ending the apprenticeship system as of August 1 of that year.

‡ [Maria Weston Chapman] "Right and Wrong in Boston," *Report of the Boston Female Anti Slavery Society; with a concise Statement of Events, previous and subsequent to the Annual Meeting of 1835* (Boston, Mass.: By the Society, 1836).

sisters could read it; they would then understand that the women of the North have engaged in this work from a sense of *religious duty,* and that nothing will ever induce them to take their hands from it until it is fully accomplished. They feel no hostility to you, no bitterness or wrath; they rather sympathize in your trials and difficulties; but they well know that the first thing to be done to help you, is to pour in the light of truth on your minds, to urge you to reflect on, and pray over the subject. This is all *they* can do for you, *you* must work out your own deliverance with fear and trembling, and with the direction and blessing of God, *you can do it.* Northern women may labor to produce a correct public opinion at the North, but if Southern women sit down in listless indifference and criminal idleness, public opinion cannot be rectified and purified at the South. It is manifest to every reflecting mind, that slavery must be abolished; the era in which we live, and the light which is overspreading the whole world on this subject, clearly show that the time cannot be distant when it will be done. Now there are only two ways in which it can be effected, by moral power or physical force, and it is for *you* to choose which of these you prefer. Slavery always has, and always will produce insurrections wherever it exists, because it is a violation of the natural order of things, and no human power can much longer perpetuate it. The opposers of abolitionists fully believe this; one of them remarked to me not long since, there is no doubt there will be a most terrible overturning at the South in a few years, such cruelty and wrong, must be visited with Divine vengeance soon. Abolitionists believe, too, that this must inevitably be the case if you do not repent, and they are not willing to leave you to perish without entreating you, to save yourselves from destruction; well may they say with the apostle, "am I then your enemy because I tell you the truth," and warn you to flee from impending judgments.

But why, my dear friends, have I thus been endeavoring to lead you through the history of more than three thousand years, and to point you to that great cloud of witnesses who have gone before, "from works to rewards"? Have I been seeking to magnify the sufferings, and exalt the character of woman, that she "might have praise of men"? No! no! my object has been to arouse *you,* as the wives and mothers, the daughters and sisters, of the South, to a sense of your duty as *women,* and as Christian women, on that great subject, which has already shaken our country, from the St. Lawrence and the lakes, to the Gulf of Mexico, and from the Mississippi to the shores of the Atlantic; *and will continue mightily to shake it,* until the polluted temple of slavery fall and crumble into ruin. I would say unto each one of you, "what meanest thou, O sleeper! arise and call upon thy God, if so be that God will think upon us that we perish not." Perceive you not that dark cloud of vengeance which hangs over our boasting Republic? Saw you not the lightnings of Heaven's wrath, in the flame which leaped from the Indian's torch to the roof of yonder dwelling, and lighted with its horrid glare the darkness of midnight? Heard you not the thunders of Divine anger, as the distant roar of the cannon came rolling onward, from the Texian country, where Protestant American Rebels are fighting with Mexican Republicans*—for what? For the reestablishment of *slavery;* yes! of American slavery in the bosom of a Catholic Republic, where that system of robbery, violence, and wrong, had been legally abolished for twelve years. Yes! citizens of the United States, after plundering Mexico of her land, are now engaged in deadly conflict for the privilege of fastening chains, and collars, and manacles—upon whom? upon the subjects of some foreign prince? No! upon native born American Republican citizens, although the fathers of these very men declared to the whole world, while struggling to free themselves from the three penny taxes of an English king, that they believed it to be a *self-evident* truth that *all men* were created equal, and had an *unalienable right to liberty.*

Well may the poet exclaim in bitter sarcasm,

> The fustian flag that proudly waves
> In solemn mockery o'er *a land of slaves.*

Can you not, my friends, understand the signs of the time; do you not see the sword of retributive justice hanging over the South, or are you still slumbering at your posts?—Are there no Shiphrahs, no Puahs among you, who will dare in Christian firmness and Christian meekness, to refuse to obey the *wicked laws* which require *woman to enslave, to degrade and to brutalize woman?* Are there no Miriams, who would rejoice to lead out the captive daughters of the Southern States to liberty and light? Are there no Huldahs there who will dare to *speak the truth* concerning the sins of the people and those judgments, which it requires no prophet's eye to see must follow if repentance is not speedily sought?

* The Mexicans won their independence from Spain in 1821, established a republic in 1824, and abolished slavery in 1829. However, the settlers from the United States, who had been invited to settle in the Texas territory, continued to bring in slaves. By 1835, some 20,000 settlers and 4,000 slaves lived in Texas, and relations between the Mexican government and the immigrants had deteriorated. Hostilities between them commenced in October 1835. The settlers established the Republic of Texas on March 2, 1836, and adopted a constitution that formally recognized the institution of slavery. Independence was won at the battle of San Jacinto, April 21, 1836. Abolitionists fought a fierce, but ultimately losing, propaganda battle against Texas' annexation as a state (1845).

Is there no Esther among you who will plead for the poor devoted slave? Read the history of this Persian queen, it is full of instruction; she at first refused to plead for the Jews: but hear the words of Mordecai, "Think not within thyself, that *thou* shalt escape in the king's house more than all the Jews, for *if thou altogether holdest thy peace at this time,* then shall there enlargement and deliverance arise to the Jews from another place: but *thou and thy father's house shall be destroyed.*" Listen, too, to her magnanimous reply to this powerful appeal; "*I will* go in unto the king, which is *not* according to law, and if I perish, I perish." Yes! if there were but *one* Esther at the South, she *might* save her country from ruin; but let the Christian women there arise, as the Christian women of Great Britain did, in the majesty of moral power, and that salvation is certain. Let them embody themselves in societies, and send petitions up to their different legislatures, entreating their husbands, fathers, brothers, and sons, to abolish the institution of slavery; no longer to subject *woman* to the scourge and the chain, to mental darkness and moral degradation; no longer to tear husbands from their wives, and children from their parents; no longer to make men, women, and children, work *without wages;* no longer to make their lives bitter in hard bondage; no longer to reduce *American citizens* to the abject condition of *slaves,* of "chattels personal"; no longer to barter the *image of God* in human shambles for corruptible things such as silver and gold.

The *women of the South can overthrow* this horrible system of oppression and cruelty, licentiousness and wrong. Such appeals to your legislatures would be irresistible, for there is something in the heart of man which *will bend under moral suasion.* There is a swift witness for truth in his bosom, which *will respond to truth* when it is uttered with calmness and dignity. If you could obtain but six signatures to such a petition in only one state, I would say, send up that petition, and be not in the least discouraged by the scoffs and jeers of the heartless, or the resolution of the house to lay it on the table. It will be a great thing if the subject can be introduced into your legislatures in any way, even by *women,* and *they* will be the most likely to introduce it there in the best possible manner, as a matter of *morals* and *religion,* not of expediency or politics. You may petition, too, the different ecclesiastical bodies of the slave states. Slavery must be attacked with the whole power of truth and the sword of the spirit. You must take it up on *Christian* ground, and fight against it with Christian weapons, whilst your feet are shod with the preparation of the gospel of peace. And *you are now* loudly called upon by the cries of the widow and the orphan, to arise and gird yourselves for this great moral conflict, with the whole armour of righteousness upon the right hand and on the left.

There is every encouragement for you to labor and pray, my friends, because the abolition of slavery as well as its existence, has been the theme of prophecy. "Ethiopia (says the Psalmist) shall stretch forth her hands unto God." And is he not doing so? Are not the Christian negroes of the south lifting their hands in prayer for deliverance, just as the Israelites did when their redemption was drawing nigh? Are they not sighing and crying by reason of the hard bondage? And think you, that He, of whom it was said, "and God heard their groaning, and their cry came up unto him by reason of the hard bondage," think you that his ear is heavy that he cannot *now* hear the cries of his suffering children? Or that He who raised up a Moses, an Aaron, and a Miriam, to bring them up out of the land of Egypt from the house of bondage, cannot now, with a high hand and a stretched out arm rid the poor negroes out of the hands of their masters? Surely you believe that his arm is *not* shortened that he cannot save. And would not such a work of mercy redound to his glory? But another string of the harp of prophecy vibrates to the song of deliverance: "But they shall sit every man under his vine, and under his fig-tree, and *none shall make them afraid;* for the mouth of the Lord of Hosts hath spoken it." The *slave* never can do this as long as he is a *slave;* whilst he is a "chattel personal" he can own *no* property; but the time *is to come* when *every* man is to sit under *his own* vine and *his own* fig-tree, and no domineering driver, or irresponsible master, or irascible mistress, shall make him afraid of the chain or the whip. Hear, too, the sweet tones of another string: "Many shall run to and fro, and *knowledge* shall be increased." Slavery is an insurmountable barrier to the increase of knowledge in every community where it exists; *slavery, then, must be abolished before* this prediction can be fulfilled. The last chord I shall touch, will be this, "They shall *not* hurt nor destroy in all my holy mountain."

Slavery, then, must be overthrown before the prophecies can be accomplished, but how are they to be fulfilled? Will the wheels of the millennial car be rolled onward by miraculous power? No! God designs to confer this holy privilege upon *man;* it is through *his* instrumentality that the great and glorious work of reforming the world is to be done. And see you not how the mighty engine of *moral power* is dragging in its rear the Bible and peace societies, anti-slavery and temperance, sabbath schools, moral reform, and missions? or to adopt another figure, do not these seven philanthropic associations compose the beautiful tints in that bow of promise which spans the arch of our moral heaven? Who does not believe, that if these societies were broken up, their constitutions burnt, and the vast machinery with which they are laboring to regenerate mankind was stopped, that the black clouds of vengeance would soon burst over our world, and every city would witness the fate of the devoted cities of the plain? Each one of these societies is walking abroad through the earth scattering the seeds of truth over the wide field of our world, not with the hundred hands of a Briareus,* but with a hundred thousand.

Another encouragement for you to labor, my friends, is, that you will have the prayers and co-operation of English and Northern philanthropists. You will never bend your knees in supplication at the throne of grace for the overthrow of slavery, without meeting there the spirits of other Christians, who will mingle their voices with ours, as the morning or evening sacrifice ascends to God. Yes, the spirit of prayer and of supplication has been poured out upon many, many hearts; there are wrestling Jacobs who will not let go of the prophetic promises of deliverance for the captive, and the opening of prison doors to them that are bound. There are Pauls who are saying, in reference to this subject, "Lord, what wilt thou have me to do?" There are Marys sitting in the house now, who are ready to arise and go forth in his work as soon as the message is brought, "the master is come and calleth for thee." And there are Marthas, too, who have already gone out to meet Jesus, as he bends his footsteps to their brother's grave, and weeps, *not* over the lifeless body of Lazarus bound hand and foot in grave-clothes, but over the politically and intellectually lifeless slave, bound hand and foot in the iron chains of oppression and ignorance. Some may be ready to say, as Martha did, who seemed to expect nothing but sympathy from Jesus, "Lord, by this time he stinketh, for he hath been dead four days." She thought it useless to remove the stone and expose the loathsome body of her brother; she could not believe that so great a miracle could be wrought, as to raise *that putrefied body* into life; but 'Jesus said, take *ye* away the stone"; and when *they* had taken away the stone where the dead was laid, and uncovered the body of Lazarus, then it was that "Jesus lifted up his eyes and said, Father, I thank thee that thou hast heard me," &c. "And when he had thus spoke, he cried with a loud voice, Lazarus, come forth." Yes, some may be ready to say of the colored race, how can *they* ever be raised politically and intellectually,

* Briareus, in Greek mythology, a giant who aided Zeus and the Olympians in their battle with the Titans.

they have been dead four hundred years? But *we* have *nothing* to do with *how* this is to be done; *our business* is to take away the stone which has covered up the dead body of our brother, to expose the putrid carcass, to show *how* that body has been bound with the grave-clothes of heathen ignorance, and his face with the napkin of prejudice, and having done all it was our duty to do, to stand by the negro's grave, in humble faith and holy hope, waiting to hear the life-giving command of "Lazarus, come forth." This is just what Anti-Slavery Societies are doing; they are taking away the stone from the mouth of the tomb of slavery, where lies the putrid carcass of our brother. They want the pure light of heaven to shine into that dark and gloomy cave; they want all men to see *how* that dead body had been bound, *how* that face has been wrapped in the *napkin of prejudice;* and shall they wait beside that grave in vain? Is not Jesus still the resurrection and the life? Did He come to proclaim liberty to the captive, and the opening of prison doors to them that are bound, in vain? Did He promise to give beauty for ashes, the oil of joy for mourning, and the garment of praise for the spirit of heaviness unto them that mourn in Zion, and will He refuse to beautify the mind, anoint the head, and throw around the captive negro the mantle of praise for that spirit of heaviness which has so long bound him down to the ground? Or shall we not rather say with the prophet, "the zeal of the Lord of Hosts *will* perform this"? Yes, his promises are sure, and amen in Christ Jesus, that he will assemble her that halteth, and gather her that is driven out, and her that is afflicted.

But I will now say a few words on the subject of Abolitionism. Doubtless you have all heard Anti-Slavery Societies denounced as insurrectionary and mischievous, fanatical and dangerous. It has been said they publish the most abominable untruths, and that they are endeavoring to excite rebellions at the South. Have you believed these reports, my friends? have *you* also been deceived by these false assertions? Listen to me, then, whilst I endeavor to wipe from the fair character of Abolitionism such unfounded accusations. You know that *I* am a Southerner; you know that my dearest relatives are now in a slave State. Can you for a moment believe I would prove so recreant to the feelings of a daughter and a sister, as to join a society which was seeking to overthrow slavery by falsehood, bloodshed, and murder? I appeal to you who have known and loved me in days that are passed, can *you* believe it? No! my friends. As a Carolinian, I was peculiarly jealous of any movements on this subject; and before I would join an Anti-Slavery Society, I took the precaution of becoming acquainted with some of the leading Abolitionists, of reading their publications and attending their meetings, at which I heard addresses both from colored and white men; and it was not until I was fully convinced that their principles were *entirely pacific,* and their efforts *only moral,* that I gave my name as a member to the Female Anti-Slavery Society of Philadelphia. Since that time, I have regularly taken the Liberator, and read many Anti-Slavery pamphlets and papers and books, and can assure you I *never* have seen a single insurrectionary paragraph, and never read any account of cruelty which I could not believe. Southerners may deny the truth of these accounts, but why do they not *prove* them to be false. Their violent expressions of horror at such accounts being believed, *may* deceive some, but they cannot deceive *me,* for I lived too long in the midst of slavery, not to know what slavery is. When *I* speak of this system, "I speak that I do know," and I am not at all afraid to assert, that Anti-Slavery publications have *not* overdrawn the monstrous features of slavery at all. And many a Southerner *knows* this as well as I do. A lady in North Carolina remarked to a friend of mine, about eighteen months since, "Northerners know nothing at all about slavery; they think it is perpetual bondage only; but of the *depth of degradation* that word involves, they have no conception; if they had, *they would never cease* their efforts until so *horrible* a system was overthrown." She did not know how faithfully some Northern men and Northern women had studied this subject; how diligently they had searched out the cause of "him who had none to help him," and how fearlessly they had told the story of the negro's wrongs. Yes, Northerners know *every* thing about slavery now. This monster of iniquity has been unveiled to the world, her frightful features unmasked, and soon, very soon will she be regarded with no more complacency by the American republic than is the idol of Juggernaut,* rolling its bloody wheels over the crushed bodies of its prostrate victims.

But you will probably ask, if Anti-Slavery societies are not insurrectionary, why do Northerners tell us they are? Why, I would ask you in return, did Northern senators and Northern representatives give their votes, at the last sitting of congress, to the admission of Arkansas Territory as a state? Take those men, one by one, and ask them in their parlours, do you *approve of slavery?* ask them on *Northern* ground, where they will speak the truth, and I doubt not *every man* of them will tell you, *no!* Why then, I ask, did *they* give their votes to enlarge the mouth

* One of the titles of the Hindu deity, Krishna. In annual processions, his idol was drawn on a huge car, and, it is said, worshipers would throw themselves under the wheels to be crushed.

of that grave which has already destroyed its tens of thousands? All our enemies tell *us* they are as much anti-slavery as we are. Yes, my friends, thousands who are helping you to bind the fetters of slavery on the negro despise you in their hearts for doing it; they rejoice that such an institution has not been entailed upon them. Why then, I would ask, do *they* lend you their help? I will tell you, "they love *the praise of men more* than the praise of God." The Abolition cause has not yet become so popular as to induce them to believe, that by advocating it in congress, they shall sit still more securely in their seats there and like the *chief rulers* in the days of our Saviour, though *many* believed on *[sic]* him, they did *not* confess him, lest they should *be put out of the synagogue;* John xii, 42, 43. Or perhaps like Pilate, thinking they could prevail nothing, and fearing a tumult, they determined to release Barabbas and surrender the just man, the poor innocent slave to be stripped of his rights and scourged. In vain will such men try to wash their hands, and say, with the Roman governor, "I am innocent of the blood of this just person." Northern American statesmen are no more innocent of the crime of slavery, than Pilate was of the murder of Jesus, or Saul of that of Stephen. These are high charges, but I appeal to *their hearts;* I appeal to public opinion ten years from now. Slavery then is a national sin.

But you will say, a great many other Northerners tell us so, who can have no political motives. The interests of the North, you must know, my friends, are very closely combined with those of the South. The Northern merchants and manufacturers are making *their* fortunes out of the *produce of slave labor;* the grocer is selling your rice and sugar; how then can these men bear a testimony against slavery without condemning themselves? But there is another reason, the North is most dreadfully afraid of Amalgamation.* She is alarmed at the very idea of a thing so monstrous, as she thinks. And lest this consequence *might* flow from emancipation, she is determined to resist all efforts at emancipation without expatriation. It is not because *she approves of slavery,* or believes it to be "the corner stone of our republic," for she is as much *anti-slavery* as we are; but amalgamation is too horrible to think of. Now I would ask *you,* is it right, is it generous, to refuse the colored people in this country the advantages of education and the privilege, or rather the *right,* to follow honest trades and callings merely because they are colored? The same prejudice exists here against our colored brethren that existed against the Gentiles in Judea. Great numbers cannot bear the idea of equality, and fearing lest, if they had the same advantages we enjoy,

* The pre–Civil War term for miscegenation.

they would become as intelligent, as moral, as religious, and as respectable and wealthy, they are determined to keep them as low as they possibly can. Is this doing as they would be done by? Is this loving their neighbor *as themselves?* Oh! that *such* opposers of Abolitionism would put their souls in the stead of the free colored man's and obey the apostolic injunction, to "remember them that are in bonds *as bound with them.*" I will leave you to judge whether the fear of amalgamation ought to induce men to oppose anti-slavery efforts, when *they* believe *slavery* to be *sinful.* Prejudice against color, is the most powerful enemy we have to fight with at the North.

You need not be surprised, then, at all, at what is said *against* Abolitionists by the North, for they are wielding a two-edged sword, which even here, cuts through the *cords of caste,* on the one side, and the *bonds of interest* on the other. They are only sharing the fate of other reformers, abused and reviled whilst they are in the minority; but they are neither angry nor discouraged by the invective which has been heaped upon them by slaveholders at the South and their apologists at the North. They know that when George Fox and William Edmundson* were laboring in behalf of the negroes in the West Indies in 1671 that the very *same* slanders were propogated against them, which are *now* circulated against Abolitionists. Although it was well known that Fox was the founder of a religious sect which repudiated *all* war, and *all* violence, yet *even he* was accused of "endeavoring to excite the slaves to insurrection and of teaching the negroes to cut their master's throats." And these two men who had their feet shod with the preparation of the Gospel of Peace, were actually compelled to draw up a formal declaration that *they were not* trying to raise a rebellion in Barbadoes. It is also worthy of remark that these Reformers did not at this time see the necessity of emancipation under seven years, and their principal efforts were exerted to persuade the planters of the necessity of instructing their slaves; but the slaveholder saw then, just what the slaveholder sees now, that an *enlightened* population *never* can be a *slave* population, and therefore they passed a law that negroes should not even attend the meetings of Friends. Abolitionists know that the life of Clarkson† was sought by slavetraders, and that even Wilberforce was denounced on the floor of Parliament

* George Fox (1624–1691), led the formation of the Society of Friends. In 1671, from Barbados, he urged Quaker slaveholders to limit the terms of service of their slaves and educate them. William Edmundson (1627–1712) was the society's leader in Ireland. He visited the American colonies on three occasions and, in 1676, wrote to Friends in Newbury, Rhode Island, clearly stating his opposition to slavery.

† Thomas Clarkson (1760–1846) worked with Wilberforce in the British antislavery campaign.

as a fanatic and a hypocrite by the present King of England [William IV], the very man who, in 1834, set his seal to that instrument which burst the fetters of eight hundred thousand slaves in his West India colonies. They know that the first Quaker who bore a *faithful* testimony against the sin of slavery was cut off from religious fellowship with that society. That Quaker was a *woman.** On her deathbed she sent for the committe[e] who dealt with her—she told them, the near approach of death had not altered her sentiments on the subject of slavery and waving her hand towards a very fertile and beautiful portion of country which lay stretched before her window, she said with great solemnity, "Friends, the time will come when there will not be friends enough in all this district to hold one meeting for worship, and this garden will be turned into a wilderness."

The aged friend, who with tears in his eyes, related this interesting circumstance to me, remarked that at that time there were seven meetings of friends in that part of Virginia, but that when he was there ten years ago, not a single meeting was held, and the country was literally a desolation. Soon after her decease, John Woolman began his labors in our society, and instead of disowning a member for testifying *against* slavery, they have for fifty-two years positively forbidden their members to hold slaves.

Abolitionists understand the slaveholding spirit too well to be surprised at any thing that has yet happened at the South or the North; they know that the greater the sin is, which is exposed, the more violent will be the efforts to blacken the character and impugn the motives of those who are engaged in bringing to light the hidden things of darkness. They understand the work of Reform too well to be driven back by the furious waves of opposition, which are only foaming out of their own shame. They have stood "the world's dread laugh," when only twelve men formed the first Anti-Slavery Society in Boston in 1831. They have faced and refuted the calumnies of their enemies, and proved themselves to be emphatically *peace men* by *never resisting* the violence of mobs, even when driven by them from the temple of God, and dragged by an infuriated crowd through the streets of the emporium of New-England, or subjected by *slaveholders* to the pain of corporal punishment. "None of these things move them"; and, by the grace of God, they are determined to persevere in this work of faith and labor of love: they mean to pray, and preach, and write, and print, until slavery is completely overthrown, until Babylon is taken up and cast into the sea, to "be

* Unable to identify.

found no more at all." They mean to petition Congress year after year, until the seat of our government is cleansed from the sinful traffic of "slaves and the souls of men." Although that august assembly may be like the unjust judge who "feared not God neither regarded man," yet it *must* yield just as he did, from the power of importunity. Like the unjust judge, Congress *must* redress the wrongs of the widow, lest by the continual coming up of petitions, it be wearied. This will be striking the dagger into the very heart of the monster, and once 'tis done, he must soon expire.

Abolitionists have been accused of abusing their Southern brethren. Did the prophet Isaiah *abuse* the Jews when he addressed to them the cutting reproofs contained in the first chapter of his prophecies, and ended by telling them, they would be *ashamed* of the oaks they had desired, and *confounded* for the garden they had chosen? Did John the Baptist *abuse* the Jews when he called them *"a generation of vipers,"* and warned them "to bring forth fruits meet for repentance"? Did Peter abuse the Jews when he told them they were the *murderers* of the Lord of glory? Did Paul abuse the Roman Governor when he reasoned before him of righteousness, temperance, and judgment, so as to send conviction home to his guilty heart, and cause him to tremble in view of the crimes he was living in? Surely not. No man will *now* accuse the prophets and apostles of *abuse,* but what have Abolitionists done more than they? No doubt the Jews thought the prophets and apostles in their day, just as harsh and uncharitable as slaveholders now, think Abolitionists; if they did not, why did they beat, and stone, and kill them?

Great fault has been found with the prints which have been employed to expose slavery at the North, but my friends, how could this be done so effectually in any other way? Until the pictures of the slave's sufferings were drawn and held up to public gaze, no Northerner had any idea of the cruelty of the system, it never entered their minds that such abominations could exist in Christian, Republican America; they never suspected that many of the *gentlemen* and *ladies* who came from the South to spend the summer months in travelling among them, were petty tyrants at home. And those who had lived at the South, and came to reside at the North, were too *ashamed of slavery* even to speak of it; the language of their hearts was, "tell it *not* in Gath, publish it *not* in the streets of Askelon"; they saw no use in uncovering the loathsome body to popular sight, and in hopeless despair, wept in secret places over the sins of oppression. To such hidden mourners the formation of Anti-Slavery Societies was as life from the dead, the first beams of hope which gleamed through the dark clouds of despondency and grief. Prints were made use of to effect the abolition of the Inquisition in Spain,* and Clarkson employed them when he was laboring to break up the Slave trade, and English Abolitionists used them just as we are now doing. They are powerful appeals and have invariably done the work they were designed to do, and we cannot consent to abandon the use of these until the *realities* no longer exist.

With regard to those white men, who, it was said, did try to raise an insurrection in Mississippi a year ago,† and who were stated to be Abolitionists, none of them were proved to be members of Anti-Slavery Societies, and it must remain a matter of great doubt whether, even they were guilty of the crimes alleged against them, because when any community is thrown into such a panic as to inflict Lynch law upon accused persons, they cannot be supposed to be capable of judging with calmness and impartiality. *We know* that the papers of which the Charleston mail was robbed, were *not* insurrectionary, and that they were *not* sent to the colored people as was reported. *We know* that Amos Dresser was *no insurrectionist* though he was accused of being so, and on this false accusation was publicly whipped in Nashville in the midst of a crowd of infuriated *slaveholders*. Was that young man disgraced by this infliction of corporal punishment? No more than was the great apostle of the Gentiles who five times received forty stripes, save one. Like him, he might have said, "henceforth I bear in my body the marks of the Lord Jesus," for it was for the *truth's sake, he suffered,* as much as did the Apostle Paul. Are Nelson, and Garrett, and Williams,‡ and other Abolitionists who have recently been banished from Missouri, insurrection-

* The Inquisition was created in 1478 to eliminate Muslims and Jews and ensure that only orthodox Catholicism would be practiced. Its power was curbed by Charles III (1759–1788).

† During the summer of 1835, rumors of a slave insurrection gripped white citizens in the Jackson area. Two "steam doctors" (itinerants prescribing steam baths as a cure for all ills) were apprehended, brought before a "Committee of Investigation," and hanged on July 4. Armed patrols scoured Madison and Hinds counties; white women and children were collected in central, heavily guarded places at night, and three more white men and between ten and fifteen blacks were executed (*The Liberator,* August 8, 1835, p. 127). Two months later, forty white citizens of Mississippi sent an open letter to Ransom G. Williams, the publishing agent of the American Anti-Slavery Society, promising him a "taste of hemp" if he ever ventured into the South.

‡ Dr. David Nelson (1793–1844) was born in Tennessee, practiced medicine in Kentucky, and became a Presbyterian minister in 1825. A colorful revivalist, he moved to Palmyra, Missouri in 1830 and established a Presbyterian church and a college to train Presbyterian preachers. Impressed with his energy and speaking ability, Weld recommended, in 1835, that Nelson be appointed the American Anti-Slavery Society agent for Missouri. At the beginning of May 1836, A. C. Garratt arrived from the East with a group of prospective students, two young blacks, and a trunkful of antislavery material. He stayed on the farm of Evan Williams. A vigilante committee seized Garratt and Williams and, under the threat of hanging, forced them and several students to leave Missouri on May 18. Four days later, another mob threatened Nelson, and he, fearing for his life, fled across the Mississippi River to Quincy, Illinois. There he continued his religious and antislavery activities.

ists? *We know* they are *not,* whatever slaveholders may choose to call them. The spirit which now asperses the character of the Abolitionists, is the *very same* which dressed up the Christians of Spain in the skins of wild beasts and pictures of devils when they were led to execution as heretics. Before we condemn individuals, it is necessary, even in a wicked community, to accuse them of some crime; hence, when Jezebel wished to compass the death of Naboth, men of Belial were suborned to bear *false* witness against him, and so it was with Stephen, and so it ever has been, and ever will be, as long as there is any virtue to suffer on the rack, or the gallows. *False* witnesses must appear against Abolitionists before they can be condemned.

I will now say a few words on George Thompson's mission to this country. This Philanthropist was accused of being a foreign emissary. Were La Fayette, and Steuben, and De Kalb,* foreign emissaries when they came over to American to fight against the tories, who preferred submitting to what was termed, "the yoke of servitude," rather than bursting the fetters which bound them to the mother country? *They* came with *carnal weapons* to engage in *bloody* conflict against American citizens, and yet, where do their names stand on the page of History. Among the honorable, or the low? Thompson came here to war aginst the giant sin of slavery, *not* with the sword and the pistol, but with the smooth stones of oratory taken from the pure waters of the river of Truth. His splendid talents and commanding eloquence rendered him a powerful coadjutor in the Anti-Slavery cause, and in order to neutralize the effects of these upon his auditors, and rob the poor slave of the benefits of his labors, his character was defamed, his life was sought, and he at last driven from our Republic, as a fugitive. But was *Thompson* disgraced by all this mean and contemptible and wicked chicanery and malice? No more than was Paul, when in consequence of a vision he had seen at Troas, he went over to Macedonia to help the Christians there, and was beaten and imprisoned, because he cast out a spirit of divination from a young damsel which had brought much gain to her masters. Paul was as much a *foreign emissary* in the Roman colony of Philippi, as George Thompson was in America, and it was because he was a *Jew,* and taught customs it was not lawful for them to receive or observe, being Romans, that the Apostle was thus treated.

* Marquis de Marie Joseph La Fayette (1757–1834), Baron Friedrich Wilhelm von Steuben (1730–1794), and Johann (Baron de) Kalb (1721–1780) were Europeans who aided the colonies in their war for independence.

It was said, Thompson was a felon, who had fled to this country to escape transportation to New Holland. Look at him now pouring the thundering strains of his eloquence, upon crowded audiences in Great Britain, and see in this a triumphant vindication of his character. And have the slaveholder, and his obsequious apologist, gained any thing by all their violence and falsehood? No! for the stone which struck Goliath of Gath, had already been thrown from the sling. The giant of slavery who had so proudly defied the armies of the living God, had received his death-blow before he left our shores. But what is George Thompson doing there? Is he not now laboring there, as effectually to abolish American slavery as though he trod our own soil, and lectured to New York or Boston assemblies? What is he doing there, but constructing a stupendous dam, which will turn the overwhelming tide of public opinion over the wheels of that machinery which Abolitionists are working here. He is now lecturing to *Britons* on *American slavery,* to the *subjects* of a *King,* on the abject condition of the *slaves of a Republic.* He is telling them of that mighty confederacy of petty tyrants which extends over thirteen States of our Union. He is telling them of the munificent rewards offered by slaveholders, for the heads of the most distinguished advocates for freedom in this country. He is moving the British Churches to sent out to the churches of American the most solemn appeals, reproving, rebuking, and exhorting them with all long suffering and patience to abandon the sin of slavery immediately. Where then I ask, will the name of George Thompson stand on the page of history? Among the honorable, or the base?

What can I say more, my friends, to induce *you* to set your hands, and heads, and hearts, to this great work of justice and mercy. Perhaps you have feared the consequences of immediate Emancipation, and been frightened by all those dreadful prophecies of rebellion, bloodshed and murder, which have been uttered. "Let no man deceive you"; they are the predictions of that same "lying spirit" which spoke through the four hundred prophets of old, to Ahab king of Israel, urging him on to destruction. *Slavery* may produce these horrible scenes if it is continued five years longer, but Emancipation *never will.*

I can prove the *safety* of immediate Emancipation by history. In St. Domingo in 1793 six hundred thousand slaves were set free in a white population of forty-two thousand.* That Island "*[sic]* marched as by

* A revolt of the blacks and mulattoes of that French island colony began in 1790 and became a full-scale slave revolt the following year. Although the French government officially abolished slavery

enchantment toward its ancient splendor, cultivation prospered, every day produced perceptible proofs of its progress and the negroes all continued quietly to work on the different plantations, until in 1802, France determined to reduce these liberated slaves again to bondage. It was at *this time* that all those dreadful scenes of cruelty occurred, which we so often *unjustly* hear spoken of, as the effects of Abolition. They were occasioned *not* by Emancipation, but by the base attempt to fasten the chains of slavery on the limbs of liberated slaves.

In Guadaloupe eighty-five thousand slaves were freed in a white population of thirteen thousand. The same prosperous effects followed manumission here, that had attended it in Hayti, every thing was quiet until Buonaparte* sent out a fleet to reduce these negroes again to slavery, and in 1802 this institution was re-established in that Island.† In 1834, when Great Britain determined to liberate the slaves in her West India colonies, and proposed the apprenticeship system; the planters of Bermuda and Antigua, after having joined the other planters in their representations of the bloody consequences of Emancipation, in order if possible to hold back the hand which was offering the boon of freedom to the poor negro; as soon as they found such falsehoods were utterly disregarded, and Abolition must take place, came forward voluntarily, and asked for the compensation which was due to them, saying, *they preferred immediate emancipation,* and were not afraid of any insurrection. And how is it with these islands now? They are decidedly more prosperous than any of those in which the apprenticeship system was adopted, and England is now trying to abolish that system, so fully convinced is she that immediate Emancipation is the *safest* and the best plan.

And why not try it in the Southern States, if it *never* has occasioned rebellion; if *not a drop* of *blood* has ever been shed in consequence of it, though it has been so often tried, why should we suppose it would produce such disastrous consequences now? "Be not deceived then, God is not mocked," by such false excuses for not doing justly and loving mercy. There is nothing to fear from immediate Emancipation, but *every thing* from the continuance of slavery.

Sisters in Christ, I have done. As a Southerner, I have felt it was my duty to address you. I have endeavored to set before you the exceeding

in 1794, the revolt, led by Toussaint L'Ouverture, continued, and his armies pushed the French, Spanish, and English off the island by 1798. A temporarily successful French invasion resulted in L'Ouverture's arrest and death, but the blacks defeated the French in 1803 and declared themselves free citizens of the independent Republic of Haiti.

* Napoleon Bonaparte (1769–1821), First Consul of France (1799–1804) and Emperor of France (1804–1814).

† The slaves in the French West Indies were not emancipated until 1848.

sinfulness of slavery, and to point you to the example of those noble women who have been raised up in the church to effect great revolutions, and to suffer for the truth's sake. I have appealed to your sympathies as women, to your sense of duty as *Christian women.* I have attempted to vindicate the Abolitionists, to prove the entire safety of immediate Emancipation, and to plead the cause of the poor and oppressed. I have done—I have sowed the seeds of truth, but I well know, that even if an Apollos* were to follow in my steps to water them, "*God only* can give the increase." To Him then who is able to prosper the work of his servant's hand, I commend this Appeal in fervent prayer, that as he "hath *chosen the weak things of the world,* to confound the things which are mighty," so He may cause His blessing, to descend and carry conviction to the hearts of many Lydias† through these speaking pages. Farewell—Count me not your "enemy because I have told you the truth," but believe me in unfeigned affection,

Your sympathizing Friend,

ANGELINA E. GRIMKÉ.

Angelina E. Grimké to Sarah M. Grimké

[W/G, Box 3.]

[Shrewsbury, N.J.] [August] 14th Evening [1836]

My Beloved Sister—

. . . Dearest—Language cannot express to thee the shock thy letter‡ was to my feelings. Such a thing had never enter'd my mind at all, & at first I knew not what to make of it. But on laying down the letter, the language rushd into my mind: I will break your bonds & set you free; so sweetly was this assurance seald that my morning was turnd into joy. I never saw before how it was possible for thee ever to leave C W M,§ but now it does seem clear to me that thy releas from Philadelphia is signd, for when the Apostles were sent out to preach, they were told to leav the hous on the city wh[ic]h would not receiv them, & shake off the dust of their feet as a memorial ag[ai]nst them. . . . Thou askest if my mind turns to Providence as an abiding place. It does to New

* Apollos, an Alexandrian Jew who became a Christian missionary c. 50 A.D.

† Lydia, the first European convert of St. Paul and his hostess at Philippi.

‡ Not found, but Angelina's opening lines indicate that Sarah had informed her that she had left Philadelphia and was on her way to Shrewsbury.

§ Catherine W. Morris, the sister of Israel Morris and an elder in the Society of Friends, had provided Sarah with a home for her entire stay in Philadelphia and Angelina for part of hers.

England. . . . So much so, that I wrote to E & L Capron* yesterday, stating to them just how I felt & querying whether *they* were willing the subjects which pressed upon my mind should be discussd & examind on Christian principle &c. & whether they thought I could be of any use in social circles in exciting an interest on behalf of the slave. I feel as if my services in this way must be freely offered to friends *first,* but it will be no surprise to me, even if N E friends are willing to receiv me, if Philadelphia friends managd to destroy my influence among them so completely as to close the door of usefulness to me altogether. If so, I believ I will be requird to labor among others. Should I go to N E this fall & winter, dearest, I need hardly tell thee it would be a great comfort to me to have thee in Providence, where I might see thee occasionally. Yea, would there not be a propriety in thy being near me, if the dear Master does order my step in that direction.

. . . I expect to go down to Quarterly Meeting tomorrow & feel as if I should hav to drink a cup of suffering there; I shall see S[amuel] B[ettle], I suppose, & perhaps we may hav that said conversation. O! for wisdom to direct my tongue. I shall surely need Divine help. No doubt he will want to know what I have been doing here, & I feel as if I could be very open. I am only afraid of being too much so. I do not expect to tell him any thing about my New England prospect, simply because I am uncertain about what the result of my letter to E & L Capron will be. I read it to dear Margaret [Parker], who has realy enterd into sympathy with me, & she approvd it, but I feel very confident that P[hiladelphia] friends will oppose this step most decidedly. Nevertheless, I shall simply say, I must obey God rather than man, & if way opens then I intend to go.

. . . [T]he more I reflect on the exclusiveness of our Society, the more I am convinced its constitution must be radically wrong, for any thing which cuts us off from christian communion with Christians of any name, & cooperation with them in works of mercy & faith, must be of *man's* invention & does partake of the nature of that spirit which divides in Jacob & scatters in Israel. As to the course now determind on by some in our Society of crushing & treading down every which opposes the peculiar views of Friends, it feels to me just like the powerful effort of the Jews, to close the lips of Jesus. . . . Some of the elders & chief priests

* Effingham L. Capron (1791–1859), a Quaker, an abolitionist, and a peace advocate, owned a textile factory in Uxbridge, Massachusetts. He was an early joiner and regular financial supporter of the New England Anti-Slavery Society, a participant at the founding convention of the American Anti-Slavery Society, and would be elected first president of the New England Non-Resistance Society (1838).

among us are trembling for the Ark, (whether it be the *Ark of God,* future events will amply testify). They think unholy hands ar about to touch it. They ar afraid that the Society will be completely broken up if they allow any difference of opinion to pass unrebuked, & they are resolved to crush all who question in any way the doctrines of Barclay,* the soundness of Fox, or the practices which are built upon them, & yet they strenuously *deny the right* of these men to rule over the opinions of any.

Very affy A E Gé

Angelina E. Grimké to Jane Smith†

[W/G, Box 3.]

Shrewsbury 9th Month 18th [1836]

My beloved Jane

. . . E Capron came to see me about my letter to him. We had two long interviews, & the substance of what he communicated was that if I went into N E with the *avowd* intention of laboring among friends on the subject of Slavery, in *any* way, that my way would be completely closed, & I would find that I could not do any thing at all. He even went so far as to say He believd there were friends there who would destroy my character if I attempted it. He then proposed my going to his hous to spend the winter & employing my time principaly in visiting for the Anti Slavery Society, cooperating with the Boston L[adies] Society & doing what I could incidentaly. It seemd as if I could not take hold of this plan at all. I feel as tho' it had been right for me to offer my poor services to *Friends first,* & I am glad I did so, but it seemd as if there was no door open among them. Besides which, when I told C W M. about this plan, she objected to it very decidedly & said I could not go without a minute‡ & a companion, & these she, of course, knew, Friends wld. not give me. I felt a little like the Apostle Paul, who, having *first* offerd the Jews the Gospel, on finding *they wld. not have it,* believd it right for him to turn to the Gentiles.

My mind was again introduced into close exercise about the proposi-

* Robert Barclay (1648–1690), Scottish Quaker whose *An Apology for the True Christian Divinity* . . . (1678) was considered the standard exposition of Friends' principles.

† Jane Smith, a Quaker, was Angelina's closest friend. Because she nursed an invalid mother, she could not offer a home to the sisters when they departed Catherine Morris'. Jane joined the Philadelphia Female Anti-Slavery Society in 1838 and attended the Anti-Slavery Convention of American Women held in Philadelphia that May.

‡ Certificate of approval from the meeting.

tion of the Anti Slavery Committee, & I tho't if only I could see some of them & talk the matter over, I would be better able to judge about it. Sister kindly offerd to go with me to N Y, & so we went. I had a short intercourse with E[lizur] W[right]. I learnd that the Comm was still desirous of my undertaking the work & that what was to be done could be done privately. Abby Ann Cox* came to see us, & we spent the next day with her . . . & talked over the matter. She tho't a *National* Female Society would be formed next mo., & we agreed if it was, I had better *ask for them* rather than for the male Society. She said she would write immediately to Maria Chapman in answer to a letter she had receivd some time before & would let me know as soon as it was determind what had best be done. M W C had herself proposed Female Agents, and the matters rests just here.

I feel as if I was given up to travel in the Cause, either for this one Society or the other, & tho' the path seems to me beset, on the one hand, with trials &, on the other, with temptations, yet I am willing to go because I believ the Master has sent me out & that he will be near to help & to guide me in every strait & difficulty. I need hardly tell thee, dear, that I hav passd thro' a great deal before I could realy giv up to do what I am almost certain will be disapprovd by nearly *all* my friends. As to dear Catherine [Morris], I am afraid she will hardly want to see me even. . . . I expect nothing less than the loss of her friendship & my membership in So[ciety of Friends]. The latter will be a far less trial than the former, for I do consider the restrictions place on our members as so very anti christian that I would rather be disownd than to be any longer bound by them. I hav borne them as long as I possibly could with peace of mind, & now that my Master has burst my fetters & set me free, I never expect to suffer myself to be manacled again. I never before was in bondage to any man, & I believ it is realy sinful to be influenced by any human authority, as to forget our individual responsibility to Him whose we ar & whom we ought to serv, independent of the opinion of man.

. . . I cannot describe to thee how my dear Sister has comfortd & strengthend me. I can not regard the change in her feelings as any other than a strong evidence that my heavenly [Father] has called me into the Anti Slavery field &, after having taxd my faith by her opposition, is now pleasd to strengthen & confirm it by her application.

. . . be *faithful* & believe in Thy affectionate A E Gé

* Abby Ann Cox, an organizer of women against slavery in New York City, provided a home for the Grimkés when they returned to New York in October.

Angelina E. Grimké to Jane Smith

[W/G, Box 3.]

[New York, N.Y.] First day noon*

My Dear Jane

The meetings of the Convention deepen in interest and hav, under the divine blessing, been the means of uniting dear Sister to our Abolition brethren in spirit & in love. . . .

We sit from 9 to 1, 3 to 5 & 7 to 9, from day to day & *never feel weary at all.* It is *better,* far better, than any Yearly Meeting I ever sat.

Very affy & gratefully Thine

Angelina

Angelina E. Grimké to Jane Smith

[W/G, Box 3.]

[New York, N.Y.] 11/19/36

My dear Jane

. . . [The meetings] are increasingly interesting, & to-day we enjoyd a moral & intellectual feast in a most notable speech from T D Weld of more than two hours on the question of what is slavery. I never heard so grand & beautiful an exposition of the dignity & nobility of man in my life. . . . He then spoke on the *duty* of immediate emancipation, regardless of all consequences, even to the slaves. . . . In the afternoon, he was followed by Beriah,† whose speech, tho' *good* was not *grand.* It was excelent but tame in comparison to that of T D W. After the meeting was over, W L Garrison introduced Weld to us. He greeted me with the appelation of my dear sister, & I felt as tho' he was a brother indeed in the holy cause of suffering humanity, a man raisd up by God & wonderfuly qualified to plead the cause of the poor & the oppressd. Perhaps thou will now want to know how this lion of the tribe Abolition *looks.* Well, at first sight, there was nothing remarkable to me in his appearance, & I wonderd whether he realy was as great as I had heard. But as soon as his countenance became animated by speaking, I found it

* The date of this letter cannot be determined precisely; it was probably written at the end of the first week of the convention.

† Beriah Green (1795–1874), professor of sacred literature at Western Reserve College, president of the Oneida Institute, and president of the founding convention of the American Anti-Slavery Society.

was one which portrayd the noblest quality of the heart & head, beaming with benevolence, intelligence & frankness.

It is truly comforting for me to find that Sister is so much pleasd with the Convention, that she acknowledges the spirit of brotherly love & condescension manifest among them, & that earnest desire that *truth* which characterizes the addresses, the querys that are thrown up &c.

. . . I am very comfortable, feeling in my right place, & Sister seems so too, tho' neither of us see much ahead. . . .

Thy Affect & grateful A E Gé

THREE

The Agency: New York

IN DECEMBER 1836, under the auspices of, but not officially employed or paid by, the American Anti-Slavery Society, Sarah and Angelina began speaking to the women of New York City about the evils of slavery in the South. At first they spoke in parlors, but the number of women desirous of hearing the Grimké sisters speak quickly outstripped the capacity of parlors to hold them.

The sisters were offered a room at a Baptist church, and, when attendance far exceeded their expectations, they began speaking there every Friday afternoon at 3:00. They discussed the laws of the slave states, read testimony from Southerners attesting to the evils of slavery, and handed out pamphlets of their writings. They also taught Sunday school classes to black children and visited their students' homes. Sarah helped to organize an association for the benefit of black orphans, and she prepared an address to southern clergymen and a critique of the Society of Friends. Weld, however, advised her not to publish the latter.[1]

By the end of February, 1837, the sisters were holding meetings in New Jersey and were actively involved in helping to organize a national women's antislavery convention. They received and replied to their first public criticism that February. A man identified only as "Clarkson" wrote a letter to the New Haven *Religious Intelligencer,* arguing that the people of the North did not need the sisters to "undeceive" them on the "wickedness, cruelty and oppression of slavery" and challenging the Grimkés to present "the *definite practicable means*" Northerners could employ to end slavery in the South. They responded with a detailed program, published in *Friend of Man,* during the first week of April.

The following month, 71 delegates gathered in New York for the Anti-Slavery Convention of American Women (103 corresponding members were listed). The convention was a response to a rule passed by the United States House of Representatives on May 26, 1836. Dubbed the "gag rule" by its opponents, it read: "all petitions relating . . . to the subject of slavery or the abolition of slavery, shall, without being either printed or referred, be laid upon the table and . . . no further action whatever shall be had thereon."[2]

The southern congressmen who had promulgated and secured the passage of this rule were determined to stifle what was perhaps the most vital means immediatists used to spread their doctrine in the North and goad the South. In addition, northern and southern congressmen alike were disturbed to note that petitioning had become a widening channel for feminist activism: increasing numbers of women carried petitions from door to door and the majority of signatures came from women.

But the immediate consequence was a new direction for the women's abolitionist movement. Shortly after the gag rule was passed, the female antislavery societies of Boston, New York, and Philadelphia decided to mount a national response, to flood Congress with many more petitions signed by many more people and to organize, at a national congress, a representative executive committee to coordinate it. The American Anti-Slavery Society, meeting at the same time, appointed Stanton, Weld, and Whittier to oversee a national petition campaign that would rely, for the most part, on women volunteers.[3]

The delegates to the woman's convention named Mary S. Parker* president, Sarah one of six vice presidents, and Angelina one of four secretaries. Following the reading of the twenty-seventh Psalm and a prayer, Sarah told the delegates that "the object of the convention was to interest women in the subject of anti-slavery, and establish a system of operations throughout every town and village in the free states, that would exert a powerful influence in the abolition of American slavery."[4] Sarah was assigned to the Committee to Prepare an "Address to Free Colored Americans," and Angelina to two committees—one to prepare "An Appeal to Women of the Nominally Free States," and one to write a letter to John Quincy Adams.†

* Mary S. Parker (1785–1841) was one of eleven children born to John and Hannah (Stearns) Parker of Lexington, Massachusetts. Her younger brother, Theodore, became a prominent Unitarian minister and reformer. Virtually nothing has been written about her, and she barely rates a mention in biographies of her brother. Parker was a charter member of the Boston Female Anti-Slavery Society and presided over the first two Anti-Slavery Conventions of American Women. She was a moderate on most issues, though, and, by 1837, began to clash regularly with Maria Weston Chapman and become the leader of an anti-Garrisonian group within the Boston Female Anti-Slavery Society.

† John Quincy Adams (1767–1848), the sixth president of the United States, had, in the privacy of his diary, registered pronounced opposition to slavery and admiration for those who devoted their lives to its abolition. He did not, however, become a public opponent of the institution until 1835, when, as a Congressman from Massachusetts, he opposed the annexation of Texas. The following year he became the most consistent, and often the only, advocate for repeal of the gag rule. Although abolitionists appreciated these acts, they were frustrated by his being unwilling to do or say more.

The sisters submitted ten motions between them, touching on the topics of the intertwined interests of North and South, fugitive slaves, the right of petition, northern men and women who marry southern slaveholders, the role of the federal government in perpetuating the slave institution, the need for women to teach the principles of peace and uphold the virtues of the abolitionists, a protest against racial prejudice, and a plea for open and equal higher education. Only two were not unanimously adopted.

Angelina's *An Appeal to the Women of the Nominally Free States* described the horrors of slavery, demonstrated how women were both victims and exploiters of it, challenged arguments denigrating the blacks' right to equality, critiqued the Colonization Society, and urged women of the North to petition, use free produce, cast out prejudice from their hearts, and pray. It also addressed the question of women and politics. The letter that she prepared to John Quincy Adams thanked him "for having defended so wisely, and so well, the right of women to be heard in the halls of legislation" and for having "asserted the right of the unpitied bondman to tell the story of his wrongs in those same proud halls," but expressed "our deep regret that your influence has not been employed, to procure the abolition of slavery in the District of Columbia."[5]

Sarah's *Address to the Free Colored People of the United States* was a sermon advising them what they should do and avoid doing to improve themselves and make further progress as a race.

The delegates agreed that their most important work was to gather signatures on petitions that asked for abolition in the District of Columbia and the Florida Territory and for ending the interstate slave trade. These petitions were to be sent in overwhelming numbers to Congress. They agreed to convene in Philadelphia the following May.

Angelina E. Grimké to Jane Smith

[W/G, Box 3.]

[New York, N.Y.] 12th Month, 17th [1836]

My Beloved Jane,

. . . After the privilege of attending the Convention (during which time my feelings were too much occupied with the business & taking notes to hav much time to think of myself), I began to feel afresh my *utter inability* to do any thing in the work I had undertaken. The more I looked at it, with the eye of reason, the more unnatural it seemd, & if I had dared to return to Philadelphia & lay down my commission, most gladly would I have done so. But one little grain of faith yet remains. I remember the deep travail of spirit thro' which I had passed at Shrewsbury & could not but believ that He who had sent me out would go before & prepare the way of the poor instruments he was pleased to employ.

Last week a Baptist minister of the name of Dunbar proposed our having a meeting in his Session room, similar to those held by Deborah Wade.* This was a great relief to our minds, for we both felt that this was just the right thing & readily closed in with the offer. The Female A S Sy embraced the opportunity of making this the commencement of Quarterly Meetings for their Sy, & it was accordingly given out in 4 churches on the Sabbath, but our names *not* mentioned. Well, after this was done, we felt almost in despair about the meeting, for we know that some persons here were exceedingly afraid that if we addressed our sisters, it would be called quaker preaching & that the prejudice here against women speaking in public life was so great that if such a view was taken, our precious cause would be injured.

The Throne of Grace was our only refuge & to it we often fled in united supplication for divine help. On 4th day morning [Wednesday], our dear brother in the Lord, G. Smith,† came to Henry Ludlow's‡ (where we are now staying) to breakfast, & when we gathered round the family altar, our hearts were melted together as he pourd out his soul in prayer for *us*, particularly, that we might be directed, strengthend & comforted in our work of mercy, & as soon as we rose from our places, the bell rung & a printed notice of the meeting was handed in, & in it our names were mentioned as intending to address the meeting. It was too much for us, & in christian freedom we opend our hearts to our dear friends. Truly, we felt as if such a thing was humanly impossible. We talkd the matter over & found that G Smith had another fear, that it would be called a Fanny Wright meeting & so on, & advised us not to make addresses except in parlors.

Well, we did not know what to do. The meeting was appointed &

* Deborah B. (Lapham) Wade (1801–1868) and her husband, Jonathan, a Baptist minister, were two of the first foreign missionaries, leaving for Burma in June 1823. During one of her returns to the United States, she spoke on the subject of "self denial and a devoted life."

† Gerrit Smith (1797–1874), an upstate New York philanthropist who had begun his antislavery career as a staunch supporter of colonization. He switched to immediatism in 1835 and presided over the New York Society from 1836–1839. He published *Friend of Man*.

‡ Reverend Henry G. Ludlow, minister of Spring Street Presbyterian Church. The Grimkés lived at his house during the winter of 1836–1837.

there was no business at all to come before it. When he left us, I went up to my room. I laid my difficulty at the feet of Jesus. I calld upon him in my trouble & he hearkened unto my cry, renewd my strength & confidence in God, & from that time I felt sure of his help in the hour of need. My burden was rolld off upon his everlasting arm, & I could rejoice in a full assurance of his mercy & power to be mouth & wisdom, tongue & utterance to us both.

Yesterday morning, T D Weld came up like a brother to sympathize with us & encourage our hearts in the Lord. He is a precious christian, bid us not to fear, but to trust in God &c. In a previous conversation on our holding meetings, he had expressed his full unity with our doing so, & grieved over that factitious state of society which bound up the energy of woman instead of allowing her to exercise them to the glory of God & the good of her fellow creatures. In the cause of the slaves, he believs, she has a *great* work to do & *must* be awakend to her responsibility &c.

His visit was realy a strength to us, & I felt *no* fear about the consequences, went to the meeting at 3 O clock & found about 300 persons. It was opend with prayer by H Ludlow. We were warmly welcomd by brother Dunbar. They soon left us &, after an opening minute, I spoke for about 40 minutes, I think, feeling perfectly unembarrassed, after which Dear Sister did her part better than I did. We then read some extrats from papers & letters & answerd a few questions, when at 5 the meeting closed, after the question had been put whether our sisters wishd another meeting to be held. A good many rose & H L says he is sure he can get his Session room for us. . . .

I know nothing of the effects on *others*. We went home with Julia Tappan* to tea, & brother Weld was all anxiety to know about it. She undertook to giv some account & among other things mentiond that a warm-heartd Abolitionist had found *his* way into the back pack of the meeting & that H L had escorted him out. Weld's countenance was instantly lighted up, & he exclaimed how extremely ridiculous to think of a man's being shoulderd out of a meeting for fear he should hear a woman speak. *We* smiled & said we did not know how it seemd to others, but it lookd *very strange* in our eyes. . . .

No doubt thou will want to know when we expect to leave N Y. We don't know. Sister is now writing an Address to Southern Clergymen & we think this had best be finished before we go hence. . . . We hope that now begining has been made, that we shall be able to hold a series of meetings here with our sisters, &, as the brethren think it will not do

* Juliana Tappan, eldest daughter of Lewis.

to hav public lectures in N Y, it seems the more necessary for us to do what we can. . . .

Very affy A E Gé

*Sarah M. Grimké, An Epistle to the Clergy of the Southern States**

> And when he was come near, he beheld the city and wept over it, saying—it thou had'st known, even thou, at least in this thy day, the things which belong unto thy peace. Luke, xix, 41–42.

Brethren Beloved in the Lord:

It is because I feel a portion of that love glowing in my heart towards you, which is infused into every bosom by the cordial reception of the Gospel of Jesus Christ, that I am induced to address you as fellow professors of this holy religion. To my dear native land, to the beloved relatives who are still breathing her tainted air, to the ministers of Christ, from some of whom I have received the emblems of a Saviour's love; my heart turns with feelings of intense solicitude, even with such feelings, may I presume to say, as brought the gushing tears of compassion from the Redeemer of the world, when he wept over the city which he loved, when with ineffable pathos he exclaimed, "O Jerusalem! Jerusalem! thou that killest the prophets, and stonest them which are sent unto thee, how often would I have gathered my children together, even as a hen gathereth her chickens under her wings, and ye would not." Nay, these are the feelings which fill the hearts of Northern Abolitionists, towards Southern slave-holders. Yes, my brethren, notwithstanding the bon fire at Charleston—the outrages at Nashville on the person of Dresser—the banishment of Birney† and [Dr. David] Nelson—the arrest and imprisonment of our colored citizens—we can still weep over you with unfeigned tenderness and anxiety, and exclaim, O that ye would now listen to the Christian remonstrances of those who feel that the principles they advocate "is not a vain thing for YOU, because it is YOUR LIFE." For you the midnight tear is shed, for you the daily and the nightly prayer ascends, that God in his unbounded mercy may open

* (New York: [American Anti-Slavery Society], 1836).

† James Gillespie Birney (1792–1857), a slaveholder who became an agent for the American Colonization Society, met Weld, converted to abolitionism, helped form the Kentucky Anti-Slavery Society, and became an agent for the American Anti-Slavery Society. When he found it impossible to establish a newspaper in Kentucky, he moved to Ohio, where he founded *The Philanthropist*. It began publication on January 1, 1836.

your hearts to believe his awful denunciations against those who "rob the poor because he is poor." And will you still disregard the supplications of those, who are lifting up their voices like the prophets of old, and reiterating the soul-touching enquiry, "Why will ye die, O house of Israel?" Oh, that I could clothe my feelings in eloquence that would be irresistible, in tones of melting tenderness that would soften the hearts of all, who hold their fellow men in bondage.

A solemn sense of the duty I owe as a southerner to every class of the community of which *I* once was a part, likewise impels one to address *you,* especially, who are filling the important and responsible station of minister of Jehovah, expounders of the lively oracles of God. It is because you sway the minds of a vast proportion of the Christian community, who regard you as the channel through which divine knowledge must flow. Nor does the fact that you are voluntarily invested by the people with this high prerogative, lessen the fearful weight of responsibility which attaches to you as watchmen of the walls of Zion. It adds rather a tenfold weight of guilt, because the very first duty which devolves upon you is to teach them not to trust in man.—Oh my brethren, is this duty faithfully performed? Is not the idea inculcated that to you they must look for the right understanding of the sacred volume, and has not your interpretation of the Word of God induced thousands and tens of thousands to receive as truth, sanctioned by the authority of Heaven, the oft repeated declaration that slavery, American slavery, stamped as it is with all its infinity of horrors, bears upon it the signet of that God whose name is LOVE?

Let us contemplate the magnificent scene of creation, when God looked upon chaos and said, "Let there be light, and there was light." The dark abyss was instantaneously illuminated, and a flood of splendor poured upon the face of the deep, and "God saw the light that it was good." Behold the work of creation carried on and perfected—the azure sky and verdant grass, the trees, the beasts, the fowls of the air, and whatsoever passeth through the paths of the sea, the greater light to rule the day, the lesser light to rule the night, and all the starry host of heaven, brought into existence by the simple command, Let them be.

But was man, the lord of this creation, thus ushered into being? No, the Almighty, clothed as he is with all power in heaven and in earth, paused when he had thus far completed his glorious work—"Omnipotence retired, if I may so speak, and held a counsel when he was about to place upon the earth the sceptered monarch of the universe." He did not say let man be, but "Let us make man in OUR IMAGE, after our likeness, and let them have dominion over the fish of the sea, and over the fowl of the air, and over the cattle, and over all the earth, and over every creeping thing, that creepeth upon the earth." Here is written in characters of fire continually blazing before the eyes of every man who holds his fellow men in bondage—In the image of God created he man. Here is marked a distinction which can never be effaced between a man and *a thing,* and we are fighting against God's unchangeable decree by depriving this rational and immortal being of those inalienable rights which have been conferred upon him. He was created a little lower than the angels, crowned with glory and honor, and designed to be God's viceregent upon earth—but slavery has wrested the sceptre of dominion from his hand, slavery has seized with an iron grasp this God-like being, and torn the crown from his head. Slavery has disrobed him of royalty, put on him the collar and chain, and trampled the image of God in the dust.

> Eternal God! when from thy giant hand
> Thou heaved the floods, and fixed the trembling hand;
> When life sprung startling at thy plastic call;
> Endless her forms and man the Lord of all—
> Say, was that lordly form, inspired by thee,
> To wear eternal chains and bow the knee?
> Was man ordained the slave of man to toil,
> Yoked with the brutes and fettered to the soil?

This, my brethren, is slavery—that is what sublimates the atrocity of that act, which virtually says, I will as far as I am able destroy the image of God, blot him from creation as a man, and convert him into a thing —"a chattel personal." Can any crime, tremendous as is the history of human wickedness, compare in turpitude with this?—No, the immutable difference, the *heaven-wide distinction* which God has established between *that* being, whom he has made a little lower than the angels, and all the other works of this wonderful creation, cannot be annihilated without incurring a weight of guilt beyond expression terrible.

And after God had destroyed the world with a flood because of the wickedness of man, every imagination of whose heart was evil, and had preserved Noah because he was righteous before him, He renewed man's delegated authority over the whole animate and inanimate creation, and again delivered into his hand every beast of the earth and every fowl of the air, and added to his former grant of power, "Every moving thing that liveth shall be meat for you, even as the green herb have I given you all things." Then, as if to impress indelibly upon the mind of man the eternal distinction between his rational and immortal creatures and the lower orders of beings, he guards the life of this most precious jewel, with a decree which would have proved all-sufficient to protect it, had not Satan infused into man his own reckless spirit.

Permission ample was given to shed the blood of all inferior creatures, but of this *being, bearing the impress of divinity,* God said, "And surely your blood of your lives will I require, at the hand of every beast will I require it, and at the hand of man, and at the hand of every man's brother will I require the life of man. Whoso sheddeth man's blood, by man shall his be shed, for in the IMAGE OF GOD made he man." Let us pause and examine this passage.—Man may shed the blood of the inferior animals, he may use them as *mere means*—he may convert them into food to sustain existence—but if the top-stone of creation, the *Image of God* had his blood shed by a beast, that blood was required even of this irrational brute: as if Deity had said, over my *likeness* I will spread a panoply divine that all creation may instinctively feel that he is precious to his Maker—so precious, that if his life be taken by his fellow man—if man degrades himself to the level of a beast by destroying his brother—"by man shall his blood be shed."

This distinction between *men and things* is marked with equal care and solemnity under the Jewish Dispensation. "If a man steal an ox, or a sheep, and kill it, or sell it, he shall restore five oxen for an ox, and four sheep for a sheep." But "he that stealeth a man and selleth him or if he be found in his hand, he shall surely be put to death." If this law were carried into effect now, what must be the inevitable doom of all those who now hold man as property? If Jehovah were to exact the execution of this penalty upon the more enlightened and more spiritually minded men who live under the Christian Dispensation, would he not instantly commission his most tremendous thunderbolts to strike from existence those who are thus trampling upon his laws, thus defacing his image?

I pass now to the eighth Psalm, which is a sublime anthem of praise to our Almighty Father for his unbounded goodness to the children of men. This Psalm alone affords irrefragable proof that God never gave to man dominion over his own image, that he never commissioned the Israelites to enslave their fellow men. This was

> Authority usurped from God not given—
> . . . Man over men

He made not Lord, such title to *himself*
Reserving, human left, from human free.

This beautiful song of glory to God was composed three thousand years after the creation, and David who says of himself, "The spirit of the Lord spake by me, and word was in my tongue," gives us the following exquisite description of the creation of man and of the power with which he was intrusted. "Thou hast made him a little lower than the angels, and crowned him with glory and honor. Thou madest him to have dominion over the works of thy hands: thou hast put all things under his feet: all sheep and oxen, yea, and all the beasts of the field, the fowl of the air and the fish of the sea, and whatsoever passeth through the paths of the sea."

David was living under that dispensation to which slave-holders triumphantly point as the charter of their right to hold men as PROPERTY; but he does not even intimate that any extension of prerogative had been granted. He specified precisely the same things which are specified at the creation and after the flood. He had been eminently instrumental in bringing into captivity the nations around about, but he does not so much as hint that Jehovah had transferred the sceptre of dominion over his immortal creatures to the hand of man. How could God create man in his own image and then invest his fellow worms with power to blot him from the world of spirits and place him on a level with the brutes that perish!

The same Psalm is quoted by the Apostle Paul, as if our heavenly Father designed to teach us through all the dispensation of his mercy to a fallen world, that man was but a little lower than the angels, God's viceregent upon earth over the inferior creatures. St. Paul quotes it in connection with that stupendous event whereby we are saved from eternal death. "But we see Jesus who was made a little lower than the angels for the suffering of death, crowned with glory and honor; that he by the grace of God should taste death for every man." Here side by side the apostle places "God manifest in the flesh" and his accredited representative man. He calls us to view the master-piece of God's creation, and then the master-piece of his mercy—Christ Jesus, wearing our form and dying for our sins, thus conferring everlasting honor upon man by declaring "both he that sanctifieth and those that are sanctified are all of one: for which cause he is not ashamed to call them brethren." It is then, the Lord's brethren whom we have enslaved; the Lord's brethren of whom we say "slaves shall be deemed, taken, reputed, and adjudged, chattels personal in the hands of their owners and possessors to all intents and purposes whatever."—*Laws of South Carolina.*

And here I cannot but advert to a most important distinction which God has made between immortal beings and beasts that perish.—No one can doubt that by the fall of man the whole creation underwent a change. The apostle says, "We know what the whole creation groaneth and travaileth in pain together." But it was for *man* alone that the Lord Jesus "made himself of no reputation and took upon him the form of a servant." When he came before his incarnation to cheer his servants with his blessed presence, when he visited Abraham and Manoah, he took upon himself a human form. Manoah's wife says, "a man of God came unto me." And when he came and exhibited on the theater of our world, that miracle of grace, "God in Christ reconciled the world unto himself," what form did he wear? "Verily," says the apostle, "he took not on him the nature of angels; but he took on him the seed of Abraham." Oh, my brethren, he has stamped with high and holy dignity the form we wear, he has forever exalted our nature by condescending to assume it, and by investing man with the high and holy privilege of being "the temple of the holy Ghost." Where then is our title deed for enslaving our equal brother?

Mr. [John A.] Chandler of Norfolk, in a speech to the House of Delegates of Virginia, on the subject of negro slavery in 1832,* speaking of our right to hold our colored brethren in bondage, says:

> As a Virginian, I do not question the master's title to his slave; but I put it to that gentleman, as a man, as a moral man, as a Christian man, whether he has not some doubts of his claim to his slaves, being as absolute and unqualified as that to other property. Let us in the investigation of this title go back to its origin—Whence came slaves into this country?—From Africa. Were they free men there? At one time they were. How came they to be converted into slaves?—By the stratagem of war and the strong arm of the conqueror; they were vanquished in battle, sold by the victorious party to the slave trader; who brought them to our shores, and disposed of them to the planters of Virginia. . . . The truth is, our

* The slave insurrection led by Nat Turner in Southampton, Virginia, in August 1831 provoked fear and horror among Virginia's white citizens and a powerful urge to address the slave institution. When the legislature met on December 5 memorials poured in: some advising stricter laws, some an end to slavery, some deportation of free blacks, and some calm. The House of Delegates met in February, 1832, to discuss legislation on the subject. Sarah had read the complete debates and had offered to prepare them for publication by the American Anti-Slavery Society (Sarah to Weld, December 9, 1836, W/G, Box 3; B/D, 1:348–349).

> ancestors had *no title* to this property, and we have acquired it only by legislative enactments.

But can "legislative enactments" annul the laws of Jehovah, or sanctify the crimes of theft and oppression? "Wo unto them that decree unrighteous decrees. . . . to take away the *right* from the poor of my people." Suppose the Saviour of the world were to visit our guilty country and behold the Christianity of our slave holding states, would not his language be, "Ye have heard that it hath been said by them of old time, enslave your fellow men, but I say unto you, "Do unto others as ye would they should do unto you," and set your captives free!

The sentiment—

> Man over man
> He made not Lord—

is the sentiment of human nature. It is written by the Almighty, on the soul, as a part of its very being. So that, urge on the work of death as we may, in the mad attempt to convert a free agent into a machine, a man into a thing, and *nature* will cry out for freedom. Hear the testimony of James McDowell [Rockbridge County] in the Virginia House of Delegates, in Virginia in 1832.

> As to the idea that the slave in any considerable number of cases can be so attached to his master and his servitude, as to be indifferent to freedom, it is wholly unnatural, rejected by the *conscious testimony* of every man's heart, and the *written testimony of the world's experience*. . . . You may place the slave where you please, you may oppress him as you please, you may dry up to the uttermost the fountain of his feelings, the springs of his thought, you may close upon his mind every avenue of knowledge, and cloud it over with artificial night, you may yoke him to your labors as the ox which liveth only to work, you may put him under any process, which without destroying his value as a slave, will debase and crush him as a rational being, and the idea that *he was born to be free* will survive it all. It is allied to his hope of immortality—it is the ethereal part of his being, which oppression cannot reach; it is a torch lit up in his soul by the hand of the Deity, and never meant to be extinguished by the hand of man.

I need not enter into an elaborate proof that Jewish servitude, as permitted by God, was as different from American slavery, as Christianity is from heathenism. The limitation laws respecting strangers and servants, entirely prohibited cruelty and oppression, whereas in our slave states, "THE MASTER MAY, AT HIS DISCRETION, INFLICT ANY SPECIES OF PUNISHMENT UPON THE PERSON OF HIS SLAVE,"* and the law throws her protecting aegis over the master, by refusing to receive under any circumstances, the testimony of a colored man against a white, except to subserve the interests of the owner.—"It is manifest," says the author (a Christian minister) of "A calm enquiry into the countenance afforded by the Scriptures to the system of British Colonial slavery" "that the Hebrews had no word in their language equivalent to slave in the West Indian use of that term. The word עבד obed [*ehvehd*],† is applied to both bond servant and hired, to kings and prophets, and even to the Saviour of the world. It was a general designation for any person who rendered service of any kind to God or man. But the term SLAVE, in the Colonial sense, could not be at all applied to a freeman." The same word in the Septuagint‡ which is translated servant, is also translated child, and as the Hebrew language is remarkable for its minute shades of distinction in things, had there been as is asserted, slaves in Judea, there would undoubtedly have been some term to designate such a condition. Our language recognizes the difference between a slave and a servant, because those two classes actually exist in our country. The Burmese language has no word to express ETERNITY, hence a missionary remarked that it was almost impossible to convey to them any conception of it.§ So likewise among the ancient Greeks and Romans there was no word equivalent to humility, because they acknowledged no such virtue. The want of any term therefore in the Hebrew, to mark the distinction between a slave in the proper sense of the term and other servants, is proof presumptive to say the least, that no such condition as that of slaves was known among the Jews of that day.

To assert that Abraham held slaves is a mere slander. The phrase translated "souls that they had gotten into Haran," Gen. 12:5, has no possible reference to slaves, and was never supposed to have any allusion to slavery until the commencement of the slave trade in England, in 1563. From that time commentators endeavored to cast upon Abraham the obloquy of holding his fellow creatures in bondage, in order to excuse this nefarious traffic. The Targum of Onkelos thus paraphrases

* Sketch of the Laws relating to slavery, in the United States of America, by George M. Stroud. [Footnote in original (Philadelphia, Pa.: Kimber and Sharpless, 1827).]

† עֶבֶד is translated as *serf* or *slave* in modern Hebrew-English dictionaries.

‡ Greek translation of the Old Testament, third century B.C.

§ The missionary was probably Jonathan Wade, who compiled an Anglo-Karen dictionary.

this passage, "souls gotten, i.e. those whom they had caused to obey the law." The Targum of Jonathan calls them "Proselytes." Jarchi, "Those whom they had brought under the wings of Shekimah." Menochius, "Those whom they converted from idolatry." Luke Franke, a Latin commentator, "Those whom they subjected to the law." Jerome calls them "Proselytes."* Here is a mass of evidence which is incontrovertible. Abraham's business as "the friend of God" was to get souls as the seal of his ministry. Would he have been called from a heathen land to be the father of the faithful in all generations, that he might enslave the converts he made from idolatry? As soon might we suspect our missionaries of riveting the chains of servitude on souls that they might have gotten, as seals of their ministry, from among those to whom they proclaim the unsearchable riches of Christ. Would heathen then, any more than now, be attracted to a standard which bore on it the inscription SLAVERY? No, my brethren; and if our downtrodden slaves did not distinguish between Christianity, and the Christians who hold them in bondage, they could never embrace a religion, which is exhibited to them from the pulpit, in the prayer-meeting, and at the domestic altar, embodied in the form of masters, utterly regardless of the divine command, "Render unto your servants that which is just." From the confidence Abraham reposed in his servants we cannot avoid the inference that they clustered voluntarily around him as the benefactor of their souls, the patriarch of that little community which his ministry had gathered.

Again, it is often peremptorily asserted that "the Africans are a divinely condemned and proscribed race." If they are, has God constituted the slave holders the ministers of his vengeance? This question can only be answered in the negative, and until it can be otherwise answered, it is vain to appeal to the curse on Canaan, or to Hebrew servitude, in support of American slavery. As well might the blood-stained Emperor of France [Napoleon I] appeal to the conquest of Canaan by the Israelites, and challenge the Almighty to reward him for the work of death which he wrought on the fields of Marengo and Leipsic† *[sic]*, because God invested his peculiar people, with authority to destroy the natives which had filled up the measure of their iniquity. The express grant to

* The Targums are translations, interpretations, and paraphrases of the Old Testament in Aramaic, made after the Babylonian Captivity (538 B.C.). They were preserved by oral transmission until about A.D. 100, when they were committed to writing. Jarchi or Solomon ben Isaac of Troyes, called RaSHI (1040–1105), *Commentaries on the Pentateuch* (in Hebrew); Menochius or Giovanni Stefano Menochio (1575–1655), *Bible Commentaries* (in Latin); Luke Franke or Franciscus Lucas (1549?–1612), *Biblia Sacra* (1583), *Concordantiae Bibliorum* (1612); Jerome (340?–420), translated the Bible into Latin, the *Vulgate*.

† Battles fought during the Napoleonic Wars: 1800 and 1813.

the Jews to reduce to subjection some of the Canaanitish nations and to exterminate others, at once condemns American slavery, because those who derive their sanction to hold their fellow men in bondage from the Bible, admit that a specific grant was necessary to empower the Israelites to make bond-men of the heathen; and unless this permission has been given, they would not have been justified in doing it. It is therefore self-evident that as *we* have never been commanded to enslave the Africans, *we* can derive no sanction for our slave system from the history of the Jews.

Another plea by which we endeavor to silence the voice of conscience is, "that the child is invariably born to the condition of the parent." Hence the law of South Carolina, says, "ALL THEIR (THE SLAVES) ISSUE AND OFFSPRING, BORN, OR TO BE BORN, SHALL BE AND THEY ARE HEREBY, DECLARED TO BE, AND REMAIN FOREVER HEREAFTER ABSOLUTE SLAVES, AND SHALL FOREVER FOLLOW THE CONDITION OF THE MOTHER." To support this assumption, recourse is had to the page of inspiration. Our colored brethren are said to be the descendants of Ham who was cursed with all his posterity, and their condition only in accordance with the declaration of Jehovah, that he visits the iniquities of the father upon the children.—I need only remark that Canaan, not Ham, was the object of Noah's prophecy, and that upon its descendants it has been amply fulfilled.

But we appeal to prophecy in order to excuse or palliate the sin of slavery, and we regard ourselves as guiltless because we are fulfilling the designs of Omnipotence. Let us read our sentence in the word of God: "And he said unto Abraham, Know of a surety that thy seed shall be a stranger in a land that is not theirs and shall serve them, and I will afflict them four hundred years, and also that nation whom they shall serve, I WILL JUDGE." That nation literally drank the blood of the wrath of Almighty God. The whole land of Egypt was a house of mourning, a scene of consternation and horror. What did it avail the Egyptians that they had been the instruments permitted in the inscrutable counsels of Jehovah to accomplish every iota of the prophecy concerning the seed of Abraham?

Appeal to prophecy! As well might the Jews who by wicked hands crucified the Messiah claim to themselves the sanction of prophecy. As well might *they* shield themselves from the scathing lightning of the Almighty under the plea that the tragedy they acted on Calvary's mount, had been foretold by the inspired penman a thousand years before. Read in the 22nd Psalm an exact description of the crucifixion of Christ. Hear the words of the dying Redeemer from the lips of the Psalmist: "My God! my God! why has thou forsaken me?" At that awful day when the dead, small and great, stand before God, and the books are opened, and another book is opened, which is the book of life, and the dead are judged out of those things which are written in the book ACCORDING TO THEIR WORKS—think you, my brethren, that the betrayer and the crucifier of the Son of God will find their names inscribed in the book of life *"because they* fulfilled prophecies[''] in killing the Prince of Peace? Think you that they will claim, or receive on this ground, exemption from the torments of the damned? Will it not add to their guilt and woe that "To Him bare *[sic]* all the prophets witness," and render more intense the anguish and horror with which they will call upon "the rocks and the mountains to fall upon them and hide them from the face of Him that sitteth upon the throne and from the wrath of the Lamb"?

Contemplate the history of the Jews since the crucifixion of Christ! Behold even in this world the awfully retributive justice, which is so accurately pourtrayed *[sic]* by the pen of Moses. "And the Lord shall scatter thee among all people from one end of the earth even unto the other, and among those nations shalt thou find no ease." And can we believe that those nations who with satanic ingenuity have fulfilled to a tittle these prophecies against this guilty people, will stand acquitted at the bar of God for their own cruelty and injustice, in the matter? Prophecy is a mirror on whose surface is inscribed in characters of light, the sentence of deep, immitigable woe which the Almighty has pronounced and executed on transgressors. Let me beseech you then, my dear, though guilty brethren, to pause and learn from the tremendour *[sic]* past what must be the inevitable destiny of those who are adding yea[r] after year, to the amount of crime which is treasuring up "wrath against the day of wrath." "A Wonderful and horrible thing is committed in the land! The *prophets prophecy falsely,* and the priests bear rule by their means. And my people love to have it so, and what will ye do in the end thereof?" "Thus saith the Lord of hosts concerning the prophets, Behold, I will feed them with wormwood, and make them drink the water of gall."

The present position of my country and of the church is one of deep and solemn interest. The times of our ignorance on the subject of slavery which God may have winked at, *have passed away.* We are no longer standing unconsciously and carelessly on the brink of a burning volcano. The strong arm of Almighty power has rolled back the dense cloud which hung over the terrific crater, and has exposed it to our view, and although no human eye can penetrate the abyss, yet enough is seen to warn us of the consequences of trifling with Omnipotence. Jehovah is calling us as he did Job out of the whirlwind, and every blast bears on its wings the sound, Repent! Repent! God, if I so may speak, is waiting to see whether we will harken unto his voice. He has sent out his light and his truth, and as regards us it may perhaps be said—there is now silence in heaven. The commissioned messengers of grace to this guilty nation are rapidly traversing our country, through the medium of the Anti-Slavery Society, through its agents and its presses, whilst the "ministering spirits" are marking with breathless interest the influence produced by these means of knowledge thus mercifully furnished to our land. Oh! if there be joy in heaven over one sinner that repenteth, what hallelujahs of angelic praise will arise, when the slave-holder and the defender of slavery bow before the footstool of mercy, and with broken spirits and contrite hearts surrender unto God that dominion over his immortal creatures which he alone can rightly exercise.

What an appalling spectacle do we now present! With one hand we clasp the cross of Christ and with the other grasp the neck of the down-trodden slave! With one eye we are gazing imploringly on the bleeding sacrifice of Calvary, as if we expected redemption through the blood which was shed there, and with the other we cast the glance of indignation and contempt at the representation of Him who there made his soul an offering for sin! My Christian brethren, if there is any truth in the Bible, and in the God of the Bible, *our hearts bear us witness* that he can no more acknowledge us as his disciples, if we willfully persist in this sin, than he did the Pharisees formerly, who were strict and punctilious in the observance of the ceremonial law, and yet devoured widows' houses. *We have added a deeper shade to their guilt,* we make widows by tearing from the victims of a cruel bondage, the husbands of their bosoms, and then devour the widow herself by robbing her of her freedom, and reducing her to the level of a brute. I solemnly appeal to your own consciences. Does not the rebuke of Christ to the Pharisees apply to some of those who are exercising the office of Gospel ministers, "wo unto you, Scribes and Pharisees, hypocrites! for ye devour widow's *[sic]* houses, and for a pretence make long prayers, therefore ye shall receive the greater damnation."

How long the space now granted for repentance may continue, is among the secret things which belong unto God, and my soul ardently desires that those who are enlisted in the ranks of abolition may regard every day as possibly the last, and may pray without ceasing to God, to grant this nation repentance and forgiveness of the sin of slavery. The time is precious, unspeakably precious, and every encouragement is offered us to supplicate the God of the master and of the slave to make a "right way" "for us, and for the little ones, and for all our substance." Ezra says, "so we fasted and besought the Lord, and he was entreated for us." Look at the marvellous effects of prayer when Peter was imprisoned. What did the church in that crisis? She felt that her weapons were not carnal, but spiritual, and "prayer was made without ceasing." These petitions offered in humble faith were mighty through God to the emancipation of Peter. "Is the Lord's arm shortened that it cannot save, or his ear grown heavy that it cannot hear?" If he condescended to work a miracle in answer to prayer when *one* of his servants was imprisoned, will he not graciously hear our supplications when two millions of his immortal creatures are in bondage? We entreat the Christian ministry to co-operate with us to unite in our petitions to Almighty God to deliver our land from blood guiltiness; to enable us to see the abominations of American slavery by the light of the gospel. "This is the condemnation, that light is come into the world, but men loved darkness rather than light, because their deeds were evil." Then may we expect a glorious consummation to our united labors of love. Then may the Lord Jesus unto whom belongeth all power in heaven and in earth condescend to answer our prayers, and by the softening influence of his holy spirit induce our brethren and sisters of the South "to undo the heavy burdens, to break every yoke and let the oppressed go free."

My mind has been deeply impressed whilst reading the account of the anniversaries* held last spring in the city of New York, with the belief that there is in America a degree of light, knowledge and intelligence which leaves us without excuse before God for upholding the system of slavery. Nay, we not only sustain this temple of Moloch; but with impious lips consecrate it to the Most High God; and call upon Jehovah himself to sanctify our sins by the presence of his Shekinah. Now mark, the unholy combination that has been entered into between

* During the 1820s, as evangelically motivated national organizations were formed, many of them scheduled their meetings around the annual meeting of the American Bible Society, in New York City, during the second week of May. Since the same people formed the nucleus of these movements, it proved more efficient to meet at the same time in the same place. This was the origin of what was called "Anniversary Week." Among the organizations that scheduled their annual meetings that week were the American Seamen's Friend Society, the American Tract Society, The American Peace Society, and the American Anti-Slavery Society. The following week, in Philadelphia, during "Ecclesiastical Week," assemblies of the Presbyterian, Episcopal, and Baptist communions and the Philadelphia and Adult Sunday School Union met. (The 1838 meeting of the Anti-Slavery Convention of American Women was scheduled for Ecclesiastical Week.) Finally, at the end of the month, in Boston, various missionary and Christian associations, held their annual meetings.

the North and the South to shut out the light on this all important subject. I copy from the speech before the "General Assembly's Board of Education." As an illustration of his position, Dr. Breckenridge* referred to the influence of the Education Board in the Southern States. "Jealous as those States were, and not without reason, of all that came to them in the shape of benevolent enterprise from the North, and ready as they were to take fire in a moment at whatever threatened *their own peculiar institutions,* the plans of this Board had *conciliated* their fullest confidence: in proof of which they had placed nearly two hundred of their sons under its care, that they might be *trained and fitted to preach to their own population.*" The inference is unavoidable that the *"peculiar institution"* spoken of is domestic slavery in all its bearings and relations; and it is equally clear that the ministry educated for the South are to be thoroughly imbued with the slave-holding spirit, that they may be *"fitted to preach to their own population," not* the gospel of Jesus Christ, which proclaims LIBERTY TO THE CAPTIVE, but a religion which grants to man the privilege of sinning with impunity, and stamps with the signet of the King of heaven a system that embraces every possible enormity. Surely if ye are ambassadors for Christ, ye are bound to promulgate the *whole* counsel of God. But can ye preach from the language of James, "Behold the hire of your laborers which is of you kept back by fraud crieth, and the cries of them which have reaped, are entered into the ears of the Lord of Sabaoth."† Multitudes of other texts must be virtually expunged from the Bible of the slave holding minister; every denunciation against oppression strikes at the root of slavery. God is in a peculiar manner the God of the poor and the needy, the despised and the oppressed. "The Lord said I have surely seen the affliction of my people, and have heard their cry by reason of their task-masters, for I know their sorrows." And he knows the sorrows of the American slave, and he will come down in mercy, or in judgment to deliver them.

In a speech before the "American Seamen's Friend Society," by Rev. William S. Plumer of Virginia,‡ it is said, "The resolution spoke of weighty considerations, why we should care for seamen, and one of these certainly was, because *as a class, they had been long and criminally*

* John Breckinridge (1797–1841), a Presbyterian minister in Kentucky and Maryland, secretary and general agent of the Board of Education of the Presbyterian church (1831), and professor of pastoral theology at Princeton Seminary (1836).

† "The wages you never paid to the men who mowed your fields are loud against you, and the outcry of the reapers has reached the ears of the Lord of the Hosts." James 5:4–5, *The New English Bible: The New Testament,* 2d ed. (Oxford University Press and Cambridge University Press, 1970), p. 394.

‡ William S. Plumer (1802–1880), Presbyterian.

neglected. Another weighty consideration was that seamen were a suffering race." . . . "And who was the cause of this? Was it not the church who withheld from these her suffering brethren, those blessed truths of God, so well calculated to comfort those who suffer?" Oh my brother! while drawing to the life a picture of a class of our fellow beings, who have been "long and criminally neglected," of "a suffering race," was there no cord of sympathy in thy heart to vibrate to the groans of the slave? Did no seraph's voice whisper in thine ear, "Remember them which are in bonds"? Did memory present no scenes of cruelty and oppression? And did not conscience say, thou art one who withholds from thy suffering colored brethren those blessed truths of God so well calculated to comfort those who suffer? Can we believe that the God of Christianity will bless the people who are thus dispensing their gifts to all, save to those by whose *unrequited* toil, we and our ancestors for generations past have subsisted?

Let us examine the testimony of Charles C. Jones,* Professor in the Theological Seminary, Columbia, S.C. relative to the condition of our slaves, and then judge whether they have not at least as great a claim as seamen to the sympathy and benevolent effort of Christian Ministers. In a sermon preached before two associations of planters in Georgia in 1831, he says: "Generally speaking, they (the slaves) appear to us to be without God and without hope in the world, a nation of HEATHEN in our very midst. We cannot cry out against the Papists for withholding the scriptures from the common people, and keeping them in ignorance of the way of life, for we *withhold the bible* from our servants, and *keep them* in ignorance of it, while we *will not* use the means to have it read and explained to them. The cry of our perishing servants comes up to us from the sultry plains as they bend at their toil; it comes up to us from their humble cottages when they return at evening, to rest their weary limbs; it comes up to us from the midst of their ignorance and superstition, and adultery and lewdness. We have manifested *no emotions* of horror at abandoning the souls of our servants to the adversary, the 'roaring lion, that walketh about, seeking whom he may devour.' "

On the 5th of December 1833, a committee of the synod of South Carolina and Georgia,† to whom was referred the subject of the reli-

* Charles C. Jones (1804–1863), a Methodist minister from a slaveholding family in Georgia, who urged the Methodist Episcopal church to establish missions to the slaves of Georgia. He taught at Columbia Theological Seminary from 1837 to 1838.

† Presbyterian Synod of South Carolina and Georgia, *Report of the Committee to whom was referred the subject of the religious instruction of the colored population of the Synod, at its late session in Columbia, South Carolina, December 5–9, 1833* (Charleston, S.C.: Charleston Observer Office Press, 1834).

gious instruction of the colored population, made a report in which this language was used.

> Who would credit it that in these years of revival and benevolent effort, in this Christian republic, there are over TWO MILLIONS of human beings in the condition of HEATHEN, and in some respects in a *worse* condition. From long continued and close observation, we believe that their moral and religious condition is such that they may be justly considered the HEATHEN of this Christian country, and will bear comparison with heathens in *any country in the world.* The negroes are destitute of the gospel, and *ever will be* under the present state of things.

In a number of the Charleston Observer (in 1834), a correspondent remarked: "Let us establish missionaries among our own negroes, who, in view of religious knowledge, are as debasingly ignorant as any on the coast of Africa; for I hazard the assertion that throughout the bounds of our Synod, there are at least ONE HUNDRED THOUSAND SLAVES, speaking the same language as ourselves, who never heard of the plan of salvation by a Redeemer." The Editor, Rev. Benjamin Gildersleeve,* who has resided at least ten years at the South, so far from contradicting this broad assertion, adds, "We fully concur with what our correspondent has said, respecting the benighted heathen among ourselves."

As Southerners, can we deny these things? As Christians, can we ask the blessing of the Redeemer of men on the system of American slavery? Can we carry it to the footstool of a God whose "compassions fail not," and pray for holy help to rivet the chains of interminable bondage on TWO MILLIONS of our fellow men, the accredited representatives of Jesus Christ? If we cannot ask in faith that the blessing of God may rest on this work of cruelty to the bodies, and destruction of the souls of men, we may be assured that his controversy is against it. Try it, my brethren, when you are kneeling around the family altar with the wife of your bosom, with the children of your love, when you are supplicating Him who hath made of one blood all nations, to justify these precious souls and prepare them for an inheritance with Jesus—then pray, *if you can* that God will grant you power to degrade to the level of brutes your colored brethren. Try it, when your little ones are twining their arms around your necks, and lisping the first fond accents of

* Benjamin Gildersleeve, a Presbyterian minister, was graduated from Middlebury College (Vermont), preached in South Carolina and Georgia, and began editing the Charleston *Observer* in January 1827.

affection in your ears; when the petition arises from the fulness of a parent's heart for a blessing on your children. At such a moment, look in upon your slave. He too is a father, and *we know* that he is susceptible of all the tender sensibilities of a father's love. He folds his cherished infant in his arms, he feels its life-pulse throb against his own, and he rejoices that he is a parent; but soon the withering thought rushes to his mind—I am a slave, and tomorrow my master may tear my darling from my arms. Contemplate this scene, while your cheeks are yet warm from the kisses of your children, and then try if you can mingle with a parent's prayer and a parent's blessing, the petition that God may enable you and your posterity to perpetuate a system which to the slave denies—

> To live together, or together die.
> By felon hands at one relenting stroke
> See the fond links of feeling nature broke;
> The fibre twisting around a parent's heart,
> Torn from their grasp and bleeding as they part.

A southern minister, Rev. Mr. Atkinson of Virginia,* in a speech before the Bible society last spring, says: "The facts which have been told respecting the destitution of some portions of our country are but samples of thousands more. Could we but feel what we owed to him who gave the Bible, we would at the same time feel that we owed it to a fallen and perishing world not merely to pass *fine resolutions,* or listen to *eloquent speeches,* but to exhibit a life devoted to the conversion of the world."

Let us now turn to the heart-sickening picture of the "destitution" of our slaves drawn by those who had the living original continually before their eyes. I extract from the report of the Synod of South Carolina and Georgia, before referred to.

> We may now enquire if they (the slaves) enjoy the privileges of the gospel in their own houses, and on our plantations? Again we return a negative answer—They have no Bibles to read by their own fire-sides—they have no family altars; and when in affliction, sickness, or death, they have no minister to address to them the consolations of the gospel, nor to bury them with solemn and appropriate services.

* Thomas Atkinson (1807–1881), Episcopalian.

This state of things, is the result of laws enacted in a free and enlightened republic. In North Carolina, to teach a slave to read or write, or to sell or give him any book, (the Bible not excepted) or pamphlet, is punished with thirty-nine lashes, or imprisonment, if the offender be a free negro, but if a white man then with a fine of two hundred dollars. The reason for this law assigned in the preamble is, that "teaching slaves to read and write tends to excite dissatisfaction in their minds, and to produce insurrection and rebellion."

In Georgia, if a white teach a free negro, or slave, to read or write, he is fined $500, and imprisoned at the discretion of the court. By this barbarous law, which was enacted in 1829, a white man may be fined and imprisoned for teaching his own child if he happens to be colored, and if colored, whether bond or free, he may be fined or whipped.

> "We have," says Mr. [Henry] Berry [Jefferson County], in a speech in the House of Delegates of Virginia in 1832, "as far as possible closed every venue by which light might enter their (the slaves) minds. If we could extinguish the capacity to see the light, our work would be completed; they would then be on a level with the beasts of the fields, and we should be safe. I am not certain that we would not do it, if we could find out the necessary process, and that on the plea of necessity."

Oh, my brethren! when you are telling to an admiring audience that through your instrumentality nearly two millions of Bibles and Testaments have been disseminated throughout the world, does not the voice of the slave vibrate on your ear, as it floats over the sultry plains of the South, and utters forth his lamentation, "Hast thou but one blessing my father? *bless me, even me also,* O my father!" Does no wail of torment interrupt the eloquent harangue?—And from the bottomless pit does no accusing voice arise to charge you with the perdition of those souls from whom you wrested, as far as you were able, the power of working out their own salvation?

Our country, I believe, has arrived at an awful crisis. God has in infinite mercy raised up those who have moral courage and religion enough to obey the divine command, "Cry aloud and spare not, lift up thy voice like a trumpet, and show my people their transgressions."—Our sins are set in order before us, and we are now hesitating whether we shall choose the curse pronounced by Jehovah, "Cursed be he that perverteth the judgment of the stranger, fatherless and widow," or the blessing recorded in the 41st Psl. "Blessed is the man that considereth the poor (or the weak) the Lord will deliver him in the time of trouble."

And is there no help? Shall we be dismayed because our mistaken countrymen burned our messengers of Truth in Charleston, S.C.? No, my brethren, *I am not dismayed!* I do not intend to stamp the anti-slavery publications as inspired writings, but the principles they promulgate are the principles of the holy Scriptures, and I derive encouragement from the recollection that Tindal* suffered martyrdom for translating and printing the New Testament—and that Tonstal, Archbishop of London,† purchased every copy which he could obtain, and had them burnt by the common hangman. Now Great Britain is doing more than any other people to scatter the Bible to every nation under heaven. Shall we be alarmed as though some new thing has happened unto us because our printing press has been destroyed at Cincinnati, Ohio?‡ The devoted Carey§ was compelled to place his establishment for the translation of the sacred volume beyond the boundary line of the British authorities. And now England would gladly have the Bible translated into every tongue.

If then there be, as I humbly trust there are among my Christian brethren some who like the prophet of old are ready to exclaim! "Wo is me! for I am undone; because I am a man of unclean lips; for mine eyes have seen the King, the Lord of Hosts"—If to some of you Jehovah has unvailed the abominations of American slavery, the guilt of yourselves and of your brethren! Oh remember the prophet of Israel and be encouraged. Your lips like his will be touched with a live coal from off the altar. The Lord will be your light and your salvation: He will go before you and the God of Israel will be your reward.

If ever there was a time when the Church of Christ was called upon to make an *aggressive* movement on the kingdom of darkness, *this is the time.* The subject of slavery is fairly before the American public.—The consciences of the slave-holders at the South and of the coadjutors at the North are aroused, notwithstanding all the opiates which are so abundantly administered under the pleas of necessity, and expediency, and the duty of obedience to man, rather than to God. In regard to slavery,

* William Tyndale (1494?–1536) translated the first printed English Bible (1526) but had to go to Germany to do it. Ten years later he was burned as a heretic in the Netherlands.

† Cuthbert Tunstall (1474–1559) had discouraged Tyndale's project when it was first proposed.

‡ On July 12, 1836, a mob broke into the printing office of *The Philanthropist* and dismantled the press. It was reassembled and printing resumed three days later. On the night of July 30 another mob dragged the press to the banks of the Ohio River and sank it.

§ Mathew Carey (1760–1839), twice driven from Ireland for his printed remarks, settled in Philadelphia where he published various newspapers, magazines, and books.

Satan has transformed himself into an angel of light, and under the false pretense of consulting the good of the slaves, pleads for retaining them in bondage, until they are prepared to enjoy the blessings of liberty. Full well he knows that if he can but gain time, he gains every thing. When he stood beside Felix, and saw that he trembled before his fettered captive, as Paul reasoned of righteousness, temperance, and judgment to come, he summoned to his aid this masterpiece of satanic ingenuity, and whispered, say to this Apostle, "Go thy way for this time, at a more convenient season, I will call for thee." The heart of Felix responded to this intimation, and his lips uttered the fatal words—fatal, because, for aught that appears, they sealed his death warrant for eternity. Let me appeal to every Christian minister, who has known what it is to repent and forsake his sins: Have you not all found that prospective repentance and future amendment are destruction to the soul? The truth is, to postpone present duty, to get ready for the discharge of future, is just putting yourselves under the hands of Satan to prepare you for the service of God. Just so, gradualism puts the slave into the hands of his master, whose interest it is to keep him enslaved, to prepare him for freedom, because that master says at a convenient season I will liberate my captive. So says the adversary of all good, serve me to-day and to-morrow thou mayest serve God. Oh lay not this flattering unction to your souls, ye that are teachers in Israel. God is not mocked, and ye may as well expect indulgence in sin to purify the heart and prepare the soul for an inheritance with the saints in light, as to suppose that slavery can fit men for freedom. That which debases and brutalizes can never fit for freedom. The chains of the slave must be sundered; he must be taught that he is "heaven-born and destined to the skies again"; he must be restored to his dignified station in the scale of creation, he must be crowned again with the diadem of glory, again ranked amongst the sons of God and invested with lordly prerogative over every living creature. If you would aid in this mighty, this glorious achievement—"preach the word" of IMMEDIATE EMANCIPATION. "Be instant in season and out of season." "If they persecute you in one city, flee ye unto another," that your sound may go out through all our land; and you may not incur the awful charge,

"YE KNEW YOUR DUTY, BUT YE DID IT NOT."

It is now twenty years since a beloved friend with whom I often mingled my tears, related to me the following circumstance, when helpless and hopeless we deplored the horrors of slavery, and I believe many are doing what we did then, weeping and praying and interceding, "but secretly, for the fear of the Jews." On the plantation adjoining her husbands, there was a slave of pre-eminent piety. His master was not a professor of religion, but the superior excellence of this disciple of Christ was not unmarked by him, and I believe he was so sensible of the good influence of his piety that he did not deprive him of the few religious privileges within his reach. A planter was one day dining with the owner of this slave, and in the course of conversation observed that all profession of religion among slaves was mere hypocrisy. The other asserted a contrary opinion, adding, I have a slave who I believe would rather die than deny his Saviour. This was ridiculed and the master urged to prove his assertion. He accordingly sent for this man of God, and peremptorily ordered him to deny his belief in the Lord Jesus Christ. The slave pleaded to be excused, constantly affirming that he would rather die than deny the Redeemer, whose blood was shed for him. His master, after vainly trying to induce obedience by threats, had him severely whipped. The fortitude of the sufferer was not to be shaken; he nobly rejected the offer of exemption from further chastisement at the expense of destroying his soul, and this blessed martyr died in consequence of this severe infliction. Oh, how bright a gem will this victim of irresponsible power be, in that crown which sparkles on the Redeemer's brow; and that many such will cluster there, I have not the shadow of a doubt.*

Brethren, you are invested with immense power over those to whom you minister in holy things—commensurate with your power is your responsibility, and if you abuse, or neglect to use it aught, great will be your condemnation. Mr. [Samuel D.] Moore [Rockbridge County], in a speech in the House of Delegates in Virginia, in 1832, says:

> It is utterly impossible to avoid the consideration of the subject of slavery. As well might the Apostle have attempted to close his eyes against the light which shone upon him from heaven, or to turn a deaf ear to the name which reached him from on high! as for us to try to stifle the spirit of enquiry which is abroad in the land. . . . THE MONSTROUS CONSEQUENCES which arise from the existence of slavery have been exposed to open day; the DANGERS

* Since writing the above, I have received information that "the perpetrators of the foul deed were in a state of inebriation," and that this martyr was an aged slave. Drunkenness instead of palliating crime aggravates it even according to human laws. But such are the men in whose hands slavery often places absolute power. [Footnote in original.]

> arising from it stare us in the face, and it becomes us as men to meet and overcome them, rather than attempt to escape by evading them. Slavery, as it exists among us, may be regarded as the heaviest calamity which has ever befallen any portion of the human race. If we look back at the long course of time which has elapsed from the creation to the present moment, we shall scarcely be able to point out a people whose situation was not in many respects preferable to our own, and that of the other states in which slavery exists. True, we shall see nations which have groaned under the yoke of despotism for hundreds and thousands of years, but the individuals composing those nations have enjoyed a degree of happiness, peace and freedom from apprehension which the holders of slaves in this country can never know.

The daughters of Virginia have borne their testimony to the evils of slavery, and have pleaded for its extinction. Will this nation continue deaf to the voice of reason, humanity, and religion? In the memorial of the female citizens of Fluvanna Co., Va. to the General Assembly of that commonwealth in 1832, they say:

> We cannot conceal from ourselves that an evil (slavery) is amongst us, which threatens to outgrow the growth, and dim the brightness of our national blessings. A shadow deepens over the land and casts its thickest gloom upon the sacred shrine of domestic bliss, darkening over us as time advances.
>
> We can only aid by ardent outpourings of the spirit of supplication at a throne of grace. . . . We conjure you by the sacred charities of kindred, by the solemn obligations of justice, by every consideration of domestic affection and patriotic duty, to nerve every faculty of your minds to the investigation of this important subject, and let not the united voices of your mothers, wives, daughters and kindred have sounded in your ears in vain.

We are cheered with the belief that many knees at the South are bent in prayer for the success of the Abolitionists. We believe, and we rejoice in the belief that the statement made by a Southern Minister of the Methodist Episcopal Church, at the session of the New York Annual Conference, in June of this year, is true: "Don't give up Abolitionism—don't bow down to slavery. You have thousands at the South who are secretly praying for you."—In a subsequent conversation with the same individual, he stated, That the South is not that unit of which the pro-slavery party boast—there is a diversity of opinion among them in reference to slavery and the REIGN OF TERROR alone suppresses the free expression of sentiment. That there are thousands who believe slave-holding to be sinful, who secretly wish the abolitionists success, and believe God will bless their efforts. That the ministers of the gospel and ecclesiastical bodies who indiscriminately denounce the abolitionists, without doing anything themselves to remove slavery, have not the thanks of thousands at the South, but on the contrary are viewed as taking sides with slaveholders and recreant to the principles of their own profession. *Zion's Watchman,* November, 1836.*

The system of slavery is necessarily cruel. The lust of dominion inevitably produces hardness of heart, because the state of mind which craves unlimited power, such as slavery confers, involves a desire to use that power, and although I know there are exceptions to the exercise of barbarity on the bodies of slaves, I maintain that there *can be no exceptions* to the exercise of the most soul-withering cruelty on the *minds* of the enslaved. All around is the mighty ruin of intellect, the appalling spectacle of the down-trodden image of God. What has caused this mighty wreck? A voice deep as hell and loud as the thunder of heaven replies, SLAVERY! Both worlds of spirits echo and re-echo, SLAVERY! And yet American slavery is palliated, is defended by slave-holding ministers at the South and their coadjutors at the North. Perhaps all of you would shrink with horror from a proposal to revive the Inquisition and give to Catholic superstition the power to enforce in this country its wicked system of bigotry and despotism. But I believe if all the horrors of the Inquisition and all the cruelty and oppression exercised by the Church of Rome, could be fully and fairly brought to view and compared with the details of slavery in the United States, the abominations of Catholicism would not surpass those of slavery, while the victims of the latter are ten fold more numerous.

But it is urged again and again, that slavery has been entailed upon us by our ancestors. We speak of this with a degree of self-complacency,

* When the managers of *Zion's Herald,* published by the Boston Wesleyan Association, refused to print articles written by immediatist Methodist ministers, LaRoy Sunderland and George Storrs founded *Zion's Watchman* in New York City. The first issue appeared on January 1, 1836, and that summer, the New York Methodist Conference censored it for its antislavery position, disapproved of any member aiding abolitionists, admonished members not to attend antislavery meetings, and refused to elect any candidate deacon or elder who did not pledge to refrain from agitating the slave question. For an overview of the response of northern churches to abolition, see Lorman Ratner, *Powder Keg: Northern Opposition to the Antislavery Movement, 1831–1840* (New York: Basic Books, 1968), pp. 88–130.

which seems to intimate that we would not do the deeds of our fathers. So to speak argues an utter want of principle, as well as an utter ignorance of duty, because as soon as we perceive the iniquity of that act by which we inherit PROPERTY IN MAN, we should surrender to the rightful owner, viz. the slave himself, a right which although legally vested in us, by the "unrighteous decrees" of our country, is vested in the slave *himself* by the laws of God. We talk as if the guilt of slavery from its first introduction to the present time, rested on our progenitors, and as if we were innocent because we had not imported slaves originally from Africa. The prophet Ezekiel furnishes a clear and comprehensive answer to this sophistry. "What means ye, that ye use this proverb saying: Thy fathers have eaten sour grapes, and the children's teeth are set on edge. . . . Behold all souls are mine, as the soul of the father, so also the soul of the son is mine. THE SOUL THAT SINNETH IT SHALL DIE. If a man be just and doeth that which is lawful and right, he shall surely live. If he shall beget a son that hath opprest the poor and needy, he shall surely die; his blood shall be upon him. Now, lo! if he beget a son that seeth all his father's sins which he hath done, and doeth not such like, that hath not opprest any, neither hath spoiled by violence; that hath taken off his hand from the poor, he shall not die for the iniquity of his father. THE SOUL THAT SINNETH IT SHALL DIE. The son shall not bear the iniquity of the father, neither shall the father bear the iniquity of the son. The righteousness of the righteous shall be upon him—and the wickedness of the wicked shall be upon him."

Upon the present generation, rests, I believe, an accumulated weight of guilt. They have the experience of more than two centuries to profit by—they have witnessed the evils and crimes of slavery, and they know that sin and misery are its legitimate fruits. They behold every where, inscribed upon the face of nature, the withering curse of slavery, as if the land mourned over the iniquity and wretchedness of its inhabitants. They contemplate in their domestic circles the living examples of that description given by Jefferson, in his "Notes on Virginia,"* of the influence of slavery, on the temper and morals of the master, and they know that there is not one redeeming quality, in the system of American slavery.

And now we have the most undeniable evidence of the safety of Immediate Emancipation, in the British West Indies. Every official account from these colonies, especially such as have rejected the appren-

* Thomas Jefferson (1743–1826), *Notes on the State of Virginia* (London: Stockdale, 1787).

ticeship system, comes fraught with encouragement to this country to deliver the poor and needy out of the hand of the oppressor.

To my brethren of the Methodist connection, with some of whom I have taken sweet counsel, and whose influence is probably more extensive than that of any other class of ministers at the South, it may avail something to the cause of humanity, which I am pleading, to quote the sentiments of John Wesley and Adam Clarke.* Speaking of slavery the former says, "The blood of thy brother crieth against thee from the earth: oh, whatever it costs, put a stop to its cry before it is too late—instantly, at any price, were it the half of thy goods, deliver thyself from blood guiltiness. Thy hands, thy bed, thy furniture, thy house and thy lands, at present are stained with blood. Surely it is enough—accumulate no more guilt, spill no more blood of the innocent. Whether thou are a Christian or not, show thyself A MAN." Adam Clarke says, "In heathen countries, slavery was in some sort excusable. Among Christians it is an enormity and crime, for which perdition has scarcely an adequate punishment."

Yet this is the crime of which the Synod of Virginia, convened for the purpose of deliberating on the state of the Church in November last, speaks thus: "The Synod solemnly affirm, that the General Assembly of the Presbyterian Church have *no right* to declare that relation (viz. the relation between master and slave) sinful, which Christ and his apostles teach to be consistent with the most unquestionable piety. And that any act of the General Assembly which would impeach the *Christian* character of any man because he is a slave holder, would be a palpable violation of the just principles on which the union of our Church was founded—as well as a daring usurpation of authority granted by the Lord Jesus."

And this is the sin which the Church is fostering in her bosom—This is the leprosy over which she is casting the mantle of charity, to hide, if possible, the "putrefying sores"—This is the monster around which she is twining her maternal arms, and before which she is placing her anointed shield inscribed "holiness to the Lord"—Oh, ye ministers of Him who so loved the slave that he gave his precious blood to redeem him from sin, can ye any longer with our eyes fixed upon the Cross of Christ, plant your foot on his injured representative, and sanction and sanctify this heart-breaking, this soul-destroying system?

* John Wesley (1703–1791), the founder of Methodism; Adam Clarke (1762?–1832), Methodist preacher and writer.

Wo to those whose hire is with the price of blood
Perverting, darkening, changing as they go
The sacred truths of the Eternal God.

Brethren, farewell! I have written under a solemn sense of my responsibility to God for the truths I have uttered: I know that all who nobly dare to speak the truth will come up to the help of the Lord, and add testimony to testimony until time would fail to hear them. To Him who has promised that "the expectation of the needy shall not perish forever" —who "hath chosen the weak things of the world to confound the things that are mighty, and the foolish things of the world to confound the wise, and base things of the world, and things which are despised, hath God chosen, yea and things which are not, to bring to naught things that are, that no flesh should glory in the presence," I commend this offering of Christian affection, humbly beseeching him so to influence the ministers of his sanctuary, and the people committed to their charge by his Holy Spirit, that from every Christian temple may arise the glorious anthem,

Blow ye the trumpet blow,
The gladly solemn sound!
Let all the nations know,
To earth's remotest bound,
The year of jubilee is come.

Yours in gospel love,
Sarah M. Grimké.
New York, 12th Mo. 1836.

Angelina E. and Sarah M. Grimké to Jane Smith

[W/G, Box 3.]

[New York, N.Y.] 1 Month 20th 1836 [1837]

My Dear Jane
. . . thou will doubtless want to know whether I find it an *easy* thing to hold such meetings—I, no! I can truly say that the day I hav to speak is always a day of suffering. . . . I feel like a totaly different being after the meeting is over, for I assure thee I do know that a fresh caption is needed for every appearance in public. It is realy delightful to see dear Sister so

happy in this work. I hav not the shadow of a doubt she is in her right place & will be made instrumental of great good. . . .

Thou mayest remark I speak of our *talks* as *lectures*. Well, this is the name that *others* have given our poor effort, & I don't know in fact what to call such novel proceedings. How little! how *very little* I supposed, when I used to say, "I wish I was a *man,* that I might go out and lecture," that *I* would ever do such a thing. The idea never crossed my mind that *as a woman* such work could possible be assigned me. But the Lord is "wonderful counsel, excelent in working," making a way for his people when there seems to be *no* way. Dear Jane, I love the work. I count myself greatly favord in being calld to it, & I often feel as if the only earthly blessing I hav to ask for is to be made the unworthy instrument of arousing the slumbering energy & dormant sympathy of my northern sisters on this deeply painful & interesting subject. . . .

Farewell Dear Jane, pray for thy poor unworthy Angelina

My Dear Jane,

. . . I am not very comfortable in the performance of those duties to which I have been calld & altho' I feel as if the circumstances which led to my present situation were many of them painful to my best feelings, yet I rejoice that God over-ruled them to work in me a willingness to do his blessed will. . . .

affy thy S M G

Angelina E. Grimké to Jane Smith

[W/G, Box 3.]

[New York, N.Y.] 2 mo: 4th 1837.

My Dear Jane,

. . . [Our meeting last week] was the largest we hav had, about 400, I should think. . . . We had one male auditor, who refused to go out when H G L[udlow] told him it was exclusively for ladys, & so there he sat & somehow I did not feel his presence at all embarrassing & went on just as tho' he was not there. Some one said he took notes, & I think he was a Southern spy & shall not be at all surprized if he publishes us in some Southern paper, for we hav heard nothing of him here. . . .

Some friends think *I* make too many gestures, one thinking females ought to be *motionless* when speaking in public, another fearing that *other* denominations might be offended by them, because they were unaccustomed to hear women speak in public. But I think the more a speaker can yield himself entirely to the nativ impulses of feeling, the better, & this is just what I do. . . .

Last 5th day [Thursday], I think not more than 200 were out. Sister spoke one hour on the effects on the soul, & I finished off with some remarks on the popular objection Slavery is a political subject, therefore *women* should not intermeddle. I admitted it was, but endeavord to show that women were citizens & had dutys to perform to their country as well as men. . . . I tryd to enlighten our sisters a little in their rights & dutys. . . .

Pray for us—

A E Gé

*Sarah M. and Angelina E. Grimké to Sarah Douglass**

[W/G, Box 3; B/D, 1:362–365.]

Newark, N.J. 2/22/37

My dear Sarah

. . . Our meetings in New York have been better attended than we expected, but it is a hard place to labor in; ten thousand cords of interest are linked with the southern slaveholder. Still there are some warm-hearted abolitionists there, & I believe the fire of Emancipation will increase until our Jubilee is proclaimed.

We came to Bloomfield [N.J.] . . . last week, held two meetings with the ladies there, & they formed a society. We have had two interesting meetings also at this place [Newark] & a society was formed here; many ladies here are much engaged on behalf of the slave & this is a very important place. Southern interest in powerful; shoes & carriages, etc. made in Newark are bartered for the gold of the South, which is gotten by the unrequited toil of the slave. Many children attended our meetings, which rejoiced us because they will soon come on the stage of action & if they are only thoro'ly abolitionized, the bastile† *[sic]* of slavery will fall. . . .

* Sarah Douglass ran a school for black children in Philadelphia. She and her mother, Grace, were Quakers who sat on the "colored bench" at the Fourth and Arch Street Meeting. They were charter members of the Philadelphia Female Anti-Slavery Society. Grace Douglass served as a vice president of the Anti-Slavery Conventions of American Women in 1837 and 1839; Sarah served on the Committee of Arrangements of the 1837 convention and as treasurer of those in 1838 and 1839.

† The Bastille, a prison in Paris liberated by a revolutionary crowd on July 14, 1789.

It is so much the fashion to publish anti slavery movements that I will just mention that our friends in N Y think the less said at present about what we are doing the better. Let us move quietly on for a while & the two "fanatical women," as the Richmond papers call us, may, thro' divine help, do a little good.

Affy thy friend

Sarah M. Grimké

My Dear Sarah—
. . . We feel as yet unprepared to go fully into our delightful work, because the subject of Slavery is one of such length and breadth, height & depth that our time has been, & ought to be for some time to come, spent in reading on & studying it in its various bearings. I long to be fully harnessed for it, & often feel as if I had no petition to ask for at a throne of Grace, but to be made a blessing to the free & bond colored people of our land. The more I mingle with your people, the more I feel for their oppressions & desire to sympathize in their sorrows. . . .

Angelina E. Grimké

Angelina E. Grimké to Jane Smith

[W/G, Box 3.]

[New York, N.Y., late February 1837]

My Dear Jane—
I think our approaching Convention will be a deeply important one. I think it ought to issue Addresses to Northern Women, Northern Clergymen, & Northern Senators & Representatives, & the Colored People of the U S—free. Wilt then go to Lucretia Mott & tell her I ask whether she would be willing to write that to the Free people. I know *she* has put away prejudice, that monster in iniquity, & therefore I believ she possesses one of the very best qualifications for such a work. . . .

Tell her also, that I should like to hav her opinion as to requesting teachers of colord scholars to send on to this meeting, specimens of the skill of their pupils in needlework, Painting, Composition &c &c, to be exhibited to the Ladys of the Convention, as a means of interesting them in this class of our fellow creatures. If she approves it, will she see that a Comm be appointed to visit such teachers in Pa, request such specimens & undertake to see that they are sent on by the Delegates from your Society, who I hope will be appointed *without distinction of color*. . . . Tell

L M. I think it best it should not be known *who* writes the different pieces which may be presented at the meeting.* Let them go out from *the Convention.*

Very Affy—

[A. E. Grimké]

Sarah M. and Angelina E. Grimké to "Clarkson"

[*Friend of Man,* April 5, 1837, p. 159 (front page); W/G, Box 3; B/D, 1:365–372.]

[New York, N.Y., early march 1837]

The communication from "Clarkson," which was published in the New Haven Intelligencer of the 11th ult. [February], was handed us a few days since, and we cheerfully embrace the earliest opportunity to comply with the request of our unknown correspondent. We shall endeavor to present him with "the *definite practicable* means," by which the Northerners can put an end to slavery in the South. Permit us then, in the first place, to enumerate all that variety of ways by which the *North* is involved in the crime of slavery. Bear with us whilst we set the *sins of the North* in order before thee, and then the way will be prepared for us to show what Northerners can do to overthrow the great Prison House of the South.

I. Slavery now exists in the District of Columbia, over which, according to the Constitution of the United States, Congress has power "to exercise exclusive legislation in all cases whatsoever."

II. Slave-traders in the District of Columbia, by the payment of $400 a piece, are licensed by Congress to buy and sell American citizens, and this "price of blood," is thrown into the coffers of the nation.

III. Northern members of Congress are striving to perpetuate slavery in the District of Columbia. It was only last year that they referred certain petitions and resolutions respecting the abolition of slavery in the District, to a select committee with the instructions to report, "That in the opinion of this House, Congress ought *not* in any way to interfere with slavery in the District of Columbia." And the present Congress have treated them with contempt. Even the Ex.-President [John Quincy Adams] who so zealously contends for the right of Petition has "de[c]lared himself *adverse* to the abolition of slavery in the District."

* Mott declined.

IV. In the District of Columbia the Prisons which are built with *northern* as well as southern money, are continually thrown open to receive innocent men, women and children, who are lodged in their gloomy cells until the slave-trader has made the necessary arrangements for dragging them into hopeless bondage. One keeper of the jail in Washington stated, that in five years 450 colored persons had been lodged there for *safe keeping,* i.e. until they could be disposed of in the course of the slave trade; besides nearly 300 who had been taken up and lodged there as runaways. In 1834, there were at one time 13 incarcerated in the prison, who claimed that they were entitled to their freedom.

V. Slavery now exists in the Territory of Florida, which is under the exclusive jurisdiction of Congress.

VI. The Internal Slave Trade, which is productive of an enormous amount of misery and crime, might be regulated or abolished by Congress; for the constitutional power to legislate on this subject is vested in that body.

VII. According to the Constitution of the United States, *northern* men are pledged to put down servile insurrections at the South: their physical strength is pledged to support this system of oppression and cruelty, heathenism and robbery.

VIII. Northern votes in Congress have admitted seven new Slave States into the Union since the Constitution was adopted. In this way northern men have enlarged "the place of the tent of slavery; stretched forth the curtains of her habitation; lengthened her cords and strengthened her stakes."

IX. Conformably to the Constitution of the U. States, the Northern States deliver up the fugitive slave into the hands of his master. But this is not all; the colored man who is taken up on suspicion that he has no right to *his own body,* is denied a trial by jury, and is thrown into *northern* prisons until his claimant is ready to return him into abject slavery. And furthermore, Pennsylvania and New Jersey have gratuitously passed laws to secure the slaveholder his *unnatural* but legal right to his slave for six months after he has voluntarily brought that slave under their jurisdiction. New York has been even more obsequious to southern convenience and extended the term to nine months. Indeed, so exceedingly lax are the laws of the Northern States with regard to colored persons, that they are constantly liable to be kidnapped. We know that they *often* are, the *free* as well as the bond, and that many a *free* citizen of color has been stolen and reduced to bondage, and sold on southern vendue tables.

X. Northern Churches receive slaveholders to their communion tables, and slaveholding ministers into their pulpits whilst at the same time they close their pulpits against anti-slavery ministers, who are pleading the cause of the dumb.

XI. Northern ministers go to the South and close their lips on the subject of slavery. They will not preach the truth to the people of their charge: many of them become slaveholders and thus strengthen the hands of the oppressor by their examples.

XII. Northern men go to the South to make their fortunes; they frequently become slaveholders, and very often *harder* masters, than those who have been born and bred at the South.

XIII. Northern men are themselves *slaveholders,* and in the city of New York alone, the merchants hold mortgages on the southern plantations and slaves to the amount of 10,000,000 dollars. This fact was ascertained last spring. And furthermore, a person interested in the Texas Insurrection, told Judge Jay* that there were two merchants in New York ready to engage in the African slave trade, to supply that country with slaves under the specious name of indented apprentices, if it was wrested from Mexico. Look at the fact that the big brig Satena of New York, which sailed for St. Thomas, last autumn, was afterwards sent to Cuba to be sold as a Guineaman.† This vessel was the property of a New York merchant.

XIV. Northern manufacturers, merchants and consumers, are constantly lending their aid to support the system of slavery, by purchasing a large amount of the products of the unrequited labor of the slave.

XV. Northern prejudice against color is grinding the colored man to the dust in our free states, and this is strengthening the hands of the oppressor continually. When the slaveholders hear that the colored citizens of the North are not permitted to erect a college at New Haven; that their schools at Canterbury and Canaan‡ are broken up; that they

* William Jay (1789–1858), judge of the Westchester County Court (1818–1843), a close friend of the Tappans, a member of the Executive Committee, and a president of the American Peace Society.

† A slave ship.

‡ In June 1831, at the First Annual Convention of the People of Color, held in Philadelphia, Arthur Tappan, Garrison, and Simeon S. Jocelyn (1799–1879; white pastor of a black New Haven church), proposed that a college for blacks be established in New Haven. Tappan pledged to fund it. But the participants at a New Haven town meeting in September denounced the proposal by a vote of 700 to 4 and vowed to oppose it "by every lawful means in our power." Even though the abolitionists decided to abandon the project, a mob stoned Tappan's house and invaded black neighborhoods, "apprehending" eighteen white males involved in "amalgamation."

Canterbury, Connecticut was the site of a school for girls headed by Prudence Crandall (1803–?), a Quaker. When she admitted a black girl in 1833 white parents removed their children. With the aid of the American Anti-Slavery Society, she made it a school for black girls. It barely lasted a year. A host of legal and extralegal harrassments and violence drove her out in September 1834.

In autumn 1834, Noyes Academy of Canaan, New Hampshire was opened to students of both are continually subject to great inconvenience and great indignities in traveling from place to place, because the pride of *Northern* aristocracy can not bear a colored person at the same table, in the same boat-cabin, in the same rail-car with the whites, or to sit side by side with them even in the temples of God:—when they hear that a Presbyterian minister was, at the last Anniversary of the Alumni of Princeton College, actually *kicked* out of the chapel, because he wore a darker skin than their own,—thinkest thou they can not discern in these things the very same spirit which leads them to degrade and brutalize their Colored brethren at home.

It is impossible, whilst speaking on the subject of prejudice, not to advert to the cause which has produced such an increase of this sinful feeling towards our colored brethren and sisters. Every one who has watched the influence of the colonization scheme upon the public mind, or who has examined the natural tendency of a plan to "separate the two races," as they are termed, must perceive that its result would be a spirit something like that spoken of by the prophet,—"stand by, I am holier than thou." This feeling of prejudice against a man whose skin is of a darker hue than their own, is said by colonizationists to be "inherent in our natures": that even divine grace, which the Bible teaches is to sanctify us wholly, leaves this spot of leprosy in the believer's heart untouched. As long as colonizationists hold up the colored man to public view, as a being who *can not rise* in his own native America to a level with his white brother; so long as they maintain, contrary to reason, religion and the judgment of our intelligent and pious colored citizens that they must go to Africa to enjoy the blessings of liberty and equality, so long they are encouraging and strengthening that unhallowed feeling of prejudice, and violating the command of Christ "whatsoever ye would that men should do to you, do ye even so to them." It is not from any wish to find fault with those who are upholding the Colonization Society, that we thus write, but simply to draw their attention, and the attention of Northerners generally to this effect of colonization, which is inflicting on our American citizens of color the most heart-withering oppression.

We now feel prepared to present our correspondent with "the definite, practicable means by which Northerners can put an end to slavery in the South." Let them petition Congress unceasingly to abolish slavery

colors on an equal basis. On August 10, 1835, following a vote by the town meeting, 100 yoke of oxen and 300 men dragged the school building from its foundation to the village common. The teacher and black students were told to leave town.

and the slave trade in the District of Columbia, and let them vote for no Senators and Representatives who will not assert the right of constituents to petition, and the duty of Congress to receive and hear those petitions, and refer them to a committee for solemn consideration and judicious action. Let them protest against the use of the national prisons for the iniquitous purpose of confining slaves, and free people of color taken up on suspicion of being runaways. Let northerns petition for the abolition of slavery in the Territory of Florida, and the entire breaking up of the inter-state slave trade. Let them respectfully ask for an alteration in that part of the constitution by which they are bound to assist the South in quelling servile insurrections. Let them see to it that they send no man to Congress who would give his vote to the admission of another slave state into the national union. Let them protest against the injustice and cruelty of delivering the fugitive slave back to his master, as being a direct infringement of the Divine command.—Deut. xxiii. 15, 16. Let them petition their different legislatures to grant a jury trial to the friendless, helpless runaway, and for the repeal of those laws which secure to the slaveholder his legal right to his slave, after he has voluntarily brought him within the verge of their jurisdiction, and for the enactment of such laws as will protect the colored man, woman and child from the fangs of the kidnapper, who is constantly walking about in the northern states, seeking whom he may devour. Let the northern churches refuse to receive slaveholders at their communion tables, or to permit slaveholding ministers to enter their pulpits. Let those northern ministers who go to the South, "cry aloud and spare not; lift up their voices like a trumpet, and show the people their transgressions, and the house of Jacob their sins"; let them refuse to countenance the system of slavery by owning slaves themselves. Let northern men who go to the South to make their fortunes, see to it that those fortunes are not made out of the unrequited toil of the slave. Let northern merchants refuse to receive mortgages on these slaves, seeing that this is a vir[t]ual acknowledgement that man can hold man as property. Let the grocer refuse to buy the rice and sugar of the South, so long as "the hire of the laborers who had reaped down their fields is kept back by fraud." Let the merchant refuse to receive the articles manufactured of slave grown cotton, and let the consumer refuse to purchase either the rice, sugar or cotton articles, to produce which has cost the slave his unpaid labor, his tears and his blood. Every northerner may, in this way, bear a faithful testimony against slavery at the South, by withdrawing his pecuniary support.

We know well that this will involve much self-denial, but we presume not any more than our revolutionary fathers voluntarily imposed on themselves, when, previous to the outbreaking of insurrectionary movements of the colonies, "they resolved to *risk all* consequences rather than submit to the use of paper required by law. By suspending their future purchases on the repeal of the Stamp Act, the colonists made it the *interest* of merchants and manufacturers to solicit for that repeal. They had usually taken so great a proportion of British manufactures, that the sudden stopping of all their orders, amounting annually to two or three million sterling, threw some thousands in the mother country out of employment, and induced them from a regard to their own interest, to advocate the measures wished for by America. The petitions of the colonists were seconded by petitions from the merchants and manufacturers. In order to remedy the deficiency of British goods, the colonists betook themselves to a variety of necessary domestic manufactures. In a little time, large quantities of common cloths were brought to market, and these, though dearer and of a worse quality, were cheerfully preferred to similar articles imported from Britain. That wool might not be wanting, they entered into resolutions to abstain from eating lamb. Foreign elegances were laid aside. The *women* were exemplary as the men, in various instances of self-denial. With great readiness they refused every article of decoration for their persons, and luxury for their tables."* Our fathers and mothers knew that there was a very important *principle* involved in the right claimed by England to lay a tax upon articles exported to the colonies, and they therefore refused to pay that tax. Now we would ask, is there not a very important principle involved in the constant purchase of slave-grown products? Does not every man who purchases them tacitly concede the right of the slaveholder to rob the laborer of his wages? Is not the language of the Psalmist applicable to such, "When thou sawest a thief, then thou consentedst with him?" Do not such purchasers offer to the Southern planter the very strongest inducements to continue his oppression of the poor? It is a maxim in law, that the receiver is as bad as the thief; is not every Northerner, then, who buys or sells the production of slave labor, involved in the guilt of slavery? Do such obey the apostle's injunction, "Have no fellowship with the unfruitful works of darkness, but rather reprove them"?

Then again we would have Northerners abandon that unholy and

* Ramsay's United States, vol. 1, page 845, 310. [Footnote in original; David Ramsay, *History of the United States . . . to the year 1808. . . . Continued to the Treaty of Ghent, by S. S. Smith and other literary gentlemen*, 3 vols. (Philadelphia, Pa.: Carey, 1816–1817).]

unreasonable prejudice which is doing the work of oppression on the free people of color in our midst. Let them learn to measure men, *not* by their complexions, but by their intellectual and moral worth. Then will they be less ashamed to be found the associates of the worthy colored citizens than the companions of those who rob "the poor because he is poor." Let them in every possible way promote their moral and intellectual elevation, and treat them as though they were men, and American citizens, whenever they meet with people of color in stages or steam boats, taverns, or places of public worship.

If Northerners were to do all we have marked out, can any one doubt the powerful influence which it would produce on southern conscience and Southern interest? Could slavery live a single year under such an organized, disinterested, noble opposition to it? No, it would wither and die, never to be revived again. If Northerners were thus to purify *their* hearts and cleanse *their* hands from the sin of slavery, then would their tongues be loosed, and they would unceasingly pour into the ears of Southerners, the calm remonstrance, the brotherly rebuke, the earnest entreaty, "to loose the bands of wickedness, to undo the heavy burdens, and to let the oppressed go free, and to break every yoke." Could the slaveholder resist such pathetic, powerful appeals? Oh no! He still has the heart of a man, and that heart would soon break under the hammer of truth.

We could say a great deal more on this subject, but fear we have already trespassed on thy patience, and therefore forbear, hoping thou wilt immediately begin to carry into operation "these definite, practicable means by which Northerners can put an end to slavery in the South." Let every Northerner only do his part and we are fully confident that the oppressor will soon release his grasp, and the trumpet of Jubilee be sounded from the Ohio and the Potomac to the Gulf of Mexico, and from the Atlantic to the borders of the Mexican Republic.

Sarah M. Grimké,
Angelina E. Grimké.

Angelina E. Grimké to Jane Smith

[W/G, Box 3.]

New York 3d Month 22d 1837.

My Dear Jane

I do not think we shall form a National Female Society at the Convention & for this reason, but it must *not be* mentiond. The Ladys [Anti-

Slavery] Sy is realy doing nothing, it is utterly inefficient & must continue so until our Sisters here are willing to giv up sinful prejudice. It is a canker worm among them & paralyzes every effort. They are doing *literaly nothing* as a Sy for the colored people. We attended their last Monthly mg. of Managers. I believed it right to throw before them our views on the state of things among them, particularly on prejudice. No colord Sister has ever been in the board, & they hav hardly any colored members even & will not admit any such in the working Sy. What we said to them was from a sense of duty in love & tears, but it was hard work, & I believ as much as they could possibly hear from us. But some were reachd, I do believ, for tears were shed, & when it was moved that a vote of thanks should be tenderd to us for our kind & sisterly counsel, it was seconded with great feeling by a female who sat opposit to us. . . .

O Jane, how this Anti Slavery does grind us in the dust, hurls us from the proud elevation of *rank* in Society & throws us right down among those who sit, as it were, on the dung pile & among the pots. This is the best, the *only* way to get our wings coverd with silver & our feathers with yellow gold. Now it does seem to us that we had better hav no National Society until we can hav one of the *right stamp,* & I do not think one can flourish in this city while Prejudice banishes our colored sisters from an equal & full participation in its deliberations & labors. I am greatly in hopes that the Boston Society will send colord Delegates to the Convention & that something may be done to break down this adamantine wall in this proud city. . . .

I am Thy A E Gé

Angelina E. and Sarah M. Grimké to Sarah Douglass

[W/G, Box 3.]

New York. 4th Month. 3d 1837.

Dear Sarah

. . . We do indeed rejoice that thou canst address us as fellow pilgrims to the heavenly city. Whenever allusion is made to that distinction which American prejudice has made between those who wear a darker skin than we do, I feel ashamed for my Country, ashamed for the church, but the time is coming when such "respect of persons" will no more be known in our land, & the children of the Lord will think no more of a difference in the color of the skin than of that of the hair or the eyes. I was very glad to hear from Sydney Ann Lewis* that thy Mother & thyself tho't of coming to our Female Convention. I am very, very glad of it, & would say all I could to urge you to do so without fail. You, my dear Sisters, hav a work to do in rooting out this wicked feeling, as well as we. You *must be willing* to come in amongst us, tho' it *may be* your feelings *may* be wounded by the "putting forth of the finger," the avoidance of a seat by you, or the glancing of the eye. To suffer these things is the sacrifice which is calld for at *your hands,* & I earnestly desire that you may be willing to bear these mortifications with christian meekness, gentleness & love. They will tend to your growth in grace, & will help your paler sisters *more* than any thing else to overcome their own sinful feelings. Come, then, I would say, for we need your help. I cannot help hoping that a place will be found for the Fortens† too. . . . If an Address to the colored people is passed by our Convention, it will be absolutely necessary that some of them should be on the Committee to examine it before it is printed. . . .

. . . [W]e spent yesterday week in Poughkeepsie, & brother [Gerrit] Smith & ourselves had a meeting with the colord people in the evening. About 300 attended, & it was a very satisfactory meeting I believe to all partys & for the first time in my life I spoke in a promiscuous assembly, but I found that the men were no more to me then, than the women. Some of the females present were very desirous we should hold a meeting with the ladys, & we would gladly have done so, had we not expected to leav town early the next morning.

I remain Thy sister in the Lord

A E Grimké

My beloved sister

I suppose thou still attends our meeting. I feel as if the seat you occupy there, is a reproach to us, & I think the Lord must send you there to be a memorial to us of our pride & our prejudice. Yet we heed it not; like many of his other lessons we let it pass unimproved. . . . I feel as if I had taken my stand by the side of the colored American, willing to share with him the odium of a darker skin, & trust, if I am permitted again to take my seat in Arch St. Mtg. House, it will be beside thee & thy dear

* Sidney Ann Lewis, a charter member of the Philadelphia Female Anti-Slavery Society; she ran a Free Produce store.

† James Forten (1766–1842) had fought in the War for Independence and became one of the most active black abolitionists. He made a great deal of money as a sail manufacturer and contributed large sums to Garrison and *The Liberator.* His daughters, Charlotte, Sarah, and Margaretta, were also active abolitionists.

mother. Will it be too painful for thee to give me a description of thy feelings under the effect of steel hearted prejudice? Dear Sarah, does it sink thy spirits, does it destroy thy comfort? I pray that I may feel more & more deeply for you, that thro' the grace of God, my soul may be in your soul's stead. . . .

[Sarah M. Grimké]

*Sarah M. Grimké to Anne Warren Weston**

[BPL, MS.A.9.2, 9; 25.]

New York 4th Mo 7th 1837

My dear sister,

. . . All who reflect on the subject with the seriousness it requires must feel that our meeting together as a national Convention is a step of great importance. The eyes of many will be fixed upon us, watching for our halting, & it is exceedingly to be desired that all the strength we have should be concentrated at that time. We hope to have the company of some of our colored sisters from your city; their voices will, we think, be needed. . . . It is all important that we begin right, & I know of no way so likely to destroy the cruel prejudices that exist as to bring our sisters in contact with those who shrink from such intercourse. The modest worth & unassuming yet dignified deportment of many of our colored friends must, I think, put the supercilious arrogance of their fairer countrywomen to the blush & compel them to acknowledge that of a truth God is no respecter of persons. . . .

Farewell my sister united in love to the dear band in Boston with thy friend in the gospel of Christ

Sarah M. Grimké

Sarah M. Grimké to Jane Smith

[W/G, Box 3.]

New York 4/11/37

My dear Jane

. . . Mass. is the place that Brother Weld &c recommended our laboring in, & altho' a disappointment to me, having a great inclination to spend

* Anne Warren Weston (1812–1890), Maria Weston Chapman's sister, was one of the founders and most active members of the Boston Female Anti-Slavery Society.

the summer in the western part of this state, yet the cause of abolition, not my gratification, is what I am anxious to promote.

thy attached S. M. G

Angelina E. Grimké to Jane Smith

[W/G, Box 3.]

New York—4th Month 17th [1837]

My Dear Jane

. . . As to the address to Northern Senators & Representatives, you must be willing to giv it up this year. If you knew Brother Weld as well as I do, I expect his judgement would hav quite as much weight with you as it has had with me. His objection to it was, that a sufficient *moral foundation* had not yet been laid in the public's mind upon which to erect a political structure, & that therefore all the energy of our first Convention ought to be directed toward laying this foundation, by working only on the moral & religious feelings. With regard to the abilities & the duty of woman, his standard is very high, for he believs they are calld even to preach, and so does H C Wright of Boston,* so that it has not been from any unworthy suspicion of their capacity to issue such an address, if the time had come fully to do it.

. . . I hav been afraid, dear, that I unintentionally gave thee the idea that Abolitionists here have treated us *unkindly*. Far from it. All I meant to say was, that on account of the strong aristocratical feeling in the Ladies Society, they were most exceedingly inefficient, & instead of being springs for our efforts, hav been dead weights which we could not throw off. We hav had serious tho'ts of forming an Anti Slavery Socety among our colord sisters & getting them to invite their white friends to join them. In this way, we think we would get the most efficient white females in the city to cooperate with them. We ar sure that this Society will never do any good—tho' they might make a great show in their annual reports. The Convention seems like a great mountain before us, but we trust the Lord will be our helper. We mean to take a firm stand on Prejudice, but whether the Society will oppose us we know not. It may be they will [be] ashamed to do so, but we can expect *no help* from them at all. In fact, if our colord sisters do not come

* Henry Clarke Wright (1797–1870), a hatmaker who became a Congregational minister, then an agent for the American Sunday School Union, the American Peace Society, and the American Anti-Slavery Society. He had been one of "the Seventy," and he and Garrison were very close.

up strongly to our support, I do not know what we shall do. On this account, we are very anxious that the Douglas's *[sic]* & Fortens should be here, & are glad to hear that two such delegates ar to be sent on from Boston. . . . Oh! I feel as tho' I could say to them with regard to this meeting: If you will go with me, then I will go, but if you will not go with me, then I will not go.

I am aff

[Angelina E. Grimké]

*Proceedings of the Anti-Slavery Convention of American Women, Held in the City of New York, May 9th, 10th, 11th, and 12th, 1837.**

MOTION OF ANGELINA E. GRIMKÉ:

"*Resolved,* That the right of petition is natural and inalienable, derived immediately from God, and guaranteed by the Constitution of the United States, and that we regard every effort in Congress to abridge this sacred right, whether it be exercised by man or woman, the bond or the free, as a high-handed usurpation of power, and an attempt to strike a death-blow at the freedom of the people. And therefore that it is the duty of every woman in the United States, whether northerner or southerner, annually to petition Congress with the faith of an Esther, and the untiring perseverance of the importunate widow, for the immediate abolition of slavery in the District of Columbia and the Territory of Florida, and the extermination of the inter-state slave trade." [Adopted.]

MOTION OF SARAH M. GRIMKÉ:

"*Resolved,* That whereas God has commanded us to 'prove all things and hold fast that which is good,'—therefore, to yield the right, or exercise of free discussion to the demands of avarice, ambition, or worldly policy, would involve us in disobedience to the laws of Jehovah, and that as moral and responsible beings, the women of America are solemnly called upon by the spirit of the age and the signs of the times, fully to discuss the subject of slavery that they may be prepared to meet

* (New York: Dorr, 1837), pp. 8–9.

the approaching exigency, and be qualified to act as women, and as Christians on this all-important subject."

"The resolution was supported by the mover, A.E. Grimké, and Lucretia Mott."

MOTION OF ANGELINA E. GRIMKÉ:

"*Resolved,* That as certain rights and duties are common to all moral beings, the time has come for woman to move in that sphere which Providence has assigned her, and no longer remain satisfied in the circumscribed limits with which corrupt custom and a perverted application of Scripture has encircled her; therefore that it is the duty of woman, and the province of woman, to plead the cause of the oppressed in our land, and to do all that she can by her voice, and her pen, and her purse, and the influence of her example, to overthrow the horrible system of American slavery." [Adopted, but not unanimously, after "an animated and interesting debate respecting the rights and duties of women." A motion by Lydia Maria Child, the next day, to reconsider Angelina's "province of women" motion was defeated.]

*An Appeal to the Women of the Nominally Free States, Issued by an Anti-Slavery Convention of American Women**

SLAVERY, A POLITICAL SUBJECT

. . . [I]t is gravely urged that as it is a *political subject, women* have no concernment with it: this doctrine of the North is a sycophantic response to the declaration of a Southern representative, that women have *no right* to send up petitions to Congress. We know, dear sisters, that the open and the secret enemies of freedom in our country have dreaded our influence, and therefore have reprobated our interference, and in order to blind us to our responsibilities, have thrown dust into our eyes, well knowing that if the organ of vision is only clear, the whole body, the moving and acting faculties will become full of light, and will soon be thrown into powerful action. Some, who pretend to be very jealous for the honor of our sex, and are very anxious that *we* should scrupulously

* (New York: Dorr, 1837), pp. 10, 13.

maintain the dignity and delicacy of female propriety, continually urge this objection to female effort. We grant that it is a political, as well as a moral subject: does this exonerate women from their duties as subjects of the government, as members of the great human family? Have women never wisely and laudably exercised political responsibilities? . . .

And, dear sisters, in a country where women are degraded and brutalized, and where their exposed persons bleed under the lash—where they are sold in the shambles of "negro brokers"—robbed of their hard earnings—torn from their husbands, and forcibly plundered of their virtue and their offspring; surely, in *such* a country, it is very natural that *women* should wish to know "the reason *why*"—especially when these outrages of blood and nameless horror are practised in violation of the principles of our national Bill of Rights and the Preamble of our Constitution. We do not, then, and cannot concede the position, that because this is a *political subject* women ought to fold their hands in idleness, and close their eyes and ears to the "horrible things" that are practised in our land. The denial of our duty to act, is a bold denial of our right to act; and if we have no right to act, then may *we* well be termed "the white slaves of the North"—for, like our brethren in bonds, we must seal our lips in silence and despair.

Address to the Free Colored People of the United States *

In the sight of God, and in our own estimation, we have no superiority over you. We are all children of one Father, who has endowed us with equal capabilities for usefulness, improvement, and happiness; but the customs of society, founded in violence, and perpetuated by pride, operate generally to deprive you of full and free opportunities to develop your moral and intellectual gifts. For these reasons, you have always needed advice and encouragement; and the present is in many respects, a season of peculiar trial. . . .

Within a few years, decided improvement has become visible among you. Parents are more careful to form neat and orderly habits in their children, and the desire for education has greatly increased. In the next generation, we trust it will be a very rare thing to find a colored person in the free states, who does not know how to read, write and cipher;

* (Philadelphia, Pa.: Merrihew and Gunn, 1837), pp. 3–5.

and this circumstance alone will do a vast deal toward the removal of existing prejudice.

However zealously the abolitionists may preach, even if all of them consistently practise what they preach, they cannot do one hundredth part so much for you as you can do for yourselves. Your sobriety, decorum, industry, neat appearance, and desire for improvement will furnish them with the most triumphant refutation of the charges brought against you by the oppressors and slanderers of your race. . . .

In view of your efforts, particularly of late years, we find much to excite our respect and to make us thankful. Considering the numerous and discouraging obstacles with which you have to contend, your progress has been truly surprising; but you have yet a great work to perform—a work requiring no ordinary degree of moral strength and courage.

Angelina E. Grimké to Jane Smith

[W/G, Box 4.]

[New York, N.Y.] 5th Month 20th—1837

My Dear Jane

. . . I would say that Mary S Parker, Lydia M Child & Anne Weston from Boston were very great helps, not only on account of their understanding the business department so well, but from the fact of their sentiments on Prejudice, the province of woman and other important topics being so similar to some of ours. They are noble hearted women & M S P—a true christian I do believe. . . .

As our meetings were not advertized at all, they were not as well attended as I am sure they would have been if public notice had been given, for I understand it was very little known that they were being held. This was brother Garrison's advice, but I do not think it was good: indeed, he surprised me on one or two other points; time perhaps may show me which was right with greater certainty. . . .

And now to the Convention. I think we were greatly favored in getting along as well as we did; much more was said in the way of *debate* than I expected, & this contributed very much to the animation & interest of the meetings, & very soon broke down all stiffness & reserve, threw open our hearts to each other's view, and produced a degree of confidence in ourselves & each other which was very essential & delightful. Some of our Resolutions will certainly frighten the weak & startle the slumbering, particularly those on Southern intermarriages, the province of woman, the right of Petition, *J Q Adams,* Bible Society &c, &c. . . .

It was really pleasant to see the No. & the So. thus meeting together in counsel & effort for the chained & stricken slave. . . .

Hast thou seen C E Beecher's book on the Slave Question?* I hope I shall not have to answer it except by letter. . . .

Thy Affect—A E Gé

* Catharine E. Beecher, *Essay on Slavery and Abolitionism, with reference to the duty of American females* (Philadelphia, Pa.: Perkins, 1837; Freeport, N.Y.: Books for Libraries, 1970).

FOUR

The Agency: Massachusetts

SARAH and Angelina left New York on May 26, 1837, and arrived in Boston on May 28. The move offered them a great opportunity for effective work, but Boston was the location where the fault lines in the national antislavery movement were beginning to open into major fissures. The combination of the Grimké sisters and the New England Garrisonians markedly altered the causes of abolition and women's rights.

Eight-thousand members of the American Anti-Slavery Society lived in Massachusetts, as compared to 20,000 in New York and 15,000 in Ohio.[1] The number of women's reform societies had grown dramatically since 1810, and it is estimated that between one-third and one-half of adult women were members of at least one reform association.[2] Female abolitionists were more active and radical in New England than elsewhere, they were creating a framework for women to act politically, and there was a strong element of male support for nontypical female activity. At the same time, difficulties would arise in Massachusetts that had been largely absent in New York. Some of the problems had nothing to do with the venue. The increasing fame of Sarah and Angelina would have provoked negative responses from those opposed to immediate abolition, to women speaking in public, and to women speaking publicly about immediate abolition, no matter where the sisters lectured. But there were problems specific to the Boston area: men became increasingly omnipresent at their meetings; antagonism to Garrison both within and without the American Anti-Slavery Society was rapidly accumulating; and many Garrisonians were moving toward incorporating the evangelical reform impulse behind their abolitionism into a more universal mode of repentance and purification: nonresistance. Sarah and Angelina Grimké and their responses to the pressures that began to be placed on them triggered several serious reactions within this critical mass.

The American Anti-Slavery Society had never been a sound organization. The Executive Committee was dominated by the New York City leadership, but it could not exert firm control over the other auxiliaries. For example, though it contributed money to the parent society, the connection of the New England Anti-Slavery Society (renamed the Massachusetts Anti-Slavery Society in February 1835) remained vague. Though it seemed as if there were three main axes on which the movement revolved (New York, Boston, and Ohio), in fact none of these areas contained monolithic entities. Not only were there factions within factions and autonomous satellites revolving around the main bodies, but personality conflicts abounded. The movement was peopled with intense, emotional, strong-willed, dedicated, intelligent, dogmatic, fiercely committed, and frequently stubborn people.

Although most had begun their involvement with the movement in a visionary surge toward spiritual purification of self and country, the moral suasion vehicle they generally agreed on employing ran into difficulty in the middle years of the decade, 1834–1837, when increasing numbers of more and more violent mobs attacked abolitionists and their enterprises. As abolitionists pondered the relationship of moral suasion and violence, a divergence occurred in their strategic thinking. Eventually, three paths would lead out of this rethinking process: those who would follow the Tappan brothers into the American and Foreign Anti-Slavery Society (1840) believed in the need for a moderate, secular message aimed at mobilizing what they saw as an emerging anti-South majority in the North; those who stayed with Garrison in the American Anti-Slavery Society were convinced that moral values in the United States had become so corrupt that a more universal message of rectification was required; and finally, there were those who believed that moral suasion had no leverage without political power, and they would form the Liberty party and nominate James G. Birney as their presidential candidate in 1840.[3]

Two aspects of the Garrisonian push toward a more broadly based moral revolution impacted on the Grimké sisters and through them on the movement as a whole: "ultra" nonresistance and women as political activists. The question of the limits of resistance to violence had long simmered within the American Peace Society. Those who argued against any form of resistance, even to foreign invasions, came to be known as "ultras"* or, by their critics, as "no-government" people. "Ultra" or

* Sydney (Owenson) lady Morgan, in her recounting of the Bourbon restoration in France (1814–1816), noted that the returning émigré aristocrats soon divided into two factions: *modérés* and *ultras*, the

radical pacifists also rejected the use of government legal machinery to punish miscreants.

In 1835, Garrison had concluded that ill-treatment should not be met by physical force or resort to law. This belief was strengthened by his correspondence with John Humphrey Noyes* and his friendship with Henry C. Wright. Noyes developed the doctrine known as Perfectionism; Wright was probably the most ultra of the peace ultraists, having been dismissed as an agent of the American Peace Society after only a few months' service (in the summer of 1836) because of the radical nature of the message he had been delivering.

Thomas S. Grimké had been one of the earliest ultras within the American Peace Society, and Sarah and Angelina had been sympathetic to that doctrine since the early 1830s. In New York, they had not had occasion to speak about it, but in Boston, especially when they stayed at the home of Henry C. Wright, it reclaimed their attention. It also attracted the attention of the New York leaders, notably Theodore Dwight Weld. For most of the leaders the antipathy toward Garrison's and Wright's nonresistance had more to do with their fear that ultras within the abolition movement were in the process of alienating the solid citizens that the Executive Committee hoped to win for antislavery by means of a moderate message.

Weld's response, however, was compounded of the personal and the political. He believed that the "no-government" doctrine invited anarchy, social disorder, or license, and that a focus on nonresistance detracted energy and attention from antislavery. Personally, he harbored a deep antagonism for Noyes,† who he thought was a charlatan, and he

---

latter a shortening of *ultraroyalistes*. The *ultras*, she wrote, were more aggressive and wanted more. *France by Lady Morgan*, 2 vols., 2d ed. (London: Colburn, 1817), 1:189. In Great Britain and the United States the term *ultra* came to denote those who held extreme religious or political opinions. Ralph Waldo Emerson's journal offers an example of what the term meant to people of the 1830s. He wrote, on October 3, 1831: "I wish the Christian principle[,] the *ultra* principle of nonresistance & returning good for ill[,] might be tried fairly." *The Journals and Miscellaneous Notebooks of Ralph Waldo Emerson*, ed. William H. Gilman and Alfred R. Ferguson (Cambridge, Mass.: Belknap, 1963), 3:295.

* John Humphrey Noyes (1811–1886) believed that it was possible to attain perfect holiness in this life, that all human institutions were obstacles to human progress, and that the only proper society was a biblically based anarchy in which perfect human beings behaved strictly according to their inner laws. When his advocacy of complete nonresistance and "come-outerism" (from established churches) failed to perfect society, he withdrew from it with a small band of followers to form the Bible Community at Putney, Vermont in 1836.

† Weld's unstable older brother, Charles, had had a wrenching experience with Noyes. Charles had embraced Perfectionism in late 1833 and developed a close, intense relationship with Noyes. Noyes broke sharply with Charles in the spring of 1835 and followed that with deprecatory remarks and a letter calling Charles a "child of the devil." Robert David Thomas, *The Man Who Would Be Perfect: John Humphrey Noyes and the Utopian Impulse* (Philadelphia, Pa.: University of Pennsylvania, 1977), pp. 50–54, 74–77, and 83.

was extremely jealous of other men having any influence over Sarah and Angelina.

But nonresistance was a minor irritant compared to the question of women's rights. During 1837, Sarah and Angelina came under attack from two formidable opponents: Catharine Beecher and the conservative Congregational ministers of Massachusetts. When the sisters decided to respond publicly (in open letters) to these broadsides and to extend the scope of their commentary beyond a simple defense of immediate abolitionism to a powerful offensive on woman's rights, it provoked consternation in New York in general and in Weld in particular.

Lyman Beecher, though in the abstract opposed to slavery, strongly opposed active agitation in the North against it. He had argued that colonizationists and immediatists should unite, discouraged student activism at Lane Seminary, helped organize a short-lived anti-Garrisonian antislavery organization (the American Union for the Relief and Improvement of the Colored Race), and helped convince the Congregationalist governing bodies of Connecticut and Massachusetts to forbid "itinerant agents and lecturers" advancing "sentiments . . . of an erroneous or questionable character" to speak in Congregational churches. Catharine, his oldest daughter, had presented his point of view at the Lane debate on February 1834, and the essay she penned criticizing the Grimkés assumed the same position. In essence, he and she believed that immediatist abolitionism caused more problems than it solved and was an obstacle in the path of the reform of slavery. In addition, Catharine Beecher's image of the role of women directly contradicted that of the Grimkés', and her *Essay on Slavery and Abolitionism, with reference to the duty of American females* marked the start of her campaign to convince women to change society via their positions in homes and schools.[4]

Six months earlier, Catharine Beecher had attacked Frances Wright in *Letters on the Difficulty of Religion:*

> Who can look without disgust and abhorrence upon such an one as Fanny Wright, with her great masculine person, her loud voice, her untasteful attire, going about unprotected, and feeling no need of protection, mingling with men in stormy debate, and standing up with bare-faced impudence, to lecture to a public assembly. . . . I cannot conceive any thing in the shape of woman, more intolerably offensive and disgusting.[5]

She had begun the *Essay on Slavery,* Beecher wrote in her preface, as an answer to a request from

> a gentleman and a friend . . . to assign reasons why he should not join the Abolition Society. While preparing a reply to this request, Miss Grimké's Address [To Christian Women of the South] was presented, and the information communicated, of her intention to visit the North, for the purpose of using her influence among northern ladies to induce them to unite with Abolition Societies. The writer then began a private letter to Miss Grimké as a personal friend. But by the wishes and advice of others, these two efforts were finally combined in the following Essay, to be presented to the public.[6]

The *Essay* was "Addressed to Miss A. D. *[sic]* Grimké," and it was mainly devoted to a polemical assault on the American Anti-Slavery Society and all of its activities, but the last third of the book addressed the question of woman's role in society.

Angelina's response to Catharine Beecher was, therefore, important on two levels: as a continuation of the immediatist critique of colonizationists and as a statement justifying the political action of women outside the home. Sarah, for her part, responding to a request of Mary S. Parker and to her own observations of women workers in the New England textile mills, had begun a series of letters to detail the historical, legal, and economic constraints limiting women and to establish their equality before God, law, and society.

No sooner had both begun writing than the Congregational ministers belonging to the General Association of Massachusetts authorized Reverend Nehemiah Adams of Boston to pen an attack on Garrisonian abolitionists and women abolitionist agents. It was read from the pulpits in early July and printed in the *New England Spectator* on July 12.[7] The third section, although it did not mention their names, was clearly aimed at the Grimké sisters. Sarah answered the ministers in her third letter.

These letters disconcerted the moderate and conservative elements in the American Anti-Slavery Society, whose unhappiness was heightened by Henry C. Wright's effort to use the sisters' lecture tour as a vehicle for criticizing the Congregational clergy and promoting his version of nonresistance. His columns in *The Liberator,* "Labors of the Miss Grimkés,"[8] particularly roused Weld's ire. He thought that Sarah and Angelina were being misled and distracted, when, in fact, they were responding to ideas that connected logically with their past thinking on peace and to a man with whom they had trained and who had offered them the comforts of his home, helped schedule their tour, and helped plan their lectures. He also supported unequivocally their position on women's rights. On three separate occasions, between June 26 and July 25, 1837, in letters to Jane Smith, Angelina had strongly praised him and his family: "one of the best men I ever met with"; "one of the holyest men I ever saw"; "we enjoyed the green pastures of christian intercourse & the still waters of *peace* in his lovely family."[9] Wright obviously cared deeply for the sisters. When he learned, at the end of July, that the Executive Committee had decided to transfer him to Pennsylvania, he wrote in his journal: "I want to stay & see the end of it. I am willing to sink or swim with them. . . . I would gladly stay & avert every arrow of scorn & obloquy from their devoted heads."[10]

Although the members of the Boston Female Anti-Slavery Society supported Sarah and Angelina, some of the New York women expressed doubts about women publicly answering male criticism. Juliana Tappan wrote to Anne Weston:

> What do you think about it? Is it not very difficult to draw the boundary line? On the one hand, we are in danger of servile submission to the opinions of the other sex. & on the other hand, in perhaps equal danger of losing that modesty, & instinctive delicacy of feeling, which our Creator has given as a safeguard to protect us from dangers, to which on account of our weakness, we are continually exposed. How difficult it is to ascertain what duty is, when we consult the stereotyped opinions of the world. . . .[11]

A mixed message appeared in the organ of the New York Anti-Slavery Society, *The Emancipator,* on August 10: "These ladies do not go out as agents of the American Anti-Slavery Society, nor in any way connected with it, yet, for ourself, we could fully justify the Society in sending them, to do just what they are doing." But privately, Weld and John Greenleaf Whittier tried to convince the sisters to concentrate on abolition, Lewis Tappan deeply regretted "that they (while in the full tide of successful experiment as it regards woman's rights) should have vaulted from the anti slavery path to vindicate by essays the course they were pursuing," and James G. Birney saw no very good reason for Sarah Grimké "writing in favor of female independence etc."[12]

Thus the controversy over women's rights in Massachusetts that summer proceeded on four tracks: 1) the attack of conservative Congregational ministers on Garrison and women abolitionists; 2) Weld's personal effort to persuade the sisters to drop the women's issue from their speeches; 3) the efforts of the moderate abolitionists to silence Wright and convince the sisters to speak only to women's groups and about slavery only; and 4) Sarah's and Angelina's determination (with the support of Garrison, Wright, and the Boston Female Anti-Slavery Society) not to be silenced on the question of women.

By November, the sisters' efforts on these various fronts had exhausted them and undermined their health. Finally, with Angelina critically ill with fever, they halted the tour on November 3. They had been on the circuit for twenty-three weeks and spoken at over eighty-eight meetings in sixty-seven towns, to more than 40,000 listeners.[13]

Angelina E. Grimké to Jane Smith

[W/G, Box 4.]

Boston. 5th Month 29th 1837.

My Dear Jane

. . . A Peace Resolution was brought up [at the Massachusetts Anti-Slavery Convention], but this occasioned some difficulty on account of non-resistance here meaning a repudiation of *civil* government, & of course we cannot expect many to be willing to do this. There was no difficulty as to war itself. Indeed, my own mind is all in a mist, & I desire earnestly to know what is the truth about it; whether *all* civil government is an usurpation of God's authority or not. Hast thou ever tho't about it, & what is thy opinion?

It has realy been delightful to mingle with our brethren & sisters in this city. On 5th day [Thursday] evening we had a pleasant meeting of Abolitionists at Francis Jackson's,* in the rooms where the Female Anti Slavery Meeting was held. On 6th day evening, we had just another such at Friend Chapman's, Ann's father.† Here I had a long talk with the brethren on the rights of women & found a very general sentiment prevailing that it was time our fetters were broken. Goodell‡ said he was well aware that women could not perform their duties as *moral*

* Francis Jackson (1791–1859), financial backer of *The Liberator* and strong supporter of the Boston Female Anti-Slavery Society.

† Henry Chapman, father-in-law of Maria Weston Chapman, was a wealthy Boston merchant. He was a strong supporter of immediatist abolition, and the second Anti-Slavery Fair organized by the Boston Female Anti-Slavery Society was held at his house. His daughter, Ann, had died in March.

‡ William Goodell (1792–1878), a member of the Executive Committee and editor of *The Emancipator* and then *Friend of Man*.

beings, under the existing state of public sentiment. M Child & M Chapman support the same views. Indeed very many seem to think that a new order of things is very desirable in this respect.

And now, my dear friend, in view of these things, I feel as if it is not the cause of the slave only which we plead, but the cause of woman as a responsible moral being, & I am ready to exclaim, "Who is sufficient for these things?" These holy causes must be injured if they are not helped by us. What an untrodden path we have entered upon! Sometimes I feel almost bewildered, amazed, confounded & wonder by what strange concatenation of events I came to be where I am & what I am. And if I look forward, I am no less bewildered. I see not to what point, all these things are leading me. I wonder whether I shall make shipwreck of the faith—I cannot tell—but one thing comforts me, I do feel as tho' the Lord had sent us, & as if I was leaning on the arm of my beloved. I do not believ we ar going [into] this warfare at our own charges (spiritually), tho' I rejoice the Lord has provided for our doing so in a pecuniary point of view.*

Tomorrow [June 6], we begin our public labor at Dorchester. . . . Pray for us, dear Jane. We need it *more* than ever. We see only in a glass darkly what results ar to grow out of this experiment. I tremble for fear. . . . Sister is to speak at the Moral Reform Society this afternoon. I will leave this open & say something about it.

We hav just returned from the meeting, & the Lord was there to help us, for I, too, opend my mouth, tho' I had refused to engage to do so. About 300, I guess, were present & appeared interested in the remarks made. We broached one part of the subject, which I doubt not was new to many, i.e., that this reform was to begin in *ourselves*. We were polluted by it, our moral being was seard & scathed by it. Look at our feelings in the society of *men*, why the restraint & embarrassment? If we regarded each other as *moral* & intellectual beings merely, how pure & elevated & dignified would be our feelings towards, & intercourse with them. How is the solemn & sacred subject of marriage regarded & talked about? My heart is pained, my womanhood is insulted, my moral being is outraged continually, & I told them so. After we had finished, many women came up & expressed their pleasure & satisfaction at this part particularly of our remarks. They were their own feelings, but had never heard them expressed before.

No doubt, thou wilt wish to know whether the Boston women hav answerd our high expectations—they hav: Maria Chapman, particu-

* The sisters refused to accept any money from the American Anti-Slavery Society.

larly, is one of the noblest women I ever saw. She has been 3 times to see us: there is real antislavery here: a heart to work, a tongue to speak. We feel ourselves surrounded by an elastic atmosphere which yields to the stroke of the wings of effort & sends up the soaring spirit still higher & swifter in its upward flight. In New York we were allowed to sit down & do nothing. Here, invitations to labor pour in from all sides. . . .

Yesterday we attended the meeting at Dorchester. It was appointed in a private house, but as about 150 attended, we had to adjourn to the town house. We talked about 2 hours. I *hope* some good was done. It was a fatiguing day, for on our way out we stopped at Quincy to see the Ex President J. Q. Adams. Garrison & Whittier had been out the day before & told us he had no idea of moral power. After conversing with him, I did not wonder at it, for he has no idea of *moral right,* the supremacy of the laws of God over those of man, thinks the Bible is written in such contradictory terms that we cannot find out what the truth is. Indeed, my dear, I could not help thinking how little was the politician & statesman, who with all his gettings, had not got wisdom & the true understanding of the ABC of moral principles. A little child might lead such an one. . . . I asked him whether women could do any thing in the abolition of Slavery. He said, smiling, if it is abolished, *they* must do it. . . .

Farewell my Dear Jane. May we often meet where spirits blend in prayer is the desire of Thy Angelina

Sarah M. Grimké to Theodore Dwight Weld

[W/G, Box 4; B/D, 1:400–403.]

Samuel Philbricks* delightful farm near Boston
6th Mo. 11th, 1837.

dear brother

. . . A few numbers of the "Perfectionist"† have fallen into my hands. Their sentiments are in many respects as transcript of my heart; subjects are there treated and elucidated which have long exercised my mind & which I have hardly dared to breathe. Civil government, Public worship, the Ministry, the sabbath, & other points connected with religion have long been matters of enquiry & doubt, & I have feared to act out

* Samuel Philbrick (1789–1859), a retired Boston merchant and treasurer of the Massachusetts Anti-Slavery Society.

† A periodical edited by John Humphrey Noyes.

the principles which have been gradually working in my mind; but I can say with Milton,* "We want new light and care not whence it comes; we want reformers worthy of the name; & we should rejoice in such a manifestation of Christianity, as would throw *all present* systems into obscurity." Sometimes I am ready to turn away from the contemplation of these subjects lest my mind should not dwell sufficiently on that of slavery; but the more I reflect, the more I am persuaded that light on every subject is a blessing & adds a qualification to labor more effectually in that department which is alloted to us. I almost rejoice in the prospect of a release from the *duty* as it has heretofore seemed to me of attending public worship, for truly it has been a weariness to my soul, & if that part of the machinery of piety is laid in the dust, then the necessity of a regular ministry, paid or unpaid, delegated by human authority, will cease, & that will be a wonderful relief to my spirit, which has been burdened with the ministry ever since I was born again. . . .

This week we are to have A. S. Mtgs. at Roxbury and Weymouth, & a meeting of the Ladies Peace Society, to discuss the Peace question. The meeting at Roxbury is to be in the evening and I believe free admittance to the brethren. I hope the time is approaching when the wicked & injurious distinctions which now prevail will vanish away & Christians feel in spirit & in truth that there is neither male nor female, but all are one in Christ.

I almost forgot to tell thee that we went to see John Quincy Adams, & came away sick at heart of political morality. . . .

[Angelina] says she is very lazy about answering C. E. Beecher's book until she gets comfortably housed for the winter. She wishes to know if she may not be excused & whether thou knowest what impression the book is making. . . .

In the bonds of fellowship of the gospel I am thy sister,

Sarah M. Grimké.

Angelina E. Grimké to Jane Smith

[W/G, Box 4.]

Danvers, Massachusetts, 6th Month [1837]

I do not know, My Beloved Jane, why it is that I have not heard from you since I left New York, but I am sure that thou wantest to hear

* John Milton (1608–1674), British Puritan poet.

something of our getting along since my last, written from Boston near three weeks ago. I will, therefore, copy a leaf from our day book since the time I wrote. 7th of 6th month. Spoke before the Anti Slavery Society in Boston, in Washington Hall, where they had been mobbed 18 months before. About 400 present; many could not get in. 5 life members. 33 annual subscribers. 8th. Held a meeting at Brookline, in the house of Saml Philbrick. 75 present. first A S meeting ever held in the town. much opposition to be felt & very hard to speak to such strong hearts. 9th. Addressed the A S Society at North Weymouth, about 120 present—great apathy—hard to speak. 9 new subscribers—near 30 men present. Pretty easy to speak. 16th. Attended a Peace meeting in the Vestry of the Old South Ch[urch] in Boston. about 250 out. took the *ultra* ground, on law & civil government also. 18th. Addressed the A S Sy of So Weymouth. about 150 out. tho' it was very rainy. 19th. A S Sy in Boston. 550 women. 50 men. very easy to speak because there was great openness to hear. about 50 new subscribers added. 21st. Attended the Anniversary of the Lynn A S Sy. Spoke on the Report & Resolutions—about 500 women present. In the *evening* of the same day, addressed our *first large mixed* audience. about 1000 present. Great openness to hear & ease in speaking. 22d. Held another in Lynn, but in a smaller house, so that it was crowded to excess. about 600 seated. many went away, about 100 stood around the door, & we were told that on each window on the outside stood three men with their heads above the lowered sash. very easy speaking indeed. 23d. Held a meeting here [Danvers]. about 200 out—a few of the brethren. very hard speaking: I gave them a complete scolding, which I afterwards found they deserved. Think it likely we shall not have much more than half as many this afternoon in consequence of it, but the truth must be told. . . .

It is wonderful to us how the way has been opened for us to address mixed audiences, for most sects here are greatly opposed to public speaking for women. . . .

Hast thou read C E Beecher's book? I am answering it by letter in the Liberator & requested that they might be sent to thee by post. I have not spared her at all, as thou wilt perceive. It was one of the most subtle things I ever saw & has been ably reviewed, I am told, by the Author of Archy Moore,* but it has yet attracted so little notice that it is tho't best *not* to publish it unless my letters turn the attention of the public to it. I do not know how I shall find language strong enough to express

* Richard Hildreth (1807–1865), *The Slave; or memoirs of Archy Moore* (Boston: Eastburn, 1836).

my indignation at the view she takes of *woman's* character & duty. . . .

Thy ever affectionate A E Grimké

*Angelina E. Grimké, Letters to Catherine [sic] E. Beecher, in reply to An Essay on Slavery and Abolitionism, addressed to A. E. Grimké. Revised by the author**

LETTER I
Fundamental Principles of Abolitionists

Brookline, Mass. 6 month, 12th, 1837.

My Dear Friend: Thy book has appeared just at a time, when, from the nature of my engagements, it will be impossible for me to give it that attention which so weighty a subject demands. Incessantly occupied in prosecuting a mission, the responsibilities of which task all my powers, I can reply to it only by desultory letters, thrown from the pen as I travel from place to place. I prefer this mode to that of taking as long a time to answer it as thou didst to determine upon the best method by which to counteract the effect of my testimony at the north—which, as the preface of thy book informs me, was thy main design.

Thou thinkest I have not been "sufficiently informed in regard to the feelings and opinions of Christian females at the North" on the subject of slavery; for that in fact they hold the same *principles* with Abolitionists, although they condemn their measures. Wilt thou permit me to receive their principles from thy pen? Thus instructed, however misinformed I may heretofore have been, I can hardly fail of attaining to accurate knowledge. Let us examine them, to see how far they correspond with the principles held by Abolitionists.

The great fundamental principle of Abolitionists is, that man cannot rightfully hold his fellow man as property. Therefore, we affirm that *every slaveholder is a man-stealer.* We do so, for the following reasons: to steal a man is to rob him of himself. It matters not whether this be done in Guinea, or Carolina; a man is a *man,* and *as* as man he has *inalienable*

* (Boston, Mass.: Isaac Knapp, 1838; New York: Arno and *New York Times,* 1969). Angelina's response, in the form of thirteen letters, was printed in *The Liberator* between June 23 and November 3, 1837, in *The Emancipator* between July and November, 1837, and in the *Friend of Man* between July and December, 1837. Weld assisted Angelina in preparing the letters for publication in book form. It is the revised letters that appear below, with the exception of Letters IX and X, from which I have deleted lengthy documentation.

rights, among which is the right to personal *liberty*. Now if every man has an *inalienable* right to personal liberty, it follows, that he cannot rightfully be reduced to slavery. But I find in these United States, 2,250,000 men, women and children, robbed of that to which they have an *inalienable* right. How comes this to pass? Where millions are plundered, are there no *plunderers?* If, then, the slaves have been robbed of their liberty, *who* has robbed them? Not the man who stole their forefathers from Africa, but he who now holds them in bondage; no matter *how* they came into his possession, whether he inherited them, or bought them, or seized them at their birth on his own plantation. The only difference I can see between the original man-stealer, who caught the African in his native country, and the American slaveholder, is, that the former committed *one* act of robbery, while the other perpetrates the same crime *continually*. Slaveholding is the perpetrating of acts, all of the same kind, in a *series,* the first of which is technically called man-stealing. The *first* act robbed the man of himself; and the same state of mind that prompted *that act, keeps up the series,* having *taken* his all from him: it *keeps* his all from him, not only *refusing* to *restore,* but still robbing him of all he gets, and as fast as he gets it. Slaveholding, then, is *the constant or habitual perpetration of the act of man-stealing. To make* a slave is *man-stealing*—the ACT *itself*—to *hold* him such is man-stealing—the *habit,* the *permanent* state, made up of *individual* acts. In other words—to *begin* to hold a slave is man-stealing—to *keep on* holding him is merely a *repetition* of the first act—a doing the same identical thing *all the time.* A series of the same acts continued for a length of time is a *habit—a permanent state.* And the *first* of this series of the *same* acts that make up this *habit* or state is just like all the rest.

If every slave has a right to freedom, then surely the man who withholds that right from him to-day is a man-stealer, though he may not be the first person who has robbed him of it. Hence we find that Wesley says—"Men-*buyers* are *exactly on a level* with men-*stealers.*" And again—"Much less is it possible that any child of man should ever be *born a slave.*" Hear also Jonathan Edwards*—"To hold a man in a state of slavery, is to be *every day guilty* of robbing him of his liberty, or of *man-stealing.*" And Grotius† says—"Those are men-stealers who abduct, *keep,* sell or buy *slaves* or freemen."

If thou meanest merely that *acts* of that *same nature,* but differently

* Jonathan Edwards (1703–1758), Congregational minister and theologian, who helped spark the Great Awakening.

† Hugo Grotius (1583–1645), Dutch philosopher, founder of the discipline of international law.

located in a series, are designated by different terms, thus pointing out their different *relative positions,* then thy argument concedes what we affirm,—the identity in the *nature* of the acts, and thus it dwindles to a mere philological criticism, or rather a mere play upon words.

These are Abolition sentiments on the subject of slaveholding; and although our principles are universally held by our opposers at the North, yet I am told on the 44th page of thy book, that "the word man-stealer has one peculiar signification, and is no more synonymous with slaveholder than it is with sheep-stealer." I must acknowledge, thou hast only confirmed my opinion of the difference which I had believed to exist between Abolitionists and their opponents. As well might Saul have declared, that he held similar views with Stephen, when he stood by and kept the raiment of those who slew him.

I know that a broad line of distinction is drawn between our principles and our measures, by those who are anxious to "avoid the appearance of evil"—very desirous of retaining the fair character of enemies to slavery. Now, our *measures* are simply the carrying out of our *principles;* and we find, that just in proportion as individuals embrace our principles, in spirit and in truth, they cease to cavil at our measures. Gerrit Smith is a striking illustration of this. Who cavilled more at Anti-Slavery *measures,* and who more ready now to acknowledge his former blindness? Real Abolitionists know full well, that the slave never has been, and never can be, a whit the better for mere abstractions, floating in the *head* of any man; and they also know, that *principles, fixed in the heart,* are things of another sort. The former have never done any good in the world, because they possess no vitality, and therefore cannot bring forth *the fruits* of holy, untiring effort; but the latter live in the lives of their possessors, and breathe in their words. And I am free to express my belief, that *all* who really and heartily approve our *principles,* will also approve our *measures;* and that, too, just as certainly as a good tree will bring forth good fruit.

But there is another peculiarity in the views of Abolitionists. We hold that the North is guilty of the crime of slaveholding—we assert that it is a *national* sin: on the contrary, in thy book, I find the following acknowledgement:—"*Most* persons in the non-slaveholding States, have considered the matter of southern slavery as one in which they were no more called to interfere, than in the abolition of the press-gang system in England, or the tithe-system in Ireland." Now I cannot see how the same principles can produce such entirely different opinions. "Can a good tree bring forth corrupt fruit?" This I deny, and cannot admit what thou art anxious to prove, viz. that "Public opinion may have been *wrong* on this point, and yet *right* on all those great *principles* of rectitude and justice relative to slavery." If Abolition principles are generally adopted at the North, how comes it to pass, that there is no abolition action here, except what is put forth by a few despised fanatics, as they are called? Is there any living faith without works? Can the sap circulate vigorously, and yet neither blossoms put forth nor fruit appear?

Again, I am told on the 7th page, that all Northern Christians believe it is a sin to hold a man in slavery for *"mere purposes of gain";* as if this was the *whole* abolition principle on this subject. I can assure thee that Abolitionists do not stop here. Our principle is, that *no circumstances can ever justify* a man in holding his fellow man as *property;* it matters not what *motive* he may give for such a monstrous violation of the laws of God. The claim to him as *property* is an annihilation of his right to himself, which is the foundation upon which all his other rights are built. It is high-handed robbery of Jehovah; for He has declared, "All souls are *mine.*" For myself, I believe there are hundreds of thousands at the South, who do *not* hold their slaves, by any means, as much "for the purposes of gain," as they do from *the lust of power:* this is the passion that reigns triumphant there, and those who do not know this, have much yet to learn. Where, then, is the similarity in our views?

I forbear for the present, and subscribe myself,

Thine, but not in the bonds of gospel Abolitionism,

A. E. Grimké.

LETTER II

Immediate Emancipation

Brookline, Mass. 6th month, 17th, 1837.

Dear Friend: Where didst thou get thy statement of what Abolitionists mean by immediate emancipation? I assure thee, it is a novelty. I never heard any abolitionist say that slaveholders "were physically unable to emancipate their slaves, and of course are not bound to do it," because in some States there are laws which forbid emancipation. This is truly what our opponents affirm; but *we* say that all the laws which sustain the system of slavery are unjust and oppressive—contrary to the fundamental principles of morality, and, therefore, null and void.

We hold, that all the slaveholding laws violate the fundamental principles of the Constitution of the United States. In the preamble of that instrument, the great objects for which it was framed are declared to be "to establish justice, to promote the *general* welfare, and to secure the blessings of *liberty* to us and to our posterity." The slave laws are flagrant violations of these fundamental principles. Slavery subverts justice, promotes the welfare of the *few* to the manifest injury of the many, and robs thousands of the *posterity* of our forefathers of the blessings of liberty. This cannot be denied, for Paxton, a Virginia slaveholder,* says, "the *best* blood in Virginia flows in the veins of slaves!" Yes, even the blood of a [Thomas] Jefferson. And every southerner knows, that it is a common thing for the *posterity of our forefathers* to be sold on the vendue tables of the South. *The posterity of our fathers* are advertised in American papers as runaway slaves. Such advertisements often contain expressions like these: "has sometimes passed himself off as a *white* man,"—"has been mistaken for a *white* man,"—"*quite white,* has *straight* hair, and would not readily be taken for a slave," &c.

Now, thou wilt perceive, that, so far from thinking that a slaveholder is bound by the *immoral* and *unconstitutional* laws of the Southern States, *we* hold that he is solemnly bound as a man, as an American, to *break* them, and that *immediately* and openly; as much so, as Daniel was to pray, or Peter and John to preach—or every conscientious Quaker to refuse to pay a militia fine, or to train, or to fight. *We* promulgate no such time-serving doctrine as that set forth by thee. When *we* talk of immediate emancipation, we speak that [sic] we do mean, and the slaveholders understand us, if thou dost not.

Here, then is another point in which we are entirely at variance, though the *principles* of abolitionism are "generally adopted by our opposers." What shall I say to these things, but that I am glad thou hast afforded me an opportunity of explaining to thee what *our principles* really are? for I apprehend that *thou* "hast not been sufficiently informed in regard to the feelings and opinions" of abolitionists.

It matters not to me what meaning "Dictionaries or standard writers" may give to immediate emancipation. My Dictionary is the Bible; my standard authors, prophets and apostles. When Jehovah commanded Pharaoh to "let the people go," he meant that they should be *immediately emancipated.* I read his meaning in the judgments which terribly rebuked Pharaoh's repeated and obstinate refusal to "let the people go." I read it in the *universal* emancipation of near 3,000,000 Israelites in *one awful*

* John D. Paxton, *Letters on Slavery; addressed to the Cumberland congregation, Virginia* . . . (Lexington, Ky.: Skillman), p. 34.

night. When the prophet Isaiah commanded the Jews "to loose the bands of wickedness, to undo the heavy burdens, and to let the oppressed go free, and that ye break every yoke," he taught no gradual or partial emancipation, but *immediate, universal emancipation*. When Jeremiah said, "Execute judgment in the MORNING, and deliver him that is spoiled out of the hand of the oppressor," he commanded *immediate deliverance*. And so also with Paul, when he exhorted masters to render unto their servants that which is just and equal. Obedience to this command would *immediately* overturn the whole system of American Slavery; for liberty is justly *due* to every American citizen, according to the laws of God and the Constitution of our country; and a fair recompense for his labor is the right of every man. Slaveholders know this is just as well as we do. John C. Calhoun* said in Congress, in 1833—"He who *earns* the money —who *digs it out of the earth* with the sweat of his brow, has a *just title* to it against the Universe. *No one* has a right to touch it *without his consent*, except his government, and *it only* to the extent of its *legitimate* wants: to take more is *robbery*."

If our fundamental principle is right, that no man can rightfully hold his fellow man as *property*, then it follows, of course, that he is bound *immediately* to cease holding him as such, and that, too, in *violation of the immoral and unconstitutional laws* which have been framed for the express purpose of "turning aside the needy from judgment, and to take away the right from the poor of the people, that widows may be their prey, and that they may rob the fatherless." Every slaveholder is bound to cease to do evil *now*, to emancipate his slaves *now*.

Dost thou ask what I mean by emancipation? I will explain myself in a few words. 1. It is "to reject with indignation, the wild and guilty phantasy, that man can hold *property* in man." 2. To pay the laborer his hire, for he is worthy of it. 3. No longer to deny him the right of marriage, but to "let every man have his own wife, and let every woman have her own husband," as saith the apostle. 4. To let the parents have their own children, for they are the gift of the Lord to *them*, and no one else has any right to them. 5. No longer to withhold the advantages of education and the privilege of reading the bible. 6. To put the slave under the protection of equitable laws.

Now, why should not *all* this be done immediately? Which of these

* John C. Calhoun (1782–1850), a South Carolina slaveholder and politician who served in the United States House of Representatives and Senate and as secretary of war and secretary of state. Twice he was vice president. In 1828, at the behest of the South Carolina legislature, he wrote (anonymously) the *South Carolina Exposition and Protest*, the main philosophical defense of the state's nullification campaign.

things is to be done next year, and which the year after? and so on. *Our* immediate emancipation means, doing justice and loving mercy *to-day*—and this is what we call upon every slaveholder to do.

I have seen too much of slavery to be a gradualist. I dare not, in view of such a system, tell the slaveholder, that "he is physically unable to emancipate his slaves." I say *he is able* to let the oppressed go free, and that such heaven-daring atrocities ought to *cease now,* henceforth and forever. Oh, my very soul is grieved to find a northern woman thus "sewing pillows under all arm-holes," framing and fitting soft excuses for the slaveholder's conscience, whilst with the same pen she is *professing* to regard slavery as a sin. "An open enemy is better than such a secret friend."

Hoping that thou mayest soon be emancipated from such inconsistency, I remain until then,

Thine *out* of the bonds of Christian Abolitionism,

A. E. Grimké.

LETTER III

Main Principle of Action

Lynn, 6th Month, 23d, 1837.

Dear Friend:—I now pass on to the consideration of "the main principle of action in the Anti-Slavery Society." Thou art pleased to assert that it "rests wholly on a false deduction from past experience." In this, also, thou "hast not been sufficiently informed." Our main principle of action is embodied in God's holy command—"Wash you, make you clean, put away the evil of your doings from before mine eyes, cease to do evil, learn to do well; seek judgment, relieve the oppressed, judge the fatherless, plead for the widow." Under a solemn conviction that it is our duty as Americans to "cry aloud and spare not, to lift up our voices as a trumpet, and to show our people their transgressions, and the house of Jacob their sins," we are striving to rouse a slumbering nation to a sense of the retributions which must soon descend upon her guilty head, unless like Ninevah she repent, and "break off her sins by righteousness, and her transgressions by showing mercy to the poor." *This* is our "main principle of action." Does it rest "wholly on a false deduction from past experience"? or on the experience of Israel's King, who exclaimed, "In keeping of them (thy commandments,) there is great reward."

Thou art altogether under a mistake, if thou supposest that our "main principle of action" is the successful efforts of abolitionists in England, in reference to the abolition of the slave-trade; for I hesitate not to pronounce the attempts of Clarkson and Wilberforce, at that period of their history, to have been a *complete failure;* and never have the labors of any philanthropists so fully showed the inefficacy of half-way principles, as have those of these men of honorable fame. The doctrines now advocated by the American Anti-Slavery Society, were not advanced by the abolitionists of that day. *They* were *not* immediate abolitionists, but just such gradualists as thou art even now. If I supposed that our labors in the cause of the slave would produce *no better* results than those of these worthies, I should utterly despair. I need not remind thee, that they bent all their energies to the annihilation of the slave-trade, under the impression that *this* was the mother of slavery; and that after toiling for twenty years, and obtaining the passage of an act to that effect, the result was a mere *nominal* abolition; for the atrocities of the slave-trade are, if possible, *greater* now than ever. I will explain what I mean. A friend of mine one evening last winter, heard a conversation between two men, one of whom had, until recently, been a slave-trader. He had made several voyages to the coast of Africa, and said that once his vessel was chased by an English man of war, and that, in order to avoid a search and the penalty of death, he threw every slave overboard; and when his companion expressed surprise and horror at such a wholesale murder, "Why," said the trader, "it was the fault of the English; they had no business to make a law to hang a man on the yard arm, if they caught him with slaves in his ship." He intimated that it was not an uncommon thing for the captains of slavers thus to save their lives.* Where, then, I ask, is this glorious success of which we *hear* so much, but *see* so little?

* And in "Laird's Expedition to Africa, &c." a work recently published in England, this assertion of the slave trader is fully sustained. Laird relates that "there is *proof* of the horrid fact, that several of the wretches engaged in this traffic, when hotly pursued, consigned *whole cargoes* to the deep." He then goes on to state several such instances from which I select the following: "In 1833, the Black Joke and Fair Rosamond fell in with the Hercule and Regule, two slave vessels off the Bonny River. On perceiving the cruisers, they attempted to regain the port, and pitched overboard upwards of 500 human beings, chained together, before they were captured; from the abundance of sharks in the river, their track was literally a blood-stained one. The slaver not only does this, but *glories in it:* the first words uttered by the captain of the Maria Isabelle, seized by captain Rose, were 'that if he had seen the man of war in chase an hour sooner, he would have thrown *every* slave in his vessel overboard, as *he was fully insured.*' " [Footnote in original; see Macgregor Laird and R. A. K. Oldfield, *Narrative of an Expedition into the interior of Africa, by the river Niger, in the steam-vessels Quonah and Alburkah, in 1832, 1833, and 1834* (London: Bentley, 1837).]

Let us travel onward, from the year 1806, when England passed her abolition act. What were British philanthropists doing for the emancipation of the slave, for the next twenty years? Nothing at all; and it was the voice of Elizabeth Heyrick which first awakened them from their dream of *gradualism* to an understanding of the simple doctrine of immediate emancipation; but even though they saw the injustice and inefficiency of *their own* views, yet several years elapsed before they had the courage to promulgate hers. And now I can point thee to the success of these efforts in the emancipation bill of 1834. But even this success was paltry, in comparison with what it would have been, had all the conspicuous abolitionists of England been true to these just and holy principles. Some of them were false to those principles, and hence the compensation and apprenticeship system. A few months ago, it was my privilege to converse with Joseph Sturge,* on his return from the West Indies, via New York, to Liverpool, whither he had gone to examine the working of England's plan of emancipation. I heard him speak of the bounty of £20,000,000 which she had put into the hands of the planters, of their mean and cruel abuse of the apprenticeship system, and of the hearty approbation he felt in the thorough-going principles of the Anti-Slavery Societies in this country, and his increased conviction that *ours* were the *only right* principles on this important subject. That even the apprenticeship system is viewed by British philanthropists as a complete failure, is evident from the fact that they are now re-organizing their Anti-Slavery Societies, and circulating petitions for the substitution of immediate emancipation in its stead.

Hence it appears, that so far from our resting "wholly upon *a false deduction from past experience,*" we are resting on *no* experience at all; for no class of men in the world ever have maintained the principles which we now advocate. Our main principle of action is "obedience to God" —our hope of success is faith in Him, and that faith is as unwavering as He is true and powerful. "Blessed is the man who trusteth in the Lord, and whose hope the Lord is."

With regard to the connection between the North and the South, I shall say but little, having already sent thee my views on that subject in the letter to "Clarkson,"† orginally published in the New Haven Reli-

* Joseph Sturge (1793–1859), British Quaker corn merchant and proponent of immediate emancipation. He was the first British antislavery leader to travel to the British West Indies (1836). He wrote, with Thomas Harvey, *The West Indies in 1837. Being the Journal of a Visit . . . for the purpose of ascertaining the actual Condition of the Negro Population of Those Islands* (London: 1837), which was an important catalyst for the legislation ending the apprenticeship system.

† See above, p. 119.

gious Intelligencer. I there pointed out fifteen different ways in which the North was implicated in the guilt of slavery; and, therefore, I deny the charge that abolitionists are endeavoring "to convince their fellow citizens of the faults of *another* community." Not at all. We are spreading out the horrors of slavery before Northerners, in order to show them *their own sin* in sustaining such a system of complicated wrong and suffering. It is because we are politically, commercially, and socially connected with our southern brethren, that we urge our doctrines upon those of the free States. We have begun our work *here,* because pro-slavery men of the North are to the system of slavery just what temperate drinkers were to the vice of intemperance. Temperance reformers did not *begin* their labors among drunkards, but among temperate drinkers: so Anti-Slavery reformers did not *begin* their labors among slaveholders, but among those who were making their fortunes out of the unrequited toil of the slave, and receiving large mortgages on southern plantations and slaves, and trading occasionally in "slaves and the souls of men," and sending men to Congress to buy up southern land to be converted into slave States, such as Louisiana and Florida, which cost *this nation* $20,000,000*—men who have admitted seven slave States into the Union—men who boast on the floor of Congress, that "there is no cause in which they would sooner buckle a knapsack on their backs and shoulder a musket, then that of putting down a servile insurrection at the South," as said the present Governor of Massachusetts, which odious sentiment was repeated by Governor Lincoln† only last winter —men who, trained up on Freedom's soil, yet go down to the South and marry slaveholders, and become slaveholders, and then return to our northern cities with slaves in their train. This is the case with a native of this town, who is now here with his southern wife and southern *slave.*‡ And as soon as we reform the recreant sons and daughters of the North,—as soon as we rectify public opinion at the North,—then

* The Louisiana Territory was purchased from France for $15,000,000 (1803); in 1819, in exchange for the cession of the Floridas, the United States government agreed to assume $5 million worth of claims that American citizens held against the government of Spain.

† Edward Everett (1794–1865); served in the United States House of Representatives from 1825 to 1835, where he was markedly deferential to southern feelings on the slave question, and as governor of Mass. from 1836 to 1839. Levi Lincoln II (1782–1868), was governor of Massachusetts, 1825–1834.

‡ According to the fifth (1830) and sixth (1840) federal censuses, no slave lived in Lynn, although four aged female slaves and one young male were counted elsewhere in the state. Nor does the Lynn Historical Society have a record of a slaveholder living in the city at that time. But visits by Northerners who had married southern women was a subject of great concern to female abolitionists and to Weld who, in November 1838, under the auspices of the American Anti-Slavery Society, sent out form letters to members asking for details on Northerners working or marrying in the South and Southerners visiting the North. In general, the response proved disappointing. W/G, Box 5; B/D, 2:717–719, 726–732, and 744–748.

I, for one, will promise to go down into the midst of slaveholders themselves, to promulgate our doctrines in the land of the slave. But how can we go now, when northern pulpits and meeting-houses are closed, and northern ministers are dumb, and northern governors are declaring that "the discussion of the subject of slavery ought to be made an offence indictable at common law,"* and northern women are writing books to paralyze the efforts of southern women, who have come up from the South, to entreat their northern sisters to exert their influence in behalf of the slave, and in behalf of the slaveholder, who is as deeply corrupted, though not equally degraded, with the slave. No! No! the taunts of a New England woman will induce no abolitionist to cease his rebuke of *northern slaveholders* and apologists for slavery. Southerners see the wisdom of *this,* if *thou* canst not; and over against thy opinion, I will place that of a Louisiana planter, who, whilst on a visit to his relatives at Uxbridge, Mass. this summer, unhesitatingly admitted that the *North was the right place to begin Anti-Slavery efforts.* Had I not been convinced of this before, surely thy book would have been all-sufficient to satisfy me of it; for a more subtle defence of the slaveholder's right to property in his helpless victims, I never saw. It is just such a defence as the hidden enemies of Liberty will rejoice to see, because, like thyself, they earnestly desire "to avoid the *appearance of evil";* they are as much opposed to slavery as we are, only they are as much opposed to Anti-Slavery as the slaveholders themselves. Is there any middle path in the reformation? Or may we not fairly conclude, that he or *she* that is not for the slave, in deed and in truth, is *against* him, no matter how specious their professions of pity for his condition?

In haste, I remain thy friend,

A. E. Grimké.

LETTER IV

Connection Between the North and South

Danvers, Mass., 7th mo., 1837.

Dear Friend:—I thank thee for having furnished me with just such a simile as I needed to illustrate the connection which exists between the North and the South. Thou sayest, "suppose two rival cities, one of which becomes convinced that certain practices in trade and business in the other are dishonest, and have an oppressive bearing on certain classes

* Everett in his annual message as governor of Mass., in 1836.

in that city. Suppose, also, that these are practices, which, by those who allow them, are considered as honorable and right. Those who are convinced of this immorality wish to alter the opinions and the practices of the citizens of their rival city, and to do this they commence the collection of facts, that exhibit the tendencies of these practices and the evils they have engendered. But, instead of going among the community in which the evil exists, and endeavoring to convince them, they proceed to form voluntary associations among their neighbors at home, and spend their time, money, and efforts to convince their fellow citizens that the inhabitants of their rival city are guilty of a great sin." Now I will take up the comparison here, and suppose a few other things about these two cities. Suppose that the people in one city were *known never* to pay the laborer his wages, but to be in the constant habit of keeping back the hire of those who reaped down their fields; and that, on examination, it was found that the people in the other city were continually going over to live with these gentlemen oppressors, and instead of rebuking them, were joining hands in wickedness with them, and were actually *more* oppressive to the poor than the native inhabitants. Suppose, too, it was found that many of the merchants in the city of Fairdealing, as it was called, were known to hold mortgages, not only upon the property which ought to belong to the unpaid laborers, but mortgages, too, on the *laborers themselves,* ay, and *their wives and children also,* a thing altogether contrary to the laws of their city, and the customs of their people, and the principles of fundamental morality. Suppose, too, it was found that the people in the city of Oppression were in the constant practice of sending over to the city of Fairdealing, and bribing their citizens to seize the poorest, most defenceless of their people for them, because they were so lazy they would not do their own work, and so mean they would not pay others for doing it, and chose thus to supply themselves with laborers, who, when they once got into the city, were placed under such severe laws, that it was almost impossible for them ever to return to their afflicted wives and children. Suppose, too, that whenever any of these oppressed, unpaid laborers happened to escape from the city of Oppression, and after lying out in the woods and fastnesses which lay between the two cities, for many weeks, "in weariness and painfulness, in watchings, in hunger and thirst, in cold and nakedness," that as soon as they reached the city of Fairdealing, they were most unmercifully hunted out and sent back to their cruel oppressors, who it was well known generally treated such laborers with great cruelty, *"stern necessity"* demanding that they should be punished and "rebuked before all, that others might fear" the consequences of such elopement. In short, suppose that the city of Fairdealing was so completely connected with the city of Oppression, that the golden strands of their interests were twisted together so as to form a bond of Union stronger than death, and that by the intermarriages which were constantly taking place, there was also a silken cord of love tying up and binding together the tender feelings of their hearts with all the intricacies of the Gordian knot; and then, again, that the identity of the political interests of these cities were wound round and round them like bands of iron and brass, altogether forming an union so complicated and powerful, that it was impossible even to *speak* in the most solemn manner, in the city of Fairdealing, of the enormous crimes which were common in the city of Oppression, without having brickbats and rotten eggs hurled at the speaker's head. Suppose, too, that although it was perfectly manifest to every reflecting mind, that a most guilty copartnership existed between these two cities, yet that the "gentlemen of property and standing" of the city of Fairdealing were continually taunting the people who were trying to represent *their* iniquitous league with the city of Oppression in its true and sinful bearings, with the query of "Why don't you go to the city of Oppression, and tell the people there, not to rob the poor?" Might not these reformers very justly remark, we cannot go there *until* we have persuaded *our own* citizens to cease *their unholy cooperation with them,* for they will certainly turn upon us in bitter irony and say—"Physician, heal thyself"; go back to your own city, and tell your own citizens "to break off *their* sins by righteousness, and *their* transgressions by showing mercy to the poor," who fly from our city into the gates of theirs for protection, but receive it not. Would not common sense bear them out in refusing to go there, until they had *first* converted *their own* people from the error of their ways? I will leave thee and my other readers to make the application of this comparison; and if thou dost not acknowledge that abolitionists have been governed by the soundest common sense in the course they have pursued at the North with regard to slavery, then I am very much disappointed in thy profession of *candor*. With regard to the parallel thou hast drawn (p. 16,) between abolitionists, and the "men (who) are daily going into the streets, and calling all bystanders around them" and pointing out certain men, some as liars, some as dishonest, some as licentious, and then bringing proofs of their guilt and rebuking them before all; at the same time exhorting all around to point at them the finger of scorn; thou sayest, "they persevere in this course till the whole community is thrown into an uproar; and assaults and even bloodshed ensue." But why, I should like to know, if these people are themselves *guiltless* of the crimes alleged against the others? I cannot understand why they should be so angry, unless, like the Jews of old, they perceived that the parable had been spoken *"against them."* To my own mind, the exasperation of the North at the discussion of slavery is an undeniable proof of *her guilt,* a certain evidence of the necessity of her plucking the beam out of her own eye, *before* she goes to the South to rebuke sin there. To thee, and to all who are continually crying out, "Why don't you go to the South?" I retort the question by asking, why don't YOU go to the South? *We* conscientiously believe that this work must be commenced *here* at the North; this is an all-sufficient answer for US; but YOU, who are "as much anti-slavery as we are," and differ *only* as to the modus operandi, believing that the South and *not* the North ought to be the field of Anti-Slavery labors—YOU, I say, have no excuse to offer, and are bound to go there now.

But there is another view to be taken of this subject. By all our printing and talking at the North, we *have actually reached the very heart of the disease at the South.* They acknowledge it themselves. Read the following confession in the Southern Literary Review. "There are *many good men even among us, who have begun to grow timid.* They think that what the virtuous and high-minded men of the North took upon as a crime and a plague-spot, *cannot* be perfectly innocent or quite harmless in a slaveholding community." James Smylie,* of Mississippi, a minister of the gospel, *so called,* tells us on the very first page of his essay, written to uphold the doctrines of Governor McDuffie,† "that the abolition maxim, viz. that slavery is *in itself sinful,* had gained on and entwined itself among the *religious* and *conscientious* scruples of *many* in the community, so far as to render them *unhappy."* I could quote other southern testimony to the same effect, but will pass on to another fact just published in the New England Spectator; a proposition from a minister in Missouri "to have separate organizations for slavery and anti-slavery professors," and indeed "all over the *slave-holding States."* Has our labor then been in vain in the Lord? Have we failed to rouse the slumbering consciences of the South?

Thou inquirest—"Have the northern States power to rectify evils at the South, as they have to remove their own moral deformities?" I

* James Smylie, *A Review of a Letter, from the Presbytery of Mississippi, on the Subject of Slavery* (Woodville, Miss.: 1836).

† George E. McDuffie, Jr. (1790–1851), governor of South Carolina (1834–1836).

answer unhesitatingly, certainly they have, for *moral* evils can be removed only by *moral* power; and the close connection which exists between these two portions of our country, affords the greatest possible facilities for exerting a *moral* influence on it. Only let the North exert as much moral influence over the South, as the South has exerted demoralizing influence over the North, and slavery would die amid the flame of Christian remonstrance, and faithful rebuke, and holy indignation. The South has told us so. In the report of the committee on federal relations in the Legislature of South Carolina* last winter, we find the following acknowledgement: "Let it be admitted, that by reason of an efficient police and judicious internal legislation, we may render abortive the designs of the fanatic and incendiary within our limits, and that the torrent of pamphlets and tracts which the abolition presses of the North are pouring forth with an inexhaustible copiousness, is arrested the moment it reaches our frontiers. Are we to wait until our enemies have built up, by the grossest misrepresentations and falsehoods, a *body of public opinion, which it would be impossible to resist,* without separating ourselves from the social system of the rest of the civilized world?" Here is the acknowledgement of a southern legislature, that it will be *impossible for the South to resist the influence* of that body of *public opinion,* which abolitionists are building up against them at the North. If further evidence is needed, that anti-slavery societies are producing a powerful influence at the South, look at the efforts made there to vilify and crush them. Why all this turmoil, and passion, and rage in the slaveholder, if we have indeed rolled back the cause of emancipation 200 years, as thy father has asserted? Why all this terror at the distant roar of free discussion, if they feel not the earth quaking beneath them? Does not the *South* understand what really will affect her interests and break down her domestic institution? Has *she* no subtle politicians, no far-sighted men in her borders, who can scan the practical bearings of these troublous times? Believe me, she has; and did they not know that we are springing a mine beneath the great bastile [*sic*] of slavery, and laying a train which will soon whelm it in ruin, she would not be quite so eager "to cut out our tongues, and hang us as high as Haman."

I will just add, that as to the committee saying that abolitionists are building up a body of public opinion at the North "by the grossest misrepresentations and falsehoods," I think it was due to *their* character for veracity, [not] to have cited and refuted some of these calumnies.

* Standing committees in both the South Carolina House of Representatives and Senate, which considered matters referred by the Governor, mainly correspondence from federal officials or agencies.

Until they do, we must believe them; and as a Southerner, I can bear the most decided testimony against slavery as the mother of *all* abominations. Farewell for the present.

I remain thy friend,

A. E. Grimké.

LETTER V

Christian Character of Abolitionism

Newburyport, 7th mo. 8th, 1837.

Dear Friend: As an Abolitionist, I thank thee for the portrait thou hast drawn of the character of those with whom I am associated. They deserve all thou hast said in their favor; and I will not endeavor to vindicate those "men of pure morals, of great honesty of purpose, of real benevolence and piety," from some objections thou hast urged against their measures.

"Much evidence," thou sayest, "can be brought to prove that the character and measures of the Abolition Society are not either peaceful or christian in tendency, but that they are in their nature calculated to generate party spirit, denunciation, recrimination, and angry passion." Now I solemnly ask thee, whether the character and measures of our holy Redeemer did not produce exactly the same effects? Why did the Jews lead him to the brow of the hill, that they might cast him down headlong; why did they go about to kill him; why did they seek to lay hands on him, if the tendency of *his* measures was so very *pacific?* Listen, too, to his own declaration: "I came not to send peace on earth, but a sword"; the effects of which, he expressly said, would be to set the mother against her daughter, and the daughter-in-law against her mother-in-law. The rebukes which he uttered against sin were eminently calculated to produce "recriminations and angry passions," in all who were determined to *cleave* to their sins; and they did produce them even against "him who did no sin, neither was guile found in his mouth." He was called a wine-bibber, and a glutton, and Beelzebub, and was accused of casting out devils by the prince of the devils. Why, then, protest against our measures as *unchristian,* because they do not smooth the pillow of the poor sinner, and lull his conscience into fatal security? The truth is, the efforts of abolitionists have stirred up the *very same spirit* which the efforts of *all thorough-going* reformers have ever done; we consider it a certain proof that the truths we utter are sharper than any two edged sword, and that they are doing the work of conviction in the hearts of our enemies. If it be not so, I have greatly mistaken the character of Christianity. I consider it pre eminently aggressive; it waits not to be assaulted, but moves on in all the majesty of Truth to *attack* the strong holds of the kingdom of darkness, carries the war into the enemy's camp, and throws its fiery darts into the midst of its embattled hosts. Thou seemest to think, on the contrary, that Christianity is just such a weak, dependent, puerile creature as thou hast described women to be. In my opinion, thou hast robbed both the one and the other of all their true dignity and glory. Thy descriptions may suit the prevailing christianity of this age, and the general character of woman; and if so, we have great cause for shame and confusion of face.

I feel sorry that thy unkind insinuations against the christian character of Wm. Lloyd Garrison, have rendered it necessary for me to speak of him individually, because what I shall feel bound to say of him may, to some like thyself, appear like flattery; but I must do what justice seems so clearly to call for at my hands. Thou sayest that "though he professes a belief in the christian religion, he is an avowed opponent of most of its institutions." I presume thou art here alluding to his views of the ordinances of baptism and the Lord's supper, and the Sabbath. Permit me to remind thee, that in *all* these opinions, he coincides entirely with the Society of Friends, whose views of the Sabbath never were so ably vindicated as by his pen: and the insinuations of hypocrisy which thou hast thrown out against him, may with just as much truth be cast upon *them*. The Quakers think that these are not *christian* institutions, but thou hast assumed it without any proof at all. Thou sayest farther, "The character and spirit of *this man* have for years been exhibited in the Liberator." I have taken that paper for two years, and therefore understand its character, and am compelled to acknowledge, that harsh and severe as is the language often used, I have never seen any expressions which *truth* did not warrant. The abominations of slavery *cannot* be otherwise described. I think Dr. Channing* exactly portrayed the char-

* William Ellery Channing (1780–1842), the most eloquent spokesman for Unitarianism and a strong peace advocate. He was Lewis Tappan's pastor during the 1820s and probably played an influential role in Tappan's decision to join the Massachusetts Peace Society. Abolitionists regularly urged Channing to speak publicly against slavery. When he did, in *Slavery*, he condemned the institution but stated that the question of the mode of ending it should be left completely to slaveholders, that the abolitionists had made an error by adopting "immediate emancipation" as their motto, that they should cease public agitation of the question, and that "individual action" should replace collective agitation as a mode of reform. See Channing, *Slavery* (Boston, Mass.: Munroe, 1836), pp. 128, 153, 154, 159, and 162. The Garrisonians criticized him for his critique of them, and the Boston establishment denounced him for endorsing the antislavery cause. He remained a consis-

acter of brother Garrison's writings when he said, "That deep feeling of evils, which is necessary to *effectual* conflict with them, which marks *God's most powerful messengers to mankind, cannot* breathe itself in soft and tender accents. The deeply moved soul *will* speak strongly, and *ought* to speak strongly, so as to move and shake nations." It is well for the slave, and well for this country, that such a man was sent to sound the tocsin of alarm before slavery had completed its work of moral death in this "hypocritical nation." Garrison begun [sic] that discussion of the subject of slavery, which J. Q. Adams declared in his oration, delivered in this town on the 4th inst. "to be the only safety-valve by which the high pressure boiler of slavery could be prevented from a most fatal explosion in this country"; and as a Southerner, I feel truly grateful for all his efforts to redeem not the slave only, but the *slaveholder,* from the polluting influences of such a system of crime.

In his character as a man and a Christian, I have the highest confidence. The assertion thou makest, "that there is to be found in that paper, or *any thing else, any* evidence of his possessing the peculiar traits of Wilberforce, (benignity, gentleness and kind heartedness, I suppose thou meanest,) not even his warmest admirers will maintain," is altogether new to me; and I for one feel ready to declare, that I have never met in any one a more lovely exhibition of these traits of character. I might relate several anecdotes in proof of this assertion, but let one suffice. A friend of mine, a member of the Society of Friends, told me that after he became interested in the Anti-Slavery cause through the Liberator, he still felt so much prejudice against its editor, that, although he wished to labor in behalf of the slaves, he still felt as if he could not identify himself with a society which recognized such a leader as he had heard Wm. L. Garrison was. He had never seen him, and after many struggles of feeling, determined to go to Boston on purpose to see "this man," and judge of his character for himself. He did so, and when he entered the office of the Liberator, soon fell into conversation with a person he did not know, and became very much interested in him. After some time, a third person came in and called off the attention of the stranger, whose benevolent countenance and benignant manners he had so much admired. He soon heard him addressed as Mr. Garrison, which astonished him very much; for he had expected to see some coarse, uncouth and rugged creature, instead of the perfect gentleman he now learned was Wm. L. Garrison. He told me that the effect upon his mind

tent defender of the rights of abolitionists to speak freely and an opponent of mob action to silence them.

was so great, that he sat down and wept to think he had allowed himself to be so prejudiced against a person, who was so entirely different from what his enemies had represented him to be. He at once felt as if he could most cheerfully labor, heart and hand, with such a man, and has for the last three or four years been a faithful co-worker with him, in the holy cause of immediate emancipation. And his confidence in him as a man of pure, *christian* principle, has grown stronger and stronger, as time has advanced, and circumstances have developed his true character. I think it is impossible thou canst be personally acquainted with brother Garrison, or thou wouldst not write of him in the way thou hast. If thou really wishest to have thy erroneous opinions removed, embrace the first opportunity of being introduced to him; for I can assure thee, that with the fire of a Paul, he does possess some of the most lovely traits in the character of Wilberforce.

In much haste, I remain thy friend,

A. E. Grimké.

LETTER VI
Colonization

Amesbury, 7th mo. 20th, 1837.

Dear Friend: The *aggressive* spirit of Anti-Slavery papers and pamphlets, of which thou dost complain, so far from being a repulsive one to me, is very attractive. I see in it that uncompromising integrity and fearless rebuke of sin, which will bear the enterprize of emancipation through to its consummation. And I most heartily desire to see these publications scattered over our land as abundantly as the leaves of Autumn, believing as I do that the principles they promulgate will be as leaves for the healing of this nation.

I proceed to examine thy objections to "one of the first measures of Abolitionists": their attack on a *benevolent* society.

That the [American] Colonization Society is a *benevolent* institution, we deny; it was absolutely necessary, in order to disabuse the public mind of the false views they entertained of its character. And it is a perfect mystery to me how men and women can *conscientiously* persevere in upholding a society, which the very objects of its professed benevolence have repeatedly, solemnly, constantly and universally condemned. To say the least, this is a very suspicious kind of benevolence, and seems too nearly allied to that, which induces some southern professors to keep their brethren in bonds *for their benefit.* Yes, the free colored people are to be exiled, because public opinion is crushing them into the dust; instead of their friends protesting against that corrupt and unreasonable prejudice, and living it down by a practical acknowledgement of their *right to every* privilege, social, civil and religious, which is enjoyed by the white man. I have never yet been able to learn, how our hatred to our colored brother is to be destroyed by driving him away from us. I am told that when a colored republic is built up on the coast of Africa, then we shall respect that republic, and acknowledge that the character of the colored man can be elevated; we will become connected with it in a commercial point of view, and welcome it to the sympathies of our hearts. Miserable sophistry! deceitful apology for present indulgence in sin! What man or woman of common sense now doubts the intellectual capacity of the colored people? Who does not know, that with all our efforts as a nation to crush and *"annihilate the mind* of this portion of our race," we have never yet been able to do it? Henry Berry of Virginia [Jefferson County], in his speech in the Legislature of that State, in 1832, expressly acknowledged, that although slaveholders had "as far as possible closed every avenue by which light might enter their minds," yet that they never had found out the process by which they "could extinguish the *capacity* to see the light." No! that capacity remains—it is indestructible—an integral part of their nature, as moral and immortal beings.

If it is true that white Americans only need a demonstration of the colored man's capacity for elevation, in order to make them willing to receive him on the same platform of human rights upon which they stand, why has not the intelligence of the Haytians convinced them? *Their* free republic has grown up under the very eye of the slaveholder, and as a nation we have for many years been carrying on a lucrative trade with her merchants; and yet we have never recognized her independence, never sent a minister there, though we have sent ambassadors to European countries whose commerce is far less important to us than that of St. Domingo.*

These professions of a wish to plant the tree of Liberty on the shores

* Although there are some who like to discant on the worthless character of the Haytians, and the miserable condition of the Island, yet it is an indisputuble [sic] fact, that a population of nearly 1,000,000 are supported on its soil, and that in 1833, the value of its exports to the United States exceeded in value those of Prussia, Sweden, and Norway—Denmark and the Danish West Indies—Ireland and Scotland—Holland—Belgium—Dutch East Indies—British West Indies—Spain—Portugal—all Italy—Turkey and the Levant, or any one Republic in South America. [Footnote in original.]

of Africa, in order to convince our Republican Despotism of the high moral and intellectual worth of the colored man, are perfectly absurd. Hayti has done that long ago. A friend of mine (not an Abolitionist) whose business called him to that island for several months, told me that in the society of its citizens, he often felt his own inferiority. He was astonished at the elegance of their manners, and the intelligence of their conversation. Instead of going into an examination of Colonization principles, I refer thee to the Appeal to the Women of the nominally free States, issued by the Convention of American Women,* in which we set forth our reasons for repudiating them.

Thou hast given a specimen of the manner in which Abolitionists deal with their Colonization opponents. Thy friend remarked, after an interview with an abolitionist, "I love truth and sound argument; but when a man comes at me with a sledge hammer, I cannot help dodging." I presume thy friend only felt the truth of the prophet's declaration, "Is not my work like as a fire, saith the Lord, and like a *hammer* that breaketh the rock in pieces?" I wonder not that he did *dodge,* when the sledge hammer of truth was wielded by an abolition army. Many a Colonizationist has been compelled to dodge, in order to escape the blows of this hammer of the Lord's word, for there is no other way to get clear. We must either *dodge* the arguments of abolitionists, or like J. G. Birney, Edward C. Delevan,† and many others, be willing to be broken to pieces by them. I greatly like this specimen of private dealing, and hope it is not the only instance which has come under thy notice, of Colonizationists acknowledging the absolute necessity of *dodging* Anti-Slavery arguments, when they were unwilling that the *rock of prejudice* should be broken to pieces by them.

Thy next complaint is against the *manner* in which this benevolent EXPATRIATION Society was attacked. "The style in which the thing was done was at once offensive, inflammatory and exasperating,"—"the feelings of many sincere, upright, and conscientious men were harrowed by a sense of the injustice, the indecorum and the unchristian treatment they received." But why, if *they* were entirely innocent of the charges brought against Colonizationists? I have been in the habit, for several years past, of watching the workings of my own mind under true and false charges against myself; and my experience is, that the more clear I am of the charge, the less I care about it. If I really feel a sweet assurance

* See above, p. 131.

† Edward C. Delavan (1793–1871), a New York wine merchant who founded the New York State Temperance Society and helped organize the American Temperance Society.

that "my witness is in heaven—my record is on high," I then realize to its fullest extent that "it is a small thing to be judged of *man's* judgment," and I can bear *false* charges unmoved; but true ones always nettle me, if I am unwilling to confess that "I have sinned"; if I am, and yield to conviction, O then! how sweet the reward! Now I am very much afraid that these sincere, upright and conscientious Colonizationists are something like the *pious professors* of the South, who are very angry because abolitionists say that all slaveholders are men-stealers. Both find it "hard to kick against the pricks" of conviction, and both are unwilling to repent. A northern man remarked to a Virginia slaveholder last winter, "that as the South denied the charges brought against her by abolitionists, he could not understand why she was so enraged; for," continued he, "if you were to accuse us at the North of being sheep-stealers, we should not care about the charge—we should ridicule it." "O!" said the Virginian with an oath, "what the abolitionists say about slaveholders is *too true,* and *that's the reason* we are vexed." Is not this the reason why our Colonization brethren and sisters are so angry? Is not what we say of them also *too true?* Let them examine these things with the bible and prayer, and settle this question between God and their own souls.

Every true friend of the oppressed American has great cause to rejoice, that the cloak of benevolence has been torn off from the monster Prejudice, which could love the colored man *after* he got to Africa, but seemed to delight to pour contumely upon him whilst he remained in the land of his birth. I confess it would be very hard for me to believe that any association of men and women loved me or my family, if, because we had become obnoxious to them, they were to meet together, and concentrate their energies and pour out their money for the purpose of transporting us back to France, whence our Hugenot* fathers fled to this country to escape the storm of persecutions. Why not let us live in America, if you really *love* us? Surely you never want to *"get rid"* of people whom you *love. I* like to have such near me; and it is because I love the colored Americans, that I want them to stay in this country; and in order to make it a happy home to them, I am trying to talk down, and write down, and live down this horrible prejudice. Sending

* *Huguenot,* a word of disputed origin denoting the French people who converted to the Reformed religion of John Calvin during the seventeenth century. The Catholic monarchy's persecution of them peaked in the St. Bartholomew's Day massacre (August 24, 1572). Thousands of Huguenots were slaughtered, provoking a religious civil war. In 1589, the French crown passed to a Protestant, Henry of Navarre; he converted to Catholicism and issued a toleration decree, the Edict of Nantes (1598). In the next century, however, as Cardinal Richelieu and Louis XIV constructed an absolutist state, they progressively stripped the Huguenots of the edict's protections, culminating in Louis' revocation of it in 1685. Some 200,000 of France's most skilled and able people emigrated as a result.

a few to Africa cannot destroy it. No—we must dig up the weed by the roots out of each of our hearts. *It is a sin,* and we must repent of it and forsake it—and then we shall no longer be so anxious to *"be clear of them," "to get rid of them."*

Hoping, though against hope, that thou mayest one day know how precious is the reward of those who can love our oppressed brethren and sisters in this day of their calamity, and who, despising the shame of being identified with these peeled and scattered ones, rejoice to stand side by side with them, in the glorious conflict between Slavery and Freedom, Prejudice and Love unfeigned, I remain thine in the bonds of universal love,

A. E. Grimké.

LETTER VII
Prejudice

Haverhill, Mass. 7th mo. 23, 1837.

Dear Friend:—Thou sayeth, "the *best* way to make a person like a thing which is disagreeable, is to try in some way to make it agreeable." So, then, instead of convincing a person by sound argument and pointed rebuke that sin is *sin,* we are to *disguise* the opposite virtue in such a way as to make him like that, in preference to the sin he had so dearly loved. We are to *cheat* a sinner out of his sin, rather than to compel him, under the stings of conviction, to give it up from deep-rooted principle.

If this is the course pursued by ministers, then I wonder not at the kind of converts which are brought into the church at the present day. Thy remarks on the subject of prejudice, show but too plainly how strongly thy own mind is imbued with it, and how little thy colonization principles have done to exterminate this feeling from thy own bosom. Thou sayest, "if a certain class of persons is the subject of unreasonable prejudice, the peaceful and christian way of removing it would be to endeavor to render the unfortunate persons who compose this class, so useful, so *humble, so unassuming,* &c. that prejudice would be supplanted by complacency in their goodness, and *pity* and sympathy for their disabilities." "If the friends of the blacks had quietly set themselves to work to increase their intelligence, their usefulness, &c. and then had appealed to the *pity* and benevolence of their fellow citizens, a very different result would have appeared." Or in other words, if one person is guilty of a sin against another person, I am to let the sinner go entirely unreproved, but to persuade the injured party to bear with humility and patience all the outrages that are inflicted upon him, and thus try to soothe the sinner "into complacency with their goodness" in "bearing all things, and enduring all things." Well, suppose I succeed:—is that sinner won from the evil of his ways by *principle?* No! Has he the principle of love implanted in his breast? No! Instead of being in love with the virtue exhibited by the individual, because *it is virtue,* he is delighted with the personal convenience he experiences from the exercise of that virtue. He feels kindly toward the individual, *because* he is an *instrument* of his enjoyment, a mere *means* to promote his wishes. There is *no* reformation there at all. And so the colored people are to be taught to be "very *humble*" and *"unassuming," "gentle"* and *"meek,"* and then the *"pity* and generosity" of their fellow citizens are to be appealed to. Now, no one who knows anything of the influence of Abolitionists over the colored people, can deny that it has been *peaceful* and Christian; had it not been so, they never would have seen those whom they had regarded as their best friends, mobbed and persecuted, without raising an arm in their defence. Look, too, at the rapid spread of thorough temperance principles among them, and their moral reform and other laudable and useful associations; look at the rising character of this people, the new life and energy which have been infused into them. Who have done it? Who have exerted by far the greatest influence on these oppressed Americans? I leave thee to answer. I will give thee one instance of this salutary influence. In a letter I received from one of my colored sisters, she incidentally makes this remark:—"Until very lately, I have lived and acted more for *myself* than for the good of others. I confess that I am *wholly indebted to the Abolition cause* for arousing me from apathy and indifference, and shedding light into a mind which has been too long wrapt in selfish darkness." The Abolition cause has exerted a powerful and healthful influence over this class of our population, and it has been done by quietly going into the midst of them, and identifying ourselves with them.

But Abolitionists are complained of, because they, at the same time, fearlessly exposed the *sin* of the unreasonable and unholy prejudice which existed against these injured ones. Thou sayest "that reproaches, rebukes and sneers were employed to convince the whites that their prejudices were sinful, and *without* any just cause." *Without any just cause!* Couldst thou think so, if thou really loved thy colored sisters *as thyself?* The unmeasured abuse which the Colonization Society was heaping upon this despised people, was no *just cause* for pointed rebuke, I suppose! The manner in which they are thrust into one corner of our meeting-houses, as if the plague-spot was on their skins; the rudeness and cruelty with which they are treated in our hotels, and steamboats, rail road cars and stages, is *no just cause* of reproach to a professed christian community, I presume. Well, all that I can say is, that I believe if Isaiah or James were now alive, they would pour their reproaches and rebukes upon the heads and *hearts* of those who are thus despising the Lord's poor, and saying to those whose spirits are clothed by God in the "vile raiment" of a *colored skin,* Stand thou there in yonder gallery, or sit thou here in "the negro-pew." "Sneers," too, are complained of. Have abolitionists ever made use of greater sarcasm and irony than did the prophet Elijah? When things are ridculous as well as wicked, it is unreasonable to expect that every cast of mind will treat them with solemnity. And what is more ridiculous than American prejudice; to proscribe and persecute men and women, because their *complexions* are of a darker hue than our own? Why, it is an outrage upon common sense; and as my brother Thomas S. Grimké remarked only a few weeks before his death, "posterity will laugh at our prejudices." Where is the harm, then, if abolitionists should laugh now at the wicked absurdity?

Thou sayest, "this tended to irritate the whites, and to increase their prejudices against the blacks." The *truth always* irritates the proud, impenitent sinner. To charge abolitionists with this irritation, is something like the charge brought against the English government by the captain of the slaver I told thee of in my second letter, who threw all his human merchandize overboard, in order to escape detection, and then charged this horrible wholesale murder upon the government; because, said he, they had no business to make a law to hang a man if he was found engaged in the slave trade. So *we* must bear the guilt of man's angry passions, because the *truth* we preach is like a two-edged sword, cutting through the bonds of interest on the one side, and the cords of caste on the other.

As to our increasing the prejudice against color, this is just like the North telling us that we have increased the miseries of the slave. Common sense cries out against the one as well as the other. With regard to prejudice, I believe the truth of the case to be this: the rights of the colored man *never* were advocated by any body of men in their length and breadth, before the rise of the Anti-Slavery Society in this country. The propagation of these ultra principles has produced in the northern States exactly the same effect, which the promulgation of the doctrine of immediate emancipation has done in the southern States. It has *developed* the latent principles of pride and prejudice, not *produced* them. Hear John Green,* a Judge of the Circuit Court of Kentucky, in reference to abolition efforts having given birth to the opposition against emancipation now existing in the South: "I would rather say, it has been the means of *manifesting* that opposition, which *previously* existed, but *laid dormant* for want of an exciting cause." And just so has it been with regard to prejudice at the North—when there was no effort to obtain for the colored man his *rights* as a man, as an American citizen, there was no opposition exhibited, because it "laid dormant for want of an exciting cause."

I know it is alleged that some individuals, who treated colored people with the greatest kindness a few years ago, have, since abolition movements, had their feelings so embittered towards them, that they have withdrawn that kindness. Now I would ask, could such people have acted from *principle?* Certainly not; or nothing that others could do or say would have driven them from the high ground they *appeared* to occupy. No, my friend, they acted precisely upon the false principle which thou hast recommended; their *pity* was excited, their *sentiments of generosity* were called into exercise, because they regarded the colored man as an *unfortunate inferior,* rather than as an *outraged* and *insulted equal.* Therefore, as soon as abolitionists demanded for the oppressed American the *very same treatment,* upon the high ground of *human rights,* why, then it was instantly withdrawn, simply because *it never had been conceded on the right* ground; and those who had previously granted it became afraid, lest, during the aera *[sic]* of abolition excitement, persons would presume *they* were acting on the fundamental principle of abolitionism —the principle of *equal rights,* irrespective of color or condition, instead of on the mere principle of *"pity and generosity."*

It is truly surprising to find a professing christian excusing the unprincipled opposition exhibited in New Haven, to the erection of a College for young men of color. Are we indeed to succumb to a corrupt public sentiment at the North, and the abominations of slavery at the South, by refraining from asserting the *right* of Americans to plant a literary institution in New Haven, or New York or *any where* on the American soil? Are we to select "some retired place," where there would be the least prejudice and opposition to meet, rather than openly and fearlessly to face the American monster, who, like the horse-leach, is continually

* John Green (1787–1838), a staunch advocate of gradual emancipation, had introduced colonization and slave nonimportation bills in the Kentucky legislature.

crying give, give, and whose demands are only increased by compromise and surrender? No! there is a spirit abroad in this country, which will not consent to barter principle for an *unholy* peace; a spirit which seeks to be "pure from the blood of all men," by a bold and christian avowal of truth; a spirit which will not hide God's eternal principles of right and wrong, but will stand erect in the storm of human passion, prejudice and interest, "holding forth the light of truth in the midst of a crooked and perverse generation"; a spirit which will never slumber nor sleep, till man ceased to hold dominion over his fellow creatures, and the trump of universal liberty rings in every forest, and is re-echoed by every mountain and rock.

Art thou not aware, my friend, that this College was projected in the year 1831, previous to the formation of the first Anti-Slavery Society, which was organized in 1832? How, then, canst thou say that the circumstances relative to it occurred "at a time when the public mind was excited on the subject"? I feel quite amused at the *presumption* which thou appearest to think was exhibited by the projectors of this institution in wishing it to be located in New Haven, where was another College "embracing a large proportion of southern students," &c. It was a great offence, to be sure, for colored men to build a College by the walls of the white man's "College, where half the shoe-blacks and waiters were *colored men.*" But why so? The other half of the shoe-blacks and waiters were *white,* I presume; and if these *white* servants could be satisfied with *their* humble occupation *under the roof* of Yale College, why might not the colored waiters be contented also, though an institution for the education of colored Americans might *presume* to lift its head "beside the very walls of this College"? Is it possible that any professing christian can calmly look back at these disgraceful transactions, and tell me that such opposition was manifested *"for the best reasons"?* And what is still worse, censure the projectors of a literary institution, in free, republican, enlightened America, because they did not meekly yield to *"such reasonable objections,"* and refused "to soothe the feelings and apprehensions of those who had been excited" to opposition and clamor by the simple fact that some American born citizens wished to give their children a liberal education in a separate College, only because the white Americans despised their brethren of a darker complexion, and scorned to share with them the privileges of Yale College? It was very wrong, to be sure, for the friends of the oppressed American to consider such outrageous conduct "as a mark of the force of sinful prejudice"! Vastly uncharitable! Great complaints are made that "the worst motives were ascribed to some of the most respectable, and venerated, and *pious* men who opposed the measure." Wonderful indeed, that men should be found so true to their principles, as to dare in this age of sycophancy to declare the truth to those who stand in high places, wearing the badges of office or honor, and fearlessly to rebuke the puerile and unchristian prejudice which existed against their colored brethren! "Pious men"! Why, I would ask, how are we to judge of men's piety—by professions or products? Do men gather thorns of grapes, or thistles of figs? Certainly not. If, then, in the lives of men we do not find the fruits of christian principle, we have no right, according to our Saviour's criterion, "by their fruits ye shall know them," to suppose that men are really pious who can be perseveringly guilty of despising others, and denying them equal rights, because they have colored skins. "A great deal was said and done that was calculated to throw the community into an angry ferment." Yes, and I suppose the friends of the colored man were just as guilty as was the great Apostle, who, by the angry, and excited, and *prejudiced* Jews, was accused of being "a pestilent fellow and a mover of sedition," because he declared himself called to preach the everlasting gospel to the Gentiles, whom they considered as "dogs," and utterly unworthy of being placed on the same platform of human rights and a glorious immortality.

Thy friend,

A. E. Grimké.

LETTER VIII
Vindication of Abolitionists

Groton, Mass. 6th month, 1837.

Dear Friend:—In my last, I commented upon the opposition to the establishment of a College in New Haven, Conn., for the education of colored young men. The same remarks are applicable to the persecutions of the Canterbury School. I leave thee and our readers to apply them. I cannot help thinking how strange and unaccountable thy soft excuses for the *sins of prejudice* will appear to the next generation, if thy book ever reached their eye.

As to Cincinnati having been chosen as the city in which the Philanthropist should be published after the retreat of its editor from Kentucky, thou hast not been "sufficiently informed," for James G. Birney pursued exactly the course which *thou* hast marked out as the most prudent and least offensive. He edited his paper in New Richmond, in Ohio, for nearly three months before he went to Cincinnati, and did not go there until the excitement appeared to have subsided.

And so, thou thinkest that abolitionists are accountable for the outrages which have been committed against them; they are the tempters, and are held responsible by God, as well as the tempted. Wilt thou tell me, who was responsible for the mob which went with swords and staves to take an innocent man before the tribunals of Annas and Pilate, some 1800 years ago? And who was responsible for the uproar at Ephesus, the insurrection at Athens, and tumults at Lystra and Iconium?* Where I a mobocrat, I should want no better excuse than thou hast furnished for such outrages. Wonderful indeed, if, in free America, her citizens cannot *choose* where they will erect their literary institutions and presses, to advocate the self-evident truths of our Declaration of Independence! And still more wonderful, that a New England woman should, *after years of reflection,* deliberately write a book to condemn the advocates of liberty, and plead excuses for a relentless prejudice against her colored brethren and sisters, and for the persecutors of those, who, according to the opinion of a *Southern* member of Congress, are prosecuting "the *only plan* that can ever overthrow slavery at the South." I am glad, *for thy own sake,* that thou hast exculpated abolitionists from the charge of the "deliberate intention of fomenting illegal acts of violence." Would it not have been still better, if thou hadst spared the remarks which rendered such an explanation necessary?

I find that thou wilt not allow of the comparison often drawn between the effects of christianity on the hearts of those who obstinately rejected it, and those of abolitionism on the hearts of people of the present day. Thou sayest, "Christianity is a system of *persuasion,* tending by kind and gentle influences to make men *willing* to leave their sins." Dost thou suppose the Pharisees and Sadducees deemed it was very *kind* and *gentle* in its influences, when our holy Redeemer called them "a generation of vipers," or when he preached that sermon "full of harshness, uncharitableness, rebuke and denunciation," recorded in the xxiii. chapter of Matthew? But I shall be told that Christ knew the hearts of all men, and therefore it was right for him to use terms which mere human beings never ought to employ. Read, then, the prophecies of Isaiah, Ezekiel, and others, and also the Epistles of the New Testament. They employed the most offensive terms on many occasions, and the

* Scenes of demonstrations against the preaching of St. Paul.

sharpest rebukes, knowing full well that there are some sinners who can be reached by nothing but death-thrusts at their consciences. An anecdote of JOHN RICHARDSON,* who was remarkable for his urbanity of manners, occurs to me. He one day preached a sermon in a country town, in which he made use of some *hard* language; a friend reproved him after meeting, and inquired whether he did not know that hard wood was split by soft knocks. Yes, said Richardson, but I also know that there is some wood so rotten at the heart, that nothing but tremendously hard blows will ever split it open. Ah! John, replied the elder, I see thou understandest *how* to do thy master's work. Now, I believe this nation is *rotten at the heart,* and that nothing but the most tremendous blows with the sledge-hammer of abolition truth, could ever have broken the false rest which we had taken up for ourselves on the very brink of ruin.

"Abolitionism, on the contrary is a system of *coercion* by public opinion." By this assertion, I presume thou "hast not been correctly informed" as to the reasons which have induced abolitionists to put forth all their energies to rectify public opinion. It is *not* because we wish to wield this public opinion like a rod of iron over the heads of slaveholders, to *coerce* them into a abandonment of the system of slavery; not at all. We are striving to purify public opinion, first, because as long as the North is so much involved in the guilt of slavery, by its political, commercial, religious, and social connexion with the South, *her own citizens* need to be converted. Second, because we know that when public opinion is rectified at the North, it will throw a flood of light from its million of reflecting surfaces upon the heart and soul of the South. The South sees full well at what we are aiming, and she is so unguarded as to acknowledge that "if she does not resist the danger in its inception, it will *soon* become *irresistible."* She exclaims in terror, "the truth is, the *moral* power of the world is against us; it is idle to disguise it." The fact is, that the slaveholders of the South, and their northern apologists, have been overtaken by the storm of free discussion, and are something like those who go down to the sea and do business in the great waters: "they reel to and fro, and stagger like a drunken man, and are at their wit's end."

Our view of the doctrine of expediency, thou art pleased to pronounce "wrong and very pernicious in its tendency." Expediency is emphatically the doctrine by which the children of this world are wont

* There were several John Richardsons in South Carolina; I have been unable to identify the one who made this remark.

to guide their steps, whilst the rejection of it as a rule of action exactly accords with the divine injunction, to "walk by faith, *not* by sight." Thy doctrine that "the wisdom and rectitude of a given course depend entirely on the *probabilities of success,*" is not the doctrine of the Bible. According to this principle, how absurd was the conduct of Moses! What probability of success was there that he could move the heart of Pharaoh? None at all; and thus did *he* reason when he said, "Who am *I*, that I should go unto Pharaoh?" And again, "Behold, they will not believe *me,* nor hearken unto my voice." The *success* of Moses's mission in persuading the king of Egypt to "let the people go," was not involved in the duty of obedience to the divine command. Neither was the success of Isaiah, Jeremiah, and others of the prophets who were singularly *unsuccessful* in their mission to the Jews. All who see the path of duty plain before them, are bound to walk in that path, end where it may. They then can realize the meaning of the Apostle, when he exhorts Christians to cast all their burden on the Lord, with the promise that He would sustain them. This is walking by *faith,* not by sight. In the work in which abolitionists are engaged, they are compelled to "walk by faith"; they feel called upon to preach the truth in season and out of season, to lift up their voices like a trumpet, to show the people their transgressions and the house of Jacob their sins. The *success* of this mission, *they* have no more to do with, than had Moses and Aaron, Jeremiah or Isaiah, with that of theirs. Whether the South will be saved by Anti-Slavery efforts, is not a question for us to settle—and in some of our hearts, the *hope of its salvation has utterly gone out.* All nations have been punished for oppression, and why should ours escape? Our light, and high professions, and the age in which we live, convict us not only of enormous oppression, but of the vilest hypocrisy. It may be that the rejection of the truth which we are now pouring in upon the South, may be the final filling up of their iniquities, just previous to the bursting of God's exterminating thunders over the Sodoms and Gomorrahs, the Admahs and Zeboims of America. The *result* of our labors is hidden from our eyes; whether the preaching of Anti-Slavery truth is to be a savor of life unto life, or of death unto death to this nation, we know not; and we have no more to do with it, than had the Appostle Paul, when he preached Christ to the people of his day.

If American Slavery goes down in blood, it will but verify the declaration of those who uphold it. A committee of the North Carolina Legislature acknowledged this to an English friend ten years ago. [Thomas] Jefferson more than once uttered his gloomy forebodings; and the Legislators of Virginia, in 1832, declared that if the opportunity of escape, through the means of emancipation, were rejected, "though they might *save themselves,* they would rear their posterity to the business of the dagger and the torch." I have myself known several families to leave the South, solely from a fear of insurrection; and this twelve and fourteen years ago, long before any Anti-Slavery efforts were made in this country. And yet I presume, *if* through the cold-hearted apathy and obstinate opposition of the North, the South should become strengthened in her desperate determination to hold on to her outraged victims, until they are goaded to despair, and if the Lord in his wrath pours out the vials of his vengeance upon the slave States, why then, Abolitionists will have to bear all the blame. Thou hast drawn a frightful picture of the final issue of Anti-Slavery efforts, as thou art pleased to call it; but none of these things move me, for with just as much truth mayest thou point to the land of Egypt, blackened by God's avenging fires, and exclaim, "Behold the issue of Moses's mission." Nay, verily! See in that smoking, and blood-drenched house of bondage, the consequences of oppression, disobedience, and an obstinate rejection of truth, and light, and love. What had Moses to do with those judgment plagues, except to lift his rod? And if the South soon finds her winding sheet in garments rolled in blood, it will *not* be because of what the North has told her, but because, like impenitent Egypt, she hardened her heart against it, whilst the voices of some of her own children were crying in agony, "O! that thou hadst known, even thou, in this thy day, the things which belong to thy peace; but now they are hid from thine eyes."

Thy friend,

A. E. Grimké.

LETTER IX
Effect on the South

Brookline, Mass. 8th month, 17th, 1837.

Dear Friend:—Thou sayest "There are cases also, where differences in age, and station, and character, forbid all interference to modify the conduct and character of others." Let us bring this to the only touchstone by which Christians should try their principles of action.

How was it when God designed to rid his people out of the hands of the Egyptian monarch? Was *his* station so exalted "as to forbid all interference to modify his character and conduct"? And *who* was sent to interfere with his conduct towards a stricken people? Was it some brother monarch of exalted station, whose elevated rank might serve to excuse such interference "to modify his conduct and character"? No. It was an obscure shepherd of Midian's desert; for let us remember, that Moses in pleading the cause of the Israelities, identified himself with the *lowest* and *meanest* of the King's subjects. Ah! he was *one of that despised caste;* for, although brought up as the son of the princess, yet he had left Egypt as an outlaw. He had committed the crime of murder, and fled because the monarch "sought to slay him." This exiled outlaw is the instrument chosen by God to vindicate the cause of his oppressed people. Moses was in the sight of Pharaoh as much an object of scorn, as Garrison now is to the tyrants of America. Some seem to think, that great moral enterprises can be made honorable only by Doctors of Divinity, and Presidents of Colleges, engaging in them: when all powerful Truth cannot be dignified by *any* man, but *it* dignifies and ennobles all who embrace it. *It* lifts the beggar from the dunghill, and sets him among princes. Whilst it needs no great names to bear it onward to its glorious consummation, it is continally making great characters out of apparently mean and unpromising materials; and in the intensity of its piercing rays, revealing to the amazement of many, the insignificance and *moral* littleness of those who fill the highest stations in Church and State.

But take a few more examples from the bible, of those in high station being reproved by men of inferior rank. Look at David rebuked by Nathan, Ahab and Jezebel by Elijah and Micaiah. What, too, was the conduct of Daniel and Shadrach, Meshach and Abednego, but a *practical* rebuke of Darius and Nebuchadnezzar? And *who* were these men, apart from these acts of daring interference? They were the Lord's prophets, I shall be told; but what cared those monarchs for *this fact?* How much credit did they give them for holding this holy office? None, And why? Because all but David were impenitent sinners, and rejected with scorn all "interference to modify their conduct or characters." Reformers are rarely estimated in the age in which they live, whether they be called prophets or apostles, or abolitionists, or what not. They stand on the rock of Truth, and calmly look down upon the careering thunder-clouds, the tempest, and the roaring waves, because they well know that where the atmosphere is surcharged with pestiliential vapors, a conflict of the elements *must* take place, before it can be purified by that moral electricity, beautifully typified by the cloven tongues that sat upon *each* of the heads of the 120 disciples who were convened on the day of

Pentecost. Such men and women expect to be "blamed and opposed, because their measures are deemed inexpedient, and calculated to increase rather than diminish the evil to be cured." They know full well, that *intellectual* greatness cannot give *moral* perception—therefore, *those who have no clear views of the irresistibleness of moral power, cannot see the efficacy of moral means.* They say with the apostle, "The natural man receiveth not the things of the Spirit of God; for they are foolishness unto him: neither can he know them, because they are spiritually discerned." We know full well, that northern men and women laugh at the inefficacy of Anti-Slavery measures; *but slaveholders never have ridiculed them:* not that their moral perceptions are any clearer than those of our northern opponents, but where men's *interests* and *lust of power* are immediately affected by moral effort, they instinctively feel that it is so, and tremble for the result.

But suppose even that our measures were calculated to *increase* the evils of slavery. *The measures adopted by Moses, and sanctioned by God, increased the burdens of the Israelites.* Were they, therefore, *inexpedient?* And yet, if *our* measures produce a similar effect, O then! they are very inexpedient indeed. The truth is, when we look at Moses and his measures, we look at them in connection with the emancipation of the Israelites. The *ultimate* and glorious success of the measures proves their wisdom and expediency. But when Anti-Slavery measures are looked at *now,* we see them long *before the end is accomplished.* We see, according to thy account, the burdens increased; but we do not yet see the triumphant march through the Red Sea, nor do we hear the song of joy and thanksgiving which ascended from Israel's redeemed host. But canst thou not give up twenty years to complete our work? Clarkson, thy much admired model, worked twenty years; and the benevolent Colonization Society has been in operation twenty years. Just give us as long a time, or half that time, and then thou wilt be a far better judge of the expediency or inexpediency of our measures. Then thou wilt be able to look at them in connection with their success or their failure, and instead of writing a book on thy opinions and my opinions, thou canst write a *history.*

I cannot agree with thee in the sentiment, that the station of a nursery maid makes it inexpedient for her to turn reprover of the master who employs her. This is the doctrine of *modern aristocracy,* not of primitive christianity; for ecclesiastical history informs us that, in the first ages of christianity, kings were converted through the faithful and solemn rebukes of their slaves and captives. I have myself been reproved by a *slave,* and I thanked her, and still thank her for it. Think how this doctrine robs the nursery maid of her responsibility, and shields the master from reproof; for it may be that she alone has seen him ill-treat his wife. Now it appears to me, so far from her station forbidding all interference to modify the character and conduct of her employer, that that station peculiarly qualifies her for the difficult and delicate task, because nursery maids often know secrets of oppression, which no other persons are fully acquainted with. For my part, I believe it is *now the duty of the slaves of the South to rebuke their masters* for their robbery, oppression and crime; and so far from believing that such "reproof would do not good, but only evil," I think it would be attended by the happiest results in the main, though I doubt not it would occasion some instances of severe personal suffering. No station or character can destroy individual responsibility, in the matter of reproving sin. I feel that a slave has a right to rebuke me, and so has the vilest sinner; and the sincere, humble christian will be thankful for rebuke, let it come from whom it may. Such, I am confident, never would think it inexpedient for their chamber maids to administer it, but would endeavor to profit by it.

Thou askest gravely, why James G. Birney did not go quietly into the southern States, and collect facts? Indeed! Why should he go to the South to collect facts, when he had lived there forty years? Thou mayest with just as much propriety ask me, why I do not go to the South to collect facts. The answer to both questions is obvious:—We have lived at the South, as *integral* parts of the system of slavery, and therefore we know from practical observation and sad experience, quite enough about it already. I think it would be absurd for either of us to spend our time in such a way. And even if J. G. Birney had not lived at the South, why should he go there to collect facts, when the Anti-Slavery presses are continually throwing them out before the public? Look, too, at the Slave Laws. What more do we need to show us the bloody hands and iron heart of Slavery?

Thou sayest on the 89th page of thy book, "Every avenue of approach to the South is shut. No paper, pamphlet, or preacher, that touches on that topic, is admitted in their bounds." Thou art greatly mistaken; every avenue of approach to the South is not *shut.* The American Anti-Slavery Society sends between four and five hundred of its publications to the South by mail, *to subscribers,* or as exchange papers. One slaveholder in North Carolina, not long since, bought $60 worth of our pamphlets, &c. which he distributed in the slave States. Another slaveholder from Louisiana, made a large purchase of our publications last fall, which he designed to distribute among professors of religion who held slaves. To these I may add another from South Carolina, another from Richmond, Virginia, numbers from Kentucky, Tennessee, and Missouri, and others from New Orleans, besides persons connected with at least three Colleges and Theological Seminaries in slave States, have applied for our publications for their own use, and for distribution. Within a few weeks, the South Carolina Delegation in Congress have sent on an order to the publishing Agent of the American Anti-Slavery Society, for all the principal bound volumes, pamphlets, and periodicals of the Society. At the same time, they addressed a very courteous letter to J. G. Birney, the Corresponding Secretary, propounding nearly a score of queries, embracing the principles, designs, plans of operation, progress and the results of the Society. I know in the large cities, such as Charleston and Richmond, that Anti-Slavery papers are not suffered to reach their destination through the mail; but *it is not so* in the smaller towns. But even in the cities, I doubt not they are read by the postmasters and others. The South may pretend that she will not read our papers, but it is all pretence; the fact is she is very anxious to see what we are doing, so that when the mail-bags were robbed in Charleston in 1835, *I know* that the robbers were very careful to select a few copies of each of the publications *before* they made the bonfire, and that these were handed round in a private way through the city, so that they were *extensively read.* This fact I had from a friend of mine who was in Charleston at the time, and *read* the publications himself. My relations also wrote me word, that they had seen and read them. . . .

The foregoing are but a few of the facts and testimonies in the possession of Abolitionists, showing that their discussions, periodicals, petitions, argument appeals and societies, have extensively moved, and are still mightily moving the slaveholding States—*for good.* Did time and space permit, I might, by a little painstaking, procure many more. Before passing from this part of the subject, I must record my amazement at the clamors of many of the opponents of Abolitionists, from whom better things might indeed be hoped. What slaveholders have you convinced? they demand. Whom have you made Abolitionists? Give us their names and places of abode. Now, those who incessantly stun us with such unreasonable clamor, know full well, that to give the public the names and residences of such persons, would be in most instance to surrender them to butchery. But be it known to the North and to the South, we have names of scores of citizens of the slaveholding states, many of them slaveholders, who are in constant correspondence with us, persons who feel so deeply on the subject as to implore us to persevere in our efforts, and not to be dismayed by Southern threats nor disheartened by Northern cavils and heartlessness. Yea more, these persons have committed to us the custody even of their lives, thus encountering imminent peril that they might cheer us onward in our work. Shall we betray their trust, or put them in jeopardy? Judge thou.

Now let me ask, when in former years Anti-Slavery tracts, with our doctrines, could be circulated at the South? The fact is, there were *none* to be circulated there; our principle of repentance is quite new. But I can tell thee of two facts, which it is probable thou "hast not been informed of." In the year 1809, the steward of a vessel, a colored man, carried some Abolition pamphlets to Charleston. Immediately on his arrival, he was informed against, and would have been tried for his life, had he not promised to leave the State, never to return.* Was South Carolina willing to receive abolition pamphlets *then?* Again, in 1820, my sister carried some pamphlets there—"Thoughts on Slavery," issued by the Society of Friends, and therefore *not* very incendiary, thou mayest be assured; and yet she was informed some time afterwards, that had it not been for the influence of our family, she would have been imprisoned; for she, too, was accused of giving one of them to a slave; just as Abolitionists have been falsely charged with sending their papers to the enslaved. What she did give away, she was *obliged* to give *privately*. Was Charleston ready to receive Abolition pamphlets *then?* Or when? please to tell me. I say that *more,* far more Anti-Slavery tracts, &c. are *now* read in the South, than ever were at any former period. As to Colonization tracts, I know they have circulated at the South; but what of that, when Southerners believed that Colonization had *no* connection with the overthrow of Slavery? Colonization papers, &c. are not Abolition papers.

As to preachers, let me assure thee, that they *never* have dared to preach on the subject of slavery in my native city, so far as my knowledge extends. Ah! I for some years sat under two *northern* ministers, but never did I hear them preach in public, or speak in private, on the *sin* of slavery. O! the *deep,* DEEP injury which such unfaithful ministers have inflicted on the South! It is well known that our young men have, to a great extent, been educated in Northern Theological Seminaries. With what principles were *their* minds imbued? What kind of religion did the *North* prepare them to preach? A slaveholding religion. What kind of religion did *northern men* come down and preach to us? A slaveholding

* He was a steward on the *Minerva,* out of New York City.

religion—and multitudes of them became slaveholders. Such was one of my *northern* pastors. And yet thou tellest me, the North has nothing to do with slavery at the South—is *not* guilty, &c. &c. "Their own clergy," thou sayest, "either entirely hold their peace, or become the defenders of a system they once lamented, and attempted to bring to an end." Do name to me one of those valiant defenders of slavery, who formerly lamented over the system, and attempted to bring it to an end. "What is his name, or what is his son's name, if thou canst tell?" Strange indeed, if, because *we* advocate the truth, others should begin to hate it; or because we expose sin, they should turn round and defend what once they lamented over! Is this in accordance with "the known laws of mind," where principle is deeply rooted in the heart?

And then thou closest these assertions *without proof,* with the triumphant exclamation, "This is the record of experience, as to the tendencies of abolitionism, as thus far developed. The South is just now in that state of high exasperation, at the sense of wanton injury and *impertinent interference,* which makes the influence of truth and reason most useless and powerless." Hadst thou been better informed as to the real tendencies of abolitionism on the South, this assertion also might have been spared. Again I repeat, the *South* does not tell us so. . . . That we have succeeded in rousing the North to reflection, thou art thyself a living proof; for let me ask, what it was that set *thee* to such serious thinking, as to induce *thee* to write a *book* on the Slave Question?

Thy friend in haste,

A. E. Grimké.

LETTER X
"The Tendency of the Age Towards Emancipation" Produced by Abolition Doctrines

Dear Friend: Thou sayest "that this evil (Slavery,) is at no distant period to come to an end, is the unanimous opinion of all who either notice the tendencies of the age, or believe in the prophecies of the Bible." But how can this be true, if Abolitionists have indeed rolled back the car of Emancipation? If our measures really tend to this result, how can this evil come to an end at no distant period? Colonizationists tell us, if it had not been for our interference, they could have done a vast deal better than they have done; and the American Unionists* say, that we have paralyzed their efforts, so that they can do nothing; and yet "the tendencies of the age" are crowding forward Emancipation. Now, what has produced this tendency? Surely every reflecting person must acknowledge, that Colonization cannot effect the work of Abolition. The American Union is doing nothing; and Abolitionists are pursuing a course which "will tend to bring slavery to an end, *if at all,* at the *most distant* period,—then do tell me, how the tendencies of the age can possibly lean towards Emancipation? Perhaps I shall be told, that the movements of Great Britain in the West Indies created this tendency. Ah! but this is a *foreign influence,* more so even than Northern influence; and if the North is "a foreign community," as thou expressly stylest it, and can on *that account* produce *no* influence on the South, how can the doings of England affect her?

Now I believe with thee, that the tendencies of the age are toward Emancipation; but I contend that nothing but free discussion has produced this tendency. Now let us turn to the South, and ask her eagle-eyed politicians what *they* are most afraid of. Read their answer in their desperate struggles to fetter the press and gag the mouths of—*whom?*—Colonizationists? Why no—*they* talk colonization *themselves,* and are not at all afraid that the expatriation of a few hundred or thousands in 20 years will ever drain the country of its millions of slaves, where they are now increasing at the rate of 70,000 every year. The American Unionists? O no! the South has not deemed them worthy of any notice! Pray, then, *whose* mouths are slaveholders so fiercely striving to seal in silence? Why the mouths of Abolitionists, to be sure—even our infant school children know this. Strange indeed, when the labors of these men are actually rolling back the car of Emancipation for one or two centuries! Why, the South ought to pour out her treasure, to support Anti-Slavery agents, and print Anti-Slavery papers and pamphlets, and do all she can to aid us in *rolling back* Emancipation. Pray, write *her a book,* and tell her she has been very needlessly alarmed at our doings, and advise her to send us a few thousand dollars: her money would be very acceptable in these hard times, and we would take it as the wages due to the unpaid laborers, though we would never admit the donors to membership with

* In the spring of 1834, a group of conservative Congregational ministers, aided by Lyman Beecher, launched a project to take the New England antislavery movement from Garrison. The result, the American Union for the Relief and Improvement of the Colored Race, was founded in January 1835 with the aid of John and Charles Tappan, Boston brothers of Arthur and Lewis. It lasted barely a year.

us. How dost thou think *she* would receive *such a book?* Just try it, I entreat thee.

Thou seemest to think that the North has *no right* to rebuke the South, and assumest the ground that Abolitionists are the enemies of the South. We say, we have the right, and mean to exercise it. I believe that every northern Legislature has a right, and ought to use the right, to send a solemn remonstrance to every southern Legislature on the subject of slavery. Just as much right as the South has to send up a remonstrance against our free presses, free pens, and free tongues. Let the North follow her example; but, instead of asking her to enslave her subjects, entreat her to *free* them. The South may pretend *now,* that we have no right to interfere, because it suits her convenience to say so; but a few years ago, (1820,) we find that our Vice President, R. M. Johnson,* in his speech on the Missouri question,† was amazed at the "cold insensibility, the eternal apathy towards the slaves in the District of Columbia," which was exhibited by *northern* men, "though they had occular demonstration continually before them of the abominations of slavery.["] *Then* the South wondered *we did not interfere with slavery*—and *now* she says we have no right to interfere.

I find, on the 57th p. a false assertion with regard to Abolitionists. After showing the folly of our rejecting the wordly doctrine of expediency, so excellent in thy view, thou then sayest that we say, the reason why we do not go to the South is, that we should be murdered. Now, if there are any half-hearted Abolitionists, who are thus recreant to the high and holy principle of "Duty is ours, and events are God's," then I must leave such to explain their own inconsistencies; but that this is the reason assigned by the Society, as a body, I never have seen nor believed. So far from it, that I have invariably heard those who understood the principles of the Anti-Slavery Society best, *deny* that it was a duty to

* Richard M. Johnson (1780–1850), a native of Kentucky, was a hero of the War of 1812. He never married, but he lived openly with a mulatto woman, Julia Chinn, and their two daughters, whom he acknowledged proudly. When he was nominated in 1836 by the Democratic party as the running mate of Martin Van Buren, the Virginia delegation walked out of the convention. When Van Buren won Virginia, the electors there refused to cast their votes for Johnson, thereby leaving him one vote shy of a majority total. The election thus devolved upon the Senate, where, with Virginia's senators voting for him, he was elected.

† In 1819, the United States consisted of eleven free and eleven slave states. When the Missouri territory applied for admission to the Union as a slave state, northern congressmen tried to amend the statehood bill to prohibit the introduction of further slavery and to emancipate gradually the slaves already there. The ensuing sectional controversy ended with the adoption of the "Missouri Compromise" in 1820. Missouri was admitted as a slave state, Maine was admitted as a free state, and a line was drawn through the Louisiana Purchase, at 36° 30′. North of that line, excepting Missouri, slavery was "forever prohibited."

go to the South, *not* because they would be killed, but because the *North was guilty,* and therefore ought to be labored with *first.* They took exactly the same view of the subject, which was taken by the southern friend of mine to whom I have already alluded. "Until northern women, (said she,) do their duty on the subject of slavery, *southern women* cannot be expected to do theirs." I therefore utterly deny this charge. Such may be the opinion of a few, but it is not and cannot be proved to be a principle of action in the Anti-Slavery Society. The fact is, we need no excuse for not going to the South, so long as the North is as deeply involved in the guilt of slavery as she is, and as blind to her duty.

One word with regard to these remarks: "Before the Abolition movements commenced, both northern and southern men expressed their views freely at the South." This, also, I deny, because, as a southerner, *I know* that *I* never could express my views freely on the abominations of slavery, without exciting anger, even in professors of religion. It is true, "the *dangers, evils* and *mischiefs* of slavery" could be, and were discussed at the South and the North. Yes, we might talk as much as we pleased about *these,* as long as we viewed slavery as a *misfortune* to the *slaveholder,* and talked of "the dangers, evils and mischiefs of slavery" to *him,* and pitied *him* for having had such a "sad inheritance entailed upon him." But could any man or woman ever "express their views freely" on the SIN of slavery at the South? I say, never! Could they express their views freely as to the dangers, mischiefs and evils of slavery to the *poor suffering slave?* No, never! It was only whilst the *slaveholder* was regarded as *an unfortunate sufferer,* and sympathized with *as such,* that he was willing to talk, and be talked to, on this "delicate subject." Hence we find, that as soon as *he* is addressed as a *guilty oppressor,* why then he is in a phrenzy of passion. As soon as we set before him the dangers, and evils, and mischiefs of slavery to *the down-trodden victims of his oppression,* O then! the slaveholder storms and raves like a maniac. Now look at this view of the subject: as a southerner, I know it is the only correct one.

With regard to the discussion of "the subject of slavery, in the legislative halls of the South," if thou hast read these debates, thou certainly must know that they did not touch on the SIN of slavery at all; they were wholly confined to "the dangers, evils and mischiefs of slavery" to the *unfortunate slaveholder.* What did the discussion in the Virginia legislature result in? In the *rejection of every* plan of emancipation, and in the passage of an act which they believed would give additional permanency to the institution, whilst it divested it of its dangers, by removing the free people of color to Liberia; for which purpose they voted $20,000,* but took very good care to provide, "that no slave to be thereafter emancipated should have the benefit of the appropriation," so fearful were they, lest masters might avail themselves of this scheme of expatriation to manumit their slaves. The Maryland scheme is altogether based on the principle of banishment and oppression. The colored people were to be "got rid of," for the benefit of their lordly oppressors—*not* set free from the noble principles of justice and mercy to *them.* If Abolitionists have put a stop to all *such* discussions of slavery, I, for one, do most heartily rejoice at it. The fact is, the South is enraged, because we have exposed her horrible hypocrisy to the world. We have torn off the mask, and brought to light the hidden things of darkness.

To prove to thee that the South, as a body, never was prepared for emancipation, I might detail historical facts, which are stubborn things; but I have not the time to go into this subject that would be necessary. I will, therefore give a few extracts from documents published by the old Abolition Societies, whose principle was gradualism. . . .

How, then, can our opponents say, that the cause of emancipation has been *rolled back by us?* We ask, when was it ever *forward?* As a southerner, I repeat my solemn conviction, from *my own experience,* and from all I can learn from historical facts, and the reports of the Gradual Emancipation Societies of this country, and the scope of the debates which took place in the Kentucky, Virginia and Maryland Legislatures, that it *never was* forward. If the tendencies of the age are towards emancipation, they are tendencies peculiar to this age in the United States, and have been brought about by free discussion, and in accordance, too, with the *known laws of mind;* for collision of mind as naturally produces light, as the striking of the flint and the steel produces fire. *Free discussion is this collision,* and the results are visible in the light which is breaking forth in every city, town and village, and spreading over the hills and valleys, through the whole length and breadth of our land. Yes! it has already reached "the dark valley of the shadow of death" in the South; and in a few brief years, He who said, "Let there be light," will gather this moral effulgence into a focal point, and beneath its burning rays, the heart of the slaveholder, and the chains of the slave, will melt like wax before the orb of day.

Let us, then, take heed lest we be found fighting against God while

* Actually, the bill debated in March 1833 appropriated $18,000 a year for five years to finance the voluntary emigration of blacks who were free at the time of the bill's passage. The American Colonization Society would be paid $30 a head, on proof of delivery to Africa.

standing idle in the market place, or endeavoring to keep other laborers out of the field now already white to the harvest.

Thy friend,

A. E. Grimké.

LETTER XI
The Sphere Of Woman And Man As Moral Beings The Same

Brookline, Mass. 8th month, 28th, 1837.

Dear Friend: I come now to that part of thy book, which is, of all others, the most important to the women of this country; thy "general views in relation to the place woman is appointed to fill by the dispensations of heaven." I shall quote paragraphs from thy book, offer my objections to them, and then throw before thee my own views.

Thou sayest, "Heaven has appointed to one sex the *superior,* and to the other the *subordinate* station, and this without any reference to the character or conduct of either." This is an assertion without proof. Thou further sayest, that "it was designed that the mode of gaining influence and exercising power should be *altogether different and peculiar.*" Does the Bible teach this? "Peace on earth, and good will to men, is the character of all the rights and privileges, the influence and the power of *woman.*" Indeed! Did our Holy Redeemer preach the doctrine of *peace to our sex* only? "A *man* may act on Society by the collision of intellect, in public debate; *he* may urge his measures by a sense of shame, by fear and by personal interest; *he* may coerce by the combination of public sentiment; *he* may drive by physical force, and *he* does *not* overstep the boundaries of his sphere." Did Jesus, then, give a different rule of action to men and women? Did he tell his disciples, when he sent them out to preach the gospel, that man might appeal to the fear, and shame, and interest of those he addressed, and coerce by public sentiment, and drive by physical force? "But (that) all the power and all the conquests that are lawful to *woman* are those only which appeal to the kindly, generous, peaceful and benevolent principles"? If so, I should come to a very different conclusion from the one at which thou hast arrived: I should suppose that *woman was the superior,* and *man the subordinate being,* inasmuch as moral power is immeasurably superior to "physical force."

"Woman is to win every thing by peace and love; by making *herself* so much respected, &c. that to yield to *her* opinions, and to gratify *her* wishes, will be the free-will offering of the heart." This principle may do as the rule of action to the fashionable belle, whose idol is *herself;* whose every attitude and smile are designed to win the admiration of others to *herself;* and who enjoys, with exquisite delight, the double-refined incense of flattery which is offered to *her* vanity, by yielding to *her* opinions, and gratifying *her* wishes, because they are *hers*. But to the humble Christian, who feels that it is *truth* which she seeks to recommend to others, *truth* which she wants them to esteem and love, and not herself, this subtle principle must be rejected with holy indignation. Suppose she could win thousands to her opinions, and govern them by her wishes, how much nearer would they be to Jesus Christ, if she presents no higher motive, and points to no higher leader?

"But this is all to be accomplished in the domestic circle." Indeed! "Who made thee a ruler and judge over all?" I read in the Bible, that Miriam, and Deborah, and Huldah, were called to fill *public stations* in Church and State. I find Anna, the prophetess, speaking in the temple "unto all them that looked for redemption in Jerusalem." During his ministry on earth, I see women following him from town to town, in the most public manner; I hear the woman of Samaria, on her return to the city, telling the *men* to come and see a man who had told her all things that ever she did. I see them even standing on Mount Calvary, around his cross, in the most exposed situation; but He never *rebuked* them; He never told them it was unbecoming *their sphere in life* to mingle in the crowds which followed his footsteps. Then, again, I see the cloven tongues of fire resting on each of the heads of the one hundred and twenty disciples, some of whom were *women;* yea, I hear *them preaching* on the day of Pentecost to the multitudes who witnessed the outpouring of the spirit on that glorious occasion; for, unless *women* as well as men received the Holy Ghost, and *prophesied,* what did Peter mean by telling them, "This is *that* which was spoken by the prophet Joel: And it shall come to pass in the last days, said *God,* I will pour out my spirit upon *all* flesh: and your sons and your *daughters shall prophesy*. . . . And on my servants and on my *handmaidens,* I will pour out in those days of my spirit; and *they shall prophesy.*" This is the plain matter of fact, as Clark and Scott, Stratton and Locke,* all allow. Mine is no "private interpretation," no mere sectarian view.

* Adam Clarke, *The Holy Bible . . . With a commentary and critical notes,* 8 vols. (London: Butterworth, 1810–1825); *The Holy Bible . . . With explanatory notes . . . by Thomas Scott. . . .Third Edition with additions . . . by the author,* 5 vols. (London: Seeley, 1810); Thomas Stratton, *The Book of the Priesthood; an argument, in three parts . . .* (London: 1830; first American edition, 1831); John Locke, *A*

I find, too, that Philip had four daughters which did *prophesy;* and what is still more convincing, I read in the xi. of I. Corinthians, some particular directions from the Apostle Paul, as to *how* women were to pray and prophesy in the assemblies of the people—*not* in the domestic circle. On examination, too, it appears that the very same word, *Diakonos,* which, when applied to Phoebe, Romans xvi. 1, is translated *servant,* when applied to Tychicus, Ephesians vi. 21, is rendered *minister.* Ecclesiastical History informs us, that this same Phoebe was pre-eminently useful, as a minister in the Church, and that female ministers suffered martyrdom in the first ages of Christianity. And what, I ask, does the Apostle mean when he says in Phillipians iv. 3.—"Help those women who labored with me in the gospel"? Did these holy women of old perform all their gospel labors in "the domestic and social circle"? I trow not.

Thou sayest, "the moment woman begins to feel the promptings of ambition, or the thirst for power, her aegis of defence is gone." Can man, then, retain his aegis when he indulges these guilty passions? Is it woman only who suffers this loss?

"All the generous promptings of chivalry all the poetry of romantic gallantry, depend upon woman's retaining her place as *dependent* and *defenceless,* and making no claims, and maintaining no rights, but what are the gifts of honor, rectitude and love."

I cannot refrain from pronouncing this sentiment as beneath the dignity of any woman who names the name of Christ. No woman who understands her dignity as a moral, intellectual, and accountable being, cares aught for any attention or any protection, vouchsafed by "the promptings of chivalry, and the poetry of romantic gallantry"? [*sic*] Such a one loathes such littleness, and turns with disgust from all such silly insipidities. Her noble nature is insulted by such paltry, sickening adulation, and she will not stoop to drink the foul waters of so turbid a stream. If all this sinful foolery is to be withdrawn from our sex, with all my heart I say, *the sooner the better.* Yea, I say more, no woman who lives up to the true glory of her womanhood, will ever be treated with such *practical contempt.* Every man, when in the presence of true moral greatness, "will find an influence thrown around him," which will utterly forbid the exercise of "the poetry of romantic gallantry."

What dost thou mean by woman's retaining her place as defenceless

---

paraphrase and notes on the Epistles of St. Paul to the Galatians, I & II, Corinthians, Romans, Ephesians. To which is prefix'd, An essay for the understanding of St. Paul's Epistles, by consulting St. Paul himself (London: Awnsham and John Churchill, 1707).

and dependent? Did our Heavenly Father furnish man with any offensive or defensive weapons? Was *he* created any less defenceless than *she* was? Are they not equally defenceless, equally dependent on Him? What did Jesus say to his disciples, when he commissioned them to preach the gospel?—"Behold, I send you forth as SHEEP in the midst of wolves; be ye wise as serpents, and *harmless as doves*.["] What could he have said to women?

Again, she must "make no claims, and maintain no rights, but what are the gifts of honor, rectitude and love." From whom does woman receive her *rights?* From God, or from man? What dost thou mean by saying, her rights are the *gifts* of honor, rectitude and love? One would really suppose that man, as her lord and master, was the gracious giver of her rights, and that these rights were bestowed upon her by "the promptings of chivalry, and the poetry of romantic gallantry"—out of the abundance of his honor, rectitude and love. Now, if I understand the real state of the case, woman's rights are not the gifts of man—no! nor the *gifts* of God. His gifts to her may be recalled at his good pleasure—but her *rights* are an integral part of her moral being; they cannot be withdrawn; they must live with her forever. Her rights lie at the foundation of all her duties; and, so long as the divine commands are binding upon her, so long must her rights continue.

"A woman may seek the aid of co-operation and combination among her own sex, to assist her in her appropriate offices of piety, charity," &c. *Appropriate* offices! Ah! here is the great difficulty. What are they? Who can point them out? Who has ever attempted to draw a line of separation between the duties of men and women, as *moral* beings, without committing the grossest inconsistencies on the one hand, or running into the most arrant absurdities on the other?

"Whatever, in any measure, throws a woman into the attitude of a combatant, either for herself or others—whatever binds her in a party conflict—whatever obliges her in any way to exert coercive influences, throws her out of her appropriate sphere." If, by a *combatant,* thou meanest one who "drives by *physical force,*" then I say, *man* has no more right to appear as *such* a combatant than woman; for all the pacific precepts of the gospel were given to *him,* as well as to her. If, by a *party conflict,* thou meanest a struggle for power, either civil or ecclesiastical, a thirst for the praise and the honor of man, why, then I would ask, is this the proper sphere of *any* moral, accountable being, man or woman? If, by *coercive influences,* thou meanest the use of force or of fear, such as slaveholders and warriors employ, then, I repeat, that *man* has no more right to exert these than *woman.* All such influences are repudiated by the precepts and examples of Christ, and his apostles; so that, after all, this appropriate sphere of woman is *just as appropriate to man.* These "general principles are correct," if thou wilt only permit them to be of *general application.*

Thou sayest that the propriety of woman's coming forward as a suppliant for a portion of her sex who are bound in cruel bondage, depends entirely on its *probable results.* I thought the disciples of Jesus were to walk by *faith, not* by sight. Did Abraham reason as to the *probable results* of his offering up Isaac? No! or he could not have raised his hand against the life of his son; because in Isaac, he had been told, his seed should be called,—that seed in whom all the nations of the earth were to be blessed. O! when shall we learn that God is wiser than man—that his ways are higher than our ways, his thoughts than our thoughts—and that "obedience is better than sacrifice, and to hearken than the fat of rams"? If we are always to *reason* on the *probable results* of performing our duty, I wonder what our Master meant by telling his disciples, that they must become like *little children.* I used to think he designed to inculcate the necessity of walking by faith, in childlike simplicity, docility and humility. But if we are to *reason* as to the *probable results* of obeying the injunctions to plead for the widow and the fatherless, and to deliver the spoiled out of the hand of the oppressor, &c., then I do not know what he meant to teach.

According to what thou sayest, the women of this country are not to be governed by principles of duty, but by the effect their petitions produce on the members of Congress, and by the opinions of these men. If they deem them "obtrusive, indecorous, and unwise," they must not be sent. If *thou* canst consent to exchange the precepts of the Bible for the opinions of *such a body of men* as now sit on the destinies of this nation, I cannot. What is this but *obeying man* rather than God, and seeking the *praise of man* rather than of God? As to our petitions increasing the evils of slavery, this is merely an opinion, the correctness or incorrectness of which remains to be proved. When I hear Senator Preston of South Carolina,* saying that "he regarded the concerted movement upon the District of Columbia as an attempt to storm the gates of the citadel—as throwing the bridge over the moat"—and declaring that "the South must resist the *danger* in its inception, or it would *soon become irresistible*"—I feel confident that petitions will effect the work of emancipation, *thy* opinion to the contrary notwithstanding.

* William C. Preston (1794–1860), United States senator, 1833–1844.

And when I hear Francis W. Pickens,* from the same State, saying in a speech delivered in Congress—"Mr. Speaker, we cannot mistake all these things. The truth is, the moral power of the world is against us. It is idle to disguise it. We must, sooner or later, meet the great issue that is to be made on this subject. Deeply connected with this, is the movement to be made on the District of Columbia. If the power be asserted in Congress to interfere here, or any approach be made toward that end, *it will give a shock to our institutions* and the country, the consequences of which no man can foretell. Sir, as well might you grapple with iron grasp into the very heart and vitals of South Carolina, as to touch this subject here." When I hear these things from the lips of keen-eyed politicians of the South, northern apologies for not interfering with the subject of slavery, "lest it should increase, rather than diminish the evils it is wished to remove," affect me little.

Another objection to woman's petition is, that they may "tend to bring females, as petitioners and partisans, into every political measure that may tend to injure and oppress their sex." As to their ever becoming partisans, i.e. sacrificing principles to power or interest, I reprobate this under all circumstances, and in *both* sexes. But I trust my sisters may always be permitted to *petition* for a redress of grievances. Why not? The right of petition is the only political right that women have: why not let them exercise it whenever they are aggrieved? Our fathers waged a bloody conflict with England, because *they* were taxed without being represented. This is just what unmarried women of property now are. *They* were not willing to be governed by laws which *they* had no voice in making; but this is the way in which women are governed in this Republic. If, then, *we* are taxed without being represented, and governed by laws *we* have no voice in framing, then, surely, we ought to be permitted at least to remonstrate against "every political measure that may tend to injure and oppress our sex in various parts of the nation, and under the various public measures that may hereafter be enforced." Why not? Art thou afraid to trust the women of this country with discretionary power as to petitioning? Is there not sound principle and common sense enough among them, to regulate the exercise of this right? I believe they will always use it wisely. I am not afraid to trust my sisters—not I.

Thou sayest, "In this country, petitions to Congress, in reference to official duties of legislators, seem, IN ALL CASES, to fall entirely without the sphere of female duty. Men are the proper persons to make

* Francis W. Pickens (1805–1869) served in the United States House of Representatives, 1834–1843.

appeals to the rulers whom they appoint," &c. Here I entirely dissent from thee. The fact that women are denied the right of voting for members of Congress, is but a poor reason why they should also be deprived of the right of petition. If their numbers are counted to swell the number of Representatives in our State and National Legislatures, the *very least* that can be done is to give them the right of petition in all cases whatsoever; and without any abridgement. If not, they are mere slaves, known only through their masters.

In my next, I shall throw out my own views with regard to "the appropriate sphere of woman"—and for the present, subscribe myself,

Thy Friend,

A. E. Grimké.

LETTER XII

Human Rights Not Founded On Sex

East Boylston, Mass. 10th mo, 2d, 1837.

Dear Friend: In my last, I made a sort of running commentary upon thy views of the appropriate sphere of woman, with something like a promise, that in my next, I would give thee my own.

The investigation of the rights of the slave has led me to a better understanding of my own. I have found the Anti-Slavery cause to be the high school of morals in our land—the school in which *human rights* are more fully investigated, and better understood and taught, than in any other. Here a great fundamental principle is uplifted and illuminated, and from this central light, rays innumerable stream all around. Human beings have *rights,* because they are *moral* beings; the rights of *all* men grow out of their moral nature; and as all men have the same moral nature, they have essentially the same rights. These rights may be wrested from the slave, but they cannot be alienated: his title to himself is as perfect *now,* as is that of Lyman Beecher: it is stamped on his moral being, and is, like it, imperishable. Now if rights are founded in the nature of our moral being, then the *mere circumstance of sex* does not give to man higher rights and responsibilities, than to woman. To suppose that it does, would be to deny the self-evident truth, that the "physical constitution is the mere instrument of the moral nature." To suppose that it does, would be to break up utterly the relations, of the two natures, and to reverse their functions, exalting the animal nature into a monarch, and humbling the moral [nature] into a slave; making the former a proprietor, and the latter its property. When human beings are regarded as *moral* beings, *sex,* instead of being enthroned upon the summit, administering upon rights and responsibilities, sinks into insignificance and nothingness. My doctrine then is, that whatever it is morally right for man to do, it is morally right for woman to do. Our duties originate, not from difference of sex, but from the diversity of our relations in life, the various gifts and talents committed to our care, and the different eras in which we live.

The regulation of duty by the mere circumstance of sex, rather than by the fundamental principle of moral being, has led to all that multifarious train of evils flowing out of the anti-christian doctrine of masculine and feminine virtues. By this doctrine, man has been converted into the warrior, and clothed with sternness, and those other kindred qualities, which in common estimation belong to his character as a *man;* whilst woman has been taught to lean upon an arm of flesh, to sit as a doll arrayed in "gold, and pearls, and costly array," to be admired for her personal charms, and caressed and humored like a spoiled child, or converted into a mere drudge to suit the convenience of her lord and master. Thus have all the diversified relations of life been filled with "confusion and every evil work." This principle has given to man a charter for the exercise of tyranny and selfishness, pride and arrogance, lust and brutal violence. It has robbed woman of essential rights, the right to think and speak and act on all great moral questions, just as men think and speak and act; the right to share their responsibilities, perils and toils; the right to fulfill the great end of her being, as a moral, intellectual and immortal creature, and of glorifying God in her body and her spirit which are His. Hitherto, instead of being a help meet to man, in the highest, noblest sense of the term as a companion, a co-worker, an equal; she has been a mere appendage of his being, an instrument of his convenience and pleasure, the pretty toy with which he wiled away his leisure moments, or the pet animal whom he humored into playfulness and submission. Woman, instead of being regarded as the equal of man, has uniformly been looked down upon as his inferior, a mere gift to fill up the measure of his happiness. In "the poetry of romantic gallantry," it is true, she has been called "the last *best* gift of God to man"; but I believe I speak forth the words of truth and soberness when I affirm, that woman never was given to man. She was created, like him, in the image of God, and crowned with glory and honor; created only a little lower than the angels,—not, as is almost universally assumed, a little lower than man; on her brow, as well as on his, was placed the "diadem of beauty," and in her hand the sceptre of universal dominion. Gen: i. 27, 28. "The last *best gift* of God to man"! Where is the scripture warrant for this "rhetorical flourish, this splendid absurdity"? Let us examine the account of her creation. "And the rib which the Lord God had taken from man, made he a woman, and brought her unto the man." Not as a gift—for Adam immediately recognized her *as part of himself*—("this is now bone of my bone, and flesh of my flesh")—a companion and equal, not one hair's breadth beneath him in the majesty and glory of her moral being; not placed under his authority as a *subject,* but by his side, on the same platform of human rights, under the government of God only. This idea of woman's being "the last gift of God to man," however pretty it may sound to the ears of those who love to discourse upon "the poetry of romantic gallantry, and the generous promptings of chivalry," has nevertheless been the means of sinking her from an *end* into a mere *means*—of turning her into an *appendage* to man, instead of recognizing her as *a part of man*—of destroying her individuality, and rights, and responsibilities, and merging her moral being in that of man. Instead of *Jehovah* being *her* king, *her* lawgiver, and *her* judge, she has been taken out of the exalted scale of existence in which He placed her, and subjected to the despotic control of man.

I have often been amused at the vain efforts made to define the rights and responsibilities of immortal beings as *men* and *women.* No one has yet found out just *where* the line of separation between them should be drawn, and for this simple reason, that no one knows just how far below man woman is, whether she be a head shorter in her moral responsibilities, or head and shoulders, or the full length of his noble stature, below him, i.e. under his feet. Confusion, uncertainty, and great inconsistencies, must exist on this point, so long as woman is regarded in the least degree inferior to man; but place her where her Maker placed her, on the same high level of human rights with man, side by side with him, and difficulties vanish, the mountains of perplexity flow down at the presence of this grand equalizing principle. Measure her rights and duties by the unerring standard of *moral being,* not by the false weights and measures of a mere circumstance of her human existence, and then the truth will be self-evident, that whatever it is *morally* right for a man to do, it is *morally* right for a woman to do. I recognize no rights but *human* rights—I know nothing of men's rights and women's rights; for in Christ Jesus, there is neither male nor female. It is my solemn conviction, that, until this principle of equality is recognised and embodied in practice, the church can do nothing effectual for the permanent reformation of the world. Woman was the first transgressor, and the first victim of power. In all heathen nations, she has been the slave of man, and Christian nations have never acknowledged her rights. Nay more, no Christian denomination or Society has ever acknowledged them on the broad basis of humanity. I know that in some denominations, she is permitted to preach the gospel; not from a conviction of her rights, nor upon the ground of her equality as a *human being,* but of her equality in spiritual gifts—for we find that women, even in these Societies, is allowed no voice in framing the Discipline by which she is to be governed. Now, I believe it is woman's right to have a voice in all the laws and regulations by which she is to be *governed,* whether in Church or State; and that the present arrangements of society, on these points, are *a violation of human rights, a rank usurpation of power,* a violent seizure and confiscation of what is sacredly and inalienably hers—thus inflicting upon woman outrageous wrongs, working mischief incalculable in the social circle, and in its influence on the world producing only evil, and that continually. *If* Ecclesiastical and Civil governments are ordained of God, *then* I contend that woman has just as much right to sit in solemn counsel in Conventions, Conferences, Associations and General Assemblies, as man—just as much right to sit upon the throne of England, or in the Presidential chair of the United States.

Dost thou ask me, if I would wish to see woman engaged in the contention and strife of sectarian controversy, or in the intrigues of political partizans? I say no! never—never. I rejoice that she does not stand on the same platform which man now occupies in these respects; but I mourn, also, that he should thus prostitute his higher nature, and vilely cast away his birthright. I prize the purity of *his* character as highly as I do that of hers. As a moral being, *whatever it is morally wrong for her to do, it is morally wrong for him to do.* The fallacious doctrine of male and female virtues has well nigh ruined all that is morally great and lovely in his character: he has been quite as deep a sufferer by it as woman, though mostly in different respects and by other processes. As my time is engrossed by the pressing responsibilities of daily public duty, I have no leisure for that minute detail which would be required for the illustration and defence of these principles. Thou wilt find a wide field opened before thee, in the investigation of which, I doubt not, thou wilt be instructed. Enter this field, and explore it; thou wilt find in it a hid treasure, more precious than rubies—a fund, a mine of principles, as new as they are great and glorious.

Thou sayest, "an ignorant, a narrow-minded, or a stupid woman, cannot feel nor understand the rationality, the propriety, or the beauty of this relation "—i.e. subordination to man. Now, verily, it does appear to me, that nothing but a narrow-minded view of the subject of human rights and responsibilities can induce any one to believe in *this subordination to a fallible* being. Sure I am, that the signs of the times clearly indicate a vast and rapid change in public sentiment on this subject. Sure I am that she is not to be, as she has been, *"a mere second-hand agent"* in the regeneration of a fallen world, but the acknowledged equal and co-worker with man in this glorious work. Not that "she will carry her measures by tormenting when she cannot please, or by petulant complaints or obtrusive interference, in matters which are out of her sphere, and which she cannot comprehend." But just in proportion as her moral and intellectual capacities become enlarged, she will rise higher and higher in the scale of creation, until she reaches that elevation prepared for her by her Maker, and upon whose summit she was originally stationed, only "a little lower than the angels." Then will it be seen that nothing which concerns the well-being of mankind is either beyond her sphere, or above her comprehension: *Then* will it be seen "that America will be distinguished above all other nations for well educated women, and for the influence they will exert on the general interests of society."

But I must close with recommending to thy perusal, my sister's Letters on the Province of Woman, published in the New England Spectator, and republished by Isaac Knapp of Boston.* As she has taken up this subject so fully, I have only glanced at it. That thou and all my country-women may better understand the true dignity of woman, is the sincere desire of

Thy Friend,

A. E. Grimké.

* See below, p. 204.

LETTER XIII
Miscellaneous Remarks,—Conclusion

Holliston, Mass. 10th month, 23d, 1837.

My Dear Friend: I resume my pen, to gather up a few fragments of thy Essay, that have not yet been noticed, and in love to bid thee farewell.

Thou appearest to think, that it is peculiarly the duty of *women* to educate the little children of this nation. But why, I would ask—why are they any more bound to engage in this sacred employment, than men? I believe, that as soon as the rights of women are understood, our brethren will see and feel that it is their duty to co-operate with us, in this high and holy vocation, of training up little children in the way they should go. And the very fact of their mingling in intercourse with such guileless and gentle spirits, will tend to soften down the asperities of their characters, and clothe them with the noblest and sublimest Christian virtues. I know that this work is deemed beneath the dignity of man; but how great the error! I once heard a man, who had labored extensively among children, say, "I never feel so near heaven, as when I am teaching these little ones." He was right; and I trust the time is coming, when the occupation of an instructor to children will be deemed the most honorable of human employment. If it is drudgery to teach these little ones, then it is the duty of men to bear a part of that burthen; if it is a privilege and an honor, then we generously invite them to share that honor and privilege with us.

I know some noble instances of this union of principles and employment, and am fully settled in the belief, that abolition doctrines are pre-eminently calculated to qualify men and women to become faithful and efficient teachers. *They alone* teach fully the doctrine of human rights; and to know and appreciate these, is an indispensable prerequisite to the wisely successful performance of the duties of a teacher. The right understanding of these will qualify her to teach the fundamental, but unfashionable doctrine, that "God is no respecter of persons," and that he that despiseth the colored man, because he is "guilty of a skin not colored like our own," reproacheth his Maker for having given him that ebon hue. I consider it absolutely indispensable, that this truth should be sedulously instilled into the mind of every child in our republic. I know of *no* moral truth of greater importance at the present crisis. Those teachers, who are not prepared to teach *this in all its fullness,* are deficient in one of the most sterling elements of moral character, and are false to the holy trust committed to them, and utterly unfit to train up the children of *this* generation. So far from urging the deficiency of teachers in this country, as a reason why women should keep out of the anti-slavery excitement, I would say to my sisters, if you wish to become pre-eminently qualified for the discharge of your arduous duties, come into the abolition ranks, enter this high school of morals, and drink from the deep fountains of philanthropy and Christian equality, whence the waters of healing are welling forth over wide desert wastes, and making glad the city of our God. Intellectual endowments are *good,* but a high standard of moral principle is *better,* is *essential.* As a nation, we have too long educated the *mind,* and left the *heart* a moral waste. We have fully and fearfully illustrated the truth of the Apostle's declaration: "Knowledge puffeth up." We have indeed been puffed up, vaunting ourselves in our mental endowments and national greatness. But we are beginning to realize, that it is "Righteousness which exalteth a nation."

Thou sayest, when a woman is asked to sign a petition, or join an Anti-Slavery Society, it is "for the purpose of contributing her measure of influence to keep up agitation in Congress, to promote the excitement of the North against the iniquities of the South, to coerce the South by fear, shame, anger, and a sense of odium, to do what she is determined not do to." Indeed! Are these the only motives presented to the daughters of America, for laboring in the glorious cause of Human Rights? Let us examine them. 1. "To keep up agitation in Congress." Yes—for I can adopt this language of Moore of Virginia, in the Legislature of that State in 1832: "I should regret at all times the existence of any unnecessary excitement in the country on any subject; but I confess, I see no reason to lament that which may have arisen on the present occasion. It is often necessary that there should be some excitement among the people, to induce them to turn their attention to questions deeply affecting the welfare of the Commonwealth; and *there never can arise any subject more worthy their attention, than that of the abolition of slavery.*" 2. "To promote the excitement of the North against the iniquities of the South." Yes, and against her own sinful copartnership in those iniquities. I believe the discussion of Human Rights at the North has already been of incalculable advantage to this country. It is producing the happiest influence upon the minds and hearts of those who are engaged in it; just such results as Thomas Clarkson tell us, were produced in England by the agitation of the subject there. Says he, "Of the immense advantages of this contest, I know not how to speak. Indeed, the very agitation of the question, which it involved, has been highly important. Never was the heart of man so expanded; never were its generous sympathies so generally and so perseveringly excited. These sympathies, thus called into existence, have been useful preservatives of national virtue." 3. "To coerce the South by fear, shame, anger, and a sense of odium." It is true, that I feel the imminent danger of the South so much, that I would fain "save them with fear, pulling them out of the fire"; for, if they ever are saved, they will indeed be "as a brand plucked out of the burning." Nor do I see any thing wrong in influencing slaveholders by a feeling of shame and odium, as well as by a sense of guilt. Why may not abolitionists speak some things *to their shame,* as the Apostle did to the Corinthians? As to anger, it is no design of ours to excite so wicked a passion. We cannot help it, if, in rejecting the truth, they become angry. Could Stephen help the anger of the Jews, when "they gnashed upon him with their teeth"?

But I had thought the principal motives urged by abolitionists were not these; but that they endeavored to excite men and women to active exertion—first, to cleanse *their own* hands of the sin of slavery, and secondly, to save the South, if possible, and the North, at any rate, from the impending judgments of heaven. The result of their mission in this country, cannot in the least affect the validity of that mission. Like Noah, they may preach in vain; if so, the destruction of the South can no more be attributed to them, than the destruction of the antediluvian world to him. "In vain," did I say? Oh no! The discussion of the rights of the slave has opened the way for the discussion of *other rights,* and the ultimate result will most certainly be, "the breaking of *every* yoke," the letting the oppressed of *every* grade and description go free,—an emancipation far more glorious than any the world has ever yet seen,—an introduction into that "liberty wherewith Christ hath made his people free."

I will now say a few words on thy remarks about Esther. Thou sayest, "When a woman is placed in similar circumstances, where death to herself and all her nation is one alternative, and there is nothing worse to fear, but something to hope as the other alternative, then she may safely follow such an example." In this sentence, thou hast conceded every thing I could wish, and proved beyond dispute just what I adduced this text to prove in my Appeal. I will explain myself. Look at the condition of our country—Church and State deeply involved in the enormous crime of slavery: ah! more—claiming the sacred volume, as our charter for the collar and chain. What then can we expect, but that the vials of divine wrath will be poured out upon a nation of oppressors and hypocrites? for we are loud in our professions of civil and ecclesiastical liberty. Now, as a Southerner, I know that reflecting slaveholders expect their peculiar institution to be overthrown in blood. Read the opinion of Moore of Virginia, as expressed by him in the House of Delegates in 1832:—"What must be the ultimate consequence of retaining the slaves amongst us? The answer to this enquiry is both obvious and appalling. It is, that *the time will come, and at no distant day, when we shall be involved in all the horrors of a servile war,* which will not end until both sides have suffered much, until the land shall everywhere be red with blood, and until the slaves or the whites are totally exterminated. If there be any truth in history, and if the time has not arrived when causes have ceased to produce their legitimate results, the dreadful catastrophe in which I have predicted that our slave system must result, if persisted in, *is as inevitable as any event which has already transpired."*

Here, then, is one alternative, and just as tremendous an alternative as that which was presented to the Queen of Persia. "There is *nothing worse* to fear" for the South, let the results of abolition efforts be what they may, whilst "there is something to hope as the other alternative"; because if she will receive the truth in the love of it, she may repent and be saved. So that, after all, according to thy own reasoning, the women of America "may safely follow such an example."

After endeavoring to show that woman has no moral right to exercise the right of petition for the dumb and stricken slave; no business to join, in any way, in the excitement which anti-slavery principles are producing in our country; no business to join abolition societies, &c. &c.; thou professest to tell our sisters what they are to do, in order to bring the system of slavery to an end. And now, my dear friend, what does all that thou hast said in many pages amount to? Why, that women are to exert their influence in private life, to allay the excitement which exists on this subject, and to quench the flame of sympathy in the hearts of their fathers, husbands, brothers and sons. Fatal delusion! Will Christian women heed such advice?

Hast thou ever asked thyself, what the slave would think of thy book, if he could read it? Dost thou know that, from the beginning to the end, not a word of compassion for *him* has fallen from thy pen? Recall, I pray, the memory of the hours which thou spent in writing it! Was the paper once moistened by the tear of pity? Did thy heart once swell with deep sympathy for thy sister *in bonds?* Did it once ascend to God in broken accents for the deliverance of the captive? Didst thou ever ask thyself, what the free man of color would think of it? Is it such an exhibition of slavery and prejudice, as will call down *his* blessings upon thy head? Hast thou thought of *these* things? or carest thou not for the blessings and the prayers of these our suffering brethren? Consider, I entreat, the reception given to thy book by the apologists of slavery. What meaneth that loud acclaim with which they hail it? Oh, listen and weep, and let thy repentings be kindled together, and speedily bring forth, I beseech thee, fruits meet for repentance, and henceforth show thyself faithful to Christ and his bleeding representative the slave.

I greatly fear that thy book might have been written just as well, hadst thou not had the heart of a woman. It bespeaks a superior intellect, but paralyzed and spell-bound by the sorcery of a worldly-minded expediency. Where, oh where, in its pages, are the outpouring of a soul overwhelmed with a sense of the heinous crimes of our nation, and the necessity of immediate repentance? Farewell! Perhaps on a dying bed thou mayest vainly wish that *"Miss Beecher on the Slave Question"* might perish with the mouldering hand which penned its cold and heartless pages. But I forbear, and in deep sadness of heart, but in tender love though I thus speak, I bid thee again, Farewell. Forgive me, if I have wronged thee, and pray for her who still feels like

Thy sister in the bonds of a common sisterhood,

A. E. Grimké.

P.S. Since preparing the foregoing letters for the press, I have been informed by a Bookseller in Providence, that some of thy books had been sent to him to sell last summer, and that one afternoon a number of southerners entered his store whilst they were lying on the counter. An elderly lady took up one of them and after turning over the pages for some time, she threw it down and remarked, here is a book written by the daughter of a northern dough face,* to apologise for our southern institutions—but for my part, I have a thousand times more respect for the Abolitionists, who openly denounce the system of slavery, than for those people, who in order to please us, cloak their real sentiments under such a garb as this. This southern lady, I have no doubt, expressed the sentiments of thousands of the most respectable slaveholders in our country—and thus, they will tell the North in bitter reproach for their sinful subserviency, after the lapse of a few brief years, when interest no

* A northerner with southern principles.

longer padlocks their lips. At present the South feels that she must at least *appear* to thank her northern apologists.

A. E. G.

*Sarah M. Grimké, Letters on the Equality of the Sexes and the Condition of Woman, addressed to Mary S. Parker, President of the Boston Female Anti-Slavery Society**

LETTER I
The Original Equality of Woman

Amesbury, [Mass.] 7th Mo. 11th, 1837.

My Dear Friend,—In attempting to comply with thy request to give my views on the Province of Woman, I feel that I am venturing on nearly untrodden ground, and that I shall advance arguments in opposition to a corrupt public opinion, and the perverted interpretation of Holy Writ, which has so universally obtained. But I am in search of truth; and no obstacle shall prevent my prosecuting that search, because I believe the welfare of the world will be materially advanced by every new discovery we make of the designs of Jehovah in the creation of woman. It is impossible that we can answer the purpose of our being, unless we understand that purpose. It is impossible that we should fulfil our duties, unless we comprehend them; or live up to our privileges, unless we know what they are.

In examining this important subject, I shall depend solely on the Bible to designate the sphere of woman, because I believe almost every thing that has been written on this subject, has been the result of a misconception of the simple truths revealed in the Scriptures, in conse-

* Boston, Mass.: Isaac Knapp, 1838; New York: Lenox Hill, 1970. The series commenced in the *New England Spectator* on July 19, 1837, p. 111; Letter III was also printed on the front page of *The Liberator,* October 6, 1837; the entire series was reprinted in that periodical in January and February 1838. I have chosen not to include five of the letters. Letters V–VII focus on the condition of women in Asia, Africa, and Europe, and were largely derived from Lydia Maria Child's *Brief History of the Condition of Women, in Various Ages and Nations* (New York: C. S. Francis, 1835) Letter X ("Heroism of Women—Women in Authority") and Letter IX ("Intellect of Women") are mainly lists of notable women, some of whose recounted deeds are now considered the stuff of legend, not fact. And I have inserted, between Letters XIV and XV, a letter that was written in the same format but, for reasons undiscovered, was included neither in the printed edition nor in the series when it was published by *The Liberator.* Whether it was published in the *New England Spectator* cannot be determined; only one issue of that periodical during the period July 19 to December 6 has survived. However, internal evidence in the unnumbered letter and the fact that Letter XV has a "Duties of Women" section indicates that this unnumbered letter probably was not printed in the *Spectator.* It was published in the *Advocate of Moral Reform,* January 1, 1838, pp. 3–5.

quence of the false translation of many passages of Holy Writ. My mind is entirely delivered from the superstitious reverence which is attached to the English version of the Bible. King James's translators certainly were not inspired. I therefore claim the original as my standard, *believing that to have been inspired,* and I also claim to judge for myself what is the meaning of the inspired writers, because I believe it to be the solemn duty of every individual to search the Scriptures for themselves, with the aid of the Holy Spirit, and not be governed by the views of any man, or set of men.

We must first view woman at the period of her creation. "And God said, Let us make man in our own image, after our likeness; and let them have dominion over the fish of the sea, and over the fowl of the air, and over the cattle, and over all the earth, and over every creeping thing that creepeth upon the earth. So God created man in his own image, in the image of God created he him, male and female created he them." In all this sublime description of the creation of man, (which is a generic term including man and woman,) there is not one particle of difference intimated as existing between them. They were both made in the image of God; dominion was given to both over every other creature, but not over each other. Created in perfect equality, they were expected to exercise the viceregency intrusted to them by their Maker, in harmony and love.

Let us pass on now to the recapitulation of the creation of man:—"The Lord God formed man of the dust of the ground, and breathed into his nostrils the breath of life; and man became a living soul. And the Lord God said, it is not good that man should be alone, I will make him an help meet for him." All creation swarmed with animated beings capable of natural affection, as we know they still are; it was not, therefore, merely to give man a creature susceptible of loving, obeying, and looking up to him, for all that the animals could do and did do. It was to give him a companion, *in all respects* his equal; one who was like himself *a free agent,* gifted with intellect and endowed with immortality; not a partaker merely of his animal gratifications, but able to enter into all his feelings as a moral and responsible being. If this had not been the case, how could she have been a help meet for him? I understand this as applying not only to the parties entering into the marriage contract, but to all men and women, because I believe God designed woman to be a help meet for man in every good and perfect work. She was a part of himself, as if Jehovah designed to make the oneness and identity of man and woman perfect and complete; and when the glorious work of their creation was finished, "the morning stars sang together, and all the sons of God shouted for joy."

This blissful condition was not long enjoyed by our first parents. Eve, it would seem from the history, was wandering alone amid the bowers of Paradise, when the serpent met with her. From her reply to Satan, it is evident that the command not to eat "of the tree that is in the midst of the garden," was given to both, although the term man was used when the prohibition was issued by God. "And the woman said unto the serpent, WE may eat of the fruit of the trees of the garden, but of the fruit of the tree which is in the midst of the garden, God hath said, YE shall not eat of it, neither shall YE touch it, lest YE die." Here the woman was exposed to temptation from a being with whom she was unacquainted. She had been accustomed to associate with her beloved partner, and to hold communion with God and with angels; but of satanic intelligence, she was in all probability entirely ignorant. Through the subtlety of the serpent, she was beguiled. And "when she saw that the tree was good for food, and that it was pleasant to the eyes, and a tree to be desired to make one wise, she took of the fruit thereof and did eat."

We next find Adam involved in the same sin, not through the instrumentality of a super-natural agent, but through that of his equal, a being whom he must have known was liable to transgress the divine command, because he must have felt that he was himself a free agent, and that he was restrained from disobedience only by the exercise of faith and love towards his Creator. Had Adam tenderly reproved his wife, and endeavored to lead her to repentance instead of sharing in her guilt, I should be much more ready to accord to man that superiority which he claims; but as the facts stand disclosed by the sacred historian, it appears to me that to say the least, there was as much weakness exhibited by Adam as by Eve. They both fell from innocence, and consequently from happiness, *but not from equality*.

Let us next examine the conduct of this fallen pair, when Jehovah interrogated them respecting their fault. They both frankly confessed their guilt. "The man said, the woman whom thou gavest to be with me, she gave me of the tree and I did eat. And the woman said, the serpent beguiled me and I did eat." And the Lord God said unto the woman, "Thou wilt be subject unto thy husband, and he will rule over thee." That this did not allude to the subjection of woman to man is manifest, because the same mode of expression is used in speaking to Cain of Abel. The truth is that the curse, as it is termed, which was pronounced by Jehovah upon woman, is a simple prophecy. The Hebrew, like the French language, uses the same word to express shall and will. Our translators having been accustomed to exercise lordship over their wives, and seeing only through the medium of a perverted judgment, very naturally, though I think not very learnedly or very kindly, translated it *shall* instead of *will,* and thus converted a prediction to Eve into a command to Adam; for observe, it is addressed to the woman and not to the man. The consequence of the fall was an immediate struggle for dominion, and Jehovah foretold which would gain the ascendency; but as he created them in his image, as that image manifestly was not lost by the fall, because it is urged in Gen. 9:6, as an argument why the life of man should not be taken by his fellow man, there is no reason to suppose that sin produced any distinction between them as moral, intellectual and responsible beings. Man might just as well have endeavored by hard labor to fulfil the prophecy, thorns and thistles will the earth bring forth to thee, as to pretend to accomplish the other, "he will rule over thee," by asserting dominion over his wife.

> Authority usurped from God, not given.
> He gave him only over beast, flesh, fowl,
> Dominion absolute: that right he holds
> By God's donation: but man o'er woman
> He made not Lord, such title to himself
> Reserving, human left from human free.

Here then I plant myself. God created us equal;—he created us free agents;—he is our Lawgiver, our King and our Judge, and to him alone is woman bound to be in subjection, and to him alone is she accountable for the use of those talents with which Her Heavenly Father has entrusted her. One is her Master even Christ.

Thine for the oppressed in the bonds of womanhood,

Sarah M. Grimké.

LETTER II

Woman Subject Only To God

Newburyport, [Mass.] 7th mo. 17, 1837.

My Dear Sister,—In my last, I traced the creation and the fall of woman from that state of purity and happiness which their beneficent

Creator designed them to enjoy. As they were one in transgression, their chastisement was the same. "So God drove out *the man,* and he placed at the East of the garden of Eden a cherubim and a flaming sword, which turned every way to keep the way of the tree of life." We now behold them expelled from Paradise, fallen from their original loveliness, but still bearing on their foreheads the image and superscription of Jehovah; still invested with high moral responsibilities, intellectual powers, and immortal souls. They had incurred the penalty of sin, they were shorn of their innocence, but they stood on the same platform side by side, acknowledging *no superior* but their God. Notwithstanding what has been urged, woman I am aware stands charged to the present day with having brought sin into the world. I shall not repel the charge by any counter assertions, although, as was before hinted, Adam's ready acquiescence with his wife's proposal, does not savor much of that superiority *in strength of mind,* which is arrogated by man. Even admitting that Eve was the greater sinner, it seems to me man might be satisfied with the dominion he has claimed and exercised for nearly six thousand years, and that more true nobility would be manifested by endeavoring to raise the fallen and invigorate the weak, than by keeping woman in subjection. But I ask no favors for my sex. I surrender not our claim to equality. All I ask of our brethren is, that they will take their feet from off our necks and permit us to stand upright on that ground which God designed us to occupy. If he has not given us the rights which have, as I conceive, been wrested from us, we shall soon give evidence of our inferiority, and shrink back into that obscurity, which the high souled magnanimity of man has assigned us as our appropriate sphere.

As I am unable to learn from sacred writ when woman was deprived by God of her equality with man, I shall touch upon a few points in the Scriptures, which demonstrate that no supremacy was granted to man. When God had destroyed the world, except Noah and his family, by the deluge, he renewed the grant formerly made to man, and again gave him dominion over every beast of the earth, every fowl of the air, over all that moveth upon the earth, and over all the fishes of the sea; into his hands they were delivered. But was woman, bearing the image of her God, placed under the dominion of her fellow man? Never! Jehovah could not surrender his authority to govern his own immortal creatures into the hands of a being, whom he knew, and whom his whole history proved, to be unworthy of a trust so sacred and important. God could not do it, because it is a direct contravention of his law, "Thou shalt worship the Lord thy God, and *him only* shalt thou serve." If Jehovah had appointed man as the guardian, or teacher of woman, he would certainly have given some intimation of this surrender of his own prerogative. But so far from it, we find the commands of God invariably the same to man and woman; and not the slightest intimation is given in a single passage of the Bible, that God designed to point woman to man as her instructor. The tenor of his language always is, "Look unto ME, and be ye saved, all the ends of the earth, for I am God, and there is none else."

The lust of dominion was probably the first effect of the fall; and as there was no other intelligent being over whom to exercise it, woman was the first victim of this unhallowed passion. We afterwards see it exhibited by Cain in the murder of his brother, by Nimrod in his becoming a mighty hunter of men, and setting up a kingdom over which to reign. Here we see the origin of that Upas* of slavery, which sprang up immediately after the fall, and has spread its pestilential branches over the whole face of the known world. All history attests that man has subjected woman to his will, used her as a means to promote his selfish gratification, to minister to his sensual pleasures, to be instrumental in promoting his comfort; but never has he desired to elevate her to that rank she was created to fill. He has done all he could to debase and enslave her mind; and now he looks triumphantly on the ruin he has wrought, and says, the being he has thus deeply injured is his inferior.

Woman has been placed by John Quincy Adams, side by side with the slave, whilst he was contending for the right side of petition. I thank him for ranking us with the oppressed; for I shall not find it difficult to show, that in all ages and countries, not even excepting enlightened republic America, woman has more or less been made a *means* to promote the welfare of man, without due regard to her own happiness, and the glory of God as the end of her creation.

During the *patriarchal* ages, we find men and women engaged in the same employments. Abraham and Sarah both assisted in preparing the food which was to be set before the three men, who visited them in the plains of Mamre; but although their occupations were similar, Sarah was not permitted to enjoy the society of the holy visitant; and as we learn from Peter, that she "obeyed Abraham, calling him Lord," we may

* A tree of tropical Asia that yields a juice used as arrow poison.

presume he exercised dominion over her. We shall pass on now to Rebecca. In her history, we find another striking illustration of the low estimation in which woman was held. Eleazur is sent to seek a wife for Isaac. He finds Rebecca going down to the well to fill her pitcher. He accosts her; and she replies with all humility, "Drink, my lord." How does he endeavor to gain her favor and confidence? Does he approach her as a dignified creature, whom he was about to invite to fill an important station in his master's family, as the wife of his only son? No. He offered incense to her vanity, and "he took a golden ear-ring of half a shekel weight, and two bracelets for her hands of ten shekels weight of gold," and gave them to Rebecca.

The cupidity of man soon led him to regard woman as property, and hence we find them sold to those, who wished to marry them, as far as appears, without any regard to those sacred rights which belong to woman, as well as to man in the choice of a companion. That women were a profitable kind of property, we may gather from the description of a virtuous woman in the last chapter of Proverbs. To work willingly with her hands, to open her hands to the poor, to clothe herself with silk and purple, to look well to her household, to make fine linen and sell it, to deliver girdles to the merchant, and not to eat the bread of idleness, seems to have constituted in the view of Solomon, the perfection of a woman's character and achievements. "The spirit of that age was not favorable to intellectual improvement; but as there were wise men who formed exceptions to the general ignorance, and were destined to guide the world into more advanced states, so there was a corresponding proportion of wise women; and among the Jews, as well as other nations, we find a strong tendency to believe that women were in more immediate connection with heaven than men."—L. M. Child's Con. of Woman.* If there be any truth in this tradition, I am at a loss to imagine in what the superiority of man consists.

Thine in the bonds of womanhood,

Sarah M. Grimké.

* Lydia Maria Child, *Brief History of the Condition of Women, in Various Ages and Nations.*

Pastoral Letter: The General Association of Massachusetts to the Churches Under Their Care

[New England Spectator, July 12, 1837, pp. 106–107.]

III.–We invite your attention to the dangers which at present seem to threaten the female character with wide spread and permanent injury.

The appropriate duties and influence of women are clearly stated in the New Testament. Those duties and that influence are unobtrusive and private, but the sources of mighty power. When the mild, dependant [*sic*], softening influence of woman upon the sternness of man's opinion is fully exercised, society feels the effects of it in a thousand forms. The power of woman is in her dependence, flowing from the consciousness of that weakness which God has given her for her protection, and which keeps her in those departments of life that form the character of individuals and of the nation. There are social influences which females use in promoting piety and the great objects of Christian benevolence which we cannot too highly commend. We appreciate the unostentatious prayers and efforts of woman in advancing the cause of religion at home and abroad; in Sabbath schools; in leading religious inquirers to the pastors for instruction; and in all such associated effort as becomes the modesty of her sex; and earnestly hope that she may abound more and more in these labors of piety and love.

But when she assumes the place and tone of man as a public reformer, our care and protection of her seem unnecessary; we put ourselves in self-defence against her; she yields the power which God has given her for protection, and her character becomes unnatural. If the vine, whose strength and beauty is to lean upon the trellis and half conceal its clusters, thinks to assume the independence and the overshading nature of the elm, it will not only cease to bear fruit, but fall in shame and dishonor into the dust. We cannot, therefore, but regret the mistaken conduct of those who encourage females to bear an obtrusive and ostentatious part in measures of reform, and countenance any of that sex who so far forget themselves as to itinerate in the character of public lecturers and teachers. We especially deplore the intimate acquaintance and promiscuous conversation of females with regard to things "which ought not to be named"; by which that modesty and delicacy which is the charm of domestic life, and which constitutes the true influence of woman in society is consumed, and the way opened, as we apprehend, for degeneracy and ruin. We say these things, not to discourage proper advances against sin, but to secure such reformation as we believe is Scriptural, and will be permanent.

LETTER III

The Pastoral Letter of the General Association of Congregational Ministers of Massachusetts

Haverhill, [Mass.] 7th Mo. 1837.

Dear Friend,—When I last addressed thee, I had not seen the Pastoral Letter of the General Association. It has since fallen into my hands, and I must digress from my intention of exhibiting the condition of women in different parts of the world, in order to make some remarks on this extraordinary document. I am persuaded that when the minds of men and women become emancipated from the thraldom of superstition and "traditions of men," the sentiments contained in the Pastoral letter will be recurred to with as much astonishment as the opinions of Cotton Mather* and other distinguished men of his day, on the subject of witchcraft; nor will it be deemed less wonderful, that a body of divines should gravely assemble and endeavor to prove that woman has no right to "open her mouth for the dumb," than it now is that judges should have sat on the trials of witches, and solemnly condemned nineteen persons and one dog to death for witchcraft.

But to the letter. It says, "We invite your attention to the dangers which at present seem to threaten the FEMALE CHARACTER with wide-spread and permanent injury." I rejoice that they have called the attention of my sex to this subject, because I believe if woman investigates it, she will soon discover that danger is impending, though from a totally different source from that which the Association apprehends,—danger from those who, having long held the reins of *usurped* authority, are unwilling to permit us to fill that sphere which God created us to move in, and who have entered into league to crush the immortal mind of woman. I rejoice, because I am persuaded that the rights of woman, like the rights of slaves, need only be examined to be understood and

* Cotton Mather (1663–1728), a prominent Congregational minister and writer, believed in diabolical possession and wrote several works concerning it. During the Salem witch persecution (1692), he did not protest; he simply urged the prosecutors and triers to examine the evidence carefully, avoid "spectral evidence," and punish the guilty vigorously, although not necessarily by execution. It was not until 1702 that he wrote that the methods of the court had been unfair and that innocent persons had been condemned.

asserted, even by some of those, who are not endeavoring to smother the irrepressible desire for mental and spiritual freedom which glows in the breast of many, who hardly dare to speak their sentiments.

"The appropriate duties and influence of women are clearly stated in the New Testament. Those duties are unobtrusive and private, but the sources of *mighty power.* When the mild, *dependent,* softening influence of woman upon the sternness of man's opinions is fully exercised, society feels the effects of it in a thousand ways." No one can desire more earnestly than I do, that woman may move exactly in the sphere which her Creator has assigned her; and I believe her having been displaced from that sphere has introduced confusion into the world. It is, therefore, of vast importance to herself and to all the rational creation, that she should ascertain what are her duties and her privileges as a responsible and immortal being. The New Testament has been referred to, and I am willing to abide by its decision, but must enter my protest against the false translation of some passages by the MEN who did that work, and against the perverted interpretation by the MEN who understood to write commentaries thereon. I am inclined to think, when we are admitted to the honor of studying Greek and Hebrew, we shall produce some various readings of the Bible a little different from those we now have.

The Lord Jesus defines the duties of his followers in his Sermon on the Mount. He lays down grand principles by which they should be governed, without any reference to sex or condition:—"Ye are the light of the world. A city that is set on a hill cannot be hid. Neither do men light a candle and put it under a bushel, but on a candlestick, and it giveth light unto all that are in the house. Let your light so shine before men, that they may see your good works, and glorify your Father which is in Heaven." I follow him through all his precepts, and find him giving the same directions to women as to men, never even referring to the distinction now so strenuously insisted upon between masculine and feminine virtues: this is one of the anti-christian "traditions of men" which are taught instead of the "commandments of God." Men and women were CREATED EQUAL; they are both moral and accountable beings, and whatever is *right* for man to do, is *right* for woman.

But the influence of woman, says the Association, is to be private and unobtrusive; her light is not to shine before man like that of her brethren; but she is passively to let the lords of the creation, as they call themselves, put the bushel over it, lest peradventure it might appear that the world has been benefitted by the rays of *her* candle. So that her quenched light, according to their judgment, will be of more use than if it were set on the candlestick. "Her influence is the source of mighty power." This has ever been the flattering language of man since he laid aside the whip as a means to keep woman in subjection. He spares her body; but the war he has waged against her mind, her heart, and her soul, has been no less destructive to her as a moral being. How monstrous, how anti-christian, is the doctrine that woman is to be dependent on man! Where, in all the sacred Scriptures, is this taught? Alas! she has too well learned the lesson which MAN has labored to teach her. She has surrendered her dearest RIGHTS, and been satisfied with the privileges which man has assumed to grant her; she has been amused with the show of power, whilst man has absorbed all the reality into himself. He has adorned the creature whom God gave him as a companion, with baubles and gewgaws, turned her attention to personal attractions, offered incense to her vanity, and made her the instrument of his selfish gratification, a plaything to please his eye and amuse his hours of leisure. "Rule by obedience and by submission sway," or in other words, study to be a hypocrite, pretend to submit, but gain your point, has been the code of household morality which woman has been taught. The poet has sung, in sickly strains, the loveliness of woman's dependence upon man, and now we find it re-echoed by those who profess to teach the religion of the Bible. God says, "Cease ye from man whose breath is in his nostrils, for wherein is he to be accounted of?" Man says, depend upon me. God says, "HE will teach us of his ways." Man says, believe it or not, I am to be your teacher. This doctrine of dependence upon man is utterly at variance with the doctrine of the Bible. In that book I find nothing like the softness of woman, nor the sternness of man: both are equally commanded to bring forth the fruits of the Spirit, love, meekness, gentleness, &c.

But we are told, "the power of woman is in her dependence, flowing from a consciousness of that weakness which God has given her for her protection." If physical weakness is alluded to, I cheerfully concede the superiority; if brute force is what my brethren are claiming, I am willing to let them have all the honor they desire; but if they mean to intimate, that mental or moral weakness belongs to woman, more than to man, I utterly disclaim the charge. Our powers of mind have been crushed, as far as man could do it, our sense of morality has been impaired by his interpretation of our duties; but no where does God say that he made any distinction between us, as moral and intelligent beings.

"We appreciate," say the Association, "the *unostentatious* prayers and efforts of woman in advancing the cause of religion at home and abroad, in leading religious inquirers TO THE PASTOR for instruction." Several points here demand attention. If public prayers and public efforts are necessarily ostentatious, then "Anna the prophetess, (or preacher,) who departed not from the temple, but served God with fastings and prayers night and day," "and spake of Christ to all them that looked for redemption in Israel," was ostentatious in her efforts. Then, the apostle Paul encourages women to be ostentatious in their efforts to spread the gospel, when he gives them directions how they should appear, when engaged in praying, or preaching in the public assemblies. Then, the whole association of Congregational ministers are ostentatious, in the efforts they are making in preaching and praying to convert souls. But woman may be permitted to lead religious inquirers to the PASTORS for instruction. Now this is assuming that all pastors are better qualified to give instruction than woman. This I utterly deny. I have suffered too keenly from the teaching of man, to lead any one to him for instruction. The Lord Jesus says,—"Come unto me and learn of me." He points his followers to no man; and when woman is made the favored instrument of rousing a sinner to his lost and helpless condition, she has no right to substitute any teacher for Christ; all she has to do is, to turn the contrite inquirer to the "Lamb of God which taketh away the sins of the world." More souls have probably been lost by going down to Egypt for help, and by trusting in man in the early stages of religious experience, than by any other error. Instead of the petition being offered to God,—"Lead me in thy truth, and TEACH me, for thou art thc God of my salvation," —instead of relying on the precious promises—"What man is he that feareth the Lord? him shall HE TEACH in the way that he shall choose,"— "I will instruct thee and TEACH thee in the way which thou shalt go—I will guide thee with mine eye"—the young convert is directed to go to man, as if he were in the place of God, and his instructions essential to an advancement in the path of righteousness. That woman can have but a poor conception of the privilege of being taught of God, what he alone can teach, who would turn the "religious inquirer aside" from the fountain of living waters, where he might slake his thirst for spiritual instruction, to those broken cisterns which can hold no water, and therefore cannot satisfy the panting spirit. The business of men and women, who are ["]ORDAINED OF GOD to preach the unsearchable riches of Christ" to a lost and perishing world, is to lead souls to Christ, and not to Pastors for instruction.

The General Association say, that "when woman assumes the place and tone of man as a public reformer, our care and protection of her seem unnecessary; we put ourselves in self-defence against her, and her character becomes unnatural." Here again the unscriptural notion is held up, that there is a distinction between the duties of men and women as moral beings; that what is virtue in man, is vice in woman; and women who dare to obey the command of Jehovah, "Cry aloud, spare not, lift up thy voice like a trumpet, and show my people their transgression," are threatened with having the protection of the brethren withdrawn. If this is all they do, we shall not even know the time when our chastisement is inflicted; our trust is in the Lord Jehovah, and in him is everlasting strength. The motto of woman, when she is engaged in the great work of public reformation should be,—"The Lord is my light and my salvation; whom shall I fear? The Lord is the strength of my life; of whom shall I be afraid?" She must feel, if she feels rightly, that she is fulfilling one of the important duties laid upon her as an accountable being, and that her character, instead of being "unnatural," is in exact accordance with the will of Him to whom, and to no other, she is responsible for the talents and the gifts confided to her. As to the pretty simile, introduced into the "Pastoral Letter," "If the vine whose strength and beauty is to lean upon the trellis work, and half conceal its clusters, thinks to assume the independence and the overshadowing nature of the elm," &c. I shall only remark that it might well suit the poet's fancy, who sings of sparkling eyes and coral lips, and knights in armor clad; but it seems to me utterly inconsistent with the dignity of a Christian body, to endeavor to draw such an anti-scriptural distinction between men and women. Ah! how many of my sex feel in the dominion, thus unrighteously exercised over them, under the gentle appellation of *protection,* that what they have leaned upon has proved a broken reed at best, and oft a spear.

Thine in the bonds of womanhood,

Sarah M. Grimké.

LETTER IV
Social Intercourse of the Sexes

Andover, 7th Mo. 27th, 1837.

My Dear Friend,—Before I proceed with the account of that oppression which woman has suffered in every age and country from her *protector,* man, permit me to offer for your consideration, some views relative to the social intercourse of the sexes. Nearly the whole of this intercourse is, in my apprehension, derogatory to man and woman, as moral and intellectual beings. We approach each other, and mingle with each other, under the constant pressure of a feeling that we are of different sexes; and, instead of regarding each other only in the light of immortal creatures, the mind is fettered by the idea which is early and industriously infused into it, that we must never forget the distinction between male and female. Hence our intercourse, instead of being elevated and refined, is generally calculated to excite and keep alive the lowest propensities of our nature. Nothing, I believe, has tended more to destroy the true dignity of woman, than the fact that she is approached by man in the character of a female. The idea that she is sought as an intelligent and heaven-born creature, whose society will cheer, refine and elevate her companion, and that she will receive the same blessings she confers, is rarely held up to her view. On the contrary, man almost always addresses himself to the weakness of woman. By flattery, by an appeal to her passions, he seeks access to her heart; and when he has gained her affections, he uses her as the instrument of his pleasure—the minister of his temporal comfort. He furnishes himself with a housekeeper, whose chief business is in the kitchen, or the nursery. And whilst he goes abroad and enjoys the means of improvement afforded by collision of intellect with cultivated minds, his wife is condemned to draw nearly all her instruction from books, if she has time to peruse them; and if not, from her meditations, whilst engaged in those domestic duties, which are necessary for the comfort of her lord and master.

Surely no one who contemplates, with the eye of a Christian philosopher, the design of God in the creation of woman, can believe that she is now fulfilling that design. The literal translation of the word "helpmeet" is a helper like unto himself; it is so rendered in the Septuagint, and manifestly signifies a companion. Now I believe it will be impossible for woman to fill the station assigned her by God, until her brethren mingle with her as an equal, as a moral being; and lose, in the dignity of her immortal nature, and in the fact of her bearing like himself the image of superscription of her God, the idea of her being a female. The apostle beautifully remarks, 'As many of you as have been baptized into Christ, have put on Christ. There is neither Jew nor Greek, there is neither bond nor free, there is neither *male* nor *female;* for ye are all one in Christ Jesus.' Until our intercourse is purified by the forgetfulness of sex,—

until we rise above the present low and sordid views which entwine themselves around our social and domestic interchange of sentiment and feelings, we never can derive that benefit from each other's society which it is the design of our Creator that we should. Man has inflicted an unspeakable injury upon woman, by holding up to her view her animal nature, and placing in the background her moral and intellectual being. Woman has inflicted an injury upon herself by submitting to be thus regarded; and she is now called upon to rise from the station where *man,* not God, has placed her, and claim those sacred and inalienable rights, as a moral and responsible being, with which her Creator has invested her.

What but these views, so derogatory to the character of woman, could have called forth the remark contained in the Pastoral Letter? "We especially deplore the intimate acquaintance and promiscuous conversation of *females* with regard to things 'which ought not to be named,' by which that modesty and delicacy, which is the charm of domestic life, and which constitutes the true influence of woman, is consumed." How wonderful that the conceptions of man relative to woman are so low, that he cannot perceive that she may converse on any subject connected with the improvement of her species, without swerving in the least from that modesty which is one of her greatest virtues! Is it designed to insinuate that woman should possess a greater degree of modesty than man? This idea I utterly reprobate. Or is it supposed that woman cannot go into scenes of misery, the necessary result of those very things, which the Pastoral letter says ought not to be named, for the purpose of moral reform, without becoming contaminated by those with whom she thus mingles?

This is a false position; and I presume has grown out of the never-forgotten distinction of male and female. The woman who goes forth, clad in the panoply of God, to stem the tide of iniquity and misery, which she beholds rolling through our land, goes not forth to her labor of love as a female. She goes as the dignified messenger of Jehovah, and all she does and says must be done and said irrespective of sex. She is in duty bound to communicate with all, who are able and willing to aid her in saving her fellow creatures, both men and women, for that destruction which awaits them.

So far from woman losing any thing of the purity of her mind, by visiting the wretched victims of vice in their miserable abodes, by talking with them, or of them, she becomes more and more elevated and refined in her feelings and views. While laboring to cleanse the minds of others from the malaria of moral pollution, her own heart becomes purified, and her soul rises to nearer communion with her God. Such a woman is infinitely better qualified to fulfil the duties of a wife and a mother, than the woman whose *false delicacy* leads her to shun her fallen sister and brother, and shrink from *naming those sins* which she knows exist, but which she is too fastidious to labor by deed and by word to exterminate. Such a woman feels, when she enters upon the marriage relation, that God designed that relation not to debase her to a level with the animal creation, but to increase the happiness and dignity of his creatures. Such a woman comes to the important task of training her children in the nurture and admonition of the Lord, with a soul filled with the greatness of the beings committed to her charge. She sees in her children, creatures bearing the image of God; and she approaches them with reverence, and treats them at all times as moral and accountable beings. Her own mind being purified and elevated, she instils into her children that genuine religion which induces them to keep the commandments of God. Instead of ministering with ceaseless care to their sensual appetites, she teaches them to be temperate in all things. She can converse with her children on any subject relating to their duty to God, can point their attention to those vices which degrade and brutify human nature, without in the least defiling her own mind or theirs. She views herself, and teaches her children to regard themselves as moral beings; and in all their intercourse with their fellow men, to lose the animal nature of man and woman, in the recognition of that immortal mind wherewith Jehovah has blessed and enriched them.

Thine in the bonds of womanhood,

Sarah M. Grimké.

LETTER VIII

On the Condition of Women in the United States

Brookline, [Mass.] 1837.

My Dear Sister,—

I have now taken a brief survey of the condition of women in various parts of the world. I regret that my time has been so much occupied by other things, that I have been unable to bestow that attention upon the subject which it merits, and that my constant change of place has prevented me from having access to books, which might probably have assisted me in this part of my work. I hope that the principles I have asserted will claim the attention of some of my sex, who may be able to bring into view, more thoroughly than I have done, the situation and degradation of woman. I shall now proceed to make a few remarks on the condition of women in my own country.

During the early part of my life, my lot was cast among the butterflies of the *fashionable* world; and of this class of women, I am constrained to say, both from experience and observation, that their education is miserably deficient; that they are taught to regard marriage as the one thing needful, the only avenue to distinction; hence to attract the notice and win the attentions of men, by their external charms, is the chief business of fashionable girls. They seldom think that men will be allured by intellectual acquirements, because they find, that where any mental superiority exists, a woman is generally shunned and regarded as stepping out of her "appropriate sphere," which, in their view, is to dress, to dance, to set out to the best possible advantage her person, to read the novels which inundate the press, and which do more to destroy her character as a rational creature, than any thing else. Fashionable women regard themselves, and are regarded by men, as pretty toys or as mere instruments of pleasure; and the vacuity of mind, the heartlessness, the frivolity which is the necessary result of this false and debasing estimate of women, can only be fully understood by those who have mingled in the folly and wickedness of fashionable life; and who have been called from such pursuits by the voice of the Lord Jesus, inviting their weary and heavy laden souls to come unto Him and learn of Him, that they may learn the high and holy purposes of their creation, and consecrate themselves unto the service of God; and not, as is now the case, to the pleasure of man.

There is another and much more numerous class in this country, who are withdrawn by education or circumstances from the circle of fashionable amusements, but who are brought up with the dangerous and absurd idea, that *marriage* is a kind of preferment; and that to be able to keep their husband's house, and render his situation comfortable, is the end of her being. Much that she does and says and thinks is done in reference to this situation; and to be married is too often held up to the view of girls as the sine qua non of human happiness and human existence. For this purpose more than for any other, I verily believe the majority of girls are trained. This is demonstrated by the imperfect education which is bestowed upon them, and the little pains taken to cultivate their minds, after they leave school, by the little time allowed them for reading, and by the idea being constantly inculcated, that although all household concerns should be attended to with scrupulous punctuality at particular seasons, the improvement of their intellectual capacities is only a secondary consideration, and may serve as an occupation to fill up the odds and ends of time. In most families, it is considered a matter of far more consequence to call a girl off from making a pie, or a pudding, than to interrupt her whilst engaged in her studies. This mode of training necessarily exalts, in their view, the animal above the intellectual and spiritual nature, and teaches women to regard themselves as a kind of machinery, necessary to keep the domestic engine in order, but of little value as the *intelligent* companions of men.

Let no one think, from these remarks, that I regard a knowledge of housewifery as beneath the acquisition of women. Far from it: I believe that a complete knowledge of household affairs is an indispensable requisite in a woman's education,—that by the mistress of a family, whether married or single, doing her duty thoroughly and *understandingly,* the happiness of the family is increased to an incalculable degree, as well as a vast amount of time and money saved. All I complain of is, that our education consists so almost exclusively in culinary and other manual operations. I do long to see the time, when it will no longer be necessary for women to expend so many precious hours in furnishing "a well spread table," but that their husbands will forego some of the accustomed indulgences in this way, and encourage their wives to devote some portion of their time to mental cultivation, even at the expense of having to dine sometimes on baked potatoes, or bread and butter.

I believe the sentiment expressed by author of "Live and Let Live,"* is true:

> Other things being equal, a woman of the highest mental endowments will always be the best housekeeper, for domestic economy, is a science that bring into action the qualities of the mind, as well as the graces of the heart. A quick perception, judgment, discrimination, decision and order are high attributes of mind, and all are in a daily exercise in the well ordering of a family. If a sensible women, an intellectual woman, a woman of genius, is not a good

* [Catharine Maria Sedgwick], *Live and let live; or, Domestic service illustrated. By the author of "Hope Leslie," . . . &C.* (New York: Harper, 1837). Catharine Sedgwick (1789–1867) was one of the most popular American female novelists in the ante-bellum era. She wrote six novels, mainly sentimental, historical romances, and a large number of moral tracts and didactic tales. Raised a Calvinist, she became a disciple of William Ellery Channing and an advocate of benevolent reform. She hated slavery but thought that the abolitionists were too extreme. She also believed that a woman's place was in the home.

housewife, it is not because she is either, or all of those, but because there is some deficiency in her character, or some omission of duty which should make her very humble, instead of her indulging in any secret self-complacency on account of a certain superiority, which only aggravates her fault.

The influence of women over the minds and character of *children* of both sexes, is allowed to be far greater than that of men. This being the case by the very ordering of nature, women should be prepared by education for the performance of their sacred duties as mothers and as sisters. A late American writer, speaking on this subject,* says in reference to an article in the Westminster Review:

> I agree entirely with the writer in the high estimate which he places on female education, and have long since been satisfied, that the subject not only merits, but *imperiously demands* a thorough reconsideration. The whole scheme must, in my opinion, be reconstructed. The great elements of usefulness and duty are too little attended to. Women ought, in my view of the subject, to approach to the best education now given to men, (I except mathematics and the classics,) far more I believe than has ever yet been attempted. Give me a host of educated, pious mothers and sisters, and I will do more to revolutionize a country, in moral and religious taste, in manners and in social virtues and intellectual cultivation, than I can possibly do, in double or treble the time, with a similar host of educated men. I cannot but think that the miserable condition of the great body of the people in all ancient communities, is to be ascribed in a very great degree to the degradation of women.

There is another way in which the general opinion, that women are inferior to men, is manifested, that bears with tremendous effect on the laboring class, and indeed on almost all who are obliged to earn a subsistence, whether it be by mental or physical exertion—I allude to the disproportionate value set on the time and labor of men and of women. A man who is engaged in teaching, can always, I believe, command a higher price for tuition than a woman—even when he teaches the same branches, and is not in any respect superior to the woman. This I know is the case in boarding and other schools with which I have been acquainted, and it is so in every occupation in which

* Thomas S. Grimké. [Footnote in original.]

the sexes engaged indiscriminately. As for example, in tailoring, a man has twice, or three times as much for making a waistcoat or pantaloons as a woman, although the work done by each may be equally good. In those employments which are peculiar to women, their time is estimated at only half the value of that of men. A woman who goes out to wash, works as hard in proportion as a wood sawyer, or a coal heaver, but she is not generally able to make more than half as much by a day's work. The low remuneration which women receive for their work, has claimed the attention of a few philanthropists, and I hope it will continue to do so until some remedy is applied for this enormous evil. I have known a widow, left with four or five children, to provide for, unable to leave home because her helpless babes demanded her attention, compelled to earn a scanty subsistence, by making coarse shirts at 12 1-2 cents a piece, or by taking in washing, for which she was paid by some wealthy persons 12 1-2 cents per dozen. All these things evince the low estimation in which woman is held. There is yet another and more disastrous consequence arising from this unscriptural notion—women being educated, from earliest childhood, to regard themselves as inferior creatures, have not that self-respect which conscious equality would engender, and hence when their virture is assailed, they yield to temptation with facility, under the idea that it rather exalts than debases them, to be connected with a superior being.

There is another class of women in this country, to whom I cannot refer, without feelings of the deepest shame and sorrow. I allude to our female slaves. Our southern cities are whelmed beneath a tide of pollution; the virtue of female slaves is wholly at the mercy of irresponsible tyrants, and women are bought and sold in our slave markets, to gratify the brutal lust of those who bear the name of Christians. In our slave States, if amid all her degradation and ignorance, a women desires to preserve her virtue unsullied, she is either bribed or whipped into compliance, or if she dares resist her seducer, her life by the laws of some of the slave States may be, and has actually been sacrificed to the fury of disappointed passion. Where such laws do not exist, the power which is necessarily vested in the master over his property, leaves the defenceless slave entiely at his mercy, and the sufferings of some females on this account, both physical and mental, are intense. Mr. [James H.] Gholson [New Brunswick County], in the House of Delegates of Virginia, in 1832, said, "He really had been under the impression that he owned his slaves. He had lately purchased four women and ten children, in whom he thought he had obtained a great bargain; for he supposed they were his own property, *as were his brood mares.*" But even if any laws existed in the United States, as in Athens formerly, for the protection of female slaves, they would be null and void, because the evidence of a colored person is not admitted against a white, in any of our Courts of Justice in the slave States. "In Athens, if a female slave had cause to complain of any want of respect to the laws of modesty, she could seek the protection of the temple, and demand a change of owners; and such appeals were never discountenanced, or neglected by the magistrate." In Christian America, the slave has no refuge from unbridled cruelty and lust.

S. A. Forrall,* speaking of the state of morals at the South, says, "Negresses when young and likely, are often employed by the planter, or his friends, to administer to their sensual desires. This frequently is a matter of speculation, for if the offspring, a mulatto, be a handsome female, 800 or 1000 dollars may be obtained for her in the New Orleans market. It is an occurrence of no uncommon nature to see a Christian father sell his own daughter, and the brother his own sister." The following is copied by the N. Y. Evening Star from the Picayune, a paper published in New Orleans. "A very beautiful girl, belonging to the estate of John French, a deceased gambler at new Orleans, was sold a few days since for the round sum of $7,000. An ugly-looking bachelor named Gouch, a member of the Council of one of the Principalities, was the purchaser. The girl is a brunette; remarkable for her beauty and intelligence, and there was considerable contention, who should be the purchaser. She was, however, persuaded to accept Gouch, he having made her princely promises." I will add but one more from the numerous testimonies respecting the degradation of female slaves, and the licentiousness of the South. It is from the Circular of the Kentucky Union, for the moral and religious improvement of the colored race. "To the female character among our black population, we cannot allude but with feelings of the bitterest shame. A similar condition of moral pollution and utter disregard of a pure and virtuous reputation, is to be found *only without the pale of Christendom.* That such a state of society should exist in a Christian nation, claiming to be the most enlightened upon earth, without calling forth any *particular attention* to its existence, though ever before our eyes and *in our* families, is a moral phenomenon at once unaccountable and disgraceful." Nor does the colored woman suffer alone: the moral purity of the white woman is deeply contaminated. In the daily habit of seeing the virtue of her enslaved sister sacrificed without hesitancy or remorse, she looks upon the crimes of

* Unable to identify.

seduction and illicit intercourse without horror, and although not personally involved in the guilt, she loses that value for innocence in her own, as well as the other sex, which is one of the strongest safeguards to virtue. She lives in habitual intercourse with men, whom she knows to be polluted by licentiousness, and often is she compelled to witness in her own domestic circle, those disgusting and heart-sickening jealousies and strifes which disgraced and distracted the family of Abraham. In addition to all this, the female slaves suffer every species of degradation and cruelty, which the most wanton barbarity can inflict; they are indecently divested of their clothing, sometimes tied up and severely whipped, sometimes prostrated on the earth, while their naked bodies are torn by the scorpion lash.

> The whip on WOMAN's shrinking flesh!
> Our soil yet reddening with the stains
> Caught from her scourging warm and fresh.

Can any American woman look at these scenes of shocking licentiousness and cruelty, and fold her hands in apathy and say, "I have nothing to do with slavery"? *She cannot and be guiltless.*

I cannot close this letter, without saying a few words on the benefits to be derived by men, as well as women, from the opinions I advocate relative to the equality of the sexes. Many women are now supported, in idleness and extravagance, by the industry of their husbands, fathers, or brothers, who are compelled to toil out their existence, at the counting house, or in the printing office, or some other laborious occupation, while the wife and daughters and sisters take no part in the support of the family, and appear to think that their sole business is to spend the hard bought earnings of their male friends. I deeply regret such a state of things, because I believe that if women felt their responsibility, for the support of themselves, or their families it would add strength and dignity to their characters, and teach them more true sympathy for their husbands, than is now generally manifested,—a sympathy which would be exhibited by actions as well as words. Our brethren may reject my doctrine, because it runs counter to common opinions, and because it wounds their pride; but I believe they would be "partakers of the benefit" resulting from the Equality of the Sexes, and would find that woman, as their equal, was unspeakably more valuable than woman as their inferior, both as a moral and an intellectual being.

Thine in the bonds of womanhood,

Sarah M. Grimké.

LETTER XI
Dress of Women

Brookline, [Mass.] 9th Mo., 1837.

My Dear Sister,—When I view woman as an immortal being, travelling through this world to that city whose builder and maker is God,—when I contemplate her in all the sublimity of her spiritual existence, bearing the image and superscription of Jehovah, emanating from Him and partaking of his nature, and destined, if she fulfils her duty, to dwell with him through the endless ages of eternity,—I mourn that she has lived so far below her privileges and her obligations, as a rational and accountable creature; and I ardently long to behold her occupying that sphere in which I believe her Creator designed her to move.

Woman, in all ages and countries, has been the scoff and the jest of her lordly master. If she attempted, like him, to improve her mind, she was ridiculed as pedantic, and driven from the temple of science and literature by coarse attacks and vulgar sarcasms. If she yielded to the pressure of circumstances, and sought relief from the monotony of existence by resorting to the theatre and the ball-room, by ornamenting her person with flowers and with jewels, while her mind was empty and her heart desolate; she was still the mark at which wit and satire and cruelty levelled their arrows.

"Woman," says Adam Clarke, "has been invidiously defined, *an animal of dress*. How long will they permit themselves to be thus degraded?" I have been an attentive observer of my sex, and I am constrained to believe that the passion for dress, which so generally characterizes them, is one cause why there so is little of that solid improvement and weight of character which might be acquired under almost any circumstances, if the mind were not occupied by the love of admiration, and the desire to gratify personal vanity. I have already adduced some instances to prove the inordinate love of dress, which is exhibited by women in a state of heathenism; I shall, therefore, confine myself now to what are called Christian countries; only remarking that previous to the introduction of Christianity into the Roman empire, the extravagance of apparel had arisen to an unprecedented height. "Jewels, expensive embroidery, and delicious perfumes, were used in great profusion by those who could afford them." The holy religion of Jesus Christ came in at this period, and stript luxury and wealth of all their false attractions. "Women of the noblest and wealthiest families, surrounded by the seductive allurements of worldly pleasure, renounced them all. Undismayed by severe edicts against the new religion, they appeared before the magistrates, and by pronouncing the simple words, "I am a Christian," calmly resigned themselves to imprisonment, ignominy and death." Could such women have had their minds occupied by the foolish vanity of ornamental apparel? No! Christianity struck at the root of all sin, and consequently we find the early Christians could not fight, or swear, or wear costly clothing. Cave, in his work entitled "Primitive Christianity,"* has some interesting remarks on this subject, showing that simplicity of dress was not then esteemed an unimportant part of Christianity.

Very soon, however, when the fire of persecution was no longer blazing, pagan customs became interwoven with Christianity. The professors of the religion of a self-denying Lord, whose kingdom was not of this world, began to use the sword, to return railing for railing, to take oaths, to mingle heathen forms and ceremonies with Christian worship, to engraft on the beautiful simplicity of piety, the feasts and observances which were usual at heathen festivals in honor of the gods, and to adorn their persons with rich and ornamental apparel. And now if we look at Christendom, there is scarcely a vestige of that religion, which the Redeemer of men came to promulgate. The Christian world is much in the situation of the Jewish nation, when the babe of Bethlehem was born, full of outside observances, which they substitute for mercy and love, for self-denial and good works, rigid in the performance of religious duties, but ready, if the Lord Jesus came amongst them and judged them by their fruits, as he did the Pharisees formerly, to crucify him as a slanderer. Indeed, I believe the remark of a late author is perfectly correct:

> Strange as it may seem, yet I do not hesitate to declare my belief that it is easier to make Pagan nations Christians, than to reform Christian communities and fashion them anew, after the pure and simple standard of the gospel. Cast your eye over Christian countries, and see what a multitude of causes combine to resist and impair the influence of Christian institutions. Behold the conform-

* William Cave, *Primitive Christianity: or, the Religion of the ancient Christians in the first ages of the Gospel*, 2 vols. (London: Chiswell, 1673).

ity of Christians to the world, in its prodigal pleasures and frivolous amusements, in its corrupt opinions and sentiments, of false honor. Behold the wide spread ignorance and degrading superstition; the power of prejudice and the authority of custom; the unchristian character of our systems of education; and the dread of the frowns and ridicule of the world, and we discover at once a host of more formidable enemies to the progress of *true religion* in Christian, than in heathen lands.

But I must proceed to examine what is the state of professing Christendom, as regards the subject of this letter. A few words will suffice. The habits and employments of fashionable circles are nearly the same throughout Christian communities. The fashion of dress, which varies more rapidly than the changing seasons, is still, as it has been from time immemorial, an all-absorbing object of interest. The simple cobbler of Agawam,* who wrote in Massachusetts as early as 1647, speaking of women, says,

> It is no marvel they wear drailes on the hinder part of their heads, having nothing, as it seems, in the fore part, but a few squirrels' brains to help them frisk from one fashion to another.

It must, however, be conceded, that although there are too many women who merit this severe reprehension, there is a numerous class whose improvement of mind and devotion to the cause of humanity justly entitle them to our respect and admiration. One of the most striking characteristics of modern times, is the tendency toward a universal dissemination of knowledge in all Protestant communities. But the character of woman has been elevated more by participating in the great moral enterprises of the day, than by anything else. It would astonish us if we could see at a glance all the labor, the patience, the industry, the fortitude which woman has exhibited, in carrying on the causes of Moral Reform, Anti-Slavery, &c. Still, even these noble and ennobling pursuits have not destroyed personal vanity. Many of those who are engaged in these great and glorious reformations, watch with eager interest, the ever varying freaks of the goddess of fashion, and are

* Nathaniel Ward (1578?–1652), the main author of the code of law (Body of Liberties) of the Massachusetts Bay Colony (1638–1639), wrote *The Simple Cobler of Aggawam [Ipswich] in America* . . . (London: F. D. and R. I. for S. Bowtell, 1647). It was a witty but serious argument against religious toleration, arbitrary government, and extravagant forms of masculine and feminine dress and ornament.

not exceeded by the butterflies of the ball-room in their love of curls, artificial flowers, embroidery and gay apparel. Many a woman will ply her needle with ceaseless industry, to obtain money to forward a favorite benevolent scheme, while at the same time she will expend on useless articles of dress, more than treble the sum which she procures by the employment of her needle, and which she might throw into the Lord's treasury, and leave herself leisure to cultivate her mind, and to mingle among the poor and the afflicted more than she can possibly do now.

I feel exceedingly solicitous to draw the attention of my sisters to this subject. I know that it is called trifling, and much is said about dressing fashionably, and elegantly, and becomingly, without thinking about it. This I do not believe can be done. If we indulge our fancy in the chameleon caprices of fashion, or in wearing ornamental and extravagant apparel, the mind must be in no small degree engaged in the gratification of personal vanity.

Lest any one may suppose from my being a Quaker, that I should like to see a uniform dress adopted, I will say, that I have no partiality for their peculiar costume, except so far as I find it simple and convenient; and I have not the remotest desire to see it worn, where one more commodious can be substituted. But I do believe one of the chief obstacles in the way of woman's elevation to the same platform of human rights, and moral dignity, and intellectual improvement, with her brother, on which God placed her, and where he designed her to act her part as an immortal creature, is her love of dress. "It has been observed," says Scott,* "that foppery and extravagance as to dress *in men* are most emphatically condemned by the apostle's silence on the subject, for this intimated that surely *they* could be under no temptation to such a childish vanity." But even those men who are superior to such a childish vanity in themselves, are, nevertheless, ever ready to encourage it in women. They know that so long as we submit to be dressed like dolls, we never can rise to the stations of duty and usefulness from which they desire to exclude us; and they are willing to grant us paltry indulgences, which forward their own design of keeping us out of our appropriate sphere, while they deprive us of essential rights.

To me it appears beneath the dignity of woman to bedeck herself in gewgaws and trinkets, in ribbons and laces, to gratify the eye of man. I believe, furthermore, that we owe a solemn duty to the poor. Many a

* *The Holy Bible . . . With explanatory notes . . . by Thomas Scott. . . .* Third edition with additions . . . by the author, 5 vols. (London: Seeley, 1810).

woman, in what is called humble life, spends nearly all her earnings in dress, because she wants to be as well attired as her employer. It is often argued that, as the birds and the flowers are gaily adorned by nature's hand, there can be no sin in woman's ornamenting her person. My reply is, God created me neither a bird nor a flower; and I aspire to something more than a resemblance to them. Besides, the gaudy colors in which birds and flowers are arrayed, create in them no feelings of vanity; but as human beings, we are susceptible of these passions, which are nurtured and strengthened by such adornments. "Well," I am often asked, "where is the limitation?" This it is not my business to decide. Every woman, as Judson remarks,* can best settle this on her knees before God. He has commanded her not to be conformed to this world, but to be transformed by the renewing of her mind, that she may know what is the good and acceptable and perfect will of God. He made the dress of the Jewish women the subject of special denunciation by his prophet—Is. 3. 16–26; yet the chains and the bracelets, the rings and the ear-rings, and the changeable suits of apparel, are still worn by Christian women. He has commanded them, through the apostles, not to adorn themselves with broidered hair, or gold, or pearls, or costly array. Not to let their adorning be the "outward adorning of plaiting the hair, or of wearing the gold, or of putting on of apparel, but let it be the hidden man of the heart, in that which is not corruptible, even the ornament of a meek and quiet spirit, which is in the sight of God of great price"; yet we disregard these solemn admonitions. May we not form some correct estimate of dress, by asking ourselves how we should feel, if we saw ministers of the gospel rise to address an audience with ear-rings dangling from their ears, glittering rings on their fingers, and a wreath of artificial flowers on their brow, and the rest of their apparel in keeping? If it would be wrong for a minister, it is wrong for every professing Christian. God makes no distinction between the moral and religious duties of ministers and people. We are bound to be "a chosen generation, a royal priesthood, a peculiar people, a holy nation; that we should show forth the praises of him who hath called us out of darkness into his marvellous light."

Thine in the bonds of womanhood,

Sarah M. Grimké.

* *Hints to Christian Females on Dress,* [followed by] Adoniram Judson, *A Letter to the Female Members of Christian Churches in America* (London: R. T. S., 1836).

LETTER XII
Legal Disabilities of Women

Concord, [Mass.] 9th Mo., 6th, 1837.

My Dear Sister,—There are few things which present greater obstacles to the improvement and elevation of woman to her appropriate sphere of usefulness and duty, than the laws which have been enacted to destroy her independence, and crush her individuality; laws which, although they are framed for her government, she has had no voice in establishing, and which rob her of some of her *essential rights.* Woman has no political existence. With the single exception of presenting a petition to the legislative body, she is a cipher in the nation; or, if not actually so in representative governments, she is only counted, like the slaves of the South, to swell the number of law-makers who form decrees for her government, with little reference to her benefit, except so far as her good may promote their own. I am not sufficiently acquainted with the laws respecting women on the continent of Europe, to say anything about them. But Prof. Follen,* in his essay on "The Cause of Freedom in our Country," says, "Woman, though fully possessed of that rational and moral nature which is the foundation of all rights, enjoys amongst us fewer legal rights than under the civil law of continental Europe." I shall confine myself to the laws of our country. These laws bear with peculiar rigor on married women. Blackstone,† in the chapter entitled "Of husband and wife," says:

> By marriage, the husband and wife are one person in law; that is, *the very being, or legal existence of the woman* is suspended during the marriage, or at least is incorporated and consolidated into that of the husband under whose wing, protection and cover she performs everything.
>
> For this reason, a man cannot grant anything to his wife, or enter into covenant with her; for the grant would be to suppose her separate existence, and to covenant with her would be to covenant with himself; and therefore it is also generally true, that all com-

* Charles Follen (1796–1840), born and educated in Germany, taught civil law in Europe and German language and literature at Harvard. He was dismissed from Harvard because of his outspoken support of immediate emancipation. He became a Unitarian minister in New York and a member of the Executive Committee of the American Anti-Slavery Society.

† William Blackstone, *Commentaries on the Laws of England,* 4 vols. (Oxford: Clarendon, 1765–1769).

pacts made between husband and wife, when single, are voided by the intermarriage. A woman indeed may be attorney for her husband, but that implies no separation from, but is rather a representation of, her love.

Here now, the very being of a woman, like that of a slave, is absorbed in her master. All contracts made with her, like those made with slaves by their owners, are a mere nullity. Our kind defenders have legislated away almost all our legal rights, and in the true spirit of such injustice and oppression, have kept us in ignorance of those very laws by which we are governed. They have persuaded us, that we have no right to investigate the laws, and that, if we did, we could not comprehend them; they alone are capable of understanding the mysteries of Blackstone, &c. But they are not backward to make us feel the practical operation of their power over our actions.

"The husband is bound to provide his wife with necessaries by laws, as much as himself; and if she contracts debts for them, he is obliged to pay for them; but for anything besides necessaries, he is not chargeable."

Yet a man may spend the property he has acquired by marriage at the ale-house, the gaming table, or in any other way that he pleases. Many instances of this kind have come to my knowledge; and women, who have brought their husbands handsome fortunes, have been left, in consequence of the wasteful and dissolute habits of their husbands, in straitened circumstances, and compelled to toil for the support of their families.

"If the wife be indebted before marriage, the husband is bound afterwards to pay the debt; for he has adopted her and her circumstances together."

The wife's property is, I believe, equally liable for her husband's debts contracted before marriage.

"If the wife be injured in her person or property, she can bring no action for redress without her husband's concurrence, and his name as well as her own: neither can she be sued, without making her husband a defendant."

This law that "a wife can bring no action," &c., is similar to the law respecting slaves. "A slave cannot bring a suit against his master, or any other person, for an injury—his master, must bring it." So if any damages are recovered for an injury committed on a wife, the husband pockets it; in the case of the slave, the master does the same.

"In criminal prosecutions, the wife may be indicted and punished separately, unless there be evidence of coercion from the fact that the offence was committed in the presence, or by the command of her husband. A wife is excused from punishment for theft committed in the presence, or by the command of her husband."

It would be difficult to frame a law better calculated to destroy the responsibility of a woman as a moral being, or a free agent. Her husband is supposed to possess unlimited control over her; and if she can offer the flimsy excuse that he bade her steal, she may break the eighth commandment with impunity, as far as human laws are concerned.

"Our law, in general, considers man and wife as one person; yet there are some instances in which she is separately considered, as inferior to him and acting by his compulsion. Therefore, all deeds executed, and acts done by her during her coverture (i.e. marriage) are void, except it be a fine, or like matter of record, in which case she must be solely and secretly examined, to learn if her act be voluntary."

Such a law speaks volumes of the abuse of that power which men have vested in their own hands. Still the private examination of a wife, to know whether she accedes to the disposition of property made by her husband is, in most cases, a mere form; a wife dares not do what will be disagreeable to one who is, in his own estimation, her superior, and who makes her feel, in the privacy of domestic life, that she has thwarted him. With respect to the nullity of deeds or acts done by a wife, I will mention one circumstance. A respectable woman borrowed of a female friend a sum of money to relieve her son from some distressing pecuniary embarrassment. Her husband was from home, and she assured the lender, that as soon as he returned, he would gratefully discharge the debt. She gave her note, and the lender, entirely ignorant of the law that a man is not obliged to discharge such a debt, actually borrowed the money, and lent it to the distressed and weeping mother. The father returned home, refused to pay the debt, and the person who had loaned the money was obliged to pay both principal and interest to the friend who lent it to her. Women should certainly know the laws by which they are governed, and from which they frequently suffer; yet they are kept in ignorance, nearly as profound, of their legal rights, and of the legislative enactments which are to regulate their actions, as slaves.

"The husband, by the old law, might give his wife moderate correction, as he is to answer for her misbehavior. The law thought it reasonable to entrust him with this power of restraining her by domestic chastisement. The courts of law will still permit a husband to restrain a wife of her liberty, in case of any gross misbehavior."

What a mortifying proof this law affords, of the estimation in which woman is held! She is placed completely in the hands of a being subject like herself to the outbursts of passion, and therefore unworthy to be trusted with power. Perhaps I may be told respecting this law, that it is a dead letter, as I am sometimes told about the slave laws; but this is not true in either case. The slaveholder does kill his slave by moderate correction, as the law allows; and many a husband, among the poor, exercises the right given him by the law, of degrading woman by personal chastisement. And among the higher ranks, if actual imprisonment is not resorted to, women are not unfrequently restrained of the liberty of going to places of worship by irreligious husbands, and of doing many other things about which, as moral and responsbile beings, *they* should be the *sole* judges. Such laws remind me of the reply of some little girls at a children's meeting held recently at Ipswich. The lecturer told them that God had created four orders of beings with which he had made us acquainted through the Bible. The first was angels, the second was man, the third beasts; and now, children, what is the fourth? After a pause, several girls replied, "WOMEN."

"A woman's personal property by marriage becomes absolutely her husband's, which at his death, he may leave entirely away from her."

And farther, all the avails of her labor are absolutely in the power of her husband. All that she acquires by her industry is his; so that she cannot, with her own honest earnings, become the legal purchaser of any property. If she expends her money for articles of furniture, to contribute to the comfort of her family, they are liable to be seized for her husband's debts; and I know an instance of a woman, who by labor and economy had scraped together a little maintenance for herself and a do-little husband, who was left, at his death, by virtue of his last will and testament, to be supported by charity. I knew another woman, who by great industry had acquired a little money which she deposited in a bank for safe keeping. She had saved this pittance whilst able to work, in hopes that when age or sickness disqualified her for exertion, she might have something to render life comfortable, without being a burden to her friends. Her husband, a worthless, idle man, discovered this hid treasure, drew her little stock from the bank, and expended it all in extravagance and vicious indulgence. I know of another woman, who married without the least idea that she was surrendering her rights to all her personal property. Accordingly, she went to the bank as usual to draw her dividends, and the person who paid her the money, and to whom she was personally known as an owner of shares in that bank, remarking the change in her signature, withdrew the money, informing her that if she were married, she had no longer a right to draw her dividends without an order from her husband. It appeared that she intended having a little fund for private use, and had not even told her husband that she owned this stock, and she was not a little chagrined, when she found that it was not at her disposal. I think she was wrong to conceal the circumstance. The relation of husband and wife is too near and sacred to admit of secrecy about money matters, unless positive necessity demands it; and I can see no excuse for any woman entering into a marriage engagement with a design to keep her husband ignorant that she was possessed of property. If she was unwilling to give up her property to his disposal, she had infinitely better have remained single.

The laws above cited are not very unlike the slave laws of Louisiana.

> All that a slave possesses belongs to his master; he possesses nothing of his own except what his master chooses he should possess.

"By the marriage, the husband is absolutely master of the profits of the wife's lands during the coverture, and if he has had a living child, and survives the wife, he retains the whole of those lands, if they are estates of inheritance, during his life; but the wife is entitled only to one third if she survives, out of the husband's estates of inheritance. But this she has, whether she has had a child or not." "With regard to the property of women, there is taxation without representation; for they pay taxes without having the liberty of voting for representatives."

And this taxation, without representation, be it remembered, was the cause of our Revolutionary war, a grievance so heavy, that it was thought necessary to purchase exemption from it at an immense expense of blood and treasure, yet the daughters of New England, as well as of all the other States of this free Republic, are suffering a similar injustice—but for one, I had rather we should suffer any injustice or oppression, than that my sex should have any voice in the political affairs of the nation.

The laws I have quoted, are, I believe, the laws of Massachusetts, and, with few exceptions, of all the States in this Union. "In Louisiana and Missouri, and possibly, in some other southern States, a woman not only has half her husband's property by right at his death, but may always be considered as possessed of half his gains during his life; having at all times power to bequeath that amount." That the laws which have generally been adopted in the United States, for the government of women, have been framed almost entirely for the exclusive benefit of men, and with a design to oppress women, by depriving them of all control over their property, is too manifest to be denied. Some liberal and enlightened men, I know, regret the existence of these laws; and I quote with pleasure an extract from Harriet Martineau's Society in America,* as a proof of the assertion. "A liberal minded lawyer of Boston, told me that his advice to testators always is to leave the largest possible amount to the widow, subject to the condition of her leaving it to the children; but that it is with shame that he reflects that any woman should owe that to his professional advice, which the law should have secured to her as a right." I have known a few instances where men have left their whole property to their wives, when they have died, leaving only minor children; but I have known more instances of "the friend and helper of many years, being portioned off like a salaried domestic," instead of having a comfortable independence secured to her, while the children were amply provided for.

As these abuses do exist, and women suffer intensely from them, our brethren are called upon in this enlightened age, by every sentiment of honor, religion and justice, to repeal these unjust and unequal laws, and restore to woman those rights which they have wrested from her. Such laws approximate too nearly to the laws enacted by slaveholders for the government of their slaves, and must tend to debase and depress the mind of that being, whom God created as a help meet for man, or "helper like unto himself," and designed to be his equal and his companion. Until such laws are annulled, woman never can occupy that exalted station for which she was intended by her Maker. And just in proportion as they are practically disregarded, which is the case to some extent, just so far is woman assuming that independence and nobility of character which she ought to exhibit.

The various laws which I have transcribed, leave women very little more liberty, or power, in some respects, than the slave. "A slave," says the civil code of Louisiana, "is one who is in the power of a master, to whom he belongs. He can possess nothing, nor acquire anything, but what must belong to his master." I do not wish by any means to intimate that the condition of free women can be compared to that of slaves in suffering, or in degradation; still, I believe the laws which deprive married women of their rights and privileges, have a tendency

* Harriet Martineau (1802–1876), *Society in America*, 3 vols. (London: Saunders and Otley, 1837), 3:122. Martineau was a British author and social critic who traveled in the United States from 1834 to 1836 and described her impressions in *Society* and in *Retrospect of Western Travel*, 2 vols. (New York: Lohman, 1838) and *The Martyr Age of the United States* (Boston: Weeks, Jordan, 1839). The first two contained critiques of slavery; the third was a paean to the abolitionists.

to lessen them in their own estimation as moral and responsible beings, and that their being made by civil law inferior to their husbands, has a debasing and mischievous effect upon them, teaching them practically the fatal lesson to look unto man for protection and indulgence.

Ecclesiastical bodies, I believe, without exception, follow the example of legislative assemblies, in excluding woman from any participation in forming the discipline by which she is governed. The men frame the laws, and, with few exceptions, claim to execute them on both sexes. In ecclesiastical, as well as civil courts, woman is tried and condemned, not by a jury of her peers, but by beings, who regard themselves as her superiors in the scale of creation. Although looked upon as an inferior, when considered as an intellectual being, woman is punished with the same severity as man, when she is guilty of moral offences. Her condition resembles, in some measure, that of the slave, who, while he is denied the advantages of his more enlightened master, is treated with even greater rigor by the law. Hoping that in the various reformations of the day, women may be relieved from some of their legal disabilities, I remain,

Thine in the bonds of womanhood,

Sarah M. Grimké.

LETTER XIII

Relation of Husband and Wife

Brookline, [Mass.] 9th Mo., 1837.

My Dear Sister,—Perhaps some persons may wonder that I should attempt to throw out my views on the important subject of marriage, and may conclude that I am altogether disqualified for the task, because I lack experience. However, I shall not undertake to settle the specific duties of husbands and wives, but only to exhibit opinions based on the word of God, and formed from a little knowledge of human nature, and close observation of the working of generally received notions respecting the dominion of man over woman.

When Jehovah ushered into existence man, created in his own image, he instituted marriage as a part of paradisaical happiness: it was a *divine ordination,* not a civil contract. God established it, and man, except by special permission, has no right to annul it. There can be no doubt that the creation of Eve perfected the happiness of Adam; hence, our all-wise and merciful Father made her as he made Adam, in his own image after his likeness, crowned her with glory and honor, and placed in her hand, as well as in his, the sceptre of dominion over the whole lower creation. Where there was perfect equality, and the same ability to receive and comprehend divine truth, and to obey divine injunctions, there could be no superiority. If God had placed Eve under the guardianship of Adam, after having endowed her, as richly as him, with moral perceptions, intellectual faculties, and spiritual apprehensions, he would at once have interposed a fallible being between her and her Maker. He could not, in simple consistency with himself, have done this; for the Bible teems with instructions not to put any confidence in man.

The passage on which the generally received opinion, that husbands are invested by divine command with authority over their wives, as I have remarked in a previous letter, is a prediction; and I am confirmed in this belief, because the same language is used to Cain respecting Abel. The text is obscure; but on a comparison of it with subsequent events, it appears to me that it was a prophecy of the dominion which Cain would usurp over his brother, and which issued in the murder of Abel. It could not allude to any thing but physical dominion, because Cain had already exhibited those evil passions which subsequently led him to become an assassin.

I have already shown, that man has exercised the most unlimited and brutal power over woman, in the peculiar character of husband,—a word in most countries synonymous with tyrant. I shall not, therefore, adduce any further proofs of the fulfilment of that prophecy, "He will rule over thee," from the history of heathen nations, but just glance at the condition of woman in the relation of wife in Christian countries.

"Previous to the introduction of the religion of Jesus Christ, the state of society was wretchedly diseased. The relation of the sexes to each other had become so gross in its manifested forms, that it was difficult to perceive the pure conservative principle in its inward essence." Christianity came in, at this juncture, with its hallowed influence, and has without doubt tended to lighten the yoke of bondage, to purify the manners, and give the spiritual in some degree an empire over the animal nature. Still, that state which was designed by God to increase the happiness of woman as well as man, often proves the means of lessening her comfort, and degrading her into the mere machine of another's convenience and pleasure. Woman, instead of being elevated by her union with man, which might be expected from an alliance with a superior being, is in reality lowered. She generally loses her individuality, her independent character, her moral being. She becomes absorbed into him, and henceforth is looked at, and acts through the medium of her husband.

In the wealthy classes of society, and those who are in comfortable circumstances, women are exempt from great corporeal exertion, and are protected by public opinion, and by the genial influence of Christianity, from much physical ill treatment. Still, there is a vast amount of secret suffering endured, from the forced submission of women to the opinions and whims of their husbands. Hence they are frequently driven to use deception, to compass their ends. They are early taught that to appear to yield, is the only way to govern. Miserable sophism! I deprecate such sentiments, as being peculiarly hostile to the dignity of woman. If she submits, let her do it openly, honorably, not to gain her point, but as a matter of Christian duty. But let her beware how she permits her husband to be her conscience-keeper. On all moral and religious subjects, she is bound to think and to act for herself. Where confidence and love exist, a wife will naturally converse with her husband as with her dearest friend, on all that interests her heart, and there will be a perfectly free interchange of sentiment; but *she is no more bound to be governed by his judgment,* than he is by hers. They are standing on the same platform of human rights, are equally under the government of God, and accountable to him, and him alone.

I have sometimes been astonished and grieved at the servitude of women, and at the little idea many of them seem to have of their own moral existence and responsibilities. A woman who is asked to sign a petition for the abolition of slavery in the District of Columbia, or to join a society for the purpose of carrying forward the annihilation of American slavery, or any other great reformation, not unfrequently replies, "My husband does not approve of it." She merges her rights and her duties in her husband, and thus virtually chooses him for a savior and a king, and rejects Christ as her Ruler and Redeemer. I know some women are very glad of so convenient a pretext to shield themselves from the performance of duty; but there are others, who, under a mistaken view of their obligations as wives, submit conscientiously to this species of oppression, and go mourning on their way, for want of that holy fortitude, which would enable them to fulfil their duties as moral and responsible beings, without reference to poor fallen man. O that woman may arise in her dignity as an immortal creature, and speak, think and act as unto God, and not unto man!

There is, perhaps, less bondage of mind among the poorer classes, because their sphere of duty is more contracted, and they are deprived of the means of intellectual culture, and of the opportunity of exercising their judgment, on many moral subjects of deep interest and of vital importance. Authority is called into exercise by resistance, and hence there will be mental bondage only in proportion as the faculties of mind are evolved, and woman feels herself as a rational and intelligent being, on a footing with man. But women, among the lowest classes of society, so far as my observation has extended, suffer intensely from the brutality of their husbands. Duty as well as inclination has led me, for many years, into the abodes of poverty and sorrow, and I have been amazed at the treatment which women receive at the hands of those, who arrogate to themselves the epithet of *protectors*. Brute force, the law of violence, rules to a great extent in the poor man's domicil *[sic]*; and woman is little more than his drudge. They are less under the restraints of education, and unaided or unbiased by the refinements of polished society. Religion, wherever it exists, supplies the place of all these; but the real cause of woman's degradation and suffering in married life is to be found in the erroneous notion of her inferiority to man; and never will she be rightly regarded by herself, or others, until this opinion, so derogatory to the wisdom and mercy of God, is exploded, and woman arises in all the majesty of her womanhood, to claim those rights which are inseparable from her existence as an immortal, intelligent and responsible being.

Independent of the fact, that Jehovah could not, consistently with his character as the King, the Lawgiver, and the Judge of his people, give the reins of government over woman into the hands of man, I find that all his commands, all his moral laws, are addressed to women as well as to men. When he assembled Israel at the foot of Mount Sinai, to issue his commandments, we may reasonably suppose he gave all the precepts, which he considered necessary for the government of moral beings. Hence we find that God says,—"Honor thy father and thy mother," and he enforces this command by severe penalties upon those who transgress it: "He that smiteth his father, or his mother, shall surely be put to death"—"He that curseth his father, or his mother, shall surely be put to death"—Ex. 21: 15, 17. But in the decalogue, there is no direction given to women to obey their husbands: both are commanded to have no other God but Jehovah, and not to bow down, or serve any other. When the Lord Jesus delivered his sermon on the Mount, full of the practical precepts of religion, he did not issue any command to wives to obey their husbands. When he is speaking on the subject of divorce,

Mark 16: 11, 12, he places men and women on the same ground. And the Apostle, 1st Cor. 7: 12, 13, speaking of the duties of the Corinthian wives and husbands, who had embraced Christianity, to their unconverted partners, points out the same path to both, although our translators have made a distinction. "Let him not put her away," 12—"Let her not leave him," 13—is precisely the same in the original. If man is constituted the governor of woman, he must be her God; and the sentiment expressed to me lately, by a married man, is perfectly correct: "In my opinion," said he, "the greatest excellence to which a married woman can attain, is to worship her husband." He was a professor of religion—his wife a lovely and intelligent woman. He only spoke out what thousands think and act. Women are indebted to Milton for giving to this false notion, "confirmation strong as proof of holy writ." His Eve is embellished with every personal grace, to gratify the eye of her admiring husband; but he seems to have furnished the mother of mankind with just intelligence enough to comprehend her supposed inferiority to Adam, and to yield unresisting submission to her lord and master. Milton puts into Eve's mouth the following address to Adam:

> My author and disposer, what thou bidst,
> Unargued I obey; so God ordains—
> God is thy law, thou mine: to know no more,
> Is woman's happiest knowledge and her praise.*

This much admired sentimental nonsense is fraught with absurdity and wickedness. If it were true, the commandment of Jehovah should have run thus: Man shall have no other gods before ME, and woman shall have no other gods before MAN.

The principal support of the dogma of woman's inferiority, and consequent submission to her husband, is found in some passages of Paul's epistles. I shall proceed to examine those passages, premising 1st, that the antiquity of the opinions based on the false construction of those passages, has no weight with me: they are the opinions of interested judges, and I have no particular reverence for them, *merely* because they have been regarded with veneration from generation to generation. So far from this being the case, I examine any opinions of centuries standing, with as much freedom, and investigate them with as much care, as if they were of yesterday. I was educated to think for myself, and it is a privilege I shall always claim to exercise. 2d. Notwithstanding my full

* John Milton, *Paradise Lost*, 4:635–638.

belief that the apostle Paul's testimony, respecting himself, is true, "I was not a whit behind the chiefest of the apostles," yet I believe his mind was under the influence of Jewish prejudices respecting women, just as Peter's and the apostles were about the uncleanness of the Gentiles. "The Jews," says Clarke, "would not suffer a woman to read in the synagogue, although a servant, or even a child, had this permission." When I see Paul shaving his head for a vow, and offering sacrifices, and circumcising Timothy, to accommodate himself to the prepossessions of his countrymen, I do not conceive that I derogate in the least from his character as an inspired apostle, to suppose that he may have been imbued with the prevalent prejudices against women.

In 1st Cor. 11:3, after praising the Corinthian converts, because they kept the "ordinances," or "traditions," as the margin reads, the apostle says, "I would have you know, that the head of every man is Christ, and the head of the woman is the man; and the head of Christ is God." Eph. 5:23, is a parallel passage. "For the husband is the head of the Church." The apostle closes his remarks on this subject, by observing, "This is a great mystery, but I speak concerning Christ and the Church." I shall pass over this with simply remarking, that God and Christ are one. "I and my Father are one," and there can be no inferiority where there is no divisibility. The commentaries on this and similar texts, afford a striking illustration of the ideas which men entertain of their own superiority. I shall subjoin Henry's* remarks on 1st Cor. 11: 5, as a specimen: "To understand this text, it must be observed, that it was a signification either of shame, or subjection, for persons to be veiled or covered in Eastern countries; contrary to the custom of ours, where the being bare-headed betokens subjection, and being covered superiority and dominion; and this will help us the better to understand the reason on which he grounds his reprehension, 'Every man praying, &c. dishonoreth his head,' i.e. Christ, the head of every man, by appearing in a habit unsuitable to the rank in which God had placed him. The woman, on the other hand, that prays, &c. dishonoreth her head, i.e. the man. She appears in the dress of her *superior,* and throws off the token of her subjection; she might with equal decency cut her hair short, or cut it off, the common dress of the man in that age. Another reason against this conduct was, that the man is the image and glory of God, the representative of that glorious dominion and headship which God has over the world. It is the man who is set at the head of this lower creation, and

* Matthew Henry, *A Commentary upon the Holy Bible, from Henry and Scott; with occasional observations and notes from other authors,* ed. George Stokes, 6 vols. (London: 1831–1835).

therein bears the resemblance of God. The woman, on the other hand, is the glory of the man: she is his representative. Not but she has dominion over the inferior creatures, and she is a partaker of human nature, and so far is God's representative too, but it is at second hand. She is the image of God, inasmuch as she is the image of the man. The man was first made, and made head of the creation here below, and therein the image of the divine dominion; and the woman was made out of the man, and shone with a *reflection of his glory,* being made superior to the other creatures here below, but in subjection to her husband, and deriving that *honor from him,* out of whom she was made. The woman was made for the man to be his help meet, and not the man for the woman. She was, naturally, therefore, made subject to him, because made for him, for HIS USE AND HELP AND COMFORT."

We see in the above quotation, what degrading views even good men entertain of women. Pity the Psalmist had not thrown a little light on this subject, when he was paraphrasing the account of man's creation. "Thou hast made him a little lower than the angels, and hast crowned him with glory and honor. Thou madest him to have dominion over the works of thy hands; thou hast put all things under his feet." Surely if woman had been placed below man, and was to shine only by a lustre borrowed from him, we should have some clear evidence of it in the sacred volume. Henry puts her exactly on a level with the beasts; they were made for the use, help and comfort of man; and according to this commentator, this was the whole end and design of the creation of woman. The idea that man, as man, is superior to women, involves an absurdity so gross, that I really wonder how any man of reflection can receive it as of divine origin; and I can only account for it, by that passion for supremacy, which characterizes man as a corrupt and fallen creature. If it be true that he is more excellent than she, as man, independent of his moral and intellectual powers, then every man is superior by virtue of his manship, to every woman. The man who sinks his moral capacities and spiritual powers in his sensual appetites, is still, as a man, simply by the conformation of his body, a more dignified being, than the woman whose intellectual powers are highly cultivated, and whose approximation to the character of Jesus Christ is exhibited in a blameless life and conversation.

But it is strenuously urged by those, who are anxious to maintain their usurped authority, that wives are, in various passages of the New Testament, commanded to obey their husbands. Let us examine these texts.

> Eph. 5, 22. "Wives submit yourselves unto your own husbands as unto the Lord." "As the church is subject unto Christ, so let the wives be to their own husbands in every thing."
>
> Col. 3, 18. "Wives, submit yourselves unto your own husbands, as it is fit in the lord."
>
> 1st Pet. 3, 2. "Likewise ye wives, be in subjection to your own husbands; that if any obey not the word, they may also without the word be won by the conversation of the wives."

Accompanying all these directions to wives, are commands to husbands.

> Eph. 5, 25. "Husbands, love your wives even as Christ loved the Church, and gave himself for it." "So ought men to love their wives as their own bodies. He that loveth his wife, loveth himself."
>
> Col. 3, 19. "Husbands, love your wives, and be not bitter against them."
>
> 1st Pet. 3, 7. "Likewise ye husbands, dwell with them according to knowledge, giving honor unto the wife as unto the weaker vessel, and as being heirs together of the grace of life."

I may just remark, in relation to the expression "weaker vessel," that the word in the original has no reference to intellect: it refers to physical weakness merely.

The apostles were writing to Christian converts, and laying down rules for their conduct towards their unconverted consorts. It no doubt frequently happened, that a husband or a wife would embrace Christianity, while their companions clung to heathenism, and husbands might be tempted to dislike and despise those, who pertinaciously adhered to their pagan superstitions. And wives who, when they were pagans, submitted as a matter of course to their heathen husbands, might be tempted knowing that they were superior as moral and religious characters, to assert that superiority, by paying less deference to them than heretofore. Let us examine the context of these passages, and see what are the grounds of the directions here given to husbands and wives. The whole epistle to the Ephesians breathes a spirit of love. The apostle beseeches the converts to walk worthy of the vocation wherewith they are called, with all lowliness and meekness, with long suffering, forbearing one another in love. The verse preceding 5, 22, is "SUBMITTING

YOURSELVES ONE TO ANOTHER IN THE FEAR OF GOD." Colossians 3, from 11 to 17, contains similar injunctions. The 17th verse says, "Whatsoever ye do in word, or in deed, do all in the name of the Lord Jesus." Peter, after drawing a most touching picture of Christ's sufferings for us, and reminding the Christians, that he had left us an example that we should follow his steps, "who did no sin, neither was guile found in his mouth," exhorts wives to be in subjection, &c.

From an attentive consideration of these passages, and of those in which the same words "submit," "subjection," are used, I cannot but believe that the apostles designed to recommend to wives, as they did to subjects and to servants, to carry out the holy principle laid down by Jesus Christ, "Resist not evil." And this without in the least acknowledging the right of the governors, masters, or husbands, to exercise the authority they claimed. The recognition of the existence of evils does not involve approbation of them. God tells the Israelites, he gave them a king in his wrath, but nevertheless as they chose to have a king, he laid down directions for the conduct of that king, and had him anointed to reign over them. According to the generally received meaning of the passages I have quoted, they directly contravene the laws of God, as given in various parts of the Bible. Now I must understand the sacred Scriptures as harmonizing with themselves, or I cannot receive them as the word of God. The commentators on these passages exalt man to the station of a Deity in relation to woman. Clarke says, "As the Lord Christ is the head, or governor of the church, and the head of the man, so is the man the head, or governor of the woman. This is God's ordinance, and should not be transgressed. 'As unto the Lord.' The word church seems necessarily to be understood here: that is, act under the authority of your husbands, as the church acts under the authority of Christ. As the church submits to the Lord, so let wives submit to their husbands." Henry goes even further—"For the husband is the head of the wife. The metaphor is taken from the head in the natural body, which being the seat of reason, of wisdom and of knowledge, and the fountain of sense and motion, is more excellent than the rest of the body." Now if God ordained man the governor of woman, he must be able to save her, and to answer in her stead for all those sins which she commits by his direction. Awful responsibility. Do husbands feel able and willing to bear it? And what becomes of the solemn affirmation of Jehovah? "Hear this, all ye people, give ear all ye inhabitants of the world, both low and high, rich and poor." "None can by any means redeem his brother, or give to God a ransom for him, for the redemption of the soul is precious, and man cannot accomplish it."—*French Bible*.*

Thine in the bonds of womanhood,
Sarah M. Grimké.

LETTER XIV
Ministry of Women

Brookline, [Mass.] 9th Mo. 1837.

My Dear Sister,—According to the principle which I have laid down, that man and woman were created equal, and endowed by their beneficent Creator with the same intellectual powers and the same moral responsibilities, and that consequently whatever is *morally* right for a man to do, is *morally* right for a woman to do, it follows as a necessary corollary, that if it is the duty of man to preach the unsearchable riches of Christ, it is the duty also of woman.

I am aware, that I have the prejudices of education and custom to combat, both in my own and the other sex, as well as "the traditions of men," which are taught for the commandements of God. I feel that I have no sectarian views to advance; for although among the Quakers, Methodists, and Christians, women are permitted to preach the glad tidings of peace and salvation, yet I know of no religious body, who entertain the Scripture doctrine of the perfect equality of man and woman, which is the fundamental principle of my argument in favor of the ministry of women. I wish simply to throw my views before thee. If they are based on the immutable foundation of truth, they cannot be overthrown by unkind insinuations, bitter sarcasms, unchristian imputations, or contemptuous ridicule. These are weapons which are unworthy of a good cause. If I am mistaken, as truth only can prevail, my supposed errors will soon vanish before her beams; but I am persuaded that woman is not filling the high and holy station which God alloted to her, and that in consequence of her having been driven from her "appropriate sphere," both herself and her brethren have suffered an infinity of evils.

Before I proceed to prove, that woman is bound to preach the gospel, I will examine the ministry under the Old Testament dispensation. Those who were called to this office were known under various names.

* Reference unclear.

Enoch, who prophesied, is designated as walking with God. Noah is called a preacher of righteousness. They were denominated men of God, seers, prophets, but they all had the same great work to perform, viz. to turn sinners from the error of their ways. This ministry existed previous to the institution of the Jewish priesthood, and continued after its abolition. *It has nothing to do with the priesthood.* It was rarely, as far as the Bible informs us, exercised by those of the tribe of Levi, and was common to all the people, women as well as men. It differed essentially from the priesthood, because there was no compensation received for calling the people to repentance. Such a thing as paying a prophet for preaching the truth of God is not even mentioned. They were called of Jehovah to go forth in his name, one from his plough, another from gathering of sycamore fruit, &c. &c. Let us for a moment imagine Jeremiah, when God says to him, "Gird up thy loins, and arise and speak unto the people all that I command thee," replying to Jehovah, "I will preach repentance to the people, if they will give me gold, but if they will not pay me for the truth, then let them perish in their sins." Now, this is virtually the language of the ministers of the present day; and I believe the secret of the exclusion of women from the ministerial office is, that that office has been converted into one of emolument, of honor, and of power. Any attentive observer cannot fail to perceive, that as far as possible, all such offices are reserved by men for themselves.

The common error that Christian ministers are the successors of the priests, is founded in mistake. In the particular directions given to Moses to consecrate Aaron and his sons to the office of the priesthood, their duties are clearly defined: see Ex. 28th, 29th and 30th chap. There is no commission to Aaron to preach to the people; his business was to offer sacrifice. Now why were sacrifices instituted? They were types of that one great sacrifice, which in the fulness of time was offered up through the eternal Spirit without spot to God. Christ assumed the office of priest; he "offered himself," and by so doing, abolished forever the order of the priesthood, as well as the sacrifices which the priests were ordained to offer.*

But it may be inquired, whether the priests were not to teach the people. As far as I can discover from the Bible, they were simply

* I cannot enter fully into this part of my subject. It is, however, one of great importance, and I recommend those who wish to examine it, to read "The Book of the Priesthood," by an English dissenter [Stratton], and Beverly's "View of the Present State of the Visible Church of Christ." [Robert Mackenzie Beverley, *Letters on the Present State of the Visible Church of Christ, addressed to John Angel James* (London: Dinnis, 1836).] they are both masterly productions. [Footnote in original.]

commanded to read the law to the people. There was no other copy that we know of, until the time of the kings, who were to write out a copy for their own use. As it was deposited in the ark, the priests were required, "When all Israel is come to appear before the Lord thy God in the place which he shall choose, thou shalt read this law before all Israel in their hearing. Gather the people together, men, women, and children, that they may hear." Deut. 31: 9–33. See also Lev. 10: 11, Deut. 33: 10, 2d Chr. 17: 7–9, and numerous other passages. When God is enumerating the means he has used to call his people to repentance, he never, as far as I can discover, speaks of sending his priests to warn them: but in various passages we find language similar to this: "Since the day that your fathers came forth out of the land of Egypt unto this day, I have even sent unto you all my servants, the PROPHETS, daily rising up early and sending them. Yet they hearkened not unto me, nor inclined their ear, but hardened their neck; they did worse than their fathers." Jer. 7: 25, 26. See also, 25: 4, 2 Chr. 36: 15, and parallel passages. God says, Is. 9: 15, 16, "The prophet that teacheth lies, he is the tail; for the leaders of this people cause them to err." The distinction between priests and prophets is evident from their being mentioned as two classes. "The prophets prophesy falsely, and the priests bear rule by their means," Jer. 5: 31. See also, Ch. 2: 8:1–10, and many others.

That women were called to the prophetic office, I believe is universally admitted. Miriam, Deborah and Huldah were prophetesses. The judgments of the Lord are denounced by Ezekiel on false prophetesses, as well as false prophets. And if Christian ministers are, as I apprehend, successors of the prophets, and not of the priests, then of course, women are now called to that office as well as men, because God has no where withdrawn from them the privilege of doing what is the great business of preachers, viz. to point the penitent sinner to the Redeemer. "Behold the Lamb of God, which taketh away the sins of the world."

It is often triumphantly inquired, why, if men and women are on an equality, are not women as conspicuous in the Bible as men? I do not intend to assign a reason, but I think one may readily be found in the act, that from the days of Eve to the present time, the aim of man has been to crush her. He has accomplished this work in various ways; sometimes by brute force, sometimes by making her subservient to his worst passions, sometimes by treating her as a doll, and while he excluded from her mind the light of knowledge, decked her person with gewgaws and frippery which he scorned for himself, thus endeavoring to render her like unto a painted sepulchre.

It is truly marvellous that any woman can rise above the pressure of circumstances which combine to crush her. Nothing can strengthen her to do this in the character of a preacher of righteousness, but a call from Jehovah himself. And when the voice of God penetrates the deep recesses of her heart, and commands her to go and cry in the ears of the people, she is ready to exclaim, "Ah, Lord God, behold I cannot speak, for I am a woman.["] I have known women in different religious societies, who have felt like the prophet. "His word was in my heart as a burning fire shut up in my bones, and I was weary with forbearing." But they have not dared to open their lips, and have endured all the intensity of suffering, produced by disobedience to God, rather than encounter heartless ridicule and injurious suspicions. I rejoice that we have been the oppressed, rather than the oppressors. God thus prepared his people for deliverance from outward bondage; and I hope our sorrows have prepared us to fulfil our high and holy duties, whether public or private, with humility and meekness; and that suffering has imparted fortitude to endure trials, which assuredly await us in the attempt to sunder those chains with which man has bound us, galling to the spirit, though unseen by the eye.

Surely there is nothing either astonishing or novel in the gifts of the Spirit being bestowed on woman: nothing astonishing, because there is no respect of persons with God; the soul of the woman in his sight is as the soul of the man, and both are alike capable of the influence of the Holy Spirit. Nothing novel, because, as has been already shown, in the sacred records there are found examples of women, as well as of men, exercising the gift of prophecy.

We attach to the word prophecy, the exclusive meaning of foretelling future events, but this is certainly a mistake; for the apostle Paul defines it to be "speaking to edification, exhortation and comfort." And there appears no possible reason, why women should not do this as well as men. At the time that the Bible was translated into English, the meaning of the word prophecy, was delivering a message from God, whether it was to predict future events, or to warn the people of the consequences of sin. Governor Winthrop, of Massachusetts,* mentions in a letter, that the minister being absent, he went to,———to prophecy to the people.

Before I proceed to prove that women, under the Christian dispensation, were anointed of the Holy Ghost to preach, or prophecy, I will mention Anna, the (last) prophetess under the Jewish dispensation. "She

* John Winthrop (1588–1649), governor of the Massachusetts Bay Colony, 1630–1634, 1637–1640, and 1646–1649.

departed not from the temple, but served God with fasting and prayers night and day." And coming into the temple, while Simeon was yet speaking to Mary, with the infant Savior in his arms, "spake of Christ to all them that looked for redemption in Jerusalem." Blackwall,* a learned English critic, in his work entitled, "Sacred Classics," says, in reference to this passage, Luke 2: 37—"According to the *original* reading, the sense will be, that the devout Anna, who attended in the temple, both night and day, spoke of the Messiah to all the inhabitants of that city, who constantly worshipped there, and who prepared themselves for the worthy reception of that divine person, whom they expected at this time. And 'tis certain, that other devout Jews, not inhabitants of Jerusalem, frequently repaired to the temple-worship, and might, as this remarkable time, and several others, hear this admirable woman discourse upon the blessed advent of the Redeemer. A various reading has Israel instead of Jerusalem, which expresses that religious Jews, from distant places, came thither to divine offices, and would with high pleasure hear the discourses of this great prophetess, so famed for her extraordinary piety and valuable talents, upon the most important and desirable subject."

I shall now examine the testimony of the Bible on this point, after the ascension of our Lord, beginning with the glorious effusion of the Holy Spirit on the day of Pentecost. I presume it will not be denied, that women, as well as men, were at that time filled with the Holy Ghost, because it is expressly stated, that women were among those who continued in prayer and supplication, waiting for the fulfilment of the promise, that they should be endured with power from on high. "When the day of Pentecost was fully come, they were ALL with one accord in one place. And there appeared unto them cloven tongues as the Spirit gave them utterance." Peter says, in reference to this miracle, "This is that which was spoken by the prophet Joel. And it shall come to pass in the last days, said God, I will pour out my Spirit upon all flesh; and your sons and your daughters shall prophesy—and on my servants and on my hand-maidens, I will pour out in those days of my Spirit, and they shall prophesy." There is not the least intimation that this was a spasmodic influence which was soon to cease. The men and women are classed together; and if the power to preach the gospel was a supernatural and short-lived impulse in women, then it was equally so in men. But we are told, those were the days of miracles. I grant it; but the men,

* Anthony Blackwall, *The Sacred Classics Defended and Illustrated* . . . (London: Rivington and Cantrell, 1725).

equally with the women, were the subjects of this marvellous fulfilment of prophecy, and of course, if women have lost the gift of prophesying, so have men. We are also gravely told, that if a woman pretends to inspiration, and thereupon grounds the right to plead the cause of a crucified Redeemer in public, she will be believed when she shows credentials from heaven, i.e. when she works a miracle. I reply, if this be necessary to prove her right to preach the gospel, then I demand of my brethren to show me their credentials; else I cannot receive their ministry, by their own showing. John Newton* has justly said, that no power but that which created a world, can make a minister of the gospel; and man may task his ingenuity to the utmost, to prove that this power is not exercised on women as well as men. He cannot do it until he has first disclaimed that simple, but all comprehensive truth, "in Christ Jesus there is neither male nor female."

Women then, according to the Bible, were, under the New Testament dispensation, as well as the Old, the recipients of the gift of prophecy. That this is no sectarian view may be proved by the following extracts. The first I shall offer is from Stratton's "Book of the Priesthood."

> While they were assembled in the upper room to wait for the blessing, in number about one hundred and twenty, they received the miraculous gifts of the Holy Spirit's grace; they became the channels through which its more ordinary, but not less saving streams flowed to three thousand persons in one day. The whole company of the assembled disciples, male and female, young and old, were all filled with the Holy Ghost, and began to speak with other tongues as the Spirit gave them utterance. They all contributed in producing that impression upon the assembled multitude, which Peter was instrumental in advancing to its decisive results.

Scott, in his commentary on this passage, says—

> At the same time, there appeared the form of tongues divided at the tip and resembling fire; one of which rested on each of the whole company. . . . They sat on every one present, as the original determines. At the time of these extraordinary appearances, the whole company were abundantly replenished with the gifts and

* John Newton (1721–1807), a brutally treated servant of a slavetrader; he became an evangelical Anglican priest, and wrote about his experiences in *An Authentic Narrative of some remarkable and interesting particulars in the life of [John Newton] . . .* (London: Johnson, 1764).

graces of the Holy Spirit, so that they began to speak with other tongues.

Henry in his notes confirms this:

It seems evident to me that not the twelve apostles only, but all the one hundred and twenty disciples were filled with the Holy Ghost alike at this time,—all the seventy disciples, who were apostolical men and employed in the same work, and all the rest too that were to preach the gospel, for it is said expressly, Eph. 4: 8–12: "When Christ ascended up on high, (which refers to this) he gave gifts unto men." The all here must refer to the all that were together.

I need hardly remark that man is a generic term, including both sexes.

Let us now examine whether women actually exercised the office of minister, under the gospel dispensation. Philip had four daughters, who prophesied or preached. Paul calls Priscilla, as well as Aquila, his helpers; or, as in the Greek, his fellow laborers* in Christ Jesus. Divers other passages might be adduced to prove that women continued to be preachers, and that *many* of them filled this dignified station.

We learn also from ecclesiastical history, that female ministers suffered martyrdom in the early ages of the Christian church. In ancient councils, mention is made of deaconesses; and in an edition of the New Testament, printed in 1574, a woman is spoken of as minister of a church. The same word, which, in our common translation, is now rendered a servant of the church, in speaking of Phebe, Rom. 16: 1, is rendered minister, Eph. 6: 21, when applied to Tychicus. A minister, with whom I had lately the pleasure of conversing, remarked, "My rule is to expound scripture by scripture, and I cannot deny the ministry of women, because the apostle says, 'help those women who labored with me IN THE GOSPEL.' He certainly meant something more than pouring out tea for him."

In the 11th Ch. of 1 Cor., Paul gives directions to women and men how they should appear when they prophesy, or pray in public assemblies. It is evident that the design of the apostle, in this and the three succeeding chapters, is to rectify certain abuses which had crept into the Christian church. He therefore admonishes women to pray with their heads covered, because, according to the fashion of that day, it was considered immodest and immoral to do otherwise. He says, "that were

* Rom 16: 3, compare Gr. text of v. 21, 2; Cor. 3:23; Phil. 2: 25; I Thes. 3: 2. [Footnote in original.]

all one as if she were shaven"; and shaving the head was a disgraceful punishment that was inflicted on women of bad character.

"These things," says Scott, "the apostle stated as decent and proper, but if any of the Corinthian teachers inclined to excite contention about time, he would only add, v. 16, that he and his brethren knew of no such custom as prevailed among them, nor was there any such in the churches of God which had been planted by the other apostles."

John Locke, whilst engaged in writing his notes on the Epistles of St. Paul, was at a meeting where two women preached. After hearing them, he became convinced of their commission to publish the gospel, and thereupon altered his notes on the 11th Ch. 1 Cor. in favor of women's preaching. He says,—

> This about women seeming as difficult a passage as most in St. Paul's Epistles, I crave leave to premise some few considerations. It is plain that this covering the head in women is restrained in some peculiar actions which they performed in the assembly, expressed by the words praying, prophesying, which, whatever they signify, must have the same meaning applied to women in the 5th verse, that they have when applied to men in the 4th, &c. The next thing to be considered is, what is here to be understood by praying and prophesying. And that seems to me the performing of some public action in the assembly, by some one person which was for that time peculiar to that person, and whilst it lasted, the rest of the assembly silently assisted. As to prophesying, the apostle in express words tells us, Ch. 14: 3, 12. that it was speaking in the assembly. The same is evident as to praying, that the apostle means by it publicly with an audible voice, ch. 14: 19.*

In a letter to these two women, Rebecca Collier and Rachel Bracken, which accompanied a little testimony of his regard, he says,

> I admire no converse like that of Christian freedom; and I fear no bondage like that of pride and prejudice. I now see that acquaintance by sight cannot reach the height of enjoyment, which acquaintance by knowledge arrives unto. Outward hearing may misguide us, but internal knowledge cannot err. . . . Women, indeed, had the honor of first publishing the resurrection of the God of love—why not again the resurrection of the spirit of love? And let

* John Locke, *A Paraphrase and Notes on St. Paul's First Epistle to the Corinthians* (London: Awnsham and John Churchill, 1707).

all the disciples of Christ rejoice therein, as doth your partner, John Locke.*

See "The Friend," a periodical published in Philadelphia.
Adam Clarke's comment on 1 Cor. 11: 5, is similar to Locke's:

Whatever be the meaning of praying and prophesying in respect to the man, they have precisely the same meaning in respect to the woman. So that some women, at least, as well as some men, might speak to others to edification and exhortation and comfort. And this kind of prophesying, or teaching, was predicted by Joel 2: 28, and referred to by Peter; and had there not been such gifts bestowed on women, the prophesy could not have had its fulfilment.†

In the autobiography of Adam Clarke, there is an interesting account of his hearing Mary Sewall and another female minister‡ preach, and he acknowledges that such was the power accompanying their ministry, that though he had been prejudiced against women's preaching, he could not but confess that these women were anointed for the office.

But there are certain passages in the Epistles of St. Paul, which seem to be of doubtful interpretation; at which we cannot much marvel, seeing that his brother Peter says, there are some things in them hard to be understood. Most commentators, having their minds preoccupied with the prejudices of education, afford little aid; they rather tend to darken the text by the multitude of words. One of these passages occurs in 1 Cor. 14. I have already remarked that this chapter, with several of the preceding, was evidently designed to correct abuses which had crept into the assemblies of Christians in Corinth. Hence we find that the men were commanded to be silent, as well as the women, when they were guilty of any thing which deserved reprehension. The apostle says, "If there be no interpreter, let him keep silence in the church." The men were doubtless in the practice of speaking in unknown tongues, when there was no interpreter present; and Paul reproves them, because this kind of preaching conveyed no instruction to the people. Again he says, "If any thing be revealed to another that sitteth by, let the first hold his

* E. S. De Beer, editor of *The Correspondence of John Locke* (Oxford: Clarendon, 1979), considers this letter spurious (5:718). The editors of the *Journal of the Friends Historical Society* note that there is no other record of the existence of these two women [April 1914], 11:67).

† Adam Clarke, *The Holy Bible . . . With a commentary and critical notes*, 8 vols. (London: Butterworth, 1810–1825).

‡ Mary Sewell and Mrs. Proudfoot preached in Norwich, where Clarke heard them in late 1783. *The Life of the Rev. Adam Clarke, L.L.D., compiled from authentic documents. By a Wesleyan preacher* (London: Allman, n.d.).

peace." We may infer from this, that two men sometimes attempted to speak at the same time, and the apostle rebukes them, and adds, "Ye may ALL prophesy one by one, for God is not the author of confusion, but of peace." He then proceeds to notice the disorderly conduct of the women, who were guilty of other improprieties. They were probably in the habit of asking questions, on any points of doctrine which they wished more thoroughly explained. This custom was common among the men in the Jewish synagogues, after the pattern of which, the meetings of the early Christians were in all probability conducted. And the Christian women, presuming on the liberty which they enjoyed under the new religion, interrupted the assembly, by asking questions. The apostle disapproved of this, because it disturbed the solemnity of the meeting: he therefore admonishes the women to keep silence in the churches. That the apostle did not allude to preaching is manifest, because he tells them, "If they will *learn* any thing, let them ask their husbands at home." Now a person endowed with a gift in the ministry, does not ask questions in the public exercise of that gift, for the purpose of gaining information: she is instructing others. Moreover, the apostle, in closing his remarks on this subject, says, "Wherefore, brethren, (a generic term, applying equally to men and women,) covet to prophesy, and forbid not to speak with tongues. Let all things be done decently and in order."

Clarke, on the passage, "Let women keep silence in the churches," says:

> This was a Jewish ordinance. Women were not permitted to teach in the assemblies, or even to ask questions. The rabbis taught that a woman should know nothing but the use of her distaff; and the saying of Rabbi Eliezer is worthy of remark and execration: "Let the words of the law be burned, rather than that they should be delivered by women."

Are there not many of our Christian brethren, whose hostility to the ministry of women is as bitter as was that of Rabbi Eliezer, and who would rather let souls perish, than that the truths of the gospel should be delivered by women?

"This," says Clarke, "was their condition till the time of the gospel, when according to the prediction of Joel, the Spirit of God was to be poured out on the women as well as the men, that they might prophesy, that is, teach. And that they did prophesy, or teach, is evident from what the apostle says, ch. 11: 5, where he lays down rules to regulate this part of their conduct while ministering in the church. But does not what the apostle says here, let your women keep silence in the churches, contradict that statement, and show that the words in ch. 11, should be understood in another sense? for here it is expressly said, that they should keep silence in the churches, for it was not permitted to a woman to speak. Both places seem perfectly consistent. It is evident from the context, that the apostle refers here to asking questions, and what we call dictating in the assemblies."

The other passage on which the opinion, that women are not called to the ministry, is founded, is 1 Tim. 2d ch. The apostle speaks of the duty of prayer and supplication, mentions his own ordination as a preacher, and then adds, "I will, therefore, that men pray everywhere, lifting up holy hands, without wrath and doubting. In like manner also, that women adorn themselves in modest apparel," &c. I shall here premise, that as the punctuation and division into chapters and verses is not part of the original arrangement, they cannot determine the sense of a passage. Indeed, every attentive reader of the Bible must observe, that the injudicious separation of sentences often destroys their meaning and their beauty. Joseph John Gurney* whose skill as a biblical critic is well known in England, commenting on this passage, says,

> It is worded in a manner somewhat obscure; but appears to be best construed according to the opinion of various commentators (See Pool's Synopsis)† as conveying an injunction, that women as well as men should pray evewhere, lifting up holy hands without wrath and doubting. 1 Tim. 2: 8, 9. "I will therefore that men pray everwhere, &c.; likewise also the women in a modest dress." (Compare 1 Cor. 11: 5.) "I would have them adorn themselves with shamefacedness and sobriety."

I have no doubt this is the true meaning of the text, and that the translators would never have thought of altering it had they not been under the influence of educational prejudice. The apostle proceeds to exhort the women, who thus publicly made intercession to God, ["]not to adorn themselves with braided hair, or gold, or pearls, or costly array, but (which becometh women professing godliness) with good works." The word in this verse translated "professing," would be more properly rendered preaching godliness, or enjoining piety to the gods,

* Joseph John Gurney (1788–1847), an English Quaker who came to the United States in 1837 to preach revival.

† Matthew Pool, *Synopsis Criticorum aliorumque S. Scripturae interpretum*, 4 vols. (London: 1669–1676).

or conducting public worship. After describing the duty of female ministers about their apparel, the apostle proceeds to correct some improprieties which probably prevailed in the Ephesian church, similar to those which he had reproved among the Corinthian converts. He says, "Let the women LEARN in silence with all subjection; but I suffer not a woman to teach, nor to usurp authority over the man, but to be in silence," or quietness. Here again it is evident that the women, of whom he was speaking, were admonished to learn in silence, which could not refer to their public ministrations to others. The verb to teach, verse 12, is one of very general import, and may in this place more properly be rendered dictate. It is highly probable that women who had long been in bondage, when set free by Christianity from the restraints imposed upon them by Jewish traditions and heathen customs, run [sic] into an extreme in their public assemblies, and interrupted the religious services by frequent interrogations, which they could have had answered as satisfactorily at home.

On a candid examination and comparison of the passages which I have endeavored to explain, viz., Cor. chaps. 11 and 14, and 1 Tim. 2, 8–12. I think we must be compelled to adopt one of two conclusions; either that the apostle grossly contradicts himself on a subject of great practical importance, and that the fulfilment of the prophecy of Joel was a shameful infringement of decency and order; or that the directions given to women, not to speak, or to teach in the congregations, had reference to some local and peculiar customs, which were then common in religious assemblies, and which the apostle thought inconsistent with the purpose for which they were met together. Not one, I suppose, will hesitate which of these two conclusions to adopt. The subject is one of vital importance. That it may claim the calm and prayerful attention of Christians, is the desire of

Thine in the bonds of womanhood,

Sarah M. Grimké.

What are the Duties of Woman at the Present Time?

Worcester, [Mass.] 10th mo. 4th, 1837.

My dear sister—The solemn and important query often arises in my mind, "What are the duties of women at this momentous crisis?" We are living in such an artificial state of society, and are so trammeled by the "tradition of men," that it is difficult to disencumber the mind of all extraneous matter, all merely human judgment, and erect a standard of duty and usefulness, from the only safe guide, the Holy Scriptures. We come to the perusal of that volume, with our minds filled with preconceived opinions and prejudices; we are ignorant of the language in which it was written, and we do not allow ourselves to investigate any points, which have been long settled in the judgment of man, predicated upon the English translation, as if the translators were under the immediate inspiration of God, and every word they wrote was infallibly the mind of the Spirit. We would rather charge the holy men of old, with contradicting themselves on important points, as we do St. Paul, when he tells us in the 11th of 1st Cor. how we are to be apparelled when we preach and pray in public assemblies—and in the 14th, that women are to keep silence in the churches, &c.; and we shrink from an examination of these things, because we love the old way of ease—we forget that it is the laborers who receive wages, and too many of us rejoice that the Bible, as we suppose, affords us a warrant for sitting down in our ceiled houses, and doing little or nothing for the regeneration of a fallen world; and those who do undertake to labor, are the scorn and ridicule of their own and the other sex. We are so little accustomed *to think for ourselves,* that we submit to the dictum of prejudice, and of usurped authority, almost without an effort to redeem ourselves from the unhallowed shackles which have so long bound us; almost without a desire to rise from that degradation and bondage, to which we have been consigned by man, and by which the faculties of our minds, and the powers of our spiritual nature, have been prevented from expanding to their full growth, and are sometimes wholly crushed.

The first duty, I believe, which devolves on our sex now, is to think for themselves, to take the volume of inspiration in their hand, to enter into their closet, and to ask wisdom. "If any of you lack wisdom, let him ask of God who giveth liberally and upbraideth not; AND IT SHALL BE GIVEN OF HIM. But let him ask in faith, nothing wavering." To comprehend our duties, we must understand our own moral nature, our heaven-inspired rights, and our vast responsibilities growing out of those rights. Heretofore, woman has been regarded and has regarded herself, as a gift to man, a *thing* created to fill up the measure of his greatness and his happiness, as the monarch of this lower world. This idea appears to be altogether at variance with the character of God, and the majesty of our immortal nature. If God created woman as a mere appendage to man, then he designed that man should be her God, and that she should have access to her Maker, through the medium of man; if I admit that woman was given to man, I must admit his unlimited power over her, both temporally and spiritually. I see no stopping place, and as I cannot charge my maker with having given one half of accountable creatures into the keeping of the other half, equally corrupt with themselves, without accusing him of absurdity and injustice, I cannot sanction the long received opinion, that woman is "God's last, best gift to man." I turn to my Bible* to see where Milton and his unthinking admirers get this idea, so fraught with injury to woman, and I find nothing there, to substantiate the notion; so far from it, I find that God created THEM in his own image, crowned THEM with the diadem of glory and honor, and gave THEM dominion over the fish of the sea, &c., and blessed THEM. At no subsequent period was this grant to woman, any more than to man, revoked, and hence I conclude they are standing on the same platform of human rights, under the immediate government of God, amenable to no tribunal but his, and that it is in vain for us to attempt to shield our unfaithfulness and disobedience, under the plausible pretext, that we must submit to the government of man. If this were true, then Jehovah should have furnished us with another Bible, where we are pointed to man as our lawgiver, our judge and our king, and provided another Savior; for as Harriet Martineau justly remarks, two orders of beings require different codes of laws, and a different mode of redemption. Nothing has enveloped the mind in more ignorance and uncertainty, than the false idea that the mere circumstance of sex, a circumstance necessary only to our present state of existence, is to be the criterion of duty, intelligence, responsibility, superiority and inferiority. We all acknowledge that facts demonstrate, that the circumstance of sex does not determine these points, and yet we cling to the notion with as much pertinacity as though the decree were immutable, and it were sin to doubt.

Until we comprehend the design of God in the creation of woman; until we take our stand, side by side with our brother; until we read all the precepts of the Bible as addressed to woman as well as to man, and lose, in our moral, intellectual, and immortal nature, the consciousness of sex, we shall never fulfil the end of our existence. We are constantly busying ourselves, with vain endeavors to discover the exact point, where the duties of men and women diverge, and setting up a standard of perfection for each to aim at, thus merging the spiritual in the physical nature, and creating a distinction which God never made. Du-

* See letters published in the N. E. Spectator, on the Province of Woman. [Footnote in original.]

ties belong to *situation*, not to sex; a mother has duties totally different from a single woman; but the rights and responsibilities of men and women as moral beings are identical, and must necessarily be so, if their nature is the same, and their relations to the supreme Being precisely similar. With regard to all moral reformations, men and women have the same duties and the same rights. The ground I take on this point is very plain. I wish to spare you, I wish to spare myself, the worthless and disgusting task of replying in detail to all the coarse attacks and flattering sophisms, by which men have endeavored to entice, or to drive women from almost every sphere of moral action. "Go home and spin," is the well meaning advice of the domestic tyrant of the old school. "Conquer by personal charms and fashionable attractions," is the brilliant career marked out for her, by the idols and the idolaters of fashion. "Never step out of the bounds of decorum, and the customary ways of doing good"; is the sage advice of maternal caution. "Rule by obedience, and by submission sway"; is the golden saying of the moralist poet, sanctioning female servitude, and pointing out a resort and a compensation, in female cunning. What with the fear of the insolent remarks about women, in which those of the dominant sex, whose bravery is the generous offspring of conscious impunity, are particularly apt to indulge; and with the still stronger fear of being thought unfeminine, it is indeed a proof of uncommon moral courage, or of an overpowering sense of religious duty and sympathy with the oppressed, the guilty, and the outcast, that a woman is induced to embrace the unpopular, unfashionable, obnoxious principle of the moral reform, or abolition societies. Popular opinion, the habits of society, are all calculated to lead women to consider the place, the privileges, and the duties, which etiquette has assigned to them, as their peculiar portion, as more important than those which nature has given them in common with men. Men have at all times been inclined to *allow* to women *peculiar privileges*, while withholding from them ESSENTIAL RIGHTS. In the progress of civilization and Christianity, one right after another has been conceded, one occupation after another has been placed within the reach of woman. Still we are far from the practical acknowledgement of the simple truth, that the rational and moral nature of man, is the foundation of all rights and duties, and that women as well as men are rational and moral beings." *[sic]*

The present, is a deeply interesting and important period in the history of woman. The Lord Jehovah, has opened before her a wide field for usefulness and exertion. The cry of misery, the call for help, comes up from the fearful haunts of licentiousness; the wail of despair, the shriek of the helpless victims of cruelty and lust, is borne to our ear on every southern breeze; the maniac howl of intemperance, reaches us from the habitations of drunkenness, and pleads with trumpet tongue for our aid in driving these unclean spirits from our land. Can woman turn from so much wretchedness, and suppose that when she has seen well to the ways of her household, and prepared a well spread table for her family, all her duties are performed and the end of her existence is answered, when she is neglecting duties equally important? In the present state of Christendom, every woman is acting for, or against the great work of moral reformation; every woman, let her sphere be ever so contracted, her influence ever so small, is retarding, or accelerating the spread of truth and righteousness on the earth, by her example and conversation. She is either exciting those with whom she mingles to good works, or she is settling them down at ease in Zion. There is so much to do, no one need be at any loss. Some have time, others have money, others can write, others can speak, others can take the periodicals and scatter them like seed over the land, that they may spring up, and bear fruit, some thirty, some sixty, some an hundred fold. Women in the present day, are placed in a solemn and responsible situation. Circumstances, and the entreaties of the ministry that they would come up to the work of moral reformation, have drawn them out of obscurity, and in some degree burst their bonds; light has shone upon their minds, and they have been enabled to rise a little out of that state of ignorance, to which they had been consigned. Sympathy has enlarged their hearts, active benevolence has elevated their moral character, a more extended sphere of usefulness and of observation has improved their intellectual faculties, and given a higher tone to their desires and their pursuits; but still, woman falls far short of the high and holy station assigned her by her Creator. Those who are engaged in the moral reformations of the day, still measure their actions by a corrupt public opinion, and while they have nobly dared to go forward in these glorious enterprises, regardless of the esteem of a portion of mankind, they are still bound by the unseen fetters of ecclesiastical censure, and know little of that liberty wherewith Christ has made us free. To these women I would say, "emancipate yourselves from every kind of bondage, if the Lord require it, and this *you* only can decide. Open your mouths with wisdom, cry aloud, and spare not, show my people their transgressions and the house of Jacob their sins." Remember, to God your account has to be rendered, and no man, or body of men, can answer for us, in that day when we shall be judged "according to the deeds done in the body." Some women who are laboring for Christ, have doubtless done all that was required of them, and in the remarks I have made, I am far from wishing to depreciate their usefulness, or undervalue their sacrifices; still I believe, there is a wealth of intellect and talents for public exercises, among some who if they yielded to the impressions of duty, would be the Huldahs and the Annas of the day in which they live.

There is one class of women, who, being timid and unaccustomed to think for themselves, and to realize that they are free agents, submit to the command or the opinion of a father, a husband, or a brother, under the false idea in which they have been educated, that man is their superior. The authority he has assumed, and which they have conceded, is felt to be binding, and the conscience being fettered by this notion, they do not dare to act out the impulses of nature, or the promotings of duty. Oh! that they would learn the all-important lesson, "Cease from man, whose breath is in his nostrils, for wherein is he to be accounted of?" Pay all proper respect and deference to the opinions of relatives, but never let those opinions turn you aside from the path of duty. I have known women thus swayed, who have left sacred obligations unperformed, stifled the voice of God's Spirit, and given a deep wound to their own peace, as well as robbed the cause of virtue of their talents and their influence.

There is another class who are glad of any excuse to relieve themselves from difficult and arduous duties—who shelter themselves under the plea, that their male friends are opposed to their uniting in moral reform, or abolition efforts. Ah, my sister, do they remember that every woman has to work out her own salvation, with fear and trembling, and that these excuses will avail nothing in the judgment of Him who saith, "All souls are mine"—"Fear not them that kill the body, and after that have no more that they can do: but I wilt forewarn you whom ye shall fear; fear him who, after he hath killed, hath power to cast into hell; yea, I pray unto you, Fear him."—They may try to pacify their consciences by these unholy subterfuges, but they can no more roll their responsibilities on another, than they can divest themselves of their rational being, and of their accountability to God. But whilst I earnestly desire that women may come up to their duties in the great work of regenerating a fallen world, I entreat them to do it openly, fearlessly, trusting in the Lord. I have known some women sign petitions for the abolition of slavery in the District of Columbia, secretly, because their husbands forbade their doing it, or disapprove of it. If any sufficient reason can be adduced, why woman should be *governed* by the opinion of man, any more than man by the opinion of woman, then let him be her counsellor, and HER GOD; but I enter my protest against her having two masters: it makes our case too hard, and compels us to be double minded, and unstable in our ways. Deception gives a mortal stab to moral rectitude. The moment we admit the idea, that we may do evil that good may come, we lose our self-respect, and adopt policy as our rule, instead of righteousness. Never deceive a man by a *show* of submission. Tell him that you cannot obey him, rather than God, and that it is your intention to sign that petition; but let him clearly understand that obedience is practised, not because it is right to exact it, but because Christ had commanded his disciples not to resist evil. Such an open and Christian course of conduct will secure the esteem and confidence of almost any man, while it will take from him the charter he now fancies he holds, to exercise all his selfish passions on a being whom he regards as his inferior, and as having been placed in subjection to him by Jehovah himself. I am persuaded, if we did not love our chains, man would, after a short resistance, yield to the power of truth, and unbind our fetters; but we love to be idolized; we enjoy the heartless attention which springs from "the generous prompting of chivalry and the poetry of romantic gallantry," to use the expressions of C. E. Beecher; we prefer the homage offered at the shrine of WOMAN, to the respect and admiration accorded to us as moral and intellectual beings. We would rather be the playthings of man, than to stand on an equality with him, because if we assume the dignified station of free agents, of moral beings, we at once avow ourselves liable to the same responsibilities which rest upon him. The more I meditate on the subject of woman's rights and duties, the more I am persuaded, that until she elevates herself to the appropriate sphere which God appointed for her, all moral reformations will move slowly forward. Her degradation was the first effect of sin, and her elevation will give an impulse to public morals and public sentiment, which nothing else can give. While woman is kept in her present unholy subjection—while she feels as if man was her master—she cannot carry forward the glorious work of reformation by being a fellow-laborer with him in the gospel of Jesus Christ.

It is of unspeakable importance to woman, to the world, that she should disenthral her mind of the opinion which spell-binds her as by sorcery, that she is to look to man as the regulator of her actions, the prescriber of the sphere in which she is to move. It is my deep and solemn conviction, that she who first tasted of the forbidden fruit, and gave of it to man, who was the honored instrument of giving birth to the Savior of the world, is designed by her gracious Creator to act a conspicuous part in bringing in the millennial glory of his kingdom, not as a subordinate agent to man, but as a being who is standing immediately under the government of Jehovah. "The Lord God is a sun and a shield, the Lord will give grace and glory: no good thing will be withheld from them that walk uprightly. O Lord of hosts, blessed is the man that trusteth in THEE."

Thine in the bonds of womanhood,

Sarah M. Grimké.

LETTER XV
Man Equally Guilty with Woman in the Fall

Uxbridge, [Mass.] 10th Mo. 20th, 1837.

My Dear Sister,—It is said that "modern Jewish women light a lamp every Friday evening, half an hour before sunset, which is the beginning of their Sabbath, in remembrance of their original mother, who first extinguished the lamp of righteousness,—to remind them of their obligation to rekindle it." I am one of those who always admit, to its fullest extent, the popular charge, that woman brought sin into the world. I accept it as a powerful reason, why woman is bound to labor with double diligence, for the regeneration of that world she has been instrumental in ruining.

But, although I do not repel the imputation, I shall notice some passages in the sacred Scriptures, where this transaction is mentioned, which prove, I think, the identity and equality of man and woman, and that there is no difference in their guilt in the view of that God who searcheth the heart and trieth the reins of the children of men. In Is. 43: 27, we find the following passage—"Thy first father hath sinned, and thy teachers have transgressed against me"—which is synonymous with Rom. 5: 12, "Wherefore, as by ONE MAN sin entered into the world, and death by sin, &c." Here man and woman are included under one term, and no distinction is made in their criminality. The circumstances of the fall are again referred to in 2 Cor. 11:3—"But I fear lest, by any means, as the serpent *beguiled* Eve through his subtility, so your mind should be beguiled from the simplicity that is in Christ." Again, 1st Tim. 2: 14—"Adam *was not deceived;* but the woman being *deceived,* was in the transgression." Now, whether the fact, that Eve was beguiled and deceived, is a proof that her crime was of deeper dye than Adam's, who was not deceived, but was fully aware of the consequences of sharing in her transgression, I shall leave the candid reader to determine.

My present object is to show, that, as woman is charged with all the sin that exists in the world, it is her solemn duty to labor for its extinction; and that this she can never do effectually and extensively, until her mind is disenthralled of those shackles which have been riveted upon her by a *"corrupt public opinion, and a perverted interpretation of the holy Scriptures."* Woman must feel that she is the equal, and is designed to be the fellow laborer of her brother, or she will be studying to find out the *imaginary* line which separates the sexes, and divides the duties of men and women into two distinct classes, a separation not even hinted at in the Bible, where we are expressly told, "there is neither male nor female, for ye are all in Christ Jesus."

My views on this subject are so much better embodied in the language of a living author than I can express them, that I quote the passage entire: "Woman's rights and man's rights are *both* contained in the same charter, and held by the *same* tenure. *All rights* spring out of the *moral* nature: they are both the root and the offspring of *responsibilities.* The physical constitution is the mere *instrument* of the *moral* nature; sex is a mere *incident* of this constitution, a provision necessary to this *form* of existence; its *only* design, not to give, nor to take away, nor in any respect to modify or even *touch* rights or responsibilities in any sense, except so far as the peculiar offices of each sex may afford less or more *opportunity* and ability for the exercise of rights, and the discharge of responsibilities; but merely to continue and enlarge the human department of God's government. Consequently, I know nothing of *man's* rights, or *woman's* rights; *human* rights are all that I recognise. The doctrine, that the *sex of the body* presides over and administers upon the rights and responsibilities of the moral, immortal nature, is to my mind a doctrine kindred to blasphemy, *when seen in its intrinsic nature.* It breaks up utterly the *relations* of the two natures, and reverses their functions; exalting the animal nature into a monarch, and humbling the moral into a slave; making the former a proprietor, and the latter its property."

To perform our duties, we must comprehend our rights and responsibilities; and it is because we do not understand, that we now fall so far short in the discharge of our obligations. Unaccustomed to think for ourselves, and to search the sacred volume, to see how far we are living up to the design of Jehovah in our creation, we have rested satisfied with the sphere marked out for us by man, never detecting the fallacy of that reasoning which forbids woman to exercise some of her noblest faculties, and stamps with the reproach of indelicacy those actions by which women were formerly dignified and exalted in the church.

I should not mention this subject again, if it were not to point out to my sisters what seems to me an irresistible conclusion from the literal interpretation of St. Paul, without reference to the context, and the peculiar circumstances and abuses which drew forth the expressions, "I suffer not a woman to teach"—"Let your women keep silence in the church," i.e. congregation. It is manifest, that if the apostle meant what his words imply, when taken in the strictest sense, then women have no right to *teach* Sabbath or day schools, or to open their lips to sing in the assemblies of the people; yet young and delicate women are engaged in all these offices; they are expressly trained to exhibit themselves, and raise their voices to a high pitch in the choirs of our places of worship. I do not intend to sit in judgment on my sisters for doing these things; I only want them to see, that they are as really infringing a *supposed* divine command, by instructing their pupils in the Sabbath or day schools, and by singing in the congregation, as if they were engaged in preaching the unsearchable riches of Christ to a lost and perishing world. Why, then, are we permitted to break this injunction in some points, and so sedulously warned not to overstep the bounds set for us by our *brethren* in another? Simply, as I believe, because in the one case we subserve *their* views and *their* interests, and act *in subordination to them;* whilst in the other, we come in contact with their interests, and claim to be on an equality with them in the highest and most important trust ever committed to man, namely, the ministry of the word. It is manifest, that if women were permitted to be ministers of the gospel, as they unquestionably were in the primitive ages of the Christian church, it would interfere materially with the present organized system of spiritual power and ecclesiastical authority, which is now vested solely in the hands of men. It would either show that all the paraphernalia of theological seminaries, &c, &c, to prepare men to become evangelists, is wholly unnecessary, or it would create a necessity for similar institutions in order to prepare women for the same office; and this would be an encroachment on that learning, which our kind brethren have so ungenerously monopolized. I do not ask any one to believe my statements, or adopt my conclusions, because they are mine; but I do earnestly entreat my sisters to lay aside their prejudices, and examine these subjects *for themselves,* regardless of the "traditions of men," because they are intimately connected with their duty and their usefulness in the present important crisis.

All who know any thing of the present system of benevolent and religious operations, know that women are performing an important part in them, in *subserviency to men,* who guide our labors, and are often the recipients of those benefits of education we toil to confer, and which we rejoice they can enjoy, although it is their mandate which deprives us of the same advantages. Now, whether our brethren have defrauded us intentionally, or unintentionally, the wrong we suffer is equally the same. For years, they have been spurring us up to the performance of our duties. The immense usefulness and the vast influence of woman have been eulogized and called into exercise, and many a blessing has been lavished upon us, and many a prayer put up for us, because we have labored by day and by night to clothe and feed and educate young men, whilst our own bodies sometimes suffer for want of comfortable garments, and our minds are left in almost utter destitution of that improvement which we are toiling to bestow upon the brethren.

> Full many a gem of purest ray serene;
> The dark unfathomed caves of ocean bear;
> Full many a flower is born to blush unseen
> And waste its sweetness on the desert air.

If the sewing societies, the avails of whose industry are now expended in supporting and educating young men for the ministry, were to withdraw their contributions to these objects, and give them where they are *more needed,* to the advancement of their *own sex* in useful learning, the next generation might furnish sufficient proof, that in intelligence and ability to master the whole circle of sciences, woman is not inferior to man; and instead of a sensible woman being regarded as she now is, as a lusses naturae,* they would be quite as common as sensible men. I confess, considering the high claim men in this country make to great politeness and deference to women, it does seem a little extraordinary that we should be urged to work for the brethren. I should suppose it would be more in character with 'the generous prompting of chivalry, and the poetry of romantic gallantry,' for which Catherine *[sic]* E. Beecher gives them credit, for them to form societies to educate their sisters, seeing our inferior capacities require more cultivation to bring them into use, and qualify us to be helps meet for them. However, though I think that would be but a just return for all our past kindnesses

* *Lusus naturae:* nature's dalliance, trifling, or amusement.

in this way, I should be willing to balance our accounts, and begin a new course. Henceforth, let the benefit be reciprocated, or else let each sex provide for the education of their own poor, whose talents ought to be rescued from the oblivion of ignorance. Sure I am, the young men who are now benefitted by the handy work of their sisters, will not be less honorable if they occupy half their time in earning enough to pay for their own education, instead of depending on the industry of women, who not unfrequently deprive themselves of the means of purchasing valuable books which might enlarge their stock of useful knowledge, and perhaps prove a blessing to the family by furnishing them with instructive reading. If the minds of women were enlightened and improved, the domestic circle would be more frequently refreshed by intelligent conversation, a means of edification now deplorably neglected, for want of that cultivation which these intellectual advantages would confer.

Duties of Women

One of the duties which devolve upon women in the present interesting crisis, is to prepare themselves for more extensive usefulness, by making use of those religious and literary privileges and advantages that are within their reach, if they will only stretch out their hands and possess them. By doing this, they will become better acquainted with their rights as moral beings, and with their responsibilities growing out of those rights: they will regard themselves, as they really are, FREE AGENTS, immortal beings, amenable to no tribunal but that of Jehovah, and bound not to submit to any restriction imposed for selfish purposes, or to gratify that love of power which has reigned in the heart of man from Adam down to the present time. In contemplating the great moral reformations of the day, and the part which they are bound to take in them, instead of puzzling themselves with the harassing, because unnecessary inquiry, how far they may go without overstepping the bounds of propriety, which separate male and female duties, they will only inquire, "Lord, what wilt thou have us do?" They will be enabled to see the simple truth, that God has made no distinction between men and women as moral beings; that the distinction now so much insisted upon between male and female virtues is as absurd as it is unscriptural, and has been the fruitful source of much mischief—granting to man a license for the exhibition of brute force and conflict on the battle field; for sternness, selfishness, and the exercise of irresponsible power in the circle of home—and to woman a permit to rest on an arm of flesh, and to regard modesty and delicacy, and all the kindred virtues, as peculiarly appropriate to her. Now to me it is perfectly clear, that WHATSOEVER IT IS MORALLY RIGHT FOR A MAN TO DO, IT IS MORALLY RIGHT FOR A WOMAN TO DO; and that confusion must exist in the moral world, until woman takes her stand on the same platform with man, and feels that she is clothed by her Maker with the *same rights,* and, of course, that upon her devolve the *same duties.*

It is not my intention, nor indeed do I think it is in my power, to point out the precise duties of women. To him who still teacheth by his Holy Spirit as never man taught, I refer my beloved sisters. There is a vast field of usefulness before them. The signs of the times give portentous evidence, that a day of deep trial is approaching; and I urge them, by every consideration of a Savior's dying love, by the millions of heathen in our midst, by the sufferings of woman in almost every portion of the world, by the fearful ravages which slavery, intemperance, licentiousness and other iniquities are making of the happiness of our fellow creatures, to come to the rescue of a ruined world, and to be found co-workers with Jesus Christ.

Ho! to the rescue, ho!
Up every one that feels—
'Tis a sad and fearful cry of woe
From a guilty world that steals.
Hark! hark! how the horror rolls,
Whence can this anguish be?
'Tis the groan of a trammel'd people's souls,
Now bursting to be free.

And here, with all due deference for the office of the ministry, which I believe was established by Jehovah himself, and designed by Him to be the means of spreading light and salvation through a crucified Savior to the ends of the earth, I would entreat my sisters not to *compel* the ministers of the present day to give their names to great moral reformations. The practice of making ministers life members, or officers of societies, when their hearts have not been touched with a live coal from the altar, and animated with love for the work we are engaged in, is highly injurious to them, as well as to the cause. They often satisfy their consciences in this way, without doing anything to promote the anti-slavery, or temperance, or other reformations; and we please ourselves with the idea, that we have done something to forward the cause of Christ, when, in effect, we have been sewing pillows like the false prophetesses of old under the arm-holes of our clerical brethren. Let us treat the ministers with all tenderness and respect, but let us be careful how we cherish in their hearts the idea that they are of more importance to a cause than other men. I rejoice when they take hold heartily. I love and honor some ministers with whom I have been associated in the anti-slavery ranks, but I do deeply deplore, for the sake of the cause, the prevalent notion, that the clergy must be had, either by persuasion or by bribery. They will not need persuasion or bribery, if their hearts are with us; if they are not, we are better without them. It is idle to suppose that the kingdom of heaven cannot come on earth, without their co-operation. It is the Lord's work, and it must go forward with or without their aid. As well might the converted Jews have despaired of the spread of Christianity, without the co-operation of Scribes and Pharisees.

Let us keep in mind, that no abolitionism is of any value, which is not accompanied with deep, heartfelt repentance; and that, whenever a minister sincerely repents of having, either by his apathy or his efforts, countenanced the fearful sin of slavery, he will need no inducement to come into our ranks; so far from it, he will abhor himself in dust and ashes, for his past blindness and indifference to the cause of God's poor and oppressed: and he will regard it as a privilege to be enabled to do something in the cause of human rights. I know the ministry exercise vast power; but I rejoice in the belief, that the spell is broken which encircled them, and rendered it all but blasphemy to expose their errors and their sins. We are beginning to understand that they are but men, and that their station should not shield them from merited reproof.

I have blushed for my sex when I have heard of their entreating ministers to attend their associations, and open them with prayer. The idea is inconceivable to me, that Christian women can be engaged in doing God's work, and yet cannot ask his blessing on their efforts, except through the lips of a man. I have known a whole town scoured to obtain a minister to open a female meeting, and their refusal to do so spoken of as quite a misfortune. Now, I am not glad that the ministers do wrong; but I am glad that my sisters have been sometimes compelled to act for themselves: it is exactly what they need to strengthen them, and prepare them to act independently. And to say the truth, there is something really ludicrous in seeing a minister enter the meeting, open it with prayer, and then take his departure. However, I only throw out these hints for the consideration of women. I believe there are solemn responsibilities resting upon us, and that in this day of light and knowledge, we cannot plead ignorance of duty. The great moral reformations now on the wheel are only practical Christianity; and if the ministry is not prepared to labor with us in these righteous causes, let us press forward, and they will follow on to know the Lord.

Conclusion

I have now, my dear sister, completed my series of letters. I am aware, they contain some new views; but I believe they are based on the immutable truths of the Bible. All I ask for them is, the candid and prayerful consideration of Christians. If they strike at some of our bosom sins, our deep-rooted prejudices, our long cherished options, let us not condemn them on that account, but investigate them fearlessly and prayerfully, and not shrink from the examination; because, if they are true, they place heavy responsibilities upon women. In throwing them before the public, I have been actuated solely by the belief, that if they are acted upon, they will exalt the character and enlarge the usefulness of my own sex, and contribute greatly to the happiness and virtue of the other. That there is a root of bitterness continually springing up in families and troubling the repose of both men and women, must be manifest to even a superficial observer; and I believe it is the mistaken notion of the inequality of the sexes. As there is an assumption of superiority on the one part, which is not sanctioned by Jehovah, there is an incessant struggle on the other to rise to that degree of dignity, which God designed women to possess in common with men, and to maintain those rights and exercise those privileges which every woman's common sense, apart from the prejudices of education, tells her are inalienable; they are a part of her moral nature, and can only cease when her immortal mind is extinguished.

One word more. I feel that I am calling upon my sex to sacrifice what has been, what is still dear to their hearts, the adulation, the flattery, the attentions of trifling men. I am asking them to repel these insidious enemies whenever they approach them; to manifest by their conduct, that, although they value highly the society of pious and intelligent men, they have no taste for idle conversation, and for that silly preference which is manifested for their personal accommodation, often at the expense of great inconvenience to their male companions. As an illustration of what I mean, I will state a fact.

I was traveling lately in a stage coach. A gentleman, who was also a passenger, was made sick by riding with his back to the horses. I offered to exchange seats, assuring him it did not affect me at all unpleasantly; but he was too polite to permit a lady to run the risk of being discommoded. I am sure he meant to be very civil, but I really thought it was a foolish piece of civility. This kind of attention encourages selfishness in woman, and is only accorded as a sort of quietus, in exchange for those *rights* of which we are deprived. Men and women are equally bound to cultivate a spirit of accommodation; but I exceedingly deprecate her being treated like a spoiled child, and sacrifices made to her selfishness and vanity. In lieu of these flattering but injurious attentions, yielded to her as an inferior, as a mark of benevolence and courtesy, I want my sex to claim nothing from their brethren but what their brethren may justly claim from them, in their intercourse as Christians. I am persuaded woman can do much in this way to elevate her own character. And that we may become duly sensible of the dignity of our nature, only a little lower than the angels, and bring forth fruit to the glory and honor of Emanuel's name, is the fervent prayer of

Thine in the bonds of womanhood,

Sarah M. Grimké.

Angelina E. Grimké to Jane Smith

[W/G, Box 4.]

New Rowley [Mass.] 7 Mo: 25 [1837]

My Dear Jane

. . . But our *womanhood*—it is as great offense to some as our abolitionism. I will let H C W tell thee what a war is waged against it. The whole land seems roused to discussion on the *province of woman,* & I am glad of it. We are willing to bear the brunt of the storm, if we can only be the means of making a breach in the wall of public opinion, which lies right in the way of woman's true dignity, honor & usefulness. Sister Sarah does preach up woman's rights most nobly & fearlessly, & we find that many of our New England sisters are ready to receive these strange doctrines, feeling as they do, that our whole sex needs an emancipation from the thraldom of public opinion. What dost thou think of some of *them walking* 2, 4, 6 *&* 8 miles to attend our meetings? . . .

I must say Fare thee well to night my dear friend.

*Sarah M. and Angelina E. Grimké to Amos A. Phelps**
[BPL, Ms.A.21.7 (31).]

Groton [Mass.] 8th Mo. 3d 1837.

Dear brother Phelps,

Thy letter, which we received yesterday at Lowell, neither surprised us nor moved us, because we are prepared to find opposition & to meet with condemnation from the ministry *generally*. We know that it is to this class of the brethren we are indebted for the false views now so prevalent on the subject of womens preaching, that they in the first place translated the Bible & have placed their own interpretations on the words of the Apostle, using expressions which convey an utterly erroneous meaning. They have written the commentaries on these passages to suit their own misconceived opinions & have thereby deprived women of those rights which God invested [in] them as moral & responsible beings. The clergy have done an infinite injury to woman, & woman in the coming conflict will, we apprehend, be much in the situation of Paul, when he said: "No man stood by me." But, my brother, we have planted our feet on the Rock of Ages, & our trust is in Him who saith, "Trust in the Lord for in the Lord Jehovah is everlasting strength." Our views & principles & practices in this matter are founded upon the immutable Truth of God, & we believe that to abandon them would be to surrender our rights as moral & responsible beings.

I will now endeavor to reply to thy objections to our present course. 1. "Because it moves a 'previous question.' " This is not our fault; we are simply doing our duty, & the consequences we must leave to him who has pointed out this path for us to walk in. If in calling us thus publicly to advocate the cause of the down-trodden slave, God has unexpectedly placed us in the fore-front of the battle which is to be waged against the rights & duties & responsibilities of woman, it would ill become us to shrink from such a contest.

Thy 2d objection is that we are precluded from making statements relative to the fearful havoc which slavery makes of female virtue. Perhaps it may shock thee, but I do not feel precluded from making the

* Amos A. Phelps (1805–1847), a Congregational minister who became an agent of the New England Anti-Slavery Society in 1834 and of the American in 1836, was a moderate, close to the Executive Committee. Though he had been generally friendly to Sarah and Angelina, he appealed to them to cease lecturing before mixed audiences and to allow him to publish his request and their concurrence.

dreadful immorality of the South known in promiscuous assemblies. I stand before them as a moral & intellectual being, pleading with moral & intellectual beings. I feel that we are one in Christ & that I have nothing to do with my audience as males & females. I do not, however, attach to this part of the subject all the importance that thou dost. I believe that to show the American public the enormity of the sin of slavery, we must go deeper than its results; we must maintain the principle that slavery is a malum in se* & that all its concomitant evils are but its legitimate fruits.

Thou sayest our present course makes the Anti Slavery cause responsible for what, in thy judgment, we should not make it responsible. We do not, & we cannot, consent to surrender our moral accountability to any society, & when we united ourselves to the A. S. S., we did not give up our free agency. I can, therefore, only repeat what I said on the first hand, that if in the performance of duty any reproach is cast on the A. S. cause thro' our instrumentality, I do not think it is our fault, however much we may regret it. To close the doors *now* against our brethren wd. be a violation of our fundamental principle that man & woman are created equal, & have the same duties & the same responsibilitys as moral beings. If, therefore, it is right for thee, my dear brother, to lecture to promiscuous assemblies, it is right for us to do the same.

With respect to thy suggestions as to the future mode we should pursue, to do when among Quakers as Quakers do &c., I do not see how we could consent to do this, because we hold no commission from the Quakers to do what we are doing, nor do we in the least defend our present course by sheltering ourselves under our Quakerism. If it is wrong for us to speak the Truths of the Gospel in mixed assemblies, our belonging to the So. of Fds. does not make it right. We, therefore, always disclaim this reason & express ourselves as acting from a conviction of duty based on the Scriptures. This subject is worthy of candid & *prayerful* investigation, & we hope that for thy own sake thou wilt be willing to examine it. We should regret that a brother whom we esteem so highly should identify himself with the men who sent forth the Pastoral Letter, a letter which aims to tear from woman her dearest rights & substitute the paltry privilege of leaning upon a fallen creature instead of the strong arm of Almighty God. We believe that this subject of womens rights & duties must come before the public for discussion, so that the Lord will help us to endure the opposition, contumely & scorn which will be cast upon womanhood & that he will make us more

* An act that is inherently evil (literally, wrong in itself).

than conquerors thro' him that loved us. We would, therefore, entreat our brethren to stand still not for our sakes, but for their own, least [sic] peradventure they be found fighting against God.

And now, dear brother, permit me to say that we believe thou hast been influenced by a love for the A. S. cause, altho' other feelings have been mingled with that love. But surely Truth cannot hurt Truth, & to assert the rights of woman in our conduct cannot hurt the cause we are advocating with our tongues. It is like supposing, as E. C. Delavan did, that his joining the A. S. ranks would injure the Temperance cause. Pity that we have got Christianity parcelled off in lots, so that we fancy that what is designed to be one beautiful & harmonious whole will be injured by the parts coming into contact.

As far as we are concerned, we are entirely willing that thou shouldst *"say publicly"* any thing thou wishes. . . .

Thy sister in the bonds of the gospel

Sarah M. Grimké

Dear Brother

I have asked for a little space in this letter just to say that in consequence of the uneasiness I have felt from the fact that I was throwing upon the Anti Slavery Society the responsibility of our promiscuous meetings, I intend to write to Elizur Wright & give the Ex. Com. a full opportunity of throwing off that responsibility. . . .

A E Grimké

Angelina E. Grimké to Jane Smith

[W/G, Box 4.]

Groton [Mass.] 7th [8th] Month 10th [1837]

My Dear Jane

. . . No doubt H C W told you that a storm was gathering all around against our *womanhood;* the Ministers especially are in great trepidation, & I should not be at all surprised, if in 3 months, almost every pulpit was closed against us. We received, about a week ago, a letter from Amos A Phelps, remonstrating very earnestly, but *kindly,* against our lecturing to *men* & women, & requesting permission to *publish the fact of his having done so* with a declaration on our parts that *we preferred* having *female* audiences only. I wish you could see the letter & sisters admirable reply to it. . . . I wrote [to Elizur Wright] last week. H. B. Stanton happened to be here at the time, & read all the letters; & he wrote to Elizur Wright, warning him by no means to publish any thing which would in the *least* degree appear to *disapprove* of what we were doing. I do not know what the result will be.* My only fear is that some of the anti-slavery brethren will commit themselves, in this excitement, against *woman's rights & duties,* before they examine the subject, & will, in a few years, regret the steps they may take. This will soon be an absorbing topic. It must be discussed whether women are moral & responsible beings, and whether there is such a thing as *male and female virtue* & *male & female* duties &c. My opinion is that there *are none* & that this false idea has driven the plowshare of ruin over the whole field of morality. . . . I am persuaded that woman is not to be as she has been, a mere second-hand agent in the regeneration of a fallen world, but the acknowledged equal & co-worker with man in this glorious work. . . . Hubbard Winslow of Boston† has just preached a sermon to set forth the proper sphere of our sex. I am truly glad that men are not ashamed to come out boldly & tell us just what is in their hearts.

On the 2d came to this lovely little village [Groton]. . . . Here Anne Weston of Boston had come to meet us. She says the Boston women will stand by us in the contest for woman's rights, that they were very glad to find we had accepted the challenge of a discussion at Amesbury,‡ on account of its bearings on the province of *woman* &c.

On the 3d brother Stanton came here, found he was sound on the subject of woman's rights. He went to meeting with us in the evening, opened it with a precious prayer & sat with us in the pulpit.§ About 500 out, the largest Anti Slavery audience that has yet attended in this place. He says he wants very much so to arrange some meeting so that *we & he* may speak at it together. This would be an *irretrievable commitment,* but I doubt whether the time has fully come for such an *anomaly* in Massachusetts. . . .

Most affy with sisters love to all of you

A E Gé

* Weld had written to the sisters on July 22 that they had no official connection with the Executive Committee, but they had not yet received it. Weld also wrote: "If any gainsay your speaking in public and to *men,* they gainsay the *Quakers* and not the *abolitionists*" (W/G, Box 4; B/D, 1:411).

† Hubbard Winslow (1799–1864), a Congregational minister, denounced women abolitionists in his sermon, which he expanded into a book, *The Appropriate Sphere of Woman* (Boston, Mass.: 1840).

‡ At Amesbury, Mass., on July 11, the sisters had responded to two men who challenged their views on slavery; they agreed to debate the men further on July 19, also at Amesbury.

§ In her August 12 letter to Weld (see below), Angelina wrote that she did not like Stanton coming to their meetings, but did not know him well enough to refuse him.

Angelina E. Grimké to Theodore Dwight Weld

[W/G, Box 4; B/D, 1:414–419.]

Groton [Mass.] 8th Month 12. [1837]

My Dear Brother

. . . [W]e are placed very unexpectedly in a very trying situation, in the forefront of an entirely new contest—a contest for the *rights* of *woman* as a moral, intelligent & responsible being. Harriet Martineau says "God & man know that the time has not come for women to make their injuries even heard of"; but it seems as tho' it had come *now* & that the exigency must be met with the firmness & faith of woman in by gone ages. I cannot help feeling some regret that this shld have come up *before* the Anti Slavery question was settled, so fearful am I that it may injure that blessed cause, & then again I think this must be the Lords time & therefore the *best* time, for it seems to have been brought about by a concatenation of circumstances over which we had no control. The fact is it involves the interests of every minister in our land, & therefore they will stand almost in a solid phalanx against woman's rights, & I am afraid the discussion of this question will divide in Jacob & scatter in Israel; it will also touch every man's interests at home, in the tenderest relation of life; it will go down into the very depths of his soul & cause great searchings of heart. I am glad H Winslow of Boston has come out so boldly & told us just what I believe is in the hearts of thousands of men in our land. I must confess my womanhood is insulted, my moral feelings outraged when I reflect on these things, & I am sure *I know just* how the free colored people feel towards the whites when they pay them more than common attention; it is *not paid as a* RIGHT, but *given as a* BOUNTY on a *little* more than *ordinary* sense. There is not one man in 500 who really understands what kind of attention is alone acceptable to a woman of pure & exalted moral & intellectual worth. . . .

Now we want thee to sustain us on the high ground of MORAL RIGHT, *not* of Quaker peculiarity. This question must be met *now;* let us do it as *moral* beings, & not try to turn a SECTARIAN *peculiarity* to the best account for the benefit of Abolitionism. WE do not stand on Quaker ground, but on Bible ground & *moral right.* What we claim for ourselves, we claim for *every* woman whom God has called & qualified with gifts & graces. Can't *thou* stand *just here* side by side with us?

. . . Mary Parker sent us word that the Boston women would stand by us if *every* body else forsook us. A Weston has been here with us & is very strong. . . .

Thy sister in the bonds of woman and the slave

A E Gé.

Sarah M. and Angelina E. Grimké to Henry C. Wright

[BPL, MS.A.1.2, 6:62; B/D, 1:419–422.]

Groton [Mass.] 8/12/37

Dear brother Wright,

I do most cordially agree with thee about our notices being given to lecture to women only. I believe that we ought not *now* to retreat from the ground we have taken & that, if we do this, it will only make harder work at some future day. Therefore, I say, keep the "honest, straight forward course." Do the Lords will in simplicity & leave the consequences in his hands. He has very unexpectedly made us the means of bringing up the discussion of the question of womans preaching, & all we have to do is to do our duty & meet the results with patience, trusting in the Lord, who is able to deliver out of the paw of the bear & the lion. . . .

We read [your] article for the N[ew] E[ngland] S[pectator] and forwarded it. We liked it much & are thankful the Lord has opened the hearts of some of the brethren to stand by those women who are laboring with them in the gospel. I hope thy faithfulness will stir up some others to examine this important subject. . . .

Farewell in the best of bonds thy sister Sarah M. Grimké.

My Dear Brother

. . . Didst thou see my friends Sidney Ann Lewis & Jane Smith, & didst thou talk to them about this blessed doctrine of Divine Government & get them to come right under the yoke of Jesus. How easy it is, how peaceful his reign of moral suasion. . . .

in the best of bonds

A. E. Gé

Angelina E. Grimké to Amos A. Phelps
[BPL, MS.A.21.7 (34).]

Brookline [Mass.]—8th Mo—17th [1837]

Dear Brother

. . . We do not remember that *any one but* thyself has ever expressed *to us* in any way their *dis*approbation of our holding promiscuous meetings—so far from it, that with regard to myself, nothing but the repeated solicitations of our Anti Slavery brethren could have induced me to consent to speak to any but women, for tho' *my principles* were all in favor of doing so, yet, as I never have done it, I felt a timidity about it, similar to that which I suppose our colored brethren felt when they first began to address *white* as well as colored persons. I am sure I know from experience just what their feelings are on account of their supposed inferiority. And like them, *I feel that I am inferior* in as much as I have not had the advantages of a liberal education.

With regard to publishing our correspondence, we have one objection to it which is this. In thy letter to us thou hast entirely waved the discussion of the *principle* upon which we are acting, therefore we have had no opportunity of indicating this principle which is all important. Every intelligent person in Massachusetts knows thy objections to our course, but they are almost entirely ignorant of our reasons for differing from thee. We, therefore, think if the correspondence is to be published, no good end can be answered by it unless thou wilt write us another letter setting forth thy reason for not thinking our course *right,* just as thou didst to show us why thou didst not think it was *wise.* If thou wilt do this, then we can vindicate ourselves just as thou wishest to vindicate thyself. But if the two letters only which have already been written are published, then *no principles* on either side will be brought out. Our correspondence will only say to the public: Amos A Phelps entirely disapproves of S M & A E Gé's course. He has told them so & stated to them why he thinks that course is *unwise,* but he gives no reason to prove it is not *right.* We know why he disapproves of their course, because we do also on the ground of principle, but we do not know at all upon what grounds *they* sustain that course. . . .

Thine Sincerely in the bonds of the slave—

A E Grimké

John Greenleaf Whittier to Sarah and Angelina Grimké

[Catharine H. Birney, *The Grimké Sisters, Sarah and Angelina Grimké: The First American Women Advocates of Abolition and Woman's Rights* (Boston, Mass.: Lee and Shepard, 1885; Westport, Conn.: Greenwood, 1969), pp. 203–205; original not found]

Office of Am. A. S. Soc. [New York City]
14th of 8 Mo. 1837.

My Dear Sisters,—

. . . I am anxious, too, to hold a long conversation with you on the subject of *war,* human government, and church and family government. The more I reflect on this subject, the more difficulty I find, and the more decidedly am I of the opinion that we ought to hold all these matters far aloof from the cause of abolition. . . .

In regard to another subject, *"the rights of woman,"* you are now doing much and nobly to vindicate and assert the rights of woman. Your lectures to crowded and promiscuous audiences on a subject manifestly, in many of its aspects, *political,* interwoven with the framework of the government, are practical and powerful assertions of the right and the duty of woman to labor side by side with her brother for the welfare and redemption of the world. Why, then, let me ask, is it necessary for you to enter the lists as controversial writers on this question? . . .

Your friend and brother,

Jno. G. Whittier.

Theodore Dwight Weld to Sarah and Angelina Grimké

[W/G, Box 4; B/D, 1:425–427.]

New York, August 15–37

My dear sisters

. . . I do most deeply regret that you have begun a series of articles in the Papers on the rights of woman. Why, my dear sisters, the best possible advocacy which you can make is just what you *are* making day by day. Thousands hear you every week who have all their lives held that woman must not speak in public. . . . You can do ten times as much on the subject of *slavery* as Mrs. Child or Mrs. Chapman. Why? Not because your powers are superior to theirs, but because you are *southerners.* You can do more at convincing the north than twenty *north-*

ern females, tho' they could speak as well as you. Now this peculiar advantage you *lose* the moment you take *another* subject. . . .

Your brother T. D. Weld

Angelina E. Grimké to Theodore Dwight Weld and John Greenleaf Whittier

[W/G, Box 4; B/D, 1:427–432.]

Brookline [Mass.] 8th Mo 20—[1837]

To Theodore D. Weld and J. G. Whittier

Brethren beloved in the Lord

As your letters came to hand at the same time & both are devoted mainly to the same subject, we have concluded to answer them on one sheet & jointly. You seem greatly alarmed at the idea of our advocating the *rights of woman*. Now we will first tell you *how* we came to begin those letters in the Spectator. Whilst we were at Newburyport,* we received a note from Mary Parker telling us that Wm S Porter† had requested her to try to obtain some one to write for his paper in order that it might be better sustained. She asked him whether *she* might choose the subject & named the *province of woman;* he said yes, he would be glad to have such pieces to publish. Just at this time, the Pastoral Letter came out, & Mary requested us to write something every week about *Woman* for the Spectator. We consulted together & viewed this unexpected opportunity of throwing our views before the public as providential. As I was writing to C E B, S M G undertook it, & as this paper was not an abolition paper, we could not see any impropriety in embracing this opening. These letters have not been the means of *arousing* the public attention to the subject of Woman's rights; it was the Pastoral Letter which did the mischief. The ministers seemed panic struck at once & commenced a most violent attack upon us. I do not say *absurd,* for in truth if it can be fairly established that women *can lecture,* then why may they not preach, & if *they* can preach, then woe! woe be unto that Clerical Domination which now rules the world under the various names of Genl Assemblies, Congregational Associations, etc. *This Letter,* then, roused the attention of the whole country to enquire what *right* we had to open our mouths for the dumb; the people were

* Early July, at the home of Henry C. Wright.

† William S. Porter, Congregational minister and editor of the *New England Spectator,* "A Family Paper, Designed to Promote the Study of the Bible, Family Religion, Active Piety, the Abolition of War, Slavery, Licentiousness, &c. and the Circulation of Useful Intelligence."

continually told "it is a *shame* for a *woman* to speak in the churches." Paul suffered not a *woman* to *teach* but commanded *her* to be in silence. The pulpit is too *sacred a place* for *woman's* foot &c. Now, my dear brothers, *this invasion of our rights* was just such an attack upon *us,* as that made upon Abolitionists generally, when they were told a few years ago that *they had no right* to discuss the subject of Slavery. Did *you* take no notice of this assertion? Why no! With one heart & one voice, you said, *We* will settle *this right before* we go one step further. *The time* to assert a right is *the* time when *that* right is denied. *We must establish this right,* for if we do not, it will be impossible for *us* to go *on with the work of Emancipation.* But you will say that notwithstand[ing] the denial of your right, you still had crowded audiences—*curiosity,* it was a new thing under the sun to see a *woman* occupy the place of a lecturer, & the people were very anxious to *hear* & *see* for themselves: but you certainly *must* know that the leaven which the ministers are so assiduously working into the minds of the people *must* take effect in process of time, & *will close every church to us,* if we give the community no reasons to counteract the sophistry of priests & levites. In this State, particularly, there is an utter ignorance on the subject. Some few noble minds bursting thro' the trammels of educational prejudice FEEL that woman does stand on the same platform of human rights with man, but even these cannot sustain their ground by argument, & as soon as they open their lips to assert her *rights,* their opponents throw perverted scripture into their faces & call O yea, clamor for *proof,* PROOF, PROOF! & this *they cannot* give & are beaten off the field in disgrace. Now, we are confident that there are scores of such minds panting after light on this subject: "the children *ask* bread & no MAN giveth it unto them." There is an eagerness to understand our views. Now, is it wrong to give those views in a series of letters in a paper NOT devoted to Abolition?

And can you not see that women *could* do, & *would* do a hundred times more for the slave if she were not fettered? Why! we are gravely told that we are out of our sphere even when we circulate petitions; out of our "appropriate sphere" when we speak to women only; & out of them when we *sing* in the churches. Silence is *our* province, submission *our* duty. If, then, we "give *no reason* for the hope that is in us," that we have *equal rights* with our brethren, how can we expect to be permitted *much longer to exercise those rights?* IF I know my own heart, I am NOT actuated by any selfish considerations (but I do sincerely thank our dear brother J G W for the suggestion), but we are actuated by the full conviction that if we are to do any good in the Anti Slavery cause, our *right* to labor in it *must* be firmly established; *not* on the ground of Quakerism, but on the only firm bases of human rights, the Bible. Indeed, I contend brethren that *this* is not *Quaker* doctrine; it is no more like *their* doctrine on Women than our Anti Slavery is like their Abolition—just about the same difference. I will explain myself. Women are regarded as equal to men on the ground of *spiritual gifts, not* on the broad ground of *humanity*. Woman may *preach;* this is a *gift;* but woman must *not* make the discipline by which *she herself* is to be governed. O that you were here that we might have a good long, *long* talk over matters and things; then I could explain myself far better, & I think we could convince you that *we* cannot push Abolitionism forward with all our might *until* we take up the stumbling block out of the road. We cannot see with brother Weld in this matter. We acknowledge the excellence of his reasons for urging us to labor in this cause of the Slave, our being Southerners, &c. But then we say how can we expect to be able to hold meetings much longer, when people are so diligently taught to *despise us* for thus stepping out of the ["]sphere of woman"! Look at this instance: after we had left Groton, the *Abolition* minister there, at a Lyceum meeting, poured out his sarcasm & ridicule upon our heads, & among other things said, he would as soon be caught robbing a hen roost as encouraging a woman to lecture. Now, brethren, if the leaders of the people thus speak of our labors, *how long* will we be allowed to prosecute them? Answer me this question. You may depend upon it, tho' to meet *this* question *may appear* to be turning out of our road, that *it is not*. IT IS NOT: we *must* meet it & meet it *now* & meet it like *women* in the fear of the Lord. Why the language of the priest & levites to us women is that of David's brother to him. "Why camest thou down hither? & with whom hast thou left those few sheep in the wilderness? I know thy pride & the naughtiness of thy heart; for thou art come down that thou mightest see the battle." They utterly deny *our right* to interfere with this or any other moral reform, except in the particular way *they* choose to mark out for us to walk in. If we dare to stand upright & do our duty according to the dictates of *our own* consciences, why then we are compared to Fanny Wright, &c. Why, my dear brothers, can you not see the deep laid scheme of the clergy against us as lecturers? They know full well that if they can persuade the people it is a *shame* for us to speak in public, & that every time we open our mouths for the dumb we are breaking a divine command, that even if we spoke with the tongues of *men* or of angels, we should have *no hearers*. They are springing a deep mine beneath our feet, & we shall *very* soon be compelled to retreat for we shall have *no* ground to stand on. If we surrender the right to *speak* to the public this year, we must surrender the right to petition next year & the right to *write* the year after &c. What *then* can *woman* do for the slave, when she is herself under the feet of man & shamed into *silence?* Now we entreat *you* to weigh candidly the *whole subject,* & then we are sure you will see this is no more than an abandonment of our first love than the effort made by Anti Slavery men to establish the *right* of free discussion.

With regard to brother Weld's ultraism* on the subject of marriage, he is quite mistaken if he fancies he has got far *ahead of us* in the human rights reform. We do *not* think his doctrine at all shocking: it is *altogether right.* But I am afraid I am *too proud* ever to exercise the right. The fact is we are living in such an artificial state of society that there are some things about which we dare not speak out, or act out the most natural & best feelings of our hearts. O! *when* shall we be "delivered from the *bondage of corruption* into the glorious liberty of the sons of God"! By the bye, it will be very important to establish this right, for the men of Mass stoutly declare that women who hold such sentiments of *equality* can never expect to be courted. They seem to hold out this as a kind of threat to deter us from asserting our rights, not *knowing whereunto this will grow.* But jesting is inconvenient says the Apostle: to business then.

Anti Slavery men are trying very hard to separate what God hath joined together. I fully believe that so far from keeping different moral reformations entirely distinct, that no such attempt can ever be successful. They are bound together in a circle, like the sciences; they blend with each other, like the colors of the rain bow; they are the parts only of our glorious whole, & that whole is Christianity, pure *practical* christianity. The fact is *I* believe—but dont be alarmed, for it is only *I*—that Men & Women will have to go out on their own responsibility, just like the prophets of old & declare the *whole* counsel of God to the people. The whole Church Government must come down; the clergy stand right in the way of reform, & I do not know but this stumbling block too must be removed *before* Slavery can be abolished, for the system is supported by *them;* it could not exist without the Church, as it is called. This grand principle must be mooted, discussed & established, viz. the

* Weld had written that "the proposition of marriage may with just the same propriety be made by the *woman* as the *man,*" and then stated: "I have never found man, woman or child who agreed with me in the 'ultraism' of woman's rights." Letter of August 15, 1837, W/G, Box 4; B/D 1:425.

Ministers of the Gospel are the successors of the *prophets,* not of the *priests;* the latter were types of the great eternal high priest of his Church; they were struck dumb as soon as the birth of his forerunner was announced. Zacharias could *not speak unto* the people after he had seen the vision in the temple. The Church is built *not* upon the priests at all but upon the *prophets & apostles,* Jesus Christ being the chief corner stone. This develops three important inferences: 1. True ministers are called, like Elisha from the plough & Amos from gathering sycamore fruit, Matthew from the receipt of custom & Peter & John from their fishing nets. 2. As prophets *never were paid,* so ministers ought not to be. 3. As there were *prophetesses* as well as prophets, so there *ought* to be now *female* as well as male ministers. Just let this one principle be established, & what will become of the power and sacredness of the pastoral office? Is brother Weld frightened at *my ultraism?* . . .

We never mention women's rights in our *lectures,* except so far as is necessary to urge them to meet their responsibilities. We speak of their *responsibilities* & leave *them* to *infer* their *rights.* . . .

I should not be at all surprised if the public demanded of us, "by what authority doest thou this thing," & if we had to lecture on this subject specifically, & call upon the men "to show cause if any they had," why *women* should not open their mouths for the dumb. . . .

May the Lord bless you my dear brothers is the prayer of your sister in Jesus

A. E. G

Angelina E. Grimké to Jane Smith

[W/G, Box 4.]

Brookline [Mass.] 8th Mon: 26th [1837]

My Dear Jane—

I am truly glad to find that Brother Wright has been with you long enough to explain his ultra peace views. O! when will the *Christian* world (as it is called) be ready to embrace Christianity. What kind of Religion have we now—a mere *theoretical* skeleton, almost entirely destitute of practice. How terrible must be the shaking which will shake down the vast structures which man has built up to fetter the mind & body of his fellow man. Can these things come to pass without relighting the torch of persecution, are *we preparing* ourselves to encounter such deadly opposition, are we living so near the fountain of all Truth as to be continually drinking of those streams which can make glad in the midst of sorrow. I fear *I* am not. . . .

Sister & myself feel quite ready for the discussion about women, but our brothers Whittier & Weld entreat us to let it alone for the present. . . . We know that *our* views on this subject are quite new to the mass of the people of this State & think it best to throw them open for their consideration, just letting them have both sides of the argument to look at, at the same time. Indeed, some of us wanted to have a meeting in Boston for us to speak on this particular subject *now,* & we went to town on 4th day [Wednesday] on purpose to hold a conference about it at Maria Chapmans. Mary Parker, M C & S M G were against it *until* we came back in the fall, fearing that it wld bring down such a storm upon our heads that we could not work in the country, & so H Sargent* & myself yielded, & I expect this is the *wisest* plan, tho' as brother Stanton says, I am ready for the battle NOW.

I am still glad of Sisters Letters & believe they are doing *great* good. Some nobleminded *women* cheer her on, & she feels encouraged to persevere, the brethren notwithstanding. I tell them that this is a part of the great doctrine of Human rights & can no more be separated from Emancipation than the light from the heat of the sun; the rights of the slave & woman blend like the colors of the rainbow. However, I rarely introduce this topic into my addresses, except so far as to urge my sisters up to duty. I should not suppose it would do for B Lundy to republish these letters, as his paper is *strictly* Anti Slavery & the organ of the State society, but M Chapman says, as they are addressed to the President of the F A S Sy of Boston, they mean to publish them with their annual report. I fear the brethren will persuade her out of this plan if they happen to hear of it, for they are dreadfully afraid of this kind of amalgamation. I am very glad to hear that Lucretia Mott addressed the moral Reform Society and am earnest in the hope that *we* are only pioneers going before a host of worthy women who will come up to the help of the Lord against the mighty. . . .

Thine as ever

A E Gé

* Henrietta Sargent, a member of the Boston Female Anti-Slavery Society and a close friend of the Garrisons.

Sarah M. and Angelina E. Grimké to Henry C. Wright

[BPL, MS.A.1.2, 6:64; B/D, 1:436–441.]

Brookline [Mass.] 8/27/37.

Dear brother Wright,

. . . My very soul is sick of the narrow minded policy of Christians, of abolitionists, trying to keep asunder the different parts of Christianity, as if it were not a beautiful & harmonious system which could not be divided. What shall we say to these times, & what shall we do, but leave the dead to bury the dead & follow Christ. Dear Angelina is quite troubled; she is more downcast than I have yet seen her, because our coming forth in the A S cause seems really to be at the bottom of this clerical defection; but the Lord knows that we did not come to forward our own interest but in simple obedience to his commands, & I do not believe we are responsible for the consequences of doing the will of God. I do most fully believe she has been called to the work of preaching the gospel & that this is but the commencement of her labors, but it requires divine assistance to sustain the present pressure of opinion from those we love. Brothers Whittier & Weld are anxious we should say nothing on the woman question, but I do not feel as if I could surrender my right to discuss any great moral subject. If my connection with A S must continue at the expence of my conscience, I had far rather be thrown out of the A S ranks; but our business at present seems to be in patience to possess our souls. How much is comprehended in thy desire that we may be entirely emancipated from *all servitude to man.* I reciprocate it & desire it for thee, my dear brother, for I expect from all I can learn of the views of the Ex. Com. of the A A S S, that it is their intention to take the consciences of their agents into their keeping; they have disclaimed, as thou wilt see by the Eman[cipator], all connexion with us, & I suppose will do the same by thee. . . .* Dear brother Garrison has been passing the day with us; as iron sharpeth iron, so doth a man the counten[ance] of his friend, & it has cheered my spirit to find that he unites fully with us on the subject of the rights of woman. I did not see how his enlightened mind could do otherwise, but it has been pleasant to hear the confirmation from his own lips. . . .

Brother Phelps came out here & spent an evening very pleasantly with us. We talked the whole matter over. He said he came to learn & listened very patiently to all our arguments in favor of womens preach-

* In fact, the Executive Committee informed Wright that his agency would not be renewed.

ing. He said his views had been of long standing, & he had not yet reexamined the matter. I hope he will do so, but really the abolitionists are in such trouble about the clerical defection that I doubt whether he will have time. However, he has given up the idea of publishing a protest against us. . . .

I think our best course will be quietly to continue to write on the "Province of Woman" but not undertake to review sermons, so that we may avoid personal controversy. . . .

We have considered the subject of a "Paper" but conclude as long as we are not shut out from the mens papers, we will use them; we do not want to separate the sexes any more into different organizations, if it can be avoided. When they refuse to publish for us, as I expect they will, we may then find it best to have a medium of communication with the public for ourselves. We talked it over with M Chapman, &c. &c. . . .

Farewell my dear brother. . . .

Sarah M. Grimké.

My Dear Brother—
What wouldst thou think of the Liberator abandoning Abolitionism as a *primary* object & becoming the vehicle of all these grand principles? Is not the time rapidly coming for such a change, say after the contract of the Mass St Sy is closed with the Editor, the 1st of next year. I trust brother G[arrison] may be divinely directed. . . . May the Lord *guide* and (bless) thee is the prayer of Thy Sister A. E. Grimké

Angelina E. Grimké to Theodore Dwight Weld

[W/G, Box 4; B/D, 1:441–442.]

[Brookline, Mass.] August 27, 1837.

Dear Brother
Today has been a day of much trial, as I have tho't of *our* being the ostensible cause of the Clerical movement: & the query has arisen, am *I* in my right place & doing my appropriate work? Was it *right* for us to come to Massachusetts? I expected to meet with trials, *personal* trials, & I (vainly perhaps) *think* I could have borne THEM, but all this unsettlement & complaint among the *friends* of the cause is so unexpected that I don't know how to bear it. My only consolation is the hope that it will drive us nearer to Him who alone can guide & sustain. O! how precious

to feel that I came out in faith, in simple obedience to what I believed was my Father's will, *not mine* own. . . .

Thine for the poor and the outcast A. E. Gé.

O! is not *worldly policy* at work in the A S cause NOW. I tremble lest, if we persist in smothering the truth, because we are not ready to hear it or receive it in love, that our souls will wither & the Lord will rebuke us in his wrath. Only think of these things & *pray* over them. Abandon the law of expediency NOW & trust in Him who can pilot us thro' every storm.

Angelina E. Grimké to Jane Smith

[W/G, Box 4.]

Townsend [Mass.] 9th Mo: 15th [1837]

My Dear Jane

Brother Weld was not satisfied with writing us *one* letter about [Sarah's Letters], but whilst at Ashburnham we received two more setting forth various reasons why we should not meet the subject of woman's rights at all, but still our judgment is *not* convinced, & we hardly know what to do about it, for we have just as high an opinion of brother Garrison's judgment, & *he says go on*. O! that the Lord would guide us in *His* wisdom & keep our feet from falling. We are utterly unable to direct our own steps, & I feel *very*, VERY unfit to fill the place I now occupy. . . .

The great effort of Abolitionists now seems to be to keep every other topic out of view & hence their opposition to H C W preaching Anti Government Doctrines & our writing on the rights of woman. O! if only I saw *they* were *right* & *we* were *wrong*, I would quit immediately. They think we will injure the Slaves cause essentially if we divert the public attention to *any* thing else just *now*. . . .

Thy affectionate Angelina.

Sarah M. and Angelina E. Grimké to Theodore Dwight Weld

[W/G, Box 4; B/D, 1:446–452.]

Fitchburg [Mass.] 9/20/37.

My dear brother,

Angelina is so wrathy that I think it will be unsafe to trust the pen in her hands to reply to thy two last ~~good~~ bad* long letters. As I feel nothing but

* Angelina had crossed out "good" and wrote "bad" above it.

gratitude for the kindness which I am sure dictated them commingled with wonder at the "marvellables" which they contain, I shall endeavor to answer them &, as far as possible, allay the uneasiness which thou seems to feel at the course we are pursuing. My astonishment is as great at thy misconceptions, as thine can be at ours. Truly, if I did not know brother Theodore as well as I think I do, I should conclude his mind was beclouded by the fears which seem to have seized some of the brotherhood, least we should usurp dominion over our lords & masters. But, as I think we are fully agreed that dominion is vested in God only, I shall proceed. The 2d marvellable is "That we magnifyed the power of the N.E. clergy." The mtgs. we have had, generally full, if not crowded, have satisfied our sister that here she was mistaken. I never tho't so. My convictions, for several years, have been that the ministry as now organized is utterly at variance with the ministry Christ established, tends to perpetuate schism & disunion, & therefore must be destroyed; & I believe verily that the Ch[urch] so called is standing right in the way of all reform. I must say a few words about brother Wright, towards whom I do not feel certain that the law of love predominated when thou wrote that part of thy letter relative to him. I do not think he designed to exhibit us as trophies of his conquests, but simply to throw his views (& ours incidentally) before the public. We feel prepared to avow the principles set forth in the "domestic scene."* To my own mind, they have long been familiar, altho' I acknowledge that coming in contact with another mind similarly exercised on these points had given additional strengths & clearness to my views. I wonder that thou canst not perceive the simplicity & beauty & consistency of the doctrine that all government, whether civil or ecclesiastical, conflicts with the govt. of Jehovah &, that by the Christian, no other govt. can be acknowledged without leaning more or less on an arm of flesh. Would God all abolitionists put their trust where I believe H. C. W. has placed his, in God alone. Brother Weld, my heart misgives me for the abolition cause when I see that A. S. men, when smitten on one cheek, as R. G. Williams† was, instead of turning the other cheek, as Jesus commands, appeal to the arm of the law for retaliation. And E. P. Lovejoy‡ keeping arms in

* "A Domestic Scene," the title of Wright's article published in *The Liberator* on July 21, 1837; it depicted the Grimkés and others approvingly discussing the doctrines of women's rights and nonresistance.

† Ransom G. Williams, publishing agent for the American Anti-Slavery Society.

‡ Elijah P. Lovejoy (1802–1837) was converted to evangelical Presbyterianism by David Nelson (1832), established the *St. Louis Observer* (1833), and, also under the influence of Nelson, became an exponent of immediate emancipation (1835). When a mob destroyed his press, he moved it to Alton,

his office! Truly, I fear we have yet to learn the lesson, "Trust in the Lord, for in the Lord Jehovah is everlasting strength." Surely, posterity will brand us as hypocrites. The slave must not raise his hand against his oppressor, but we are at liberty to revenge our wrongs. Oh consistency, where art thou?

Thou sayest, the point at issue between us is whether "you, S. M. & A. E. G., should engage in the public discussion of the rights of women as a distinct topic. Here you affirm & I deny." Now, dear brother, I do not think we ever affirmed that we ought to engage in a public discussion on this subject: all either of us had or now have in view was to throw our views before the public. I have not the least idea of spending any time in answering objections to my letters in the N. E. Spectator; I do not feel bound to take up any caviller. There are my opinions on what I regard as a very important branch of human rights, second to no other. Those who read may receive or reject, or find fault. I have nothing to do with all that. . . . Nehemiah disregarded the scoffs of his enemies, & continued his work; but nevertheless he set half the people in the lower places behind the wall, with their swords, their spears & their bows to guard the workmen. This is all we have done. We have kept steadily on with our A. S. work; we have not held one mtg. less, because we gave a little attention to guard the workmen from the thrusts of the enemies. Thou takes it for granted that our heads are so full of *woman rights, womans rights* that our hearts have grown cold in the cause of the slave, that we have started aside like broken bows. Now, we think thou hast verily misjudged us. My cough rendered me incapable of speaking in public. Of course, I did not require time to prepare lectures, & I really cannot see where is the harm of my writing on any other subject that [is] presented to my mind. I am amazed at thy talking of us as Reformers in the A. S. cause; such a tho't never entered my head. We were the followers & aiders of the Reformers, but we bro't no new artillery into the field; we used the weapons others had used before us. Thou seems to overlook the fact that before a word was written on the subject of womans rights, the Pastoral letter had been issued & that in every place that we lectured the subject of our speaking in public was up for discussion. My reason for giving my views with my name was

Illinois. Mobs there destroyed three of his presses, and shortly after helping to form the Illinois Anti-Slavery Society, in October 1837, he brought in a fourth, which he tried to protect with armed guards. On November 7, 1837, he and a member of the crowd, Lyman Bishop, were killed. Sarah wrote a letter to Garrison criticizing Lovejoy and his followers for taking up arms to defend themselves (*The Liberator*, January 5, 1838, p. 2).

simply because I wished to be answerable for those views. The idea that my name gave any currency to the opinions I advanced never presented itself; so far from it, that I regretted that M. W. Chapman had not undertaken it, because I believed her name would give weight to the sentiments. . . . Nor did I intend to involve myself in any controversy which would take all my time & strength. Truly, my brother, thou hast called up a host of difficulties, which, if they arise, I shall not encounter; and as to absorbing the public mind, I do not see much like it. My letters are quietly received, & if any of the subjects therein discussed attract attention, I cannot see why minds may not be exercised on more than one point without injury to any. I was not aware that the ministers were playing the part of hypocrites when they said women had no right to speak in public. I believed they tho't what they said.

I do not think women being *permitted* to pray & tell their experience in revivals is any proof that Christians do not think it wrong for women to preach. This is the touchstone, to presume to teach the brethren. Let a woman who has prayed in a revival claim to be the appointed minister of Jesus, & to exercise that office by teaching regularly on the sabbath, & she will at once be regarded as a fanatic, or a fool. I know the opposition "arises (in part) from habitually regarding women as inferior beings" but chiefly, I believe, from a desire to keep them in unholy subjection to man, & one way of doing this is to deprive us of the means of becoming their equals, by forbidding us the privileges of education to fit us for the performance of duty. I am greatly mistaken if most men have not a desire that women should be silly. Thou says I have summoned the ministers & churches to surrender. Not I, truly. I do not believe, if I remember right, that I have said one word yet in my letters on the subjects of womens preaching; we have done exactly what thou sayest we ought to have done, gone right among the ministers & lectured just when & where we could. I agree with thee that moral reform is successfully advanced "by uplifting a great self-evident central principle before all eyes." This has been done by proclaiming human rights, & thus the way was prepared for the reception of the doctrine of womans rights. I have read the New Testament, my dear brother, I tho't to edification; but I cannot agree with thee in the application of that text, "I have many things to say," &c. I do not suppose Christ had allusion to the truth of the gospel—these he had declared again & again—but to the sufferings which awaited his disciples after his death; these sufferings he left time & circumstances to unfold as they were strengthened to bear them. If Jesus alluded to any great & important truth, why is none such revealed in the scripture after his ascension? I rejoice with thee that the cause of the slave cannot be destroyed by our misconception of duty, if indeed we have misconceived it, but we believe that if women exercised their rights of thinking & acting for themselves, they would labor ten times more efficiently than they now do for the A. S. cause & all other reformations. Do not wrong us by supposing that in our movements the slave is overlooked. . . .

—thy sister in Jesus

S. M. G.

Sister seems very much afraid that my pen will be transformed into a venomous serpent when it is employed in addressing thee, my Dear Brother, & no wonder, for I like to pay my debts, & as I received $10's worth of scolding, I should be guilty of injustice did I not return the favor. Well—*such* a lecture, I never before received. What is the matter with thee? One would really suppose that we had actually abandoned the A Sly cause & were scouring the country preaching *nothing* but *women's rights,* when in fact I can truly say that whenever I lecture I forget *every thing but the* SLAVE. He is all in all for the time being. And what is the reason that *I* am to be scolded because *Sister* writes letters in the Spectator? Please let every woman bear *her own* burden. Indeed. I should like to know what *I have done* yet. And dost thou really think in my answer to C E B's absurd views of woman that I had better suppress my own? If so, I will do it, as thou makest such a monster out of the molehill; but my judgment is *not* convinced that in this incidental way it is wrong to throw light on the subject. We miss Brother W very much, for he used to appoint all our meetings, & since I find the Ex Com have sent S Gould* in his place, *which shows some agent was tho't necessary here,* I do feel as tho' *they* had *not* regarded *our* comfort as much as I think they ought to have done; for S G does not approve our course & therefore cannot be expected to appoint our meetings. *This burden we did not expect to have to bear, & is often perplexing.* Brother Lincoln† of Gardener treated us very handsomely, says he felt very doubtful as to our public lectures until lately when he examined the subject & found we were *fully sustained by the Bible.* He asked us to give him our views in order that he might be furnished with the best arguments in our favor & remarked his *mind was perfectly clear,* & that he never had introduced any

* Samuel Gould, a recruit from Oberlin College, became the first American Anti-Slavery Society agent for Pennsylvania (October 1835–February 1837). He was then transferred to New York and Massachusetts, where he earned a reputation as a very successful fund raiser.

† Reverend J. Sumner Lincoln, a Congregational minister.

minister into his pulpit with more pleasure than he had us. My *keen sense of justice* compels me to admire such nobility. He hoped sister S would give her views on this branch of the subject in the Spectator, tho't they were needed, & *we* are well convinced that they are, T D W notwithstanding. So much for my bump of obstinacy, for not even thy sledge hammer can beat it down. Could we not travel in Penn[sylvani]a this winter, near the Virg[ini]a line, if the Ex Com will please to let us have brother W to appoint our meetings? They seem so afraid of letting us heretics be together, that I am very much afraid he will be sent back here as soon as we go there. . . .

[September] 21. I feel in no jesting humor this morning. . . . Suppose in fact that what has frightened thee so, was that public lecture I wanted to give in Boston on Womans rights: H B S[tanton] must have told thee about it, but our friend[s] there tho't I had best not, so I did *not* commit the sin, tho' we talked of giving it when we went back. Why not? I want that meeting, but I will not give it if it is tho't best not to. I cant have as many meetings this week as I want because I have not brother *Wright to appoint them.* We have not been treated considerately at any rate —thine for the poor stricken slave—A. E. Gé

"The Connection which S. M. Grimké and A. E. Grimké sustained to the system of slavery"

[*The Liberator,* October 13, 1837, p. 16; *National Enquirer,* October 26, 1837.]

As we are frequently asked, what relation we have in past years sustained to the system of slavery, and as we feel that individuals have a *perfect right to know,* we have thought it best to publish the following facts.

When S. M. G. was quite young, her father gave her a little African girl to wait upon her; but after a few years, she died. This was the only slave she ever owned. It must have been 30 years ago.

In the year 1827, our mother gave A. E. G. a young woman. She soon became uneasy with holding her a slave, and in a few months returned her to the donor. *No* money transactions ever passed about it —*none* was paid, and *none* was received. Still, she at that time only saw men as trees walking, and was not sensible of the sin she was committing in returning a fellow creature into bondage. She only felt that she did not want the responsibility of such an ownership, but had no clear conception of the intrinsic principles of slavery. In 1835, she began to read anti-slavery publications, and for the first time saw that slavery, under all circumstances, was sinful; she had always mourned over the ignorance, degradation and cruelty of slavery; but never before understood the chattel principle, out of which all these abominations grew as naturally as the trunk and branches from the foot of the tree. During the eight years which had elapsed since the time of her being a slaveholder, the slave had been sold, and had become the mother of three or four children. A. E. G. felt conscience-stricken at what she had done, and wrote to the then owner of the woman and her children, offering to *redeem* them from slavery at any price that might be named; and at the same time stating the change in her views, and the reasons why she could not offer to *buy* them, as that would be a recognition of the right of one man to hold another as property. The owners would not accede to the proposition, so that this slave is still in bondage. This is the only slave she ever owned.

We have been induced to state these facts, because many persons have heard that we had slaves and liberated them; and we do not wish the credit of doing what we had no opportunity of doing.

S. M. and A. E. Grimké.
East Boylston, 2d inst.

Angelina E. Grimké to Jane Smith

[W/G, Box 4.]

Holliston [Mass.] 10th Mo: 26th [1837]

My Dear Jane

. . . With regard to speaking on the rights of women, it has really be[en] wonderful to me that tho' I meet the prejudice against our speaking every where, that still in addressing our audiences I never think of introducing any thing about it. I was particularly struck with this two days ago. In riding with Dr Miller* to the meeting at Franklin, I found from conversation with him that I had a great amount of prejudice to meet at that town, & very much in his own mind. I threw out my views on women's preaching in the course of the ride & verily believe I convinced him, for he said he had no idea so much could be adduced from the Bible to sustain the ground I had taken, & remarked this will be quite new to the people, & I believe they will be glad to hear these things & pressed me so much to speak on the subject at the close of my lecture, that I was obliged to promise I would, *if* I could remember to

* Unable to identify.

do so. After speaking two hours, he remarked at tea, why did you not tell the people *why* you believed you had a right to speak. In fact, I had entirely forgotten all about it until his enquiry revived the conversation we had had on the road. Now, I believe the Lord orders these things so, driving out of my mind what I ought *not* to speak on. If the time ever comes when this will be a part of my public work, then I shall not be able to forget it. . . .

Some Abolitionists seem to think that the Clerical Appeal* was not worth noting but such sees not the *root* out of which it sprung. I should be greatly mistaken if Abolitionism & Ministerial influences have not a *hard battle* to fight in Mass: & I think Garrison & Phelps did the very best thing that could be done when they boldly exhibited the insidious character of it. The Clergy are alarmed, & they have great cause to be so, & they will cling with a death-grasp to their pay & their power, but their doom is sealed, I believe. I sincerely hope that Brother Garrison will see his way clear to throw open the columns of the Liberator to all the great moral questions. We ought to have at least one unfettered paper where *all* unpopular truth may be fearlessly spoken & hungering spirits fed. I feel that the time is rapidly approaching when the Lord will raise up men & women not to proclaim *our* truth only, but to cry aloud against *all* the sins of our guilty land, & great will be the shaking in our midst, great the persecution that will arise, but "he that endureth unto the end shall be saved."

Farewell dear Jane, I am still thy Aff A E Gé

Sarah M. And Angelina E. Grimké to Queen Victoria†

[BPL, MS. 957.]

Boston [Mass.] 10th Mo. 26th 1837.

Dear Sister

. . . We write now to entreat thee on behalf of the down trodden millions in our own country, & the hundreds of thousands in thy dominions, to abolish the system of apprenticeship which is fraught with so much suffering to the slaves, to open thy ear to the cry of the

* "Appeal of Clerical Abolitionists on Antislavery Measures" appeared in the *New England Spectator* (August 2, 1837) and was reprinted in *The Liberator* (August 11). It consisted of a harsh critique of the tone and methods of the Garrisonians. Women were not mentioned. It was signed by five Congregational ministers.

† Victoria (1819–1901) reigned as queen of the United Kingdom of Great Britain and Ireland, 1837–1901.

oppressed & rid them of the hand of the oppressor. As Americans, as Christians, we feel deeply interested in this cause. The moral power of England will be felt in every part of our beloved country, aiding & animating those, who are laboring for the overthrow of slavery. We are grateful for the thrilling appeals which thy countrymen & countrywomen have sent to the United States; they have been stirring & have strengthened the hands and comforted the hearts of abolitionists. . . .

Our hearts have been gladdened by the information, that the women of Great Britain are preparing a petition to be presented to thee, relative to the Apprenticeship system. May the Lord incline thine ear to hear, and thy heart to grant their prayer. . . .

Sarah M. Grimké
Angelina E. Grimké

Sarah M. Grimké to Sarah Douglass

[W/G, Box 4; B/D, 1:480–482.]

Brookline [Mass.] 11/23/37.

My dear Sarah

. . . When I look at the present state of affairs in the abolition cause, I am ready to think, dear sister, that this is the hour and power of darkness, not for the slave but for our country. The fearful catastrophe of Alton* seem[s] to me to indicate that God will take the work of abolishing slavery out of our hands. He gave us a great *moral* enterprise to carry forward. He gave us arms of heavenly temper to use, the sword of the spirit, prayer, preaching the truth. He has given us, thro' these means, access to the hearts of thousands. What are we rendering to him? Is our trust in him? Can we believe it when abolitionists resort to physical force, to the weapons of death to defend the cause of God? If, as we profess to believe, as I do most surely believe, that the abolition of slavery, or rather the principles of A. S. are a part of the gospel of Jesus Christ, how can we expect his blessing upon our efforts, if we take carnal weapons to fight his battles? Are we walking in his steps: Is that mind in us which was also in Christ Jesus? How appalling the spectacle! a minister of Jesus Christ engaged in the work of killing his brother man, of sending to the bar of judgment beings who were mad with fury. This event seems to me like a victory which Satan has gained over us, & altho' my faith never swerves about the abolition of slavery, yet at

* The killing of Lovejoy and Bishop.

present I have little hope that it will be brought about by peaceful means. The blood spilt at Alton will be the seed of future discord; those who were engaged in the mob, as well as the defenders of the press, will thirst for more & who can foresee the calamities that await us. See, too, in Penn. the desperate effort made against the colored citizens to deprive them of the right of voting.* Should the whites succeed, unless there is more of the spirit of Christ among my brethren who are thus unrighteously oppressed than I fear there is, it must create feelings of resentment that will some day burst out. In New York, oppression reigns. The fugitive there as well as in Pennsylvania is hunted like a partridge on the mountain & denied the right of Jury trial. My very soul sickens in utter agony at these things. All my desire for my oppressed countrymen is, that their trust may be in the Lord Jehovah in whom is everlasting strength. Is it true that men of color went armed to the polls in Bucks county? If they do thus, our country cannot be saved. I have looked towards them as a remnant whose sufferings were preparing them to do a great work in the Ch[urc]h of Christ, but God will not so honor them if their trust is in an arm of flesh. Oh, what need we all have to go to Jesus & be taught of Him, to pray to him for fresh supplies of his spirit to lead us into all truth, to comfort, to sustain us. I hope thy dear mother may be right about the conversion of the slaves and masters thro' them. Should the Lord open a way for us into the slave holding states & permit us to be instrumental in opening the eyes of the benighted slaves, I pray that we may be willing to go. To myself, the future is wrapt in impenetrable darkness. I see not beyond the present hour & live in waiting on the Lord to know his holy will, whether it be for life or death. . . .

Thine in the Peace and Love of Jesus, S. M. Grimké

Sarah M. Grimké to Theodore Dwight Weld

[W/G, Box 4; B/D, 1:486–487.]

Brookline [Mass.] 11/30/37.

. . . Now altho' we do not contemplate public speaking this winter, we do not wish or expect to be idle; we feel very ignorant still on the great

* Freed blacks had voted in Pennsylvania since 1790, but a state court ruled in 1836 *(Fogg vs. Hobbs)* that the term "freemen" did not encompass blacks. The Constitution of 1837 added the word "white" to the voting qualification clause. Blacks wrote appeals and mounted demonstrations, but to no avail.

subjects which are agitating the public mind. Thou sayest thou canst cut out work enough to employ a dozen; what wilt thou allot to us? We should like some definite object to accomplish, but I must tell thee I feel fit only to copy. I do not know whether I could write just now, for my mind was very weary when we stopt lecturing & my body has not had much rest in a sick chamber. Angelina said she really enjoyed being sick, and to say the truth, I almost envied her the entire repose of mind & body. . . . I feel the truth of what thou sayest about our keeping silence till spring & hope we many not be tempted to do otherwise, unless I can have one or two mtgs. with the colored people. My very soul yearns toward them, & I long to preach the gospel of peace and salvation *to them*. But Gods will be done in all things. . . .

thy sister S. M. G.

FIVE

Angelina Moves to Center Stage

SARAH informed Anne Weston, on December 1, 1837, that the sisters might not be able to lecture any more that winter, but they did "not contemplate being withdrawn from the A. S. cause."[1] However, for the first time in a year, Sarah and Angelina did not have a schedule, and the direction they should take was not obvious. They found an opening at the end of January, took the initiative, and widened it into what would become four triumphant months for Angelina. As the venue shifted from lectures to small groups to speeches before large audiences, Sarah was pushed into the background by her health and negative responses from male abolitionists to the quality of her speaking.

On January 5, the sisters attended a debate between males on the question: "Would the condition of society and of woman be improved, by placing the two sexes on an equality in respect to civil rights and duties?" The sisters also attended the annual meeting of the Massachusetts Anti-Slavery Society in January. Its session on Texas was reputed to be the largest meeting ever held in Boston; so large, in fact, that the society was granted the hall of the Massachusetts House of Representatives for the rest of its sessions, and a committee of the House was appointed to consider antislavery petitions.

Meanwhile, Sarah and Angelina maintained a constant, lengthy correspondence with Weld, who regularly criticized the way they wrote, spoke, thought, and dressed. To the modern ear, many of Weld's letters have the sound of an Old Testament patriarch denouncing the misguided. He was especially harsh on the subject of nonresistance. A phrase in a letter Angelina had written on December 24—"Sister S & myself are grieved that thou art *not* a Peace Man. O! wilt thou promise to examine this subject on the bended knee of thy soul?"[2]—sparked a response from Weld, in which he stated he was "a peace man" but not a " 'no government' man." He criticized the Garrisonian doctrine of nonresistance and the quality of the sisters' thinking about it:

> I do think both of you are greatly in danger of presumptuous confidence. Surrounded as you have been for many mo[n]ths and are still by those who commend and eulogize your powers of mind as highly as language can ascend, and who possibly have never in a single instance pointed out a defect, in the habit also of seeing those around you *defer* to your opinions and reasonings, it would be a marvel indeed if you were not tempted to loose and blind reliance on your own power in *this respect,* a reliance *unwarranted* by the reality. . . . That your habits of *investigation* are all wrong, and that you are exceedingly liable to arrive at conclusions without either stating your premises at all or from false ones, I believe. . . . Do, pray tell me, in your next what are the *premises* in your "No government argument." For my life, I can't find them. . . . That you will both *be at a loss,* I venture to predict. If so, what does it teach as to your *habits of reasoning?*[3]

Boston's abolitionists, on the other hand, could not have been more appreciative of Angelina. Following her presentation to the committee of the Massachusetts House of Representatives, Garrison wrote: "The effort of Angelina E. Grimké before our legislative committee, has been of incalculable benefit to the cause." Lydia Maria Child thought "it was a spectacle of the greatest moral sublimity I ever witnessed." Wendell Phillips,* speaking at her funeral, could still recall that "the profound impression then made on a class not often found in our meetings was never wholly lost."[4]

Sarah delivered two lectures to black people at the Adelphic Union in early March 1838, on the theme: "the universal dissemination of knowledge among all classes of society, the only safeguard against oppression."[5] But, when invited by a woman in Providence to address their "annual meeting," Sarah replied that she and Angelina would only do so if it were a public meeting, open to men and women.[6] In any event, the schedule became too crowded: the Boston Female Anti-Slavery Society scheduled six lectures at the Odeon on the subject of woman's rights, and Angelina and Weld, who had confessed their mutual love in a series of letters in February, decided to marry in Philadelphia in May, the day before the opening of the Anti-Slavery Convention of American Women.

* Wendell Phillips (1811–1884), the son of a wealthy Boston family, attended Harvard College and Law School. He married a militant abolitionist, Anne Terry Greene, and himself became a dedicated spokesman for the movement in late 1837. He was one of the best speakers of his time and remained a loyal follower of Garrison.

The original plan for the Odeon lectures was for the sisters to alternate, but Sarah's opening lecture on March 22 was not considered a success by Weld and other male abolitionists. He wrote her, saying that those who had heard her speak had said:

> that the great and sole object of getting the Odeon and of having lectures there would be mainly frustrated if Angelina did not deliver them. . . . [T]hey all said that the lack of interest in your lectures was not at all for lack of excellent *matter,* but for lack of an interesting and happy manner of speaking; that your manner is monotonous and heavy and instead of increasing the power of the *truth* uttered, weakens it.

Sarah thought that it was " a loving and faithful letter," stepped aside, and allowed Angelina to deliver the remainder of the lectures.[7]

The Odeon lecture series concluded on April 19. Again, abolitionists raved. Garrison wrote, on April 24: "Yesterday, the Grimkés bid farewell to Boston and to the Commonwealth, having accomplished more for the cause of God's suffering ones, in the course of a year, than any of us realize, or dare to measure. . . . Angelina's closing lecture at the Odeon . . . was the keystone of the arch. Its peroration was of a melting and thrilling character. The audience was truly immense, and her mastery over it was wonderful."[8]

On May 14, Angelina married Theodore Dwight Weld in Philadelphia. The next day, Angelina and Sarah attended the opening session of the Anti-Slavery Convention of American Women. Again, Mary Parker presided, and Sarah was one of ten vice presidents. Angelina was appointed a vice president on the last day of the meeting by a motion of Lucretia Mott. Raging antiabolitionist mobs surrounded the meeting place, the newly built Pennsylvania Hall for Free Discussion, for two days, making it difficult to conduct business. Sarah and Angelina introduced motions criticizing prejudice, offering "sympathy and prayers" to Southerners "who feel and mourn over the guilt of slavery," calling the end of the apprenticeship system in the British West Indies "a triumphant proof of the safety of immediate emancipation," and hailing the stimulus of the example of their British sisters in the cause of immediate emancipation.[9]

During the first two days of the hall's existence, May 14–15, a dedicatory address was delivered by a black lawyer, David Paul Brown, two temperance speeches were given, and meetings of the Philadelphia Lyceum, the Anti-Slavery Convention of American Women, and the

Pennsylvania State Anti-Slavery Society for the Eastern District were held. Garrison spoke at the Hall on the fifteenth. His speech and the presence of the two antislavery organizations provoked some of the citizens of Philadelphia to post handwritten placards around the city on the night of the fifteenth, calling on the people to assemble at the hall at 11:00 a.m. to disperse the antislavery meetings. The abolitionists decided to respond by holding a general meeting the night of the sixteenth, but it was not officially sponsored by either antislavery organization. Samuel Webb, the hall's treasurer, wrote that "many of the members of [the Anti-Slavery Convention of American Women] disapproved of the public addresses of women to promiscuous assemblies."[10]

That evening, May 16, William Lloyd Garrison, Maria Weston Chapman, Angelina, Abby Kelley,* and Lucretia Mott spoke. Angelina's speech was the centerpiece of the occasion; it would be her last public speech for twenty-five years. Garrison described the circumstances: "As the tumult from without increased, and the brickbats fell thick and fast, (no one, however, being injured), her eloquence kindled, her eyes flashed, and her cheeks glowed."[11]

The Anti-Slavery Convention of American Women met in the hall on the following morning and adopted an "Address to Anti-Slavery Societies," rejecting the argument "that it is not within the 'province of woman,' to discuss the subject of slavery."[12] It was the last meeting held in the hall. That night a mob broke into the building and set fire to it; it burned to the ground.

The women convened for their final session on May 18 in a schoolroom. Angelina offered the meeting's final resolution on the burning of the hall. The women then adjourned, to meet the following May, again in Philadelphia.

Angelina E. Grimké to Jane Smith

[W/G, Box 4.]

Brookline [Mass.] 1st Mo: 5 [1838]

My dear Jane

. . . Altogether I must confess the discussion has elevated my hopes of the Woman Question, tho' I forgot to say it was decided against us by

* Abigail (Kelley) Foster (1811–1887), Quaker schoolteacher who became secretary of the Lynn Female Anti-Slavery Society in 1835 and a staunch supporter of Garrison. When Weld heard her speak at the 1838 Anti-Slavery Convention of American Women he urged her to cease school teaching and become an antislavery lecturer.

acclamation, "our enemies themselves being judges." It certainly was conducted with a respect & delicacy & dignity I did not expect, & I believe many minds were roused to reflection, some new ideas thrown out. W L G has just been here & wants me to write a piece about it for the Liberator, which I think I shall under the signature of woman. . . .*

Very affy Thy

A E Gé

Angelina E. Grimké to Theodore Dwight Weld
[W/G, Box 4; B/D, 2:520–525]

Brookline [Mass.]—21 inst—[January 1838]

Very Dear Brother

. . . & now let me tell you how often I have thanked God for such a friend as you have proved to me, one who *will* tell me my faults. I solemnly believe there is, *there can be* no true friendship without it—at any rate I value none else, therefore I have no FRIENDS but J S and Sister. They tell me my faults *if* they *see* them, but you, dear brother, have, I must acknowledge, dived deeper into the *hidden* sins of my heart than any one ever did before, & you can therefore do me more good. I know I find it *very hard* to bear, but this only proves the dire necessity which exists that you should probe deep, not suffering your hand to spare or your eye to pity. I never needed *such* friendship half so much as *now*. The Lord saw my need & He supplied it, blessed be His *Holy* name. & yet, Brother, I think in some things you wronged me in *that letter never to be forgotten* [October 10, 1837], but never mind, YOU DID NOT HURT ME—even that did me good. I *tho't* too that it was *not* written in the spirit of love, but I will not say *it was not,* for I know I *was* but a poor judge *then,* & to be candid, I have never read it over since. I have often wished to, but I am never alone for any length of time, & I can't read it. I have not the courage to read it in any other way. You know, too, whilst the wound rankles we feel but little inclination to examine critically the weapon which has inflicted it, even tho' we may love the hand which dealt the blow & above all *bless God* for the chastisement. But enough of self for the present. If we ever meet & *can*

* *The Liberator* (January 19, 1838, p. 10) printed an account of the meeting, "Lyceum Meeting at the Odeon," by "A Friend of Woman," but it appears to be a composite of responses. Though it contains some of the phrases Angelina used in her letter to Jane Smith, it emphasizes topics that Angelina had not discussed elsewhere: the right of women to vote, be a part of civil government, and enlist in the army.

talk these things over, I think it will do my heart good. Be sure to keep that letter of mine which you said I ought to be ashamed of [September 20, 1837]—all the rest better be destroyed. There will be no use in writing about it—WE CANNOT UNDERSTAND EACH OTHER, & I have unintentionally said too much perhaps.

Thanks for your warnings, too, to trust not in our intellectual powers. I am *sure* I cannot with any safety. I *know* that I have just the defects you have pointed out, therefore I feel very unwilling to make up my mind *fully* on *great* subjects, such as the no human Government Question. When asked what I think of this, I believe I *always* say, my opinion is so & so, *with the light I now have,* but I feel that I *need* more & *want* more. In writing, I think I never have *committed myself;* for instance, in my 12th Let to C E B my language is "*If* civil government is a divine ordinance" &c. As this was the case, I was at a loss to know *what I* had written on the subject. I don't know to what you allude in your letter, neither does Sister, for neither of us have ever pretended to write anything like an *argument* about it, tho' she is certainly more fixed in her views than I am. As to our premises, they are simply these, & these they have been for *many months.* Civil Government is based on physical force, physical force is forbidden by the Law of Love. If I have no right to *resist evil myself,* I have no right to call upon another to resist it for me, & if *I must not* call upon the Magistrate to redress my grievances, if *I* have no *right* to do so, then he can have no right to render me any such aid. Now, the puzzle in my mind is this. If these things ARE SO, then God *has changed* the moral government of his people, & yet *my* favorite theory has been the *unchangeableness* of this government. I have believed, I still am strongly inclined to the opinion, that it is *our* ignorance of the Jewish Dispensation which makes us believe there is such a *contrast* between that & the Christian, & I never shall be satisfied until I get hold of principles which will reconcile them to each other & *both* to the holiness, justice, *immutability* and love of our Heavenly Father—these are the principles for which I have been seeking for many years. Can you help me to find them?

With regard to yourself, I will tell you just how I felt wh[ic]h induced me to urge the Peace subject upon you so earnestly. I tho't that times which would try men's souls were assuredly coming, & altho' I know how *faithfully you had acted out* the principle of *non* resistance when a Lecturer, yet I did not see why, if you believed in the *right* of the magistrates sword, you should not do just what E P L[ovejoy] did *under the order of a Mayor,* if you should ever be placed in similar circumstances. My soul was moved within me therefore to entreat you to examine this subject *fully*, so that you might have *fixed principles before* the hour of trial came; you know you said you had *not yet* examined it. But if you *never* can take up arms under *any* circumstances, then I shall feel easy, but for you ever to die as he did, I could not endure to think of it. . . .

[Angelina E. Grimké]

Angelina E. Grimké to Jane Smith

[W/G, Box 4.]

[Brookline, Mass., February 7, 1838]

My Dear Jane

I snatch a few moments with a trembling heart & hand to tell thee something of my prospect of speaking before the Committee of the Legislature appointed to take into consideration the petitions on the subject of Slavery. Brother Stanton was here on 7th day [Saturday], & half in jest & half in earnest asked us whether I would speak before the Committee. I laughed at the proposal, for I had no idea such a thing could be required of me. He, however, maintained it seriously before he went away & remarked that as the names of some thousands of women were before the Com, as signers of petitions, he tho't it would be a good thing if I felt as tho' I could do it. I still tried to throw it from me, but after he had gone, I began to *feel*, & that very unexpectedly to myself, real exercise of mind about it &, on 2d day, sent him word that I had tho't of the proposition & was willing to accede to it, if the friends of the cause tho't well of it. It seems that even the stout hearted tremble for the consequences when the Woman Question is really to be *acted out* in force, & tho' he is right in the *abstract* on this subject, yet now he greatly fears the consequences of *such* a bold assertion of our equality. Jackson, Fuller, Phelps & Quincy were committed.* The former [Francis Jackson] is sound to the core & went right up to the State House to enquire of the Chairman of the Committee† whether I could be heard. Wonder-

* John E. Fuller, cofounder of the New England Anti-Slavery Society, who would break with Garrison later that year; Edmund Quincy (1808–1877), member of the Massachusetts Anti-Slavery Society and a strong believer in nonresistance.

† James C. Alvord, an antislavery writer and speaker who would be elected to the United States House of Representatives as a Whig opponent of the gag rule but die before he could take his seat (1838).

ful to tell, he said yes without the least hesitation & actually helped to remove the scruples of some of the timid hearted Abolitionists. The Com of the A S Sy, who have the business under their care, are Jackson, Phelps & Quincy. Of course, A A Phelps will veto the bill. I have not heard what E Q thinks about it, but I send the[e] a hasty note of M Chapmans which will give thee her opinion & her belief as to Quincy. Fuller & Stanton were here yesterday, but they seemed rather to dodge the question, so I said but very little about it, believing it best to let the responsibility rest with the Comm—if they cant bear it, just to let them say *No!* to my offer, or what is most likely, take no further notice of it. Perhaps it is best *I* should bear the responsibility *wholly* myself. I feel willing to do it, & at present think the course I shall pursue will be this —say nothing further about it, but let Birney & Stanton make the speeches they expect to before the Com. this week, & *when* they have done, make an independent application to the Chairman, as a woman, as a Southerner, as a moral being.

I feel, dear, that this is the most important step I have ever been called to take—important to woman, to the slave, to my country & the world. I know that of myself I can do nothing, but thro' Christ strengthening me, I can do all things. Sister feels with me that it will [be] *right* for me to do it, but O, Jane, no earthly arm can support me in such a duty, & were it not that I had the promise of *better* help, I should sink under the bare prospect. But I am calm, my soul is staid on God, & I wait his time & way, feeling that it will be "woe unto me" if I open not my mouth for the dumb now & just in this way. . . .

Farewell—I am as ever thy true but poor & needy—Angelina

Theodore Dwight Weld to Angelina E. Grimké

[W/G, Box 4; B/D, 2:532–536.]

New York, Feb. 8, '38

Private

A paragraph in your last letter Angelina, went *to my soul.* You feel that I have "wronged" you and think that what I said "was not written in the spirit of love." . . .

I *would* explain the mystery of the *seeming* unkindness and cruelty of my spirit toward you in reproof, did not higher considerations than *inclination* or self interest forbid me to do it, until I have *first* fulfilled an obligation which I am *now* convinced should have been discharged long ago—a *sacred* duty which I owed to *you,* to my own soul, and to our Father who knoweth the thoughts and intents of the heart. . . .

I know it will surprise and even amaze you, Angelina, when I say to you as I now do, that for a long time, *you have had my whole heart.* . . .

If (and I have hardly a hope that it is otherwise) your heart, Angelina, does not reciprocate my love, I charge you before a risen Lord not to shrink for a moment, thro fear of giving me pain, from declaring to me the *whole truth.* . . .

Theodore D. Weld.

Angelina E. and Sarah M. Grimké to Theodore Dwight Weld

[W/G, Box 4; B/D, 2:536–539.]

Brookline [Mass.] Febr'y 11th [1838]

Your letter was indeed a great surprise, My Brother, & yet it was no surprise at all. It was a surprise because you have so mastered your feelings as never to betray them; it was no surprise because in the depths of my own heart *there was found a response* which I could not but believe was produced there by an undefinable feeling in yours. Not even the word "private" prepared me for such a disclosure, so full of strength & power. I tho't you had found it your duty to reprove me again for some darling sin & determined to save my feelings by hidden admonition, & my heart was lifted in prayer to receive it in the spirit of meekness & love. You say that my letter revealed to you that you had inflicted *"abiding pain";* Yes! you did, & it was love for you which caused reproof to sink so deep into my heart. I tho't, with such views of my character, it was impossible you could love me, save as a poor unworthy sinner—the love which we bear in *pity* to one who is sunk in moral pollution. But enough of this, you have broken the precious box of ointment over my wounded spirit, & it is healed.

As to explanations, I ask for *none* now, as it is likely they would involve your opinions & fears relative to those whose influence I was measurably under, & perhaps it will not be *right* for me to have any. I am content; my heart trusts you wholly.

. . . You talk too of "the long conflict" you have had with yourself on account of your affection for me. I confess I have had the same on account of mine for you. I felt it in N York. I was frightened when I found that my happiness was becoming bound up in you, & I wrestled in prayer to be delivered from a state of mind which, if it continued, must unfit me for the work to which I believed myself called. By the providence of God, we were separated, & tho' I sorrowed, yet still I rejoiced, hoping that now I should be able thro' grace to *conquer,* & for many months anxiety was destroyed, & I was strengthened in a great measure to view you as my christian *brother* only. But within the last few weeks, my former feelings have returned with increased strength. I have prayed earnestly against them at times, whilst at others I have gone to my Heavenly Father like a little child & asked Him *if* it was wrong to love you *as* I did; WHY He had constituted me a being imperfect, a *half* only of myself, as it were; why He had created these restless longings of my heart after communion & union, deep & pure & chaste & indestructible? Did He mean to mock the misery of his helpless ones, of the stranger whom He had severed from all that was nearest by nature, & thrown down in the midst of those who knew her not? I felt in my inmost soul that *He* could not, *He* would not, & this was my only hope that He had awakened corresponding feelings in your soul.

You say you are *now* convinced that the sacred duty you have by your letter discharged ought to have been performed long ago. I doubt it. I am sure I never was prepared for it before, tho' I doubt not both of us would have been saved much suffering by an earlier developement [sic], but it would have been immature, & we should have lost the benefit of the discipline thro' which we have passed. We have had to surrender each other in *heart:* the Lord knows that we *feel* that without His approbation & smile we should prove to be but empty cisterns which can hold *no* water. He knows that even if He were not to say, "hitherto shall you go and NO *further,*" we would pray for grace to bow in humble submission to His holy will. We CAN trust Him tho' He take from us the dearest earthly treasure, for we *know* that He knows *best* what is good for us.

[Angelina E. Grimké]

Brother Beloved in the Lord—

. . .Thy letter to my precious sister was not unexpected to me, altho' I sometimes thought circumstances would impose silence. Since our first meeting I have felt as if you were kindred spirits, and that if the Lord inclined your hearts to each other I could bless his holy name. . . . You have my prayers, my love, my sympathy. . . .

Thy sister in Jesus S. M. G

Sarah M. Grimké to Theodore Dwight Weld

[W/G, Box 4; B/D, 2:552–553.]

Brookline [Mass.] Feb. 16th 1838.

My dear brother

As we heard nothing from the Committee of the A. S. Society relative to our addressing the Committee of the Legislature, we concluded to write to them ourselv[e]s, & accordingly we did so on wednesday last, & they cordially assented to our request & appointed next wednesday & thursday at three o'clock in the afternoon. I expect to occupy the first & A. the second, & if she cannot get thro', she will probably ask for another hearing, as the Committee said they did not wish to restrict us as to time.

Thine in the bonds and fellowship of a Saviors love.

S. M. G.

Angelina E. Grimké, Speech to a Committee of the Massachusetts House of Representatives, February 21, 1838*

[*The Liberator,* March 2, 1838, p. 35; reprinted in Gerda Lerner, *The Grimké Sisters from South Carolina: Rebels Against Slavery* (Boston, Mass.: Houghton Mifflin, 1967), pp. 371–374; original manuscript not found.]

Mr. Chairman—More than 2000 years have rolled their dark and bloody waters down the rocky, winding channel of Time into the broad ocean of Eternity, since woman's voice was heard in the palace of an eastern monarch, and woman's petition achieved the salvation of millions of her race from the edge of the sword. The Queen of Persia,—if Queen she might be called, who was but the mistress of her voluptuous lord,—trained as she had been in the secret abominations of an oriental harem, had studied too deeply the character of Ahaseurus not to know that the sympathies of his heart could not be reached, except through the medium of his sensual appetites. Hence we find her arrayed in royal apparel, standing in the inner court of the King's house, hoping by her personal charms to win the favor of her lord. And after the golden sceptre had been held out, and the inquiry was made, "What wilt thou,

* Sarah became ill, and Angelina made the presentation, appearing three times in all. Aside from this extract, there are no transcripts of the speeches Sarah and Angelina delivered in Boston during these months.

Queen Esther, and what is thy request? it shall be given thee to the half of the kingdom"—even then she dared not ask either for her own life, or that of her people. She felt that if her mission of mercy was to be successful, his animal propensities must be still more powerfully wrought upon—the luxurious feast must be prepared, the banquet of wine must be served up, and the favorable moment must be seized when, gorged with gluttony and intoxication, the king's heart was fit to be operated upon by the pathetic appeal, "If I have found favor in thy sight, O King, and if it please the King let my life be given at my petition; and my people at my request." It was thus, through personal charms, and sensual gratification, and individual influence, that the Queen of Persia obtained the precious boon she craved,—her own life, and the life of her beloved people. Mr. Chairman, it is my privilege to stand before you on a similar mission of life and love; but I thank God that we live in an age of the world too enlightened and too moral to admit of the adoption of the same means to obtain as holy an end. I feel that it would be an insult to the Committee, were I to attempt to win their favor by arraying my person in gold, and silver, and costly apparel, or by inviting them to partake of the luxurious feast, or the banquet of wine. I understand the spirit of the age too well to believe that you could be moved by such sensual means—means as unworthy of you, as they would be beneath the dignity of the cause of humanity. Yes, I feel that if you are reached at all, it will not be by me, but by the truths I shall endeavor to present to your understandings and your hearts. The heart of the eastern despot was reached through the lowest propensities of his animal nature, by personal influence; yours, I know, cannot be reached but through the loftier sentiments of the intellectual and moral feelings.

Let the history of the world answer these queries. Read the denunciations of Jehovah against the follies and crimes of Israel's daughters. Trace the influence of woman as a courtezan and a mistress in the destinies of nations, both ancient and modern, and see her wielding her power too often to debase and destroy, rather than to elevate and save. It is often said that women rule the world, through their influence over men. If so, then may we well hide our faces in the dust, and cover ourselves with sackcloth and ashes. It has not been by moral power and intellectual, but through the baser passions of man.—This dominion of women must be resigned—the sooner the better; "in the age which is approaching, she should be something more—she should be a citizen; and this title, which demands an increase of knowledge and of reflection, opens before her a new empire."

I stand before you as a southerner, exiled from the land of my birth, by the sound of the lash, and the piteous cry of the slave. I stand before you as a repentant slaveholder. I stand before you as a moral being, endowed with precious and inalienable rights, which are correlative with solemn duties and high responsibilities; and as a moral being I feel that I owe it to the suffering slave, and to the deluded master, to my country and the world, to do all I can to overturn a system of complicated crimes, built up upon the broken hearts and prostrate bodies of my countrymen in chains, and cemented by the blood and sweat and tears of my sisters in bonds.

[The orator then proceeded to discuss the merits of the petitions.]

Angelina E. and Sarah M. Grimké to Jane Smith

[W/G, Box 4.]

Brookline [Mass.] 2d Mo: 22d [1838]

My Beloved Jane

Private

And now my dear Jane—art thou prepared to hear what I have to speak unto thee in thine ear. Art thou ready to hear that I have entered into a solemn engagement with T D W? Art thou willing that my heart & hand should be *his?* I believe this is *no* more than what thou hast expected, for I fear I betrayed *more* than a sisters love for him even when I was in Phila. I wish thou knewest him, for I am sure thou wouldst love him. Such childlike simplicity & power of intellect & moral sublimity I have never before seen united in one human being. . . .

Thine in love . . .

My beloved sister—

[Angelina] has told thee about dear Brother Weld. I need hardly say my heart is filled with thanksgiving praise that these two beloved in the Lord, these kindred spirits, are united by ties so powerful & tender & sacred. I try *only* to rejoice with them, to keep self out of sight, but sometimes it is hard work. I feel as if I had come to a full stop in every thing & am waiting the Lords time to see what next awaits me. I can trust him, tho' he take from me the nearest earthly love. . . .

. . . thy affectionate & grateful S. M. G.

Angelina E. Grimké to Theodore Dwight Weld

[W/G, Box 4.]

[Boston, Mass.] Monday 26th Febry [1838]

My beloved Theodore

. . . Some of our friends want me to deliver a course of lectures in Boston as soon as I am entirely rested. They think *now* is the time to make an effort there—that the Aristocracy will come out. What do you think of it? Darkness covers my future prospects entirely, except that I must go to Phila to attend the Woman's convention. I trust I may be enabled to see *when* to leave this quiet, lovely place & be willing to work again when the command is given to break up my encampment & enter again upon public duty . . . .

I am *your* Angelina

Angelina E. Grimké to Theodore Dwight Weld

[W/G, Box 5.]

[Brookline, Mass.] March 8th [1838]

My well beloved

. . . M Chapman tho't the Odeon might be got for a Lecture. I can choose the times. If it is, I must speak, but indeed it seems almost too much whilst my mind is passing thro' so much exercise. If such a sure & steady light did not shine down upon the union of our hearts, I should be ready to think we were wrong to indulge the hopes we cherish, because I fear we will hurt each others *usefulness* in the cause of the slave. My dear Theodore, have you *tho't of this?* Do tell me the result of your reflections.

Farewell, my heart is full—*full* but I must [unintelligible]. The Lord bless & keep thee forevermore

Sarah M. Grimké to Theodore Dwight Weld

[W/G, Box 5; B.D, 2:616.]

Brookline [Mass.] 1st Ap./38

I thank thee, my dear brother, for thy letter. I know it was the offspring of duty. It spake as the voice of Jehovah, & I trembled in his presence. It seemed like the thunders of Almighty wrath, but I fell at his feet and said "Tho' he slay me yet will I trust in him." It seemed as if God rebuked me in anger for daring to set my unhallowed foot on sacred ground, & I was ready to covenant never again to open my lips for the slave. I cannot, I must not trust myself to say much. Oh, it has seemed as if God mocked me. But this cannot be. And on a calm & prayerful review of the lecture at the Odeon, I dare not say I regret what I did. I believed it right for me to bear a part of the burden. I was anxious to relieve my precious child, but fearing to do wrong I wrote to M. Chapman. Her reply, received previous to thy letter, decided me not to speak again at the Odeon. I send her letters, not because they encourage me to speak again at the Odeon but because they give the views of one prominent abolitionist & of other persons. With regard to the Odeon not being obtained if the ab[olitionists] supposed I would speak, it was obtained by the women, who wrote more than once to say it was the wish of the So. that I sh[oul]d speak. But for this I might not have opened my lips. . . .

Thine in the bonds of the everlasting love of Jesus S. M. G.

Sarah M. Grimké to Jane Smith

[W/G, Box 5.]

Brookline [Mass.] 3d Mo. 24th 1838.

Beloved Sister

. . . [W]e intend to try to keep the secret [of Angelina and Weld's engagement], because we do not want the public gaze attracted to Angelina as the future wife of T. D. W. & by that means perhaps diverted, during the lectures at the Odeon, from the great subject we are holding up before the public mind. . . . We shall not return to Mass. It is likely we may be located in N. Y. State the coming year. . . . We greatly hope dear M. Chapman will commence lecturing & that the spark we have been permitted to kindle on the Woman question will never go out. . . .

Thine in near love & tender affection—S. M. G.

Angelina E. Grimké to Jane Smith

[W/G, Box 5.]

[Brookline, Mass.]—27th of 3d Month [1838]—

My Beloved Jane—

. . . As he [Theodore] expects to be engaged in writing for the A S Sy for some time, it seemed necessary that he should be near enough to N Y. to have access to the Public Libraries & the Printing press. We, therefore, tho't of hiring a place (a few acres so as to have a garden for fruits & vegetables) about 10 or 20 miles from the city. This he will look for immediately on his return. There we hope to spend our time in mutual improvement & in writing for the A S cause, & as way opens, we can occasionally go out & lecture, but we are fully convinced that we never ought to labor so unremittingly in this way as we have done. . . .

Our dear Sister Sarah expects to go with us & abide with us. This I regard as a great favor, for separation from her was my only fear, but Theodore loves her as a sister, & she is very much attached to him, so that the arrangement is mutually pleasant to all of us.

Our marriage is to be a very uncommon one, dear, both of us feeling that we must bear our testimonies against all the follies of such occasions. We can have no bridesmaids nor groomsmen, nor wedding cake, nor wine &c &c. We must have some of our colored friends at it. . . .

Very Affy Thy Friend A E Gé

Angelina E. Grimké to Theodore Dwight Weld

[W/G, Box 5.]

[Brookline, Mass.] Friday—13 [April 1838]

My *best* beloved one—

. . . [My mother writes], ". . . after you are married, I hope you will feel that *retirement* is best suited to your station, & that you will desire to *retire* from the busy scenes of *publicity* & enjoy that happiness which I hope your *home* will yield you." And Sister E[liza] hopes I "will enjoy a great deal of happiness in *private life.*" So thou mayest imagine how sadly disappointed they will be when they hear that *thou* hast abundantly strengthened my hands in the iniquity of public speaking. . . .

Farewell my beloved one [unintelligible] only

Angelina E. Grimké to Theodore Dwight Weld

[W/G, Box 5; B/D, 2:647–649.]

[Brookline, Mass.] Wednesday morning [April 29, 1838]

My best beloved

. . . Thou askest what Lewis Tappan meant by saying that in marrying me at this juncture thou wast showing great moral courage. Why didst *thou* not *know* that no *other* man *would marry me*—no, not even a good Abolitionist? This is just what A Weston said to me—altho' a great many will go to hear you & may admire you, Angelina, yet I have believed you had thrown yourself *entirely* beyond the ordinary lot of woman, & *no man* would wish to have such a wife. I have felt this very sensibly & been thankful for it as a shield from that kind of attention. Besides, there are a great many who despise me & would delight to insult me. Could I have placed in thy hand an anonymous letter which I received at the time thy last was handed me, I think thou wouldst be convinced of this, & understand a little better what thou wast *daring to do*. I agree with L T perfectly, but thou art blind to the *danger* of marrying a woman who feels and acts out the principle of *equal* rights. . . .

. . . We *must take time* to *talk all* those matters over relative to our anticipated union whilst we are in Phil'a'; *duty* requires that we should *understand* each others views as thoroughly as possible; this will prevent those constant jarrings which we see between husband & wife. O! how often has my heart mourned over the *misery* of married life, & prayed to be saved from it, & saved from the responsibilities of a family until my Father *had prepared* me to enter upon them in his fear and to *his glory*. I believe He has heard my prayers, for altho' I indeed tremble in view of them & exclaim "who is sufficient for these things," yet still I can & *do* trust him for *help*, unceasing help in the discharge of my new duties. . . . Beloved, I *believe* thou wilt find me *most* happy in our little Cottage & in the kitchen of that cottage when duty calls me there; still *as I have never been tried*, I will not speak positively. May the Lord Jesus help me for thy sake, & for *woman's* sake, to prove that well regulated minds can with *equal ease* occupy high & low stations & find *true happiness in both*. Yes, thou art trying a *dangerous experiment*, one which I do believe *no other man* would try, because I tho't *no other* understands my principles or myself.

[Angelina E. Grimké]

*Sarah M. Grimké to Elizabeth Pease**

[Catherine H. Birney, *The Grimké Sisters. Sarah and Angelina Grimké: The First American Women Advocates of Abolition and Woman's Rights* (Boston, Mass.: Lee and Shepard, 1885; Westport, Conn.: Greenwood, 1969), pp. 232–233; B/D, 2:678–679; original manuscript not found.]

[Manlius, N.Y., May 20?, 1838]

. . . I must now give thee some account of my dear sister's marriage, which probably thou hast already heard of. Her precious husband is emphatically a man of God, a member of the Presbyterian Church. Of course Angelina will be disowned for forming the connection, and I shall be for attending the marriage. We feel no regret at this circumstance, believing that the discipline which cuts us off from membership for an act so strictly in conformity with the will of God, and so sanctioned by His word as is the marriage of the righteous, must be anti-Christian, and I am thankful for the opportunity to testify against it. The marriage was solemnized at the house of our sister, Anna R. Frost, in Philadelphia, on the 14th instant. By the law of Pennsylvania a marriage is legal if witnessed by twelve persons. Neither clergyman nor magistrate is required to be present. Angelina could not conscientiously consent to be married by a clergyman, and Theodore D. Weld cheerfully consented to have the marriage solemnized in such a manner as compared with her views. We all felt that the presence of a magistrate, a stranger, would be unpleasant to us at such a time, and we therefore concluded to invite such of our friends as we desired, and have the marriage solemnized as a religious act, in a religious and social meeting. Neither Theodore nor Angelina felt as if they could bind themselves to any preconceived form of words, and accordingly uttered such as the Lord gave them at the moment. Theodore addressed Angelina in a solemn and tender manner. He alluded to the unrighteous power vested in a husband by the laws of the United States over the person and property of his wife, and he abjured all authority, all government, save the influence which love would give to them over each other as moral and immortal beings. I would give much to recall his words, but I cannot. Angelina's address to him was brief but comprehensive, con-

* Elizabeth (Pease) Nichol (1807–1897), the daughter of a very wealthy British Quaker woolen manufacturer and abolitionist and sister of the first Quaker member of Parliament, was extremely active in the British antislavery movement and other reform causes. She was considered a "British Garrisonian."

taining a promise to honor him, to prefer him above herself, to love him with a pure heart fervently. Immediately after this we knelt, and dear Theodore poured out his soul in solemn supplication for the blessing of God on their union, that it might be productive of enlarged usefulness, and increased sympathy for the slave. Angelina followed in a melting appeal to our Heavenly Father, for a blessing on them, and that their union might glorify Him, and then asked His guidance and overshadowing love through the rest of their pilgrimage. A colored Presbyterian minister then prayed, and was followed by a white one, and then I felt as if I could not restrain the language of praise and thanksgiving to Him who had condescended to be in the midst of this marriage feast, and to pour forth abundantly the oil and wine of consolidation and rejoicing. The Lord Jesus was the first guest invited to be present, and He condescended to bless us with His presence, and to sanction and sanctify the union which was thus consummated. The certificate was then read by William Lloyd Garrison, and was signed by the company. The evening was spent in pleasant social intercourse. Several colored persons were present, among them two liberated slaves, who formerly belonged to our father, had come by inheritance to sister Anna, and had been freed by her. They were our invited guests, and we thus had an opportunity to bear our testimony against the horrible prejudice which prevails against colored persons, and the equally awful prejudice against the poor. . . .

[Sarah M. Grimké]

Angelina Emily Grimké Weld, Speech at Pennsylvania Hall, May 16, 1838*

[Samuel Webb, ed., *History of Pennsylvania Hall, Which Was Destroyed by a Mob, on the 17th of May, 1838* (Philadelphia, Pa.: Merrihew and Gunn, 1838; New York: Negro Universities, 1969), pp. 123–126; reprinted in Elizabeth Cady Stanton, Susan B. Anthony, and Matilda Joslyn Gage, eds., *History of Woman Suffrage,* vol. 1, *1848–1861* (New York: Fowler and Wells, 1881; New York: Arno and *New York Times,* 1969), pp. 334–336; also reprinted in Lerner, pp. 375–381.]

Men, brethren and fathers—mothers, daughters and sisters, what came ye out to see? A reed shaken with the wind? Is it curiosity merely,

*Webb, the treasurer of the Board of Managers of Pennsylvania Hall and a member of the Pennsylvania Anti-Slavery Society for the Eastern District, wrote the bracketed comments that appear in the speech.

or a deep sympathy with the perishing slave, that has brought this large audience together? [A yell from the mob without the building.] Those voices without ought to awaken and call out our warmest sympathies. Deluded beings! "they know not what they do." They know not that they are undermining their own rights and their own happiness, temporal and eternal. Do you ask, "what has the North to do with slavery?"' Hear it—hear it. Those voices without tell us that the spirit of slavery is *here,* and has been roused to wrath by our abolition speeches and conventions: for surely liberty would not foam and tear herself with rage, because her friends are multiplied daily, and meetings are held in quick succession to set forth her virtues and extend her peaceful kingdom. This opposition shows that slavery has done its deadliest work in the hearts of our citizens. Do you ask, then, "what has the North to do?" I answer, cast out first the spirit of slavery from your own hearts, and then lend your aid to convert the South. Each one present has a work to do, be his or her situation what it may, however limited their means, or insignificant their supposed influence. The great men of this country will not do this work; the church will never do it. A desire to please the world, to keep the favor of all parties and of all conditions, makes them dumb on this and every other unpopular subject. They have become worldly-wise, and therefore God, in his wisdom, employs them not to carry on his plans of reformation and salvation. He hath chosen the foolish things of the world to confound the wise, and the weak to overcome the mighty.

As a Southerner I feel that it is my duty to stand up here tonight and bear testimony against slavery. I have seen it—I have seen it. I know it has horrors that can never be described. I was brought up under its wing: I witnessed for many years its demoralizing influences, and its destructiveness to human happiness. It is admitted by some that the slave is not happy under the *worst* forms of slavery. But I have *never* seen a happy slave. I have seen him dance in his chains, it is true; but he was not happy. There is a wide difference between happiness and mirth. Man cannot enjoy the former while his manhood is destroyed, and that part of the being which is necessary to the making, and to the enjoyment of happiness, is completely blotted out. The slaves, however, may be, and sometimes are, mirthful. When hope is extinguished, they say, "let us eat and drink, for to-morrow we die." [Just then stones were thrown at the windows,—a great noise without, and commotion within.] What is a mob? What would the breaking of every window be? What would the levelling of this Hall be? Any evidence that we are wrong, or that slavery is a good and wholesome institution? What if the mob should now burst in upon us, break up our meeting and commit violence upon our persons—would this be anything compared with what the slaves endure? No, no: and we do not remember them "as bound with them," if we shrink in the time of peril, or feel unwilling to sacrifice ourselves, if need be, for their sake. [Great Noise.] I thank the Lord that there is yet left life enough to feel the truth, even though it rages at it—that conscience is not so completely seared as to be unmoved by the truth of the living God.

Many persons go to the South for a season, and are hospitably entertained in the parlor and at the table of the slaveholder. They never enter the huts of the slaves; they know nothing of the dark side of the picture, and they return home with praises on their lips of the generous character of those with whom they had tarried. Or if they have witnessed the cruelties of slavery, by remaining silent spectators they have naturally become callous—an insensibility has ensued which prepares them to apologize even for barbarity. Nothing but the corrupting influence of slavery on the hearts of the Northern people can induce them to apologize for it; and much will have been done for the destruction of Southern slavery when we have so reformed the North that no one here will be willing to risk his reputation by advocating or even excusing the holding of men as property. The South know it, and acknowledge that as fast as our principles prevail, the hold of the master must be relaxed. [Another outbreak of mobocratic spirit, and some confusion in the house.]

How wonderfully constituted is the human mind! How it resists, as long as it can, all efforts made to reclaim from error! I feel that all this disturbance is but an evidence that our efforts are the best that could have been adopted, or else the friends of slavery, would not care for what we say and do. The South know what we do. I am thankful that they are reached by our efforts. Many times have I wept in the land of my birth over the system of slavery. I knew of none who sympathized in my feelings—I was unaware that any efforts were made to deliver the oppressed—no voice in the wilderness was heard calling on the people to repent and do works meet for repentance—and my heart sickened within me. Oh, how should I have rejoiced to know that such efforts as these were being made. I only wonder that I had such feelings. I wonder when I reflect under what influence I was brought up, that my heart is not harder than the nether millstone. But in the midst of temptation, I was preserved, and my sympathy grew warmer, and my hatred of slavery more inveterate, until at last I have exiled myself from my native land because I could no longer endure to hear the wailing of the slave. I fled to the land of Penn;* for here, thought I, sympathy for the slave will surely be found. But I found it not. The people were kind and hospitable, but the slave had no place in their thoughts. Whenever questions were put to me as to his condition, I felt that they were dictated by an idle curiosity, rather than by that deep feeling which would lead to effort for his rescue. I therefore shut up my grief in my own heart. I remembered that I was a Carolinian, from a state which framed this iniquity by law. I knew that throughout her territory was continued suffering, on the one part, and continual brutality and sin on the other. Every Southern breeze wafted to me the discordant tones of weeping and wailing, shrieks and groans, mingled with prayers and blasphemous curses. I thought there was no hope; that the wicked would go on his wickedness, until he had destroyed both himself and his country. My heart sunk within me at the abominations in the midst of which I had been born and educated. What will it avail, cried I in bitterness of spirit, to expose to the gaze of strangers the horrors and pollutions of slavery, when there is no ear to hear nor heart to feel and pray for the slave. The language of my soul was, "Oh tell it not in Gath, publish it not in the streets of Askelon." But how different do I feel now! Animated with hope, nay, with an assurance of the triumph of liberty and good will to man, I will lift up my voice like a trumpet, and show this people their transgression, their sins of omission towards the slave, and what they can do towards affecting Southern mind[s], and overthrowing Southern oppression.

We may talk of occupying neutral ground, but on this subject, in its present attitude, there is no such thing as neutral ground. He that is not for us is against us, and he that gathereth not with us, scattereth abroad. If you are on what you suppose to be neutral ground, the South look upon you as on the side of the oppressor. And is there one who loves his country willing to give his influence, even indirectly, in favor of slavery—that curse of nations? God swept Egypt with the besom of destruction, and punished Judea also with a sore punishment, because of slavery. And have we any reason to believe that he is less just now?—or that he will be more favorable to us than to his own "peculiar people"? [Shoutings, stones thrown against the windows, &c.]

* William Penn (1644–1718), a British Quaker who was awarded a proprietory charter in 1681 for Pennsylvania, the colony named after his father.

There is nothing to be feared from those who would stop our mouths, but they themselves should fear and tremble. The current is even now setting fast against them. If the arm of the North had not caused the Bastille of slavery to totter to its foundations, you would not hear those cries. A few years ago, and the South felt secure, and with a contemptuous sneer asked, "Who are the abolitionists? The abolitionists are nothing"?—Ay, in one sense they were nothing, and they are nothing still. But in this we rejoice, that "God has chosen things that are not to bring to nought things that are." [Mob again disturbed the meeting.]

We often hear the question asked, "What shall we do?" Here is an opportunity for doing something now. Every man and every woman present may do something by showing that we fear not a mob, and, in the midst of threatenings and revilings, by opening our mouths for the dumb and pleading the cause of those who are ready to perish.

To work as we should in this cause, we must know what Slavery is. Let me urge you then to buy the books which have been written on this subject and read them, and then lend them to your neighbors. Give your money no longer for things which pander to pride and lust, but aid in scattering "the living coals of truth" upon the naked heart of this nation, —in circulating appeals to the sympathies of Christians in behalf of the outraged and suffering slave. But, it is said by some, our "books and papers do not speak the truth." Why, then, do they not contradict what we say? They cannot. Moreover the South has entreated, nay commanded us to be silent; and what greater evidence of the truth of our publications could be desired?

Women of Philadelphia! allow me as a Southern woman, with much attachment to the land of my birth, to entreat you to come up to this work. Especially let me urge you to petition. *Men* may settle this and other questions at the ballot-box, but you have no such right; it is only through petitions that you can reach the Legislature. It is therefore peculiarly *your* duty to petition. Do you say, "It does no good?" The South already turns pale at the number sent. They have read the reports of the proceedings of Congress, and there have seen that among other petitions were very many from the women of the North on the subject of slavery. This fact has called the attention of the South to the subject. How could we expect to have done more as yet? Men who hold the rod over slaves, rule in the councils of the nation: and they deny our right to petition and to remonstrate against abuses of our sex and of our kind. We have these rights, however, from our God. Only let us exercise them: and though often turned away unanswered, let us remember the influence of importunity upon the unjust judge, and act accordingly. The fact that the South look with jealousy upon our measures shows that they are effectual. There is, therefore, no cause for doubting or despair, but rather for rejoicing.

It was remarked in England that women did much to abolish Slavery in her colonies. Nor are they now idle. Numerous petitions from them have recently been presented to the Queen, to abolish the apprenticeship with its cruelties nearly equal to those of the system whose place it supplies. One petition two miles and a quarter long has been presented. And do you think these labors will be in vain? Let the history of the past answer. When the women of these States send up to Congress such a petition, our legislators will arise as did those of England, and say, "When all the maids and matrons of the land are knocking at our doors we must legislate." Let the zeal and love, the faith and works of our English sisters quicken ours—that while the slaves continue to suffer, and when they shout deliverance, we may feel that satisfaction of *having done what we could.*

SIX

Domesticity

As soon as the sisters settled in Fort Lee, New Jersey, at the end of May, 1838, Sarah wrote to Jane Smith: "we have sat down under the shadow of our own roof & gathered around our humble board. Peace has flowed sweetly thro' our souls."[1] Mary Smith Grimké hoped Sarah would "be employed in what will be more suitable to the Female character, & be less offensive to the public," and warned Angelina, "[i]t will be your own fault if you do not enjoy a calm & quiet life."[2] The Philadelphia Friends notified them, in September, that both had been disowned: Angelina for marrying out of the faith and Sarah for attending the wedding.[3]

At first, they continued with public activities. Sarah helped organize a convention in Philadelphia on the use of free labor goods, the sisters petitioned in the area around their home, and they discussed the best site for the next women's convention. But they surprised, perhaps even dismayed, their Massachusetts friends both by their sedentary life-style and their coolness toward the "Principles of Peace" Henry C. Wright had written for the Peace Convention that met in Boston on September 18.[4] The invitation to attend, deliberate, and vote had been extended to women; several women, Abby Kelley and Maria Weston Chapman among them, were assigned to convention committees; the constitution opened the New England Non-Resistance Society to anyone, regardless of color, sex, or creed, who subscribed to "ultra" peace principles; Anne Weston and Thankful Southwick* were elected to the Executive Committee; and Maria Weston Chapman was elected recording secretary and would be coeditor of the *Non-Resistant.* Some abolitionists personally

* Thankful Southwick (1792–1857) in 1836 had led a group of black women onto a ship in Boston harbor, freed two black slaves, secured a hearing on a writ of *habeas corpus* when the slaves were recaptured, and, during the hearing, managed to spirit them from the courtroom and out of the city.

close to Garrison chose not to join: Lydia Maria Child and Wendell Phillips, among others.[5]

This new example of Garrisonian "ultraism" strengthened a concerted effort against Garrison and his followers, which had begun at the May 1838 New England Anti-Slavery Convention, when a group of moderate and conservative clerics, led by the Reverend Charles T. Torrey (1813–1846) and Amos A. Phelps, failed to prevent passage of a motion inviting women to participate on equal terms with men.[6]

Then, at the January 1839 anniversary of the Massachusetts Anti-Slavery Society, Torrey again tried to prevent women from participating and called for a new weekly newspaper. Defeated again, he and his followers launched their own newspaper, the *Massachusetts Abolitionist,* on February 7. Vehement attacks and counterattacks commenced, and Phelps resigned from the board of the Massachusetts Anti-Slavery Society, saying that it was no longer simply an antislavery society but "a woman's-rights, non-government anti-slavery society.[7]

In May, at the American Anti-Slavery Society convention, the Massachusetts clergymen, joined by Birney and Lewis Tappan, tried and failed to pass a resolution preventing women from being seated, speaking, or acting on committees. Abby Kelley both spoke and served on a committee.[8]

At the New England Anti-Slavery Convention, May 28–30, Phelps offered a resolution that only "gentlemen" should be enrolled in the organization. When it was defeated, Phelps, Elizur Wright, and others seceded and formed the Massachusetts Abolition Society.[9]

There had also been a particularly bitter quarrel among the members of the Boston Female Anti-Slavery Society. Antagonism between the conservative members, central among whom was Mary S. Parker, and the Garrisonians, led by Maria Weston Chapman, had been building since 1837. It erupted at the spring 1839 meeting. When the conservatives succeeded in defeating motions to raise money for the Massachusetts Anti-Slavery Society and support *The Liberator* with subscriptions, Mrs. Chapman and her sisters organized a fund-raising antislavery fair on their own.[10]

It seems evident that these schisms and the vituperations accompanying them played a significant part in Sarah's reluctance to return to Massachusetts and resume her career as a lecturer. The sisters had friends and connections on both sides, and their experience with the debate over the "woman question" in the summer of 1837 probably did not predispose them to become immersed in another major controversy. It is also possible that Weld's critique of Sarah's speaking ability had stung her more deeply than she acknowledged. First the Elders at the Philadelphia Friends' meetings, now Weld—perhaps Sarah decided never again to place herself in such a situation.

Angelina E. Grimké Weld to Anne Warren Weston

[BPL, MS.A.9.2. v. 10, p. 38.]

Fort Lee [N.J.] 7th Month 15 [1838]

My Dear Anna

. . . I thank thee also for thy account of the N E Convention in regard to the Woman Question. Like all other truth, when brought out *practically,* it is causing deep searchings of heart & revealing the secrets of the soul. I believe this can no more be driven back from the field of investigation than the doctrine of Human Rights, of which it is a part, & a very important part. And N E will be the battleground, for she is most certainly the moral light house of our nation. . . . I cannot help hoping [Abby] will yet come out as a lecturer in the cause of the poor slave. Such practical advocacy of the rights of woman are worth every thing to *every* reform, at least, so I believe. . . .

We keep no help & therefore are filling up "the appropriate sphere of woman" to admiration, in the kitchen with baking pans & pots & steamers &c., & in the parlor & chambers with the broom & the duster. Indeed, I think our enemies wld rejoice, could they only look in upon us from day to day & see us toiling in domestic life, instead of lecturing to *promiscuous* audiences. Now I verily believe that we are *thus* doing *as much* for the cause of woman as we did by public speaking. For it is absolutely necessary that we should show that we are *not* ruined as domestic characters, but so far from it, *as soon* as duty calls us home, we can & do rejoice in the release from public service, & are as anxious to make good bread as we ever were to deliver a good lecture. . . . [A] little more experience will enable us to save much anxiety, time & labor, so that we are looking forward to a much easier time than we have had yet. . . .

. . . I remain Thine—Angelina G Weld

Sarah M. Grimké to Anne Warren Weston

[BPL, MS.A.9.2., 10:39.]

Fort Lee [N.J.] July 17th 1838

Dear Anna

I hope my letter will not be altogether unacceptable because it contains a negative to the request contained in the resolutions about me returning to Mass. I do truly rejoice that I have been there; it was a season of improvement to my own heart & mind & had no other benefit resulted, I should be grateful for the privilege of laboring in the A. S. cause amongst you. Now, dear, it rather strikes me that one reason you mention for my returning, viz., that a door is open for the public labors of women, in Mass., renders it less necessary that I should be there than elsewhere. *The door is open,* the field has had one ploughing, & those who take the plough next will find the soil more yielding, I think. I do not know but my business is simply to open doors, or do the first rough work. If I know my own heart, I am as anxious to help the cause as when I was engaged in lecturing, & I pray to be preserved in a state of watchfulness & prayer, that I may know if my heavenly father calls me again to public labors. At present, I feel contented & happy & grateful in our sweet retirement, which the Lord has abundantly blessed, and we all desire to use the leisure we may be favored with in acquiring further information & preparing for future usefulness. . . . I do not know what the Lord designs for me in future. I only know that now he says, "in quietness & confidence should be thy strength.["] With love to thy sisters, believe me thine for the slave, Sarah M. Grimké—

A. Kelly *[sic]* I hope will be released from her school ere long & be at liberty to prepare herself for a public lecturer. And surely the women of Massachusetts are able to enter in & carry on the work. Abby Kelly *[sic]* doubtless helped it at the [American Anti-Slavery Society] Convention. I think what was done there very important.

Angelina E. Grimké Weld to Elizabeth Pease

[W/G, Box 5.]

Fort Lee New Jersey 8th Month [August 10, 1838]

My Dear Friend

With all my heart, I thank God & take courage" *[sic]* & pray that I may, yet again, feeble & unworthy as I am, be permitted to open my mouth for the dumb & "plead the cause of all that are drawn unto death["]. . . . I cannot tell thee how I love this hidden life—how I have thanked my heavenly father for this respite from public labor, or how earnestly I have prayed, that whilst I am thus dwelling at ease, I may not forget the captives of my land, or be unwilling to go forth again on the high places of the field, to combat the giant sin of slavery with the smooth stones of the pure river of Truth, if called to do so, by Him who put me forth & went before me in days that are past. My dear Theodore entertains the noblest views of the rights & responsibilities of woman, & will never lay a straw in the way of my lecturing. He has many times strengthened my hands in this work, & often tenderly admonished me to keep my eye upon my great Leader, & my heart in a state of readiness to go forth when ever I am called out. I humbly trust I may, but as earnestly desire to be preserved from going before I hear a voice saying unto me, "this is the way, walk in it," & ["] *I* will be thy shield & thy exceeding great reward." This was the promise that was given me before, & O how faithfully it was fulfilled, *"my soul knoweth right well."*

. . . believe me Thine for the slave

A G Weld

Angelina E. Grimké Weld to Lydia Maria Child

[Gratz Collection, The Historical Society of Pennsylvania, Case 7, Box 20.]

[Fort Lee, N.J.] 8th Mo: 10th [1838]

Dear Maria

When I received thy letter of June 3d I did not expect so long a time would elapse before I should answer it, but really my new vocations of cook & chambermaid, house servant & seamstress, have so engrossed my time & thought as to leave but little of the former for the book or the pen, & this I hope will be to *thee* a good excuse for apparent neglect. By the way, I ought to say that my dear Sister is a co worker with me in these *delightful* duties, & that it is our own free choice thus to live without a servant, for I was utterly ashamed to let any stranger see how ignorant I was of every part of housekeeping, & therefore determined to *learn, learn,* before I undertook to direct others. And so pleased are we with our threefold cord of peerless harmony & love, that nothing but *necessity* will induce us to employ a domestic. It is so sweet to feel our independence & serve one another in love: my dear husband bearing our burden with us, & never complaining of our ignorance & mistakes.

Indeed, Maria, considering we are Southerners & *public lecturers,* I think we do wonders, & hope if thy husband & thyself should come to New York, you will pay a visit at Fort Lee to see us moving in our "appropriate spheres." . . .

Angelina G. Weld

Angelina E. Grimké Weld to Anne Warren Weston

[BPL, MS.A.9.2, 10:58.]

Fort Lee [N.J.] 10 Mo: 14th [1838]

Dear Anna

. . . For my own part, I have always seen some difficulties connected with this question, which I could not solve & which kept me from lecturing in the Odeon upon it when applied to by Amasa Walker.* For many years, I have been convinced that the fundamental principles of morality upon which the Jewish system was founded was the *same* upon which the Gospel system was built. I never so fully examined this great subject as to be able to reconcile them in every particular, tho' I am convinced they are reconcilable. Of course, then, I could not sign the Declaration, which solemnly asserts that Jesus Christ revoked the penal code of the Old Testament & substituted for it the forgiveness of enemies. . . .

Another objection I have to the Declaration is the assumption that those who do not take the ultra Peace ground do believe that the existing governments of the world are ordained of God, that they, "the powers that be," are approvingly ordained by Him. Surely no reflecting Christian can think so with regard to such a government as ours. Nevertheless, I am glad the Society has been formed & the Convention held, because I believe it will elicit discussion & bring out the truth. But do tell me how you can consistently petition government to exercise a power which you believe to be usurped. Perhaps thou wilt be amazed to find I am not ultra, for thou appearest to think my mind was altogether settled, but the fact is it never has been, for I am sure I never have seen to the bottom of the question & am still panting after the Truth.

I thank thee for the sympathy in my new cares, & am not surprized at the fear expressed in thy last that I shall like them *Too well,* for this is my only fear. I assure thee that I can now make very nice bread & am

* Amasa Walker (1799–1876), abolitionist and coorganizer of the Peace Convention. He opposed establishing the Non-Resistance Society.

far fonder of it than I ever was [of] my lectures. I do not agree with thee that I can NOW be doing any thing of more importance than superintending my household affairs, because in doing so I am proving that public lecturing does not unfit woman for private duties. No one, then, but Sister & myself can do our work & demonstrate this for the benefit of our sex at large. . . .

With love to thy Sisters & our other Boston [friends] & love from Theodore & Sister to thyself, I [unintelligible] affy A G Weld

Sarah M. Grimké to Henry C. Wright

[BPL, MS.A.1.2, 7:75.]

Fort Lee [N.J.] 19/11/38.

Dear brother Wright

. . . I do not think I should have signed the Declaration of Sentiments, or the Constitution. Perhaps thou mayest be surprised at this, & query what change has taken place in my views. I can reply none that I am conscious of, but the more I reflect on that great subject, the more I feel that to comprehend its length & breadth & height & depth requires *deep searching of my own heart* & a fuller insight into the mysteries of Gods kingdom, than I have yet attained. . . . It is a solemn thing to come out in a public document and say that we believe Jehovah has abrogated his own laws. I do not feel prepared to take this stand. I am still looking for light on this point. . . . Whatever my sentiments may be as a private Christian, I think I cannot publicly commit myself to the principle that one of Jehovah's dispensations is contrary to the other in those principles of fundamental morality on which they are based. I like the Dec. of Sen. much, with that exception. It breathes the spirit of Jesus Christ, & I shall rejoice if the non-resistance principle is carried out in all its fullness & sweetness, by those who have entered into convenant not to resist evil. May they remember that home is the first place to exhibit the meekness & lowliness of Him, whom they have called master. . . .

I have given the subject of my returning to Mass. all the consideration which I could; still I am willing to acknowledge that it never has pressed much on my mind, altho' when I left N. E. I really desired that the Lord might send me back. But I have not been able to see that he wills me to be any where but at Fort Lee. His loving kindness has provided me a sweet harbor of rest, after years of tossing & buffeting. He has given me two children [Angelina and Theodore] with whom I enjoy sweet communion & who delight to do me good. He has given me that peace in the enjoyment of these blessings which the world cannot give. . . . A call has come from Ohio & Pennsylvania as urgent as the call from N. E., but none of them reach the [wit]ness for God in my soul. . . .

Thine in the bonds of Peace & love for Jesus & the oppressed

Sarah M. Grimké

Angelina E. Grimké Weld to Sarah Douglass

[W/G, Box 6.]

Fort Lee [N.J.] 3/21/39.

My dear Sister

. . . Thou inquirest what we think of things in Mass. I can hardly tell thee, for the truth is we have no time to read the statements. We have been all winter & still are so busily engaged in preparing the work on the condition of slaves at the South, that our anti slavery papers (&, of course, all others) are laid aside, generally without being read. Besides, we feel that it is almost impossible to judge in the case: our correspondents in Boston are all the friends of brother Garrison &, of course, we know little except thro' them. We mourn that there are divisions amongst us, that abolitionists have their Pauls & their Apollos' but we rejoice that Jehovah reigns, that the cause of the slave is his cause, & that altho' this falling out by the way may retard, it cannot prevent the triumph of truth. We pray for our dear brethren & sisters that they may not forget the slave, but may labor with a pure heart fervently for the overturning of the abomination which maketh desolate. . . .

I am as ever *Your* Angelina

Sarah M. Grimké to Elizabeth Pease

[W/G, Box 6.]

Fort Lee [N.J.] 4th Mo. 10th 1839.

My dear friend

. . . I have been busily engaged in searching for testimony on the subject of slavery, for a work Theodore is preparing on the condition of slaves in the U.S. Notwithstanding all that has been written, the public is comparatively ignorant of the sufferings of the slave, & we are every where met by the assertion that they are "well treated." . . . The state of our cause loudly demanded a work which would not *prove by argument* that slavery & cruelty were inseparable; but which would contain a mass of *incontrovertible facts,* that would exhibit the horrid barbarity of a system which embrutes Gods rational creatures. In order to procure the testimony, Angelina & myself have been engaged all winter in looking thro' files of Southern papers, which God in his providence placed in our possession, & have collected an abundance of testimony which Theodore has arranged. . . . I do not see, as many abolitionists do, that our cause goes on prosperously at present. Many circumstances, especially the divisions among abolitionists, cause some of us to mourn. . . . I have felt it a sweet privilege & blessing to be hidden in this sequestered spot, & to have had so much to do for the slaves that I have had no time to read the articles relative to the controversies, & my mind has been so intensively & exclusively occupied with the work that we have had in hand, that investigation into the merits of the opponents has been wholly out of the question. . . . The book of which I have spoken is now in the hands of the printer. . . .

In near love & unity. S. M. G

Narrative and Testimony of Sarah M. Grimké

[Theodore Dwight Weld, ed. *American Slavery As It Is: Testimony of a Thousand Witnesses* (New York: American Anti-Slavery Society, 1839), pp. 22–24.*]

Miss Grimké is a daughter of the late Judge Grimké, of the Supreme Court of South Carolina, and sister of the late Hon. Thomas S. Grimké.

As I left my native state on account of slavery, and deserted the home of my fathers to escape the sound of the lash and the shrieks of tortured victims, I would gladly bury in oblivion the recollection of those scenes with which I have been familiar; but this may not, cannot be; they come over my memory like gory spectres, and implore me with resistless power, in the name of a God of mercy, in the name of a crucified Savior, in the name of humanity; for the sake of the slaveholder, as well as the slave, to bear witness to the horrors of the southern prison house. I feel impelled by a sacred sense of duty, by my obligations to my country, by sympathy for the bleeding victims of tyranny and lust, to give my testimony respecting the system of American slavery,—to detail a few facts, most of which came under my *personal observation*. And here I may

* It sold over 100,000 copies in its first year, more than any antislavery pamphlet ever written, and it was widely distributed in Great Britain.

premise, that the actors in these tragedies were all men and women of the highest respectability, and of the first families in South Carolina, and, with one exception, citizens of Charleston; and that their cruelties did not in the slightest degree affect their standing in society.

A handsome mulatto woman, about 18 or 20 years of age, whose independent spirit could not brook the degradation of slavery, was in the habit of running away: for this offence she had been repeatedly sent by her master and mistress to be whipped by the keeper of the Charleston work-house.* This had been done with such inhuman severity, as to lacerate her back in a most shocking manner; a finger could not be laid between the cuts. But the love of liberty was too strong to be annihilated by torture; and, as a last resort, she was whipped at several different times, and kept a close prisoner. A heavy iron collar, with three long prongs projecting from it, was placed round her neck, and a strong and sound front tooth was extracted, to serve as a mark to describe her, in case of escape. Her sufferings at this time were agonizing; she could lie in no position but on her back, which was sore from scourgings, as I can testify, from personal inspection, and her only place of rest was on the floor, on a blanket, These outrages were committed in a family where the mistress daily read the scriptures, and assembled her children for family worship. She was accounted, and was really, so far as alms-giving was concerned, a charitable woman, and tender hearted to the poor; and yet this suffering slave, who was the seamstress of the family, was continually in her presence, sitting in her chamber to sew, or engaged in her other household work, with her lacerated and bleeding back, her mutilated mouth, and heavy iron collar, without, so far as appeared, exciting any feelings of compassion.

A highly intelligent slave, who panted after freedom with ceaseless longings, made many attempts to get possession of himself. For every offence he was punished with extreme severity. At one time he was tied up by his hands to a tree, and whipped until his back was one gore of blood. To this terrible infliction he was subjected at intervals for several weeks, and kept heavily ironed while at his work. His master one day accused him of a fault, in the usual terms dictated by passion and arbitrary power; the man protested his innocence, but was not credited. He again repelled the charge with honest indignation. His master's temper rose almost to frenzy; and seizing a fork, he made a deadly plunge at the breast of the slave. The man being far his superior in

* A prison or house of correction for petty offenders, also called a "sugar house."

strength, caught his arm, and dashed the weapon on the floor. His master grasped at his throat, but the slave disengaged himself, and rushed from the apartment. Having made his escape, he fled to the woods; and after wandering about for many months, living on roots and berries, and enduring every hardship, he was arrested and committed to jail. Here he lay for a considerable time, allowed scarcely food enough to sustain life, whipped in the most shocking manner, and confined in a cell so loathsome, that when his master visited him, he said the stench was enough to knock a man down. The filth had never been removed from the apartment since the poor creature had been immured in it. Although a black man, such had been the effect of starvation and suffering, that his master declared he hardly recognized him—his complexion was so yellow, and his hair, naturally thick and black, had become red and scanty; an infallible sign of long continued living on bad and insufficient food. Stripes, imprisonment, and the gnawings of hunger, had broken his lofty spirit for a season; and, to use his master's own exulting expression, he was "as humble as a dog." After a time he made another attempt to escape and was absent so long, that a reward was offered for him, *dead or alive.* He eluded every attempt to take him, and his master, despairing of ever getting him again, offered to pardon him if he would return home. It is always understood that such intelligence will reach the runaway; and accordingly, at the entreaties of his wife and mother, the fugitive once more consented to return to his bitter bondage. I believe this was the last effort to obtain his liberty. His heart became touched with the power of the gospel; and the spirit which no inflictions could subdue, bowed at the cross of Jesus, and with the language on his lips—"the cup that my father hath given me, shall I not drink it?" submitted to the yoke of the oppressor, and wore his chains in unmurmuring patience till death released him. The master who perpetrated these wrongs upon his slave, was one of the most influential and honored citizens of South Carolina, and to his equals was bland, and courteous, and benevolent even to a proverb.

A slave who had been separated from his wife, because it best suited the convenience of his owner, ran away. He was taken up on the plantation where his wife, to whom he was tenderly attached, then lived. His only object in running away was to return to her—no other fault was attributed to him. For this offence he was confined in the stocks *six weeks,* in a miserable hovel, not weather-tight. He received fifty lashes weekly during that time, was allowed food barely sufficient to sustain him, and when released from confinement, was not permitted to return to his wife. His master, although himself a husband and a father, was unmoved by the touching appeals of the slave, who entreated that he might only remain with his wife, promising to discharge his duties faithfully; his master continued inexorable, and he was torn from his wife and family. The owner of this slave was a professing Christian, in full membership with the church, and this circumstance occurred when he was confined to his chamber during his last illness.

A punishment dreaded more by the slaves than whipping, unless it is unusually severe, is one which was invented by a female acquaintance of mine in Charleston—I heard her say so with much satisfaction. It is standing on one foot and holding the other in the hand. Afterwards it was improved upon, and a strap was contrived to fasten around the ankle and pass around the neck; so that the least weight of the foot resting on the strap would choke the person. The pain occasioned by this unnatural position was great; and when continued, as it sometimes was, for an hour of more, produced intense agony. I heard this same woman say, that she had the ears of her waiting maid *slit* for some petty theft. This she told me in the presence of the girl, who was standing in the room. She often had the helpless victims of her cruelty severely whipped, not scrupling herself to wield the instrument of torture, and with her own hands inflict severe chastisement. Her husband was less inhuman than his wife, but he was often goaded on by her acts of great severity. In his last illness I was sent for, and watched beside his death couch. The girl on whom he had so often inflicted punishment, haunted his dying hours; and when at length the king of terrors approached, he shrieked in utter agony of spirit, "Oh, the blackness of darkness, the black imps, I can see them all around me—take them away!" and amid such exclamations he expired. These persons were of one of the first families in Charleston.

A friend of mine, in whose veracity I had entire confidence, told me that about two years ago, a woman in Charleston, with whom I was well acquainted, had starved a female slave to death. She was confined in a solitary apartment, kept constantly tied, and condemned to the slow and horrible death of starvation. This woman was notoriously cruel. To those who have read the narrative of James Williams* I need only say,

* The *Narrative of James Williams* (London: 1837) contained the testimony of a black slave redeemed by Joseph Sturge during his trip to Jamaica and brought back with him.

that the character of young Larrimore's wife is an exact description of this female tyrant, whose countenance was ever dressed in smiles when in the presence of strangers, but whose heart was as the nether millstone toward her slaves.

As I was traveling in the lower country in South Carolina, a number of years since, my attention was suddenly arrested by an exclamation of horror from the coachman, who called out, "Look there, Miss Sarah, don't you see?"—I looked in the direction he pointed, and saw a human head stuck up on a high pole. On inquiry I found that a runaway slave, who was outlawed, had been shot there, his head severed from his body, and put upon the public highway, as a terror to deter slaves from running away.

On a plantation in North Carolina, where I was visiting, I happened one day, in my rambles, to step into a negro cabin; my compassion was instantly called forth by the object which presented itself. A slave, whose head was white with age, was lying in one corner of the hovel; he had under his head a few filthy rags, but the boards were his only bed, it was the depth of winter, and the wind whistled through every part of the dilapidated building—he opened his languid eyes when I spoke, and in reply to my question, "What is the matter?" he said, "I am dying of a cancer in my side."—As he removed the rags which covered the sore, I found that it extended halfway round the body, and was shockingly neglected. I inquired if he had any nurse. "No, missey," was his answer, "but de people (the slaves) very kind to me, dey often steal time to run and see me and fetch me some ting to eat; if dey did not, I might starve." The master and mistress of this man, who had been worn out in their service, were remarkable for their intelligence, and their hospitality knew no bounds toward those who were of their own grade in society: the master had for some time held the highest military office in North Carolina, and not long previous to the time of which I speak, was the Governor of the State.*

On a plantation in South Carolina, I witnessed a similar case of suffering—an aged woman suffering under an incurable disease in the same miserably neglected situation. The "owner" of this slave was proverbially kind to her negroes; so much so, that the planters in the neighborhood said she spoiled them, and set a bad example, which

* Benjamin Smith (1750–1829), Sarah's uncle, had been an aide to George Washington and served as governor from 1810 to 1811. Sarah had spent several months on the North Carolina plantation of his younger brother, James, in 1820.

might produce discontent among the surrounding slaves; yet I have seen this woman tremble with rage, when her slaves displeased her, and heard her use language to them which could only be expected from an inmate of Bridewell; * and have known her in a gust of passion send a favorite slave to the workhouse to be severely whipped.

Another fact occurs to me. A young woman about eighteen, stated some circumstances relative to her young master, which were thought derogatory to his character; whether true or false, I am unable to say; she was threatened with punishment, but persisted in affirming that she had only spoken the truth. Finding her incorrigible, it was concluded to send her to the Charleston workhouse and have her whipt; she pleaded in vain for a commutation of her sentence, not so much because she dreaded the actual suffering, as because her delicate mind shrunk from the shocking exposure of her person to the eyes of brutal and licentious men; she declared to me that death would be preferable; but her entreaties were vain, and as there was no means of escaping but by running away, she resorted to it as a desperate remedy, for her timid nature never could have braved the perils necessarily encountered by fugitive slaves, had not her mind been thrown into a state of despair.—She was apprehended after a few weeks, by two slave-catchers, in a deserted house, and as it was late in the evening they concluded to spend the night there. What inhuman treatment she received from them has never been revealed. They tied her with cords to their bodies, and supposing they had secured their victim, soon fell into a deep sleep, probably rendered more profound by intoxication and fatigue; but the miserable captive slumbered not; by some means she disengaged herself from her bonds, and again fled through the lone wilderness. After a few days she was discovered in a wretched hut, which seemed to have been long uninhabited; she was speechless; a raging fever consumed her vitals, and when a physician saw her, he said she was dying of a diseases brought on by over fatigue; her mother was permitted to visit her, but ere she reached her, the damps of death stood upon her brow, and she had only the sad consolation of looking on the death-struck form and convulsive agonies of her child. . . .

Fort Lee, Bergen County, New Jersey, 3rd Month, 26th, 1839.

* A prison located near Blackfriars Bridge, London, until 1864.

Testimony of Angelina Grimké Weld

[[Theodore Dwight Weld, ed. *American Slavery As It Is: Testimony of a Thousand Witnesses* (New York: American Anti-Slavery Society, 1839), pp. 52–57.]

Mrs. Weld is the youngest daughter of the late Judge Grimké, of the Supreme Court of South Carolina, and a sister of the late Hon. Thomas S. Grimké, of Charleston.

Fort Lee, Bergen Co., New Jersey, Fourth Month 6th, 1839.

I sit down to comply with thy request, preferred in the name of the Executive Committee of the American Anti-Slavery Society. The responsibility laid upon me by such a request, leaves me no option. While I live, and slavery lives, I *must* testify against it. If I should hold my peace, "the stone would cry out of the wall, and the beam out of the timber would answer it." But though I feel a necessity upon me, and "a woe unto me," if I withhold my testimony, I give it with a heavy heart. My flesh crieth out, "if it be possible, let *this* cup pass from me"; but, "Father, *thy* will be done," is, I trust, the breathing of my spirit. Oh, the slain of the daughter of my people! they lie in all the ways; their tears fall as the rain, and are their meat day and night; their blood runneth down like water; their plundered hearths are desolate; they weep for their husbands and children, because they are not; and the proud waves do continually go over them, while no eye pitieth, and no man careth for their souls.

But it is not alone for the sake of my poor brothers and sisters in bonds, or for the cause of truth, and righteousness, and humanity, that I testify; the deep yearnings of affection for the mother that bore me, who is still a slaveholder, both in fact and in heart; for my brothers and sisters, (a large family circle,) and for my numerous other slaveholding kindred in South Carolina, constrain me to speak: for even were slavery no curse to its victims, the exercise of arbitrary power works such fearful ruin upon the hearts of *slaveholders,* that I should feel impelled to labor and pray for its overthrow with my last energies and latest breath.

I think it important to premise, that I have seen almost nothing of slavery on *plantations*. My testimony will have respect exclusively to the treatment of *"house-servants,"* and chiefly those belonging to the first families in the city of Charleston, both in the religious and in the fashionable world. And here let me say, that the treatment of *plantation* slaves cannot be fully known, except by the poor sufferers themselves, and their drivers and overseers. In a multitude of instances, even the master can know very little of the actual condition of his own field-slaves, and his wife and daughters far less. A few facts concerning my own family will show this. Our permanent residence was in Charleston; our country-seat (Bellemont), was 200 miles distant, in the north-western part of the state; where, for some years, our family spent a few months annually. Our *plantation* was three miles from the family mansion. There, all the field-slaves lived and worked. Occasionally, once a month, perhaps, some of the family would ride over to the plantation, but I never visited the *fields where the slaves were at work,* and knew almost nothing of their condition; but this I do know, that the overseers who had charge of them, were generally unprincipled and intemperate men. But I rejoice to know, that the general treatment of slaves in that region of country, was far milder than on the plantations in the lower country.

Throughout all the eastern and middle portions of the state, the planters very rarely reside permanently on their plantations. They have almost invariably *two* residences, and spend less than half the year on their estates. Even while spending a few months on them, politics, fieldsports, races, speculations, journeys, visits, company, literary pursuits, &c., absorb so much of their time, that they must, to a considerable extent, take the condition of their slaves on *trust,* from the reports of their overseers. I make this statement, because these slaveholders (the wealthier class,) are, I believe, almost the only ones who visit the north with their families;—and northern opinions of slavery are based chiefly on their testimony.

But not to dwell on preliminaries, I wish to record my testimony to the faithfulness and accuracy with which my beloved sister, Sarah M. Grimké, has, in her "narrative and testimony," on a preceding page, described the condition of the slaves, and the effect upon the hearts of slaveholders, (even the best,) caused by the exercise of unlimited power over moral agents. Of the *particular acts* which she has stated, I have no personal knowledge, as they occurred before my remembrance; but of the spirit that prompted them, and that constantly displays itself in scenes of similar horror, the recollections of my childhood, and the effaceless imprint upon my riper years, with the breaking of my heart-strings, when, finding that I was powerless to shield the victims, I tore myself from my home and friends, and became an exile among strangers —all these throng around me as witnesses, and their testimony is graven on my memory with a pen of fire.

Why I did not become totally hardened, under the daily operation of this system, God only knows; in deep solemnity and gratitude, I say, it was the *Lord's* doing, and marvellous in mine eyes. Even before my heart was touched with the love of Christ, I used to say, "Oh that I had the wings of a dove, that I might flee away and be at rest"; for I felt that there could be no rest for me in the midst of such outrages and pollutions. And yet I saw *nothing* of slavery in its most vulgar and repulsive forms. I saw it in the *city,* among the fashionable and the honorable, where it was garnished by refinement, and decked out for show. A few *facts* will unfold the state of society in the circle with which I was familiar, far better than any general assertions I can make.

I will first introduce the reader to a woman of the highest respectability—one who was foremost in every benevolent enterprise, and stood for many years, I may say, at the *head* of the fashionable elite of the city of Charleston, and afterwards at the head of the moral and religious female society there. It was after she had made a profession of religion, and retired from the fashionable world, that I knew her; therefore I will present her in her religious character. This lady used to keep cowhides, or small paddles, (called "pancake sticks,") in four different apartments in her house; so that when she wished to punish, or to have punished, any of her slaves, she might not have the trouble of sending for an instrument of torture. For many years, one or another, and *often* more of her slaves, were flogged *every day;* particularly the young slaves about the house, whose faces were slapped, or their hands beat with the "pancake stick," for every trifling offence—and often for no fault at all. But the floggings were not all; the scoldings and abuse daily heaped upon them all, were worse: "fools" and "liars," "sluts" and "husseys," "hypocrites" and "good-for-nothing creatures," were the *common* epithets with which her mouth was filled, when addressing her slaves, adults as well as children. Very often she would take a position at her window, in an upper story, and scold at her slaves while working in the garden, at some distance from the house, (a large yard intervening,) and occasionally order a flogging. I have known her thus on the watch, scolding for more than an hour at a time, in so loud a voice that the whole neighborhood could hear her; and this without the least apparent feeling of shame. Indeed, it was *no disgrace among slaveholders,* and did not in the least injure her standing, either as a lady or a Christian, in the aristocratic circle in which she moved. After the "revival" in Charleston, in 1825, she opened her house to social prayer-meetings. The room in which they were held in the evening, and where the voice of prayer was heard around the family altar, and where she herself retired for private devotion thrice each day, was the very place in which, when her slaves were to be whipped with the cowhide, they were taken to receive the infliction; and the wail of the sufferer would be heard, where, perhaps only a few hours previous, rose the voices of prayer and praise. This mistress would occasionally send her slaves, male and female, to the Charleston work-house to be punished. One poor girl, who was accordingly stripped *naked* and whipped, showed me the deep gashes on her back—I might have laid my whole finger in them—*large pieces of flesh had actually been cut out by the torturing lash*. She sent another female slave there, to be imprisoned and worked on the tread-mill.* This girl was confined several days, and forced to work the mill while in a state of suffering from another cause. For ten days or two weeks after her return, she was lame, from the violent exertion necessary to enable her to keep the step on the machine. She spoke to me with intense feelings of this outrage upon her, as a *woman*. Her men servants were sometimes flogged there; and so exceedingly offensive has been the putrid flesh of their lacerated backs, for days after the infliction, that they would be kept out of the house—the smell arising from their wounds being too horrible to be endured. They were always stiff and sore for some days, and not in a condition to be seen by visitors.

This professedly Christian woman was a most awful illustration of the ruinous influence of arbitrary power upon the temper—her bursts of passion upon the heads of her victims were dreaded even by her own children, and very often, all the pleasure of social intercourse around the domestic board, was destroyed by her ordering the cook into her presence, and storming at him, when the dinner or breakfast was not prepared to her taste, and in the presence of all her children, commanding the waiter to slap his face. *Fault-finding,* was with her the constant accompaniment of every meal, and banished that peace which should hover around the social board, and smile on every face. It was common for her to order brothers to whip their own sisters, and sisters their own brothers, and yet no woman visited among the poor more than she did, or gave more liberally to relieve their wants. This may seem perfectly unaccountable to a northerner, but these seeming contradictions vanish when we consider that over *them* she possessed no arbitrary power, they

* A large drum with broad steps on which a slave's feet were placed, while his or her hands were tied to a rail above his or her head. The drum revolved rapidly, and if, as often happened, the slave slipped from the steps, he or she was left dangling, the steps regularly slapping against the victim's entire body.

were always presented to her mind as unfortunate sufferers, towards whom her sympathies most freely flowed; she was ever ready to wipe the tears from *their* eyes, and open wide her purse for *their* relief, but the others were her *vassals,* thrust down by public opinion beneath her feet, to be at her beck and call, ever ready to serve in all humility, her, whom God in his providence had set over them—it was their *duty* to abide in abject submission, and hers to *compel* them to do so—*it was thus that she reasoned.* Except at family prayers, none were permitted to *sit* in her presence, but the seamstresses and waiting maids, and they, however delicate might be their circumstances, were forced to sit upon low stools, without backs, that they might be constantly reminded of their inferiority. A slave who waited in the house, was guilty on a particular occasion of going to visit his wife, and kept dinner waiting a little, (his wife was the slave of a lady who lived at a little distance.) When the family sat down to the table, the mistress began to scold the waiter for the offence—he attempted to excuse himself—she ordered him to hold his tongue—he ventured another apology; her son then rose from the table in a rage, and beat the face and ears of the waiter so dreadfully that the blood gushed from his mouth, and nose, and ears. This mistress was *a professor of religion;* her daughter who related the circumstance, was a *fellow member* of the Presbyterian church *with the poor outraged slave*—instead of feeling indignation at this outrageous abuse of her brother in the church, she justified the deed, and said "he got just what he deserved." I solemnly believe this to be a true picture of *slaveholding religion.*

The following is another illustration of it:

A mistress in Charleston sent a grey headed female slave to the workhouse, and had her severely flogged. The poor old woman went to an acquaintance of mine and begged her to buy her, and told her how cruelly she had been whipped. My friend examined her *lacerated back,* and out of compassion did purchase her. The circumstance was mentioned to one of the former owner's relatives, who asked her if it were true. The mistress told her it was, and said that she had made the severe whipping of this aged woman a *subject of prayer,* and that she believed she had done right to have it inflicted upon her. The last "owner" of the poor old slave, said she, had no fault to find with her as a servant.

I remember very well that when I was a child, our next door neighbor whipped a young woman so brutally, that in order to escape his blows she rushed through the drawing-room window in the second story, and fell upon the street pavement below and broke her hip. This circumstance produced no excitement or inquiry.

The following circumstance occurred in Charleston, in 1828:

A slaveholder, after flogging a little girl about thirteen years old, set her on a table with her feet fastened in a pair of stocks. He then locked the door and took out the key. When the door was opened she was found dead, having fallen from the table. When I asked a prominent lawyer, who belonged to one of the first families in the State, whether the murderer of this helpless child could not be indicted, he coolly replied, that the slave was Mr. ———'s property, and if he chose to suffer the *loss,* no one else had any thing to do with it. The loss of *human life,* the distress of the parents and other relatives of the little girl, seemed utterly out of his thoughts: it was the loss of *property* only that presented itself to his mind.

I knew a gentleman of great benevolence and generosity of character, so essentially to injure the eye of a little boy, about ten years old, as to destroy its sight, by the blow of a cowhide, inflicted whilst he was whipping him.* I have heard the same individual speak of "breaking down the spirit of a slave under the lash" as perfectly right.

I also know that an aged slave of his, (by marriage,) was allowed to get a scanty and precarious subsistence, by begging in the streets of Charleston—he was too old to work, and therefore, *his allowance was stopped,* and he was turned out to make his living by begging.

When I was thirteen years old, I attended a seminary, in Charleston, which was superintended by a man and his wife of superior education. They had under their instruction the daughters of nearly all the aristocracy. Their cruelty to their slaves, both male and female, I can never forget. I remember one day there was called into the school room to open a window, a boy whose head had been shaved in order to disgrace him, and he had been so dreadfully whipped that he could hardly walk. So horrible was the impression produced upon my mind by his heart-broken countenance and crippled person that I fainted away. The sad and ghastly countenance of one of their female mulatto slaves who used to sit on a low stool at her sewing in the piazza, is now fresh before me. She often told me, secretly, how cruelly she was whipped when they

* The Jewish law would have set this servant free, for his eye's sake, but he was held in slavery and sold from hand to hand, although, besides this title to his liberty according to Jewish law, he was a *mulatto,* and therefore free under the Constitution of the United States, in whose preamble our fathers declare that they established it expressly to "secure the blessings of *liberty* to themselves and *their posterity.*"—Ed. [Footnote in original.]

sent her to the work house. I had known so much of the terrible scourgings inflicted in that house of blood, that when I was once obliged to pass it, the very sight smote me with such horror that my limbs could hardly sustain me. I felt as if I was passing the precincts of hell. A friend of mine who lived in the neighborhood, told me she often heard the screams of the slaves under their torture.

I once heard a physician of a high family, and of great respectability in his profession, say, that when he sent his slaves to the work-house to be flogged, he always went to *see* it done, that he might be sure they were properly, i.e. *severely* whipped. He also related the following circumstance in my presence. He had sent a youth of about eighteen to this horrible place to be whipped and *afterwards* to be worked upon the treadmill. From not keeping the step, which probably he COULD NOT do, in consequences of the lacerated state of his body; his arm got terribly torn, from the shoulder to the wrist. This physician said, he went every day to attend to it himself, in order that he might use those restoratives, which *would inflict the greatest possible pain*. This poor boy, after being imprisoned there for some weeks, was then brought home, and compelled to wear iron clogs on his ankles for one or two months. I saw him with those irons on one day when I was at the house. This man was, when young, remarkable in the fashionable world for his elegant and fascinating manners, but the exercise of the slaveholder's power has thrown the fierce air of tyranny even over these.

I heard another man* of equally high standing say, that he believed he suffered far more than his waiter did, whenever he flogged him, for he felt the *exertion* for days after! and yet he never felt it to be his duty to instruct him, or have him instructed, even in the common principles of morality. I heard the mother of this man say, it would be no surprise to her, if he killed a slave some day, for, that, when transported with passion he did not seem to care what he did. He once broke a *large* stick over the back of a slave, and at another time the ivory butt-end of a long coach whip over the *head* of another. This last was attacked with epileptic fits some months after, and has ever since been subject to them, and occasionally to violent fits of insanity.

Southern mistresses sometimes flog their slaves themselves, though generally one slave is compelled to flog another. Whilst staying at a friend's house some years ago, I one day saw the mistress with a cowhide in her hand, and heard her scolding in an under tone, her waiting

* Angelina is describing her brother, Henry.

man, who was about twenty-five years old. Whether she actually inflicted the blows I do not know, for I hastened out of sight and hearing. It was not the first time I had seen a mistress thus enraged. I knew she was a cruel mistress, and had heard her daughters disputing, whether their mother did right or wrong, to send the slave *children,* (whom she sent out to sweep chimneys) to the workhouse to be whipped if they did not bring in their wages regularly. This woman moved in the most fashionable circle in Charleston. The income of this family was derived mostly from the hire of their slaves, about one hundred in number. Their luxuries were blood-bought luxuries indeed. And yet what stranger would ever have inferred their cruelties from the courteous reception and bland manners of the parlor. Every thing cruel and revolting is carefully concealed from strangers, especially those from the north. Take an instance:—I have known the master and mistress of a family send to their friends to *borrow* servants to wait on company, because their own slaves had been so cruelly flogged in the workhouse, that they could not walk without limping at every step, and their putrified flesh emitted such an intolerable smell that they were not fit to be in the presence of company. How can northerners know these things when they are hospitably received at southern tables and firesides? I repeat it, no one who has not been an *integral part* of a slaveholding community, can have any idea of its abominations. It is a whited sepulchre full of dead men's bones and all uncleanness. Blessed be God, the Angel of *Truth* has descended and rolled away the stone from the mouth of the sepulchre, and *sits upon it.* The abominations so long hidden are now brought forth before all Israel and the sun. Yes, the Angel of Truth *sits upon this stone,* and it can never be rolled back again.

The utter disregard of the comfort of the slaves, in *little* things, can scarcely be conceived by those who have not been a *component part* of slaveholding communities. Take a few particulars out of hundreds that might be named. In South Carolina musketoes *[sic]* swarm in myriads, more than half the year—they are so excessively annoying at night, that no family thinks of sleeping without nets or "musketoe-bars" hung over their bedsteads, yet slaves are never provided with them, unless it be the favorite old domestics who get the cast-off pavilions; and yet these very masters and mistresses will be so kind to their *horses* as to provide them with *fly* nets. Bedsteads and bedding too, are rarely provided for any of the slaves—if the waiters and coachmen, waiting maids, cooks, washers, &c., have beds at all, they must generally get them for themselves. Commonly they lie down at night on the bare floor, with a small blanket wrapped round them in winter, and in summer a coarse osnaburg sheet,* or nothing. Old slaves generally have beds, but it is because when younger *they have provided them for themselves.*

Only two meals a day are allowed the house slaves—the *first at twelve* o'clock. If they eat before this time, it is by stealth, and I am sure there must be a good deal of suffering among them from *hunger,* and particularly by children. Besides this, they are often kept from their meals by way of punishment. No table is provided for them to eat from. They know nothing of the comfort and pleasure of gathering round the social board—each takes his plate or tin pan and iron spoon and holds it in the hand or on the lap. I *never* saw slaves seated round a *table* to partake of any meal.

As the general rule, no lights of any kind, no firewood—no towels, basins, or soap, no tables, chairs, or other furniture, are provided. Wood for cooking and washing *for the family* is found, but when the master's work is done, the slave must find wood for himself if he has a fire. I have repeatedly known slave children kept the whole winter's evening, sitting on the stair-case in a cold entry, just to be at hand to snuff candles or hand a tumbler of water from the side-board, or go on errands from one room to another. It may be asked why they were not permitted to stay in the parlor, when they would be still more at hand. I answer, because waiters are not allowed to *sit* in the presence of their owners, and as children who were kept running all day, would of course get very tired of standing for two or three hours, they were allowed to go into the entry and sit on the staircase until rung for. Another reason is, that even slaveholders at times find the presence of slaves very annoying; they cannot exercise entire freedom of speech before them on all subjects.

I have also known instances where seamstresses were kept in cold entries to work by the stair-case lamps for one or two hours, every evening in winter—they could not see without standing up all the time, though the work was often too large and heavy for them to sew upon it in that position without great inconvenience, and yet they were expected to do their work as *well* with their cold fingers, and standing up, as if they had been sitting by a comfortable fire and provided with the necessary light. House slaves suffer a great deal also from not being allowed to leave the house without permission. If they wish to go even for a draught of water, they must *ask leave,* and if they stay longer than

* A coarse linen sheet, originally made in Osnabrück, Germany.

the mistress thinks necessary, they are liable to be punished, and often are scolded or slapped, or kept from going down to the next meal.

It frequently happens that relatives, among slaves, are separated for weeks or months, by the husband or brother being taken by the master on a journey, to attend on his horses and himself.—When they return, the white husband seeks the wife of his love; but the black husband must wait to see *his* wife, until mistress pleases to let her chambermaid leave her room. Yes, such is the despotism of slavery, that wives and sisters dare not run to meet their husbands and brothers after such separations, and hours sometimes elapse before they are allowed to meet; and, at times, a fiendish pleasure is taken in keeping them asunder—this furnishes an opportunity to vent feelings of spite for any little neglect of "duty."

The sufferings to which slaves are subjected by separations of various kinds, cannot be imagined by those unacquainted with the working out of the system behind the curtain. Take the following instances.

Chambermaids and seamstresses often sleep in their mistresses' apartments, but with no bedding at all. I know an instance of a woman who has been married eleven years, and yet has never been allowed to sleep out of her mistress's chamber.—This is a *great* hardship to slaves. When we consider that house slaves are rarely allowed social intercourse during *the day,* as their work generally *separates* them; the barbarity of such an arrangement is obvious. It is peculiarly a hardship in the above case, as the husband of the woman does not "belong" to her "owner"; and because he is subject to dreadful attacks of illness, and can have but little attention from his wife in the *day*. And yet her mistress, who is an old lady, gives her the highest character as a faithful servant, and told a friend of mine, that she was "entirely dependent upon her for *all* her comforts; she dressed and undressed her, gave her all her food, and was so *necessary* to her that she could not do without her." I may add, that this couple are tenderly attached to each other.

I also know an instance in which the husband was a slave and the wife was free: during the illness of the former, the latter was *allowed* to come and nurse him; she was obliged to leave the work by which she had made a living, and come to stay with her husband, and thus lost weeks of her time, or he would have suffered for want of proper attention; and yet his "owner" made her no compensation for her services. He had long been a faithful and a favorite slave, and his owner was a woman very benevolent to the poor whites.—She went a great deal among these, as a visiting commissioner of the Ladies' Benevolent Society, and was in the constant habit of *paying* the *relatives of the poor whites* for nursing *their* husbands, fathers, and other relations; because she thought it very hard, when their time was taken up, so that they could not earn their daily bread, that they should be left to suffer. Now, such is the stupifying influence of the *"chattel* principle" on the minds of slaveholders, that I do not suppose it ever occurred to her that this poor *colored* wife ought to be paid for her services, and particularly as she was spending her time and strength in taking care of *her "property."* She no doubt only thought how kind she was, to *allow* her to come and stay so long in her yard; for, let it be kept in mind, that slaveholders have unlimited power to separate husbands and wives, parents and children, however and whenever they please; and if this mistress had chosen to do it, she could have debarred this woman from all intercourse with her husband, by forbidding her to enter her premises.

Persons who own plantations and yet live in cities, often take children from their parents as soon as they are weaned, and send them into the country; because they do not want the time of the mother taken up by attendance upon her own children, it being too valuable to the mistress. As a *favor,* she is, in some cases, permitted to go to see them once a year. So, on the other hand, if field slaves happen to have children of an age suitable to the convenience of the master, they are taken from their parents and brought to the city. Parents are almost never consulted as to the disposition to be made of their children; they have as little control over them, as have domestic animals over the disposal of their young. Every natural and social feeling and affection are violated with indifference; slaves are treated as though they did not possess them.

Another way in which the feelings of slaves are trifled with and often deeply wounded, is by changing their names; if, at the time they are brought into a family, there is another slave of the same name; of if the owner happens, for some other reason, not to like the name of the new comer. I have known slaves very much grieved at having the names of their children thus changed, when they had been called after a dear relation. Indeed it would be utterly impossible to recount the multitude of ways in which the *heart* of the slave is continually lacerated by the total disregard of his feelings as a social being and a human creature.

The slave suffers also greatly from being continually *watched.* The system of espionage which is constantly kept up over slaves is the most worrying and intolerable that can be imagined. Many mistresses are, in fact, during the absence of their husbands, really their drivers; and the pleasure of returning to their families often, on the part of the husband, is entirely destroyed by the complaints preferred against the slaves when he comes home to his meals.

A mistress of my acquaintance asked her servant boy, one day, what was the reason she could not get him to do his work whilst his master was away, and said to him, "your master works a great deal harder than you do; he is at his office all day, and often has to study his law cases at night." "Master," said the boy, "is working for himself, and for you, ma'am, but I am working for *him*." The mistress turned and remarked to a friend, that she was so struck with the truth of the remark, that she could not say a word to him.

But I forbear—the sufferings of the slaves are not only insufferable, but they are *indescribable*. I may paint the agony of kindred torn from each other's arms, to meet no more in time; I may depict the inflictions of the blood-stained lash, but I *cannot describe* the daily, hourly, ceaseless torture, endured by the heart that is constantly trampled under the foot of despotic power. This is a part of the horrors of slavery which, I believe, no one has ever attempted to delineate; I wonder not at it, it mocks all power of language. Who can describe the anguish of that mind which feels itself impaled upon the iron of arbitrary power—its living, writhing, helpless victim! every human susceptibility tortured, its sympathies torn, and stung, and bleeding—always feeling the death-weapon in its heart, and yet not so deep as to *kill* that humanity which is made the curse of its existence.

In the course of my testimony I have entered somewhat into the *minutiae* of slavery, because this is a part of the subject often overlooked, and cannot be appreciated by any but those who have been witnesses, and entered into sympathy with the slaves as human beings. Slaveholders think nothing of them, because they regard their slaves as *property*, the mere instruments of their convenience and pleasure. *One who is a slaveholder at heart never recognises a human being in a slave.*

As thou hast asked me to testify respecting the *physical condition* of the slaves merely, I say nothing of the awful neglect of their *minds* and *Souls* and the systematic effort to imbrute them. A wrong and an impiety, in comparison with which all the other unutterable wrongs of slavery are but as the dust of the balance.

Epilogue

> It is truly a wonderful dispensation of Providence, that these two women should come forth from the bosom of a proud and fashionable family in South Carolina, and by becoming Quakers should prepare themselves for the great work, which the Lord had for them to do in the unseen future.
>
> Lydia Maria Child

> The example and teaching of the Grimkés wrought conviction as to the rights and consequent duties of women in the minds of multitudes. . . . Probably our children's children, our sons no less than our daughters, will dwell on the memory of these women, as the descendants of the bondman of today will cherish the name of Garrison.
>
> Maria Weston Chapman

FOLLOWING the publication of *American Slavery As It Is,* the sisters' letters make little mention of slavery and none of women's rights. Angelina's pregnancy, their move to a new home in Belleville (which was in dire need of repair), the making of winter clothes, the large number and frequency of visitors, and the arrival of Stephen, a family slave, all made crushing demands on their time and energy. Abby Kelley visited them in the spring of 1839 and wrote Anne Warren Weston:

> I went there with a determination to rebuke them severely for absenting themselves from the N. Y. meetings, but found to my own mortification that I had passed judgement before examining the witnesses. Angelina is truly very feeble. Their opinion is, that her labors in lecturing were altogether too great for a constitution naturally very slender and that she will never recover from it. Shockity. Then last winter she applied herself too closely in assisting

> to get out "Slavery as it is," which has entirely prostrated her physical as well as mental energies. How many changes have come over "the spirit of her dream." *Look at her history.* Sarah did not think it proper for her to leave A under such circumstances, as they expected much company and as A exerted herself far too much in order to keep up *appearances* when in company.
>
> But alas for their sentiments on non-resistance. S. and A. say they have not examined, and think they *ought* not examine it, so long as so much is to be done for the slave, and, although there appeared to be a design not to commit themselves on the point, they have evidently adopted the doctrine that any other unpopular cause, if espoused by abolitionists, will retard the progress of the cause, and therefore must be "tabued." As for Theodore, he is unsparingly severe upon us.[1]

The causes that mattered most to the sisters, abolitionism and women's rights, suffered severe setbacks during the next year as cleavages rent the antislavery movement. Women were excluded from the convention that met in Albany in July 1839 to discuss political activity by members of the American Anti-Slavery Society. The following April the members of the Boston Female Anti-Slavery Society, unable to agree on any important issue, voted to dissolve. The society was, however, immediately reconstituted by Lydia Maria Child and Maria Weston Chapman, without the conservatives; Mary Parker and the conservatives would later form the Massachusetts Female Emancipation Society.[2]

Then, when Abby Kelley was appointed to the business committee at the American Anti-Slavery Society's national convention in May 1840, the conservative minority walked out and founded the American and Foreign Anti-Slavery Society. Though its membership was strictly limited to males, the schism benefited women. The women who remained in the American Anti-Slavery Society dissolved many female auxiliaries and generally obliterated all distinctions between men's and women's activities. Lydia Maria Child, Maria Weston Chapman, and Lucretia Coffin Mott became members of the Executive Committee of the American Anti-Slavery Society; Child would become editor of its newspaper, the *National Anti-Slavery Standard* (in 1844) and Abby Kelley one of its best speakers and organizers.[3] Weld, without giving any reasons, wrote Gerrit Smith: "We feel *impelled* to stand *aloof* from both of the National A. S. Societies."[4]

Although Sarah and Angelina remained on the sidelines, their thinking had not shifted as radically as Abby Kelley seemed to think. When the British sponsors of the World's Antislavery Convention (London, June 1840) engineered a vote against seating the females delegated by antislavery societies in Massachusetts and Pennsylvania, Sarah wrote Elizabeth Pease:

> It seemed to me, at first view, that it was [a] cause of regret that the woman question as it is called was introduced, as it has I fear carried with it some of those unchristian feelings which characterized the controversy in this country, but I forbear to judge. It may induce an examination of this subject which may be a blessing to the women of G. B. Certain it is that we are under bondage to men & that our rights & privileges as human beings are little understood, & less appreciated, by our own, as well as the other sex. I apprehended injury to the cause of the slave, the cause which called the Convention together, but it may be the means of extending the usefulness of woman in that very cause. One thing is very clear, I think, viz. that the Convention had no right to reject the female delegates; as members of the A. S. S. they were entitled to a seat, unless it could be proved they were not persons.[5]

The sisters, then, remained interested but uninvolved in the future course of abolitionism and the events that led to the convening of the first women's rights convention at Seneca Falls, New York (1848). Though they did not attend, their example and their words had helped steel those women who did. Angelina did attend the conventions held at Rochester in 1851 and New York in 1863, and they wrote letters of support to the Syracuse convention of 1852.

But Sarah and Angelina had not simply served as a template for future feminists. They had made an immediate, concrete contribution to a very important area of the antislavery cause—petitioning, which built antislavery strength in communities by strengthening, organization, enhancing fund raising, and more widely distributing literature. The years following the convening of the first Anti-Slavery Convention of American Women witnessed a sharp increase in the number of petitions and signers: for example, the average number of signers per petition sent to Congress increased from 32 in 1836–1837 to 107 in 1839–1840.[6] Thirty-four of the forty-four petitions circulated in Massachusetts during the 1837–1838 period came from towns in which the sisters lectured. New female antislavery societies formed in eight of them. Angelina brought a petition with 20,000 signatures with her when she testified before the committee of the Massachusetts House of Representatives.[7] The sisters thus helped strengthen the women's and abolitionist networks that had given them their opportunity to speak and supported them during their lecture tour.

They also set a precedent in interracial relationships. In a vehement and frequently violent racist society, they fought against color bars in the organizations to which they belonged, they actively recruited black women, and—which was more unusual—formed a lifelong, intimate friendship with Sarah Douglass and, several decades later, publicly embraced as Grimkés two mulatto offspring of their brother, Henry, and a slave woman, Nancy Weston: Archibald Henry Grimké and James Francis Grimké.

After a few years of domesticity, the sisters resumed active careers as school administrators and teachers. Sarah researched and partially wrote several essays on the condition of women, but none were completed or published. The sisters kept themselves apprised of events in the realms of rights for women and blacks and occasionally worked on behalf of those causes, but they did not resume public careers. Nevertheless, they had accomplished more for slaves and women in the few years of their public lives than all but a few women or men did in an entire lifetime. And they left behind pages of eloquent testimony to the quality of their motives and the radical nature of their goals.

Endnotes

INTRODUCTION

1. Charles I. Foster, *An Errand of Mercy: The Evangelical United Front, 1790–1837* (Chapel Hill: University of North Carolina Press, 1960), p. 123.
2. Barbara J. Berg, *The Remembered Gate: Origins of American Feminism. The Woman and the City, 1800–1860* (New York: Oxford University Press, 1978), p. 156.
3. Nancy Woloch, *Women and the American Experience* (New York: Knopf, 1984), p. 172.
4. *Elizabeth Cady Stanton, Susan B. Anthony: Correspondence, Writings, Speeches,* Ellen Carol DuBois, ed. (New York: Schocken, 1981), p. 81.
5. See the bibliography for a more detailed discussion of these books.
6. Thomas E. Drake, *Quakers and Slavery in America* (New Haven, Conn.: Yale University Press, 1950), p. 133; Margaret H. Bacon, *The Quiet Rebels: The Story of the Quakers in America* (New York: Basic, 1969), p. 111.
7. P. J. Staudenraus, *The African Colonization Movement, 1816–1855* (New York: Columbia University Press, 1961), p. 251.
8. Charles Grandison Finney, *Lectures on Revival of Religion,* William J. McLoughlin, ed. (Cambridge, Mass.: Belknap, 1960), p. 404.
9. *The Liberator,* April 23, 1831, p. 65; William Lloyd Garrison, *Thoughts on African Colonization; or An Impartial Exhibition of the Doctrines, Principles and Purposes of the American Colonization Society. Together with the Resolutions, Addresses and Remonstrances of the Free People of Color.* (Boston, Mass.: Garrison and Knapp, 1832), pp. 12 and 14.
10. Donald M. Scott, "Abolitionism as a Sacred Vocation," in Lewis Perry and Michael Fellman, eds., *Antislavery Reconsidered: New Perspectives on the Abolitionists* (Baton Rouge, La.: Louisiana State University Press, 1979), p. 72; Anne C. Loveland, "Evangelism and 'Immediate Emancipation' in American Antislavery Thought," *Journal of Southern History,* 32:172–188.
11. James Brewer Stewart, *Holy Warriors: The Abolitionists and American Slavery* (New York: Hill and Wang, 1976), p. 51.
12. Jane H. Pease and William H. Pease, *They Who Would Be Free: Blacks' Search for Freedom, 1830–1861* (New York: Atheneum, 1974), pp. 24–25.

13. *Walker's Appeal, in Four Articles; Together with a Preamble, to the Colored Citizens of the World, But in Particular and Very Expressly, to Those of the United States of America, Written in Boston, State of Massachusetts, September 28, 1829,* reprinted in William H. Pease and Jane H. Pease, eds., *The Antislavery Argument* (Indianapolis, Ind.: Bobbs-Merrill, 1965), p. 309.

14. Pease and Pease, *They Who Would Be Free,* pp. 120–122.

15. Frances Wright, *Views of Society and Manners in America,* Paul R. Baker, ed. (Cambridge, Mass.: Belknap, 1963), pp. 22–23, 39, and 41–42.

16. Frances Wright, *Course of Popular Lectures . . . , with Three Addresses on Various Public Occasions . . .* (New York: Free Enquirer, 1829), p. 44.

17. Elizabeth [Coltman] Heyrick, *Immediate, Not Gradual Abolition; or, An inquiry into the shortest, safest, and most effectual means of getting rid of West Indian slavery* (London: Hatchard, 1824), pp. 9, 22.

18. Elizabeth Margaret Chandler, "Woman," in *Essays, Philanthropic and Moral, by Elizabeth Margaret Chandler: Principally Relating to the Abolition of Slavery in America* (Philadelphia, Pa.: Howell, 1836; Miami, Fla.: Mnemosyne, 1969), pp. 64–65.

19. Alma Lutz, *Crusade for Freedom: Women of the Antislavery Movement* (Boston, Mass.: Beacon, 1968), p. 12; Heyrick, *NO British Slavery, or An invitation to the people to put a speedy end to it,* 3d ed. (London: [R. Clay, printer], 1825).

20. Ruth Kettering Nuermberger, *The Free Produce Movement: A Quaker Protest Against Slavery* (Durham, N.C.: Duke University Press, 1942; New York: AMS, 1970), pp. 16, 19–20.

21. *The Liberator,* January 7, 1832, p. 2, and July 14, 1832, p. 110.

22. Lydia Maria Child, *An Appeal in Favor of that Class of Americans Called Africans* (Boston, Mass.: Allen and Ticknor, 1833; New York: Arno and *New York Times,* 1968), pp. iii, 216.

23. Samuel J. May, *Some recollections of our antislavery conflict* (Boston, Mass.: Fields, Osgood, 1869), p. 98.

24. Lydia Maria Child, *The Evils of Slavery and the Cure of Slavery: The first proved by the opinions of southerners themselves, the last shown by historical evidence* (Newburyport, Mass.: Whipple, 1836); Lydia Maria Child, *Anti-Slavery Catechism* (Newburyport, Mass.: Whipple, 1836).

25. Lydia Maria Child, *Brief History of the Condition of Women, in Various Ages and Nations,* 2 vols., 5th ed. (New York: Francis, 1845), 1:iii.

26. May, *Some recollections,* p. 93.

27. Blanche Glassman Hersh, *The Slavery of Sex: Feminist-Abolitionists in America* (Urbana, Ill.: University of Illinois, 1978), pp. 13–14; Lutz, *Crusade,* pp. 48–51.

28. Elizabeth Cady Stanton, Susan B. Anthony, and Matilda Joslyn Gage, eds., *History of Woman Suffrage,* vol. 1, *1848–1861* (New York: Fowler and Wells, 1881; New York: Arno and *New York Times,* 1969), p. 324.

29. Otelia Cromwell, *Lucretia Mott* (Cambridge, Mass.: Harvard University Press, 1958), pp. 50–51.
30. May, *Some recollections,* p. 232.
31. Lawrence J. Friedman, *Gregarious Saints: Self and Community in American Abolitionism, 1830–1870* (Cambridge: Cambridge University Press, 1982), p. 134.

ONE: The Sisters

1. See the bibliography for a discussion of these books.
2. Elizabeth Cady Stanton, "Angelina Grimké: Reminiscences by E. C. S.," in Elizabeth Cady Stanton, Susan B. Anthony, and Matilda Joslyn Gage, eds., *History of Woman Suffrage* (New York: Fowler and Wells, 1881; New York: Arno and *New York Times,* 1969), 1:392–406.
3. Catherine H. Birney, *The Grimké Sisters, Sarah and Angelina Grimké: The First American Women Advocates of Abolition and Woman's Rights* (Boston, Mass.: Lee and Shepard, 1885; Westport, Conn.: Greenwood, 1969); Katherine Du Pre Lumpkin, *The Emancipation of Angelina Grimké* (Chapel Hill, N.C.: University of North Carolina, 1974).
4. Gerda Lerner, *The Grimké Sisters from South Carolina: Rebels Against Slavery* (Boston, Mass.: Houghton Mifflin, 1967); Blanche Glassman Hersh, *The Slavery of Sex: Feminist-Abolitionists in America* (Urbana, Ill.: University of Illinois, 1978); Ellen C. DuBois, "Women's Rights and Abolition: The Nature of the Connection," in Lewis Perry and Michael Fellman, eds., *Antislavery Reconsidered: New Perspectives on the Abolitionists* (Baton Rouge, La.: Louisiana State University Press, 1979). Keith E. Melder quotes Lerner's analysis approvingly, but shies from using the term "radical feminist." He instead, variously, refers to them and their words as "militant" or "radical" and to them as "rebels." See his *Beginnings of Sisterhood: The American Woman's Rights Movement, 1800–1850* (New York: Schocken, 1977), pp. 80, 88, and 91. Similarly, Alma Lutz refers to them as strong advocates of woman's rights. See her *Crusade for Freedom: Women of the Antislavery Movement* (Boston, Mass.: Beacon, 1968).
5. Anne Firor Scott, *The Southern Lady: From Pedestal to Politics, 1830–1930* (Chicago, Ill.: University of Chicago Press, 1970), pp. 7, 20–21.
6. *Ibid.*, pp. 46, 48.
7. Catherine Clinton, *The Plantation Mistress: Woman's World in the Old South* (New York: Pantheon, 1982), pp. 56, 85.
8. Scott, *The Southern Lady,* p. 51; L. Minor Blackford, *Mine Eyes Have Seen the Glory: The Story of a Virginia Lady, Mary Berkeley Minor Blackford, 1802–1869, who taught her sons to hate slavery and to love the Union* (Cambridge, Mass.: Harvard University Press, 1954), p. 44.
9. Clinton, *The Plantation Mistress,* pp. 12, 186–187.
10. Donald G. Matthews, *Slavery and Methodism: A Chapter in American*

Morality, 1780–1845 (Princeton, N.J.: Princeton University Press, 1965), pp. 116–117.

11. Adrienne Koch, "Two Charlestonians in Pursuit of Truth: The Grimké Brothers," *The South Carolina Historical Magazine* (July 1968), 69:161.

12. Sarah M. and Angelina E. Grimké, "Sketch of Mr. Grimké's Life," *The Calumet* (January and February 1835), 2(5): 138.

13. Frederick Grimké, *Considerations Upon the Nature and Tendency of Free Institutions* (Cincinnati, Ohio: Denby; New York: Barnes, 1848); reprinted as *The Nature and Tendency of Free Institutions,* John William Ward, ed. (Cambridge, Mass.: Belknap, 1968).

14. Grimké, *The Nature and Tendency of Free Institutions,* pp. 418, 428, and 436.

15. William Warren Sweet, *Religion in the Development of American Culture, 1765–1840* (New York: Scribner's, 1952; Gloucester, Mass.: Smith, 1963), pp. 229–233; Lerner, *The Grimké Sisters,* pp. 89–90.

16. Thomas E. Drake, *Quakers and Slavery in America* (New Haven, Conn.: Yale University Press, 1950), pp. 120–121, 177; Ralph Korngold, *Two Friends of Man: The Story of William Lloyd Garrison and Wendell Phillips and Their Relationship with Abraham Lincoln* (Boston, Mass.: Little, Brown, 1950), p. 75; Mary Maples Dunn, "Women of Light," in Carol Ruth Berkin and Mary Beth Norton, eds., *Women of America: A History* (Boston, Mass.: Houghton Mifflin, 1979), p. 132. See also Jean R. Soderlund, *Quakers and Slavery: A Divided Spirit* (Princeton, N.J.: Princeton University Press, 1985) and Margaret Hope Bacon, *Mothers of Feminism: The Story of Quaker Women in America* (New York: Harper, 1986).

17. P. J. Staudenraus, *The African Colonization Movement, 1816–1855* (New York: Columbia University Press, 1961), p. 126; Birney, *The Grimké Sisters,* p. 91.

TWO: The Commitment

1. Oliver Johnson, *William Lloyd Garrison and His Times; or, Sketches of the Anti-Slavery Movement in America, and of the man who was its founder and moral leader* (Boston, Mass.: Houghton Mifflin, 1881), p. 184.

2. Leonard R. Richards, *"Gentlemen of Property and Standing": Anti-Abolition Mobs in Jacksonian America* (New York: Oxford University Press, 1970), p. 18.

3. *The Liberator,* August 15, 1835, p. 131.

4. *The Liberator,* August 22, 1835, p. 135.

5. Letter of September 12, 1835, *The Letters of William Lloyd Garrison,* Walter M. Merrill, ed. (Cambridge, Mass.: Belknap, 1971–1981), 1:527.

6. Catherine H. Birney, *The Grimké Sisters. Sarah and Angelina Grimké: The First American Women Advocates of Abolition and Woman's Rights* (Boston, Mass.: Lee and Shepard, 1885; Westport, Conn.: Greenwood, 1969), p. 138.

7. Letter of November 4, 1836, *The Letters of William Lloyd Garrison,* Louis Ruchames, ed., 2:182.
8. Diary entry, August 3, 1836, W/G, Box 22.
9. Sarah M. Grimké to Jane Smith, August 11, 1836, W/G, Box 3.
10. Letter of November 22, 1836, *The Letters of William Lloyd Garrison,* 2:185.
11. Letter of December 3, 1836, *Ibid.*, p. 187.
12. Gilbert Hobbs Barnes, *The Antislavery Impulse, 1830–1844* (New York: Appleton-Century, 1933; Gloucester, Mass.: Smith, 1957), pp. 134–135; Louis Filler, *The Crusade Against Slavery, 1830–1860* (New York: Harper, 1960), p. 67.
13. John L. Myers, "The Early Antislavery Agency System in Pennsylvania, 1833–1837," *Pennsylvania History* (January 1964), 31:62–63; Filler, *The Crusade,* p. 67.

THREE: The Agency: New York

1. Sarah referred to a "Remonstrance" in a letter to Weld of January 14, 1837. She discussed it in greater detail in a letter of March 10. Weld did not respond until July 22. That manuscript no longer exists, but Sarah wrote, in 1839, a critical account of Friends' discrimination against blacks which she sent, accompanied by the testimony of Sarah Douglass, to British Friends. The letters are in W/G, Boxes 3 and 4, and the two later notes are reprinted in Gilbert H. Barnes and Dwight L. Dumond, *Letters of Theodore Dwight Weld, Angelina Grimké Weld, and Sarah Grimké, 1822–1844* (New York: Appleton-Century, 1934; New York: Da Capo, 1970), 1:373, 414. The 1839 material—"Letter on the Subject of Prejudice Against Colour Amongst the Society of Friends in the United States"—is held by the Rare Books and Manuscripts department of the Boston Public Library (MS.qA.11). Two letters which accompanied it are reprinted in Barnes and Dumond, *Letters of Theodore Dwight Weld,* 2:829–832.
2. Gilbert Hobbs Barnes, *The Antislavery Impulse, 1830–1844* (New York: Appleton-Century, 1933; Gloucester, Mass.: Smith, 1957), p. 110.
3. *Ibid.*, pp. 133 136, and 142.
4. *Proceedings of the Anti-Slavery Convention of American Women, Held in the City of New York, May 9th, 10th, 11th, and 12th, 1837* (New York: Dorr, 1837), pp. 3–4.
5. *The Liberator,* June 9, 1837, p. 95.

FOUR: The Agency: Massachusetts

1. Gilbert Hobbs Barnes, *The Antislavery Impulse, 1830–1844* (New York: Appleton-Century, 1933; Gloucester, Mass.: Smith, 1957), pp. 134–135.
2. Kathyrn Kish Sklar, "The Founding of Mount Holyoke College," in

Ruth Berkin and Mary Beth Norton, eds., *Women of America: A History* (Boston, Mass.: Houghton Mifflin, 1979), p. 187.

3. James Brewer Stewart, "Peaceful Hopes and Violent Experiences: The Evolution of Reforming and Radical Abolitionism," *Civil War History* (December 1971), 17:293–309; James Brewer Stewart, *Holy Warriors: The Abolitionists and American Slavery* (New York: Hill and Wang, 1976). See also Ronald G. Walters, "The Boundaries of Abolitionism," in Lewis Perry and Michael Fellman, eds., *Antislavery Reconsidered: New Perspectives on the Abolitionists* (Baton Rouge, La.: Louisiana State University Press, 1979), pp. 14–15.

4. Barnes, *The Antislavery Impulse*, pp. 65–67, 95–96; Kathryn Kish Sklar, *Catharine Beecher: A Study in American Domesticity* (New Haven, Conn.: Yale University Press, 1973), p. 132.

5. Celia Morris Eckhardt, *Fanny Wright: Rebel in America* (Cambridge, Mass.: Harvard University Press, 1984), pp. 249–250.

6. Catharine E. Beecher, *Essay on Slavery and Abolitionism, with reference to the duty of American females* (Philadelphia, Pa.: Perkins, 1837; Freeport, N.Y.: Books for Libraries, 1970), p. 3.

7. *New England Spectator,* July 12, 1837, pp. 106–107; *The Liberator,* August 11, 1837, p. 129; partially reprinted in Aileen S. Kraditor, ed., *Up from the Pedestal: Selected Writings in the History of American Feminism* (Chicago, Ill.: Quadrangle, 1968), pp. 51–52. The "Pastoral Letter" was closely followed by four other clerical protests: an "Appeal of Clerical Abolitionists on Antislavery Measures," signed by five orthodox Congregationalist ministers (*New England Spectator,* August 16, 1837, p. 127; *The Liberator,* August 11, 1837, pp. 130–131); an "Appeal of Abolitionists, of the Theological Seminary, Andover, Mass.," signed by thirty-nine seminarians (*New England Spectator,* August 16, 1837, p. 127; *The Liberator,* August 25, 1837, p. 139); and two follow-up letters to the "Appeal of Clerical Abolitionists," signed by Charles Fitch and Joseph H. Towne (*The Liberator,* September 8, 1837, p. 145 and September 29, 1837, p. 157).

8. *The Liberator,* July 7, 1837, p. 110; July 21, p. 118; July 28, p. 122; August 4, p. 126.

9. Letters of June 26, July 16, and July 25, 1837, W/G, Box 4.

10. Journals of Henry Clarke Wright, Rare Books and Manuscripts, Boston Public Library, Ms.qAm.1859, 12:69.

11. Letter of July 21, 1837, Rare Books and Manuscripts, Boston Public Library, MS.A.9.2, 9:49.

12. *The Emancipator,* August 10, 1837, p. 59; letter to Amos A. Phelps, August 22, 1837, Rare Books and Manuscripts, Boston Public Library, MS.A.21.7 (42); letter to Lewis Tappan, August 22, 1837, Dwight L. Dumond, ed., *Letters of James Gillespie Birney, 1831–1857* (New York: Appleton-Century, 1938), 1:418.

13. Gerda Lerner, *The Grimké Sisters from South Carolina: Rebels Against Slavery* (Boston, Mass.: Houghton Mifflin, 1967), p. 227.

FIVE: Angelina Moves to Center Stage

1. Letter of December 1, 1837, Rare Books and Manuscripts, Boston Public Library, MS.A.9.2, 9:93.
2. W/G, Box 4; Gilbert H. Barnes and Dwight L. Dumond, eds., *Letters of Theodore Dwight Weld, Angelina Grimké Weld and Sarah Grimké, 1822–1844* (New York: Appleton-Century, 1934; New York: Da Capo, 1970), 1:501.
3. Letter of January 5, 1838, W/G, Box 4; Barnes and Dumond, *Letters of Theodore Dwight Weld,* 2:513–515.
4. Letter of March 10, 1838, *The Letters of William Lloyd Garrison,* Louis Ruchames, ed. (Cambridge, Mass.: Belknap, 1971–1981), 2:342; letter of March 20, 1838, *Lydia Maria Child: Selected Letters, 1817–1880,* ed. Milton Meltzer and Patricia G. Holland (Amherst, Mass.: University of Massachusetts Press, 1982), p. 71; [Theodore Dwight Weld], *In Memory. Angelina Grimké Weld. Printed only for private circulation* (Boston, Mass.: Ellis, 1880), pp. 28–29.
5. *The Liberator,* March 16, 1838, p. 43.
6. Letter to Elizabeth J. Davis, March 18, 1838, Rare Books and Manuscripts, Boston Public Library, MS. 957.
7. Letter of March 27, 1838, W/G, Box 5; Barnes and Dumond, *Letters of Theodore Dwight Weld,* 2:605.
8. Letter of April 24, 1838, *The Letters of William Lloyd Garrison,* 2:347.
9. *Proceedings of the Anti-Slavery Convention of American Women, held in Philadelphia, May 15th, 16th, 17th and 18th, 1838* (Philadelphia, Pa.: Merrihew and Gunn, 1838).
10. [Samuel Webb], *History of Pennsylvania Hall, which was Destroyed by a Mob, on the 17th of May, 1838* (Philadelphia, Pa.: Merrihew and Gunn, 1838; New York: Negro Universities, 1969), pp. 117, 136.
11. Letter of May 19, 1838, *The Letters of William Lloyd Garrison,* 2:363.
12. [Webb], *History of Philadelphia Hall,* p. 133.

SIX: Domesticity

1. Letter of June 5, 1838, W/G, Box 5.
2. Letters of June 18, 1838, *ibid.*
3. Letter from Mary Horner and Edith Kite to Sarah M. Grimké and Angelina E. G. Weld, September 11, 1838, W/G, Box 5; Gilbert H. Barnes and Dwight L. Dumond, eds., *Letters of Theodore Dwight Weld, Angelina Grimké Weld and Sarah Grimké, 1822–1844* (New York: Appleton-Century, 1934; New York: Da Capo, 1970), 2:701–702.
4. Sarah M. Grimké to Henry C. Wright, March 29, 1838, Rare Books and Manuscripts, Boston Public Library, MS.A.1.2, 7:17.
5. Merle E. Curti, "Non-Resistance in New England," *New England Quarterly* (January 1929), 2:42–46; Peter Brock, *Pacifism in the United States: From the Colonial Era to the First World War* (Princeton, N.J.: Princeton

University Press, 1968), p. 548; Wendell Phillips Garrison and Francis Jackson Garrison, *William Lloyd Garrison, 1805–1879: The Story of His Life, Told By His Children* (New York: Century, 1885–1889; New York: Arno and *New York Times,* 1969), 2:227–229; Carlton Mabee, *Black Freedom: The Nonviolent Abolitionists from 1830 Through the Civil War* (New York: Macmillan, 1970), pp. 67–88.

6. Aileen S. Kraditor, *Means and Ends in American Abolitionism: Garrison and His Critics on Strategy and Tactics, 1834–1850* (New York: Pantheon, 1969), p. 48.

7. Garrison and Garrison, *William Lloyd Garrison,* 2:296.

8. *Ibid.,* 2:297.

9. *Ibid.,* 2:305–306.

10. Alma Lutz, *Crusade For Freedom: Women of the Antislavery Movement* (Boston, Mass.: Beacon, 1968), pp. 151–152; Jane H. Pease and William H. Pease, *Bound With Them in Chains: A Biographical History of the Antislavery Movement* (Westport, Conn.: Greenwood, 1972), pp. 42–44.

EPILOGUE

Epigraphs: L. M. Child, letter of April 6, 1838, *Lydia Maria Child: Selected Letters, 1817–1880,* ed. Milton Meltzer and Patricia G. Holland, (Amherst, Mass.: University of Massachusetts Press, 1982), p. 73; Maria Weston Chapman, "Right and Wrong in Boston," *Annual Report of the Boston Female Anti-Slavery Society with a sketch of the obstacles thrown in the way of Emancipation by certain Clerical Abolitionists and Advocates for the subjection of woman in 1837* (Boston, Mass.: By the Society, 1837), p. 61.

1. Letter of May 29, 1839, Rare Books and Manuscripts, Boston Public Library, MS.A.9.2, 11:112.

2. Alma Lutz, *Crusade For Freedom: Women of the Antislavery Movement* (Boston, Mass.: Beacon, 1968), p. 152; Jane H. Pease and William H. Pease, *Bound With Them in Chains: A Biographical History of the Antislavery Movement* (Westport, Conn.: Greenwood, 1972), pp. 43–44.

3. Lawrence J. Friedman, *Gregarious Saints: Self and Community in American Abolitionism, 1830–1870* (Cambridge: Cambridge University Press, 1982), pp. 142–143.

4. Letter of June 18, 1840, Gilbert H. Barnes and Dwight L. Dumond, eds., *Letters of Theodore Dwight Weld, Angelina Grimké Weld and Sarah Grimké, 1822–1844* (New York: Appleton-Century, 1934; New York: Da Capo, 1970), 2:843.

5. Letter of December 20, 1840, Rare Books and Manuscripts, Boston Public Library, MS.A.1.2, 10:46.

6. Gilbert Hobbs Barnes, *The Antislavery Impulse, 1830–1840* (New York: Appleton-Century, 1933; Gloucester, Mass.: Smith, 1957), p. 266, n. 39; Edward Magdol, "A Window on the Abolitionist Constituency: Antislavery Petitions, 1836–1839," in Alan M. Kraut, ed., *Crusaders and Compromis-*

ers: Essays on the Relationship of the Antislavery Struggle to the Antebellum Party System (Westport, Conn.: Greenwood, 1983), p. 46.

7. Gerda Lerner, "The Political Activities of Antislavery Women," in Gerda Lerner, *The Majority Finds Its Past: Placing Women in History* (New York: Oxford University Press, 1979), pp. 123, 124, and 127.

Biographical Notes

THERE ARE two biographies of the Grimké sisters and one of Angelina; all are valuable. Catherine H. Birney, *The Grimké Sisters; Sarah and Angelina Grimké: The First American Women Advocates of Abolition and Woman's Rights* (Boston, Mass.: Lee and Shepard, 1885; Westport, Conn.: Greenwood, 1969), was the daughter-in-law of James G. Birney. She met the sisters when she and her husband visited Birney, who had moved to the Raritan Bay community in 1853. Mrs. Birney became good friends with them—especially, it would seem from the evidence of the book, with Sarah. She had complete access to their diaries and letters. The book lacks notes, references, a bibliography, and an index; however, there are extensive excerpts from the letters and diaries. She is very sympathetic and empathetic; her account is highly personal and extolling. She closely examines the changes in their thinking, but records none of the family problems, e.g., the hostility that Angelina felt toward Weld during the first several years of their marriage, the break between the sisters, and the illness of the second child, Thody.

Gerda Lerner, *The Grimké Sisters from South Carolina: Rebels Against Slavery* (Boston, Mass.: Houghton Mifflin, 1967), has written the most thorough, objective, and critical book available on the sisters. She subjects their ideas to close examination and, though there are a few places where she arguably anticipates developments and projects onto the sisters' struggles a feminist consciousness and purposefulness not warranted by the evidence, Lerner has solidly rooted them as the forerunners of conscious radical feminism in the United States. She describes the intrafamily problems but does not provide an in-depth analysis of them. The bibliography is excellent.

Katherine Du Pre Lumpkin, *The Emancipation of Angelina Grimké* (Chapel Hill, N.C.: University of North Carolina Press, 1974), quotes extensively from the diaries and letters and captures effectively the sisters' intensity, inner conflicts, and relational connections and difficulties. This is a sympathetic account of their lives but does not discuss their ideas or place them in an intellectual or theoretical context. It contains a useful bibliography.

Two articles are also useful. Keith E. Melder, "Forerunners of Freedom: The Grimké Sisters in Massachusetts, 1837–38," *Essex Institute Historical*

Collections (July 1967) 103:223–249, provides a well-researched account of the sisters' speaking tour and the controversies engendered by it. Ellen Du Bois succinctly analyzes the ways in which the door of domesticity shut the sisters off from their intention to combine a settled and activist life in "Struggling Into Existence—The Feminism of Sarah and Angelina Grimké," *Women: A Journal of Liberalism* (Spring 1970), 1:4–11.

There is a valuable selection of the sisters' letters in Gilbert H. Barnes and Dwight L. Dumond, eds., *Letters of Theodore Dwight Weld, Angelina Grimké Weld, and Sarah Grimké, 1822–1844* (New York: Appleton-Century, 1934; New York: Da Capo, 1970). However, the editors state in the introduction that they made their selections according to "those which had biographical significance to the life of Weld and those which threw light upon the antislavery agitation" (p. xxvi). They thus reprinted only four of the twenty-five letters the sisters wrote between 1835 and April 1837 (W/G, Box 3); twenty-five of the forty-nine they wrote between May 1837 and February 1838 (W/G, Box 4); twelve of the twenty-one written between March and June 1838 (W/G, Box 5); and two of twenty for the period between 1839 and September 1840 (W/G, Box 6). Very few of Angelina's letters to Jane Smith, for example, were chosen.

Elizabeth Ann Bartlett has compiled a collection of Sarah's writings on feminist issues, but she has not provided the reader with any assistance in understanding the sources on which Sarah relied or why the unfinished, unpublished essays of the 1850s remained so. See Elizabeth Ann Bartlett, ed., *Letters on the Equality of the Sexes and Other Essays. By Sarah Grimké* (New Haven, Conn.: Yale University Press, 1988).

Two biographies of Theodore Dwight Weld complement one another. Robert H. Abzug, *Passionate Liberator: Theodore Dwight Weld and the Dilemma of Reform* (New York: Oxford University Press, 1980), begins with a Freudian analysis of Weld's childhood that is generally plausible, because the author is cognizant of the thinness of the source material and proceeds with caution. By carefully grounding all the influences that affected Weld in detailed background sketches, Abzug provides a useful cultural history of the era. However, he has no particular insight into or in-depth penetration of the sisters, who are treated only as supporting characters. Indeed, all of the other personalities appear as cardboard replicas. Benjamin F. Thomas, *Theodore Weld: Crusader for Freedom* (New York: Octagon, 1973), on the other hand, is descriptive, not analytical. He does not provide a cultural context, but treats the important people in Weld's life in greater depth than does Abzug. There is very little on the marriage and parenting of Weld and Angelina.

Treatments of the contexts from which the Grimkés came and within which they worked vary in number and quality. Much more needs to be done on women of the South during the first half of the nineteenth century, but an excellent beginning has been made by Anne Firor Scott, *The Southern Lady: From Pedestal to Politics, 1830–1930* (Chicago, Ill.: University of Chicago Press, 1970), Catherine Clinton, *The Plantation Mistress: Woman's World in the Old South* (New York: Pantheon, 1982), Elizabeth Fox-Genovese, *Within the Plantation Household: Black and White Women of the Old South* (Chapel Hill, N.C.: University of North Carolina Press, 1988), and Suzanne Lebsock, *The Free Women of Petersburg: Status and Culture in a Southern Town, 1784–1860* (New York: Norton, 1984). Clinton's and Fox-Genovese's books do not fully cover the southern woman's world; the lives of upper-class women who lived in cities, middle-class women, the wives and daughters of yeomen farmers, and working-class and poor women still need to be examined. Lebsock, by focusing her study on a single city, was able to illuminate the situations of married women, separated, single, and widowed white women, free women of color, and women who worked, both inside and outside the home.

There is also a need for greater in-depth treatment of Quaker women during that time period. Useful overviews are available from Mary Maples Dunn, "Women of Light," in Carol Ruth Berkin and Mary Beth Norton, eds., *Women of America: A History* (Boston, Mass.: Houghton Mifflin, 1979), pp. 114–133 and Margaret Hope Bacon, *Mothers of Feminism: The Story of Quaker Women in America* (New York: Harper, 1986).

There are several first-rate books on the women's movement during the period 1800–1850: Alma Lutz, *Crusade for Freedom: Women of the Antislavery Movement* (Boston, Mass.: Beacon, 1968); Aileen Kraditor, *Means and Ends in American Abolitionism: Garrison and His Critics on Strategy and Tactics, 1834–1850* (New York: Pantheon, 1969), ch. 3; Carroll Smith-Rosenberg, *Religion and the Rise of the American City: The New York City Mission Movement, 1812–1870* (Ithaca, N.Y.: Cornell University Press, 1971); Keith E. Melder, *Beginnings of Sisterhood: The American Woman's Rights Movement, 1800–1850* (New York: Schocken, 1977); Nancy F. Cott, *The Bonds of Womanhood: "Woman's Sphere" in New England, 1780–1835* (New Haven, Conn.: Yale University Press, 1977); Barbara J. Berg, *The Remembered Gate: Origins of American Feminism—The Woman and the City, 1800–1860* (New York: Oxford University Press, 1978); Blanche Glassman Hersh, *The Slavery of Sex: Feminist-Abolitionists in America* (Urbana, Ill.: University of Illinois Press, 1978); Ellen C. DuBois, *Feminism and Suffrage: The Emergence of an Independent Women's Movement in America, 1848–1869* (Ithaca, N.Y.: Cornell University Press, 1978) and "Women's Rights and Abolition: The Nature of the Connection," in Lewis Perry and Michael Fellman, eds., *Antislavery Reconsidered: New Perspectives on the Abolitionists* (Baton Rouge, La.: Louisiana State University Press, 1979), pp. 238–251; Christine Stansell, *City of Women: Sex and Class in New York, 1789–1860* (New York: Knopf, 1986); and several of the essays in Gerda Lerner, *The Majority Finds Its Past: Placing Women in History* (New York: Oxford University Press, 1979), notably "Black and White Women in Interaction and Confrontation," and "The Political Activities of Antislavery Women." Nancy Woloch's *Women and the American Experience* (New York: Knopf, 1984) provides the best currently available synthesis of the sweep of women's history in the United States. There is valuable primary source material in Elizabeth Cady Stanton, Susan B. Anthony, and Matilda Joslyn Gage, eds., *History of Woman Suffrage,* vol. 1, *1848–1861* (New York: Fowler and Wells, 1881; New York: Arno and *New York Times,* 1969).

Individual women have not been as fortunate. There are only a handful of good biographies presently available. The best, and a model for all to follow, is Kathryn Kish Sklar, *Catharine Beecher, A Study in American Domesticity* (New Haven, Conn.: Yale University Press, 1973). Professor Sklar provides an in-depth understanding of Beecher as well as a social and intellectual history of her time. Jeanne Boydston, Mary Kelley, and Anne Margolis have provided a useful introduction to the contradictions in the reform careers of the three most active Beecher sisters, Catharine, Harriet, and Isabella, combining analysis with a selection of documents: *The Limits of Sisterhood: The Beecher Sisters on Women's Rights and Woman's Sphere* (Chapel Hill, N.C.: University of North Carolina Press, 1988).

Elizabeth Margaret Chandler is mentioned in most of the overviews, but presently lacks a full biography. The most detailed treatment of her is Merton L. Dillon, "Elizabeth Chandler and the Spread of Antislavery Sentiment to Michigan," *Michigan History* (December 1955), 39:481–494. But she is probably best approached through her own writings: *The Poetical Works of Elizabeth Margaret Chandler, With a memoir of her life and character by Benjamin Lundy* (Philadelphia, Pa.: Howell, 1836; Miami, Fla.: Mnemosyne, 1969).

There are two biographies devoted to Lydia Maria Child, but both are merely serviceable narratives that are lacking depth and written in irritating prose styles: Helene G. Baer, *The Heart Is Like Heaven: The Life of Lydia Maria Child* (Philadelphia, Pa.: University of Pennsylvania Press, 1964); and Milton Meltzer, *Tongue of Flame: The Life of Lydia Maria Child* (New York: Crowell, 1965). Here again, the best approach to her is through her letters: *Lydia Maria Child: Selected Letters, 1817–1880,* ed. Milton Meltzer and Patricia G. Holland (Amherst, Mass.: University of Massachusetts Press, 1982).

There is no biography of Maria Weston Chapman, nor have her papers been compiled and edited. A chapter is devoted to her in Jane H. Pease and William H. Pease, *Bound With Them in Chains: A Biographical History of the Antislavery Movement* (Westport, Conn.: Greenwood, 1972).

Otelia Cromwell has written a good biography of Lucretia Mott: *Lucretia Mott* (Cambridge, Mass.: Harvard University Press, 1958); and there are two good biographies of Frances Wright: A. J. G. Perkins and Theresa Wolfson, *Frances Wright, Free Enquirer: The Study of a Temperament* (New York: Harper, 1939); and Celia Morris Eckhardt, *Fanny Wright: Rebel in America* (Cambridge, Mass.: Harvard University Press, 1984).

As of the moment, the handiest means of gaining information on the other women mentioned in this book is by consulting Edward T. James, ed., *Notable American Women, 1607–1950: A Biographical Dictionary*, 4 vols. (Cambridge, Mass.: Belknap, 1971).

The time is ripe for an in-depth, full-scale treatment of the abolitionist movement. The older books by Gilbert H. Barnes, *The Antislavery Impulse, 1830–1844* (New York: Appleton-Century, 1933) and Louis Filler, *The Crusade Against Slavery, 1830–1860* (New York: Harper, 1960) and the newer one by Merton L. Dillon, *The Abolitionists: The Growth of a Dissenting Minority* (De Kalb, Ill.: Northern Illinois University Press, 1974) are generally skimpy and particularly weak on the women members. The most useful, though obviously biased, contemporary account, and the best written of them all, is Samuel J. May, *Some recollections of our antislavery conflict* (Boston, Mass.: Fields, Osgood, 1869).

An up-to-date, comprehensive history will need to depart from the focus on the New York and Boston axes and provide far more details on local auxiliaries and the black abolitionist organizations. The best current introduction to the historical problems concerning the study of abolitionism, which also describes some of the most interesting research paths to be taken, is Lewis Perry and Michael Fellman, eds., *Antislavery Reconsidered: New Perspectives on the Abolitionists* (Baton Rouge, La.: Louisiana State University Press, 1979). The approach of Aileen Kraditor *(Means and Ends in American Abolitionism),* though important for moving away from the exclusively personal account of schisms within abolitionist ranks, focuses too much on the ideological and is too bipolar in its treatment of the movement; her abolitionist universe is basically composed of radicals and conservatives. Lewis Perry, in *Radical Abolitionism: Anarchy and the Government of God in Antislavery Thought* (Ithaca, N.Y.: Cornell University Press, 1973), takes a much closer look at the impulses behind Garrisonian doctrines. Attitudes, emotions, personalities, and ideas are examined in a more meaningful social and cultural context in Ronald G. Walters, *The Antislavery Appeal: American Abolitionists After 1830* (Baltimore, Md.: Johns Hopkins University Press, 1976); James Brewer Stewart, *Holy Warriors: The Abolitionists and American Slavery* (New York: Hill and Wang, 1976); and Lawrence J. Friedman, *Gregarious Saints: Self and Community in American Abolitionism, 1830–1870* (Cambridge: Cambridge University Press, 1982). All three are suggestive, but all remain overviews. The role of the Society of Friends in the antislavery movement receives detailed treatment in Thomas E. Drake, *Quakers and Slavery in America* (New Haven, Conn.: Yale University Press, 1950).

There are shelves full of books on William Lloyd Garrison, none wholly satisfactory. In fact, the further removed in time historians get from him, the less sympathetic to him they seem to be. The most recent biographies are either distantiated—Walter M. Merrill, *Against Wind and Tide: A Biography of Wm. Lloyd Garrison* (Cambridge, Mass.: Harvard University Press, 1963)—or so unsympathetic (to him and everyone else in the movement) that one finally distrusts the author's personality assessments—John L.

Thomas, *The Liberator: William Lloyd Garrison, a Biography* (Boston, Mass.: Little, Brown, 1963). Somewhat older ones tend to be more understanding: Russel B. Nye, *William Lloyd Garrison and the Humanitarian Reformers* (Boston, Mass.: Little, Brown, 1955); Ralph Korngold, *Two Friends of Man: The Story of William Lloyd Garrison and Wendell Phillips and Their Relation with Abraham Lincoln* (Boston, Mass.: Little, Brown, 1950)—the most balanced and perceptive treatment; John Jay Chapman, *William Lloyd Garrison*, 2d ed. (Boston, Mass.: Atlantic Monthly, 1921). The oldest, by his friend and editorial assistant, Oliver Johnson, is well written and contains useful information, but is biased: *William Lloyd Garrison and His Times; or, Sketches of the Anti-Slavery Movement in America, and of the man who was its founder and moral leader* (Boston, Mass.: Houghton Mifflin, 1881). Archibald H. Grimké wrote a frankly hero worshiping book marred by flights of rhetorical excess: *William Lloyd Garrison: The Abolitionist* (New York: Funk and Wagnalls, 1891). The most comprehensive biography by far, containing massive documentation, is the one prepared by his children: Wendell Phillips Garrison and Francis Jackson Garrison, *William Lloyd Garrison, 1805–1879: The Story of His Life, Told By His Children*, 4 vols. (New York: Century, 1885–1889; New York: Arno and *New York Times*, 1969). As with many other abolitionists, Garrison is best approached through his letters: *The Letters of William Lloyd Garrison*, eds. Walter M. Merrill and Louis Ruchames, 6 vols. (Cambridge, Mass.: Belknap, 1971–1981).

A good introduction to the nonresistance movement is provided by Merle E. Curti, "Non-Resistance in New England," *New England Quarterly* (January 1929), 2:34–57. The most encyclopedic approach is by Peter Brock, *Pacifism in the United States: From the Colonial Era to the First World War* (Princeton, N.J.: Princeton University Press, 1968); Chapters 10–17 were reprinted separately as *Radical Pacifists in Antebellum America* (Princeton, N.J.: Princeton University Press, 1968). One can also profitably consult Garrison and Garrison, *William Lloyd Garrison*, 2:221–257 and Alice Felt Tyler, *Freedom's Ferment: Phases of American Social History to 1860* (Minneapolis, Minn.: University of Minnesota Press, 1944).

Index

Note: There are no entries for abolition, Christianity, the Grimké sisters, North, slavery, and South. No biblical references are indexed, and all Bible commentaries and commentators are grouped under one heading: Bible commentaries.